ASEAN AND GLOBAL VALUE CHAINS
LOCKING IN RESILIENCE AND SUSTAINABILITY

MARCH 2023

ASIAN DEVELOPMENT BANK

ADB

Notes:
In this publication, "$" refers to United States dollars.
ADB recognizes "China" as the People's Republic of China, "Hanoi" as "Ha Noi," "Korea" and
"South Korea" as the Republic of Korea, "Russia" as the Russian Federation, and "Vietnam" as
Viet Nam.

Cover design by Mike Cortes.

Contents

Tables, Figures, and Boxes   vi
Foreword   xi
About the Editors   xiii
About the Authors   xiv
Acknowledgments   xvii
Abbreviations   xviii

1   Toward Future-Proofing Global Value Chains   1
by Mia Mikic

ASEAN Is Facing an Evolving "New Normal"   2
ASEAN Remains a Value Chain Hub with Greater Reliance   5
    on Intraregional Links
Global Value Chains Can Create More and Better Jobs in ASEAN   15
Innovation and Technology Can Increase Participation   20
    in ASEAN Global Value Chains
Decarbonization in ASEAN's Global Value Chain-Driven Economies   25
Deepening Regional Integration and Cooperation under an   32
    Evolving "New Normal"
Future-Proofing ASEAN Participation in Global Value Chains   37
References   40

2   The State of Play of ASEAN Global Value Chains   44
by Adrian Mendoza and James Villafuerte

Introduction   45
Global Value Chains Prior to the COVID-19 Pandemic: 48
    Global Trends and ASEAN's Experience
ASEAN Global Value Chains after the Global Financial Crisis   62
The Development Impact of Global Value Chains on ASEAN   66
The Impact of COVID-19 on ASEAN Global Value Chains   68
The Future of ASEAN Global Value Chains   90
References   96

3   Jobs and Global Value Chains in Southeast Asia   **104**
by Christian Viegelahn, Phu Huynh, and Kee Beom Kim

Introduction   105
How Many Jobs in Southeast Asia Are Linked   108
    to Global Value Chains?
How Is Backward and Forward Participation Linked to Jobs   118
    in Southeast Asia?
Conclusion and Way Forward   128
Appendixes   135
References   143

4   Technology, Global Value Chains, and Jobs: Continuing   **148**
    ASEAN's Role in Transformed Global Value Chains
by Gloria Pasadilla

Introduction   149
Technology and Value Chains   150
Skills Bias in New Technologies   151
Transformation of the Automotive Manufacturing   152
    Global Value Chain
ASEAN in the New Automotive Value Chain   161
Electronics and Electrical Industry   170
ASEAN in the Electronics and Electrical Value Chain   176
What Can ASEAN Expect in a Transformed Electronics   180
    and Electrical Value Chain?
The Human Capital and Innovation Challenge   184
References   189

5   Decarbonization and Global Value Chains in ASEAN   **193**
by Sindhu Bharathi, Sumathi Chakravarthy,
and Badri Narayanan Gopalakrishnan
Introduction   194
Literature Review   199
Methodology   206
Results and Analysis   210
Conclusion   249
Policy Implications   251
Appendix   253
References   255

**6   Scenarios for a Global "New Normal" and ASEAN   258
      Global Value Chains**
      by Peter Petri and Michael Plummer

      Diverging Prospects   259
      Research Strategy   264
      Simulation Results   276
      Implications for Global Value Chains   292
      Conclusions   300
      Appendixes   302
      References   310

Tables, Figures, and Boxes

Tables

2.1 Impact of COVID-19 Policies on Global Value Chain Participation Rate in 2021, Marginal Effects   82

A3.1 Jobs in Global Value Chains—Sectors   137

A3.2 Jobs in Global Value Chains—Economies   138

A3.3 Jobs in Global Value Chains—Aggregate Sectors   142

4.1 Automotive Industry Transformation: Partnership, Acquisition, Joint Venture Highlights   159

4.2 Examples of Parts of Traditional Cars Not Needed in Electric Vehicles   163

4.3 Policy Support for Electric Vehicle Development in ASEAN   167

4.4 ASEAN Semiconductor Component Exports By Category, 2018   177

4.5 Types of Upgrades in ASEAN   182

5.1 ASEAN's Renewable Power Capacity   210

5.2 Emissions and Renewable Power Capacity—Brunei Darussalam   211

5.3 Change in Macroeconomic Variables—Brunei Darussalam   211

5.4 Percent Change in Domestic and Foreign Value Added—Brunei Darussalam   214

5.5 Emissions and Renewable Power Capacity—Cambodia   215

5.6 Change in Macroeconomic Variables—Cambodia   216

5.7 Percent Change in Domestic and Foreign Value Added—Cambodia   218

5.8 Emissions and Renewable Power Capacity—Indonesia   220

5.9 Change in Macroeconomic Variables—Indonesia   220

5.10 Percent Change in Domestic and Foreign Value Added—Indonesia   223

5.11 Emissions and Renewable Power Capacity—Lao People's Democratic Republic   224

5.12 Change in Macroeconomic Variables—Lao People's Democratic Republic   225

5.13 Percent Change in Domestic and Foreign Value Added—Lao People's Democratic Republic   228   228

5.14 Emissions and Renewable Power Capacity—Malaysia   229

5.15 Change in Macroeconomic Variables—Malaysia   229

5.16 Percent Change in Domestic and Foreign Value Added—Malaysia   232

5.17 Emissions and Renewable Power Capacity—Philippines   233

5.18 Change in Macroeconomic Variables—Philippines   233

5.19 Percent Change in Domestic and Foreign Value Added—Philippines   236

5.20 Emissions and Renewable Power Capacity—Singapore   237

5.21 Change in Macroeconomic Variables—Singapore   237

5.22 Percent Change in Domestic and Foreign Value Added—Singapore   240

5.23 Emissions and Renewable Power Capacity—Thailand   241

5.24 Change in Macroeconomic Variables—Thailand   241

5.25 Percent Change in Domestic and Foreign Value Added—Thailand 244
5.26 Emissions and Renewable Power Capacity—Viet Nam 245
5.27 Change in Macroeconomic Variables—Viet Nam 246
5.28 Percent Change in Domestic and Foreign Value Added—Viet Nam 248
6.1   Specification of Alternative Baselines 270
6.2A Specification of Geopolitical Interventions 272
6.2B Specification of Trade Cooperation Scenarios 275
6.3   World Growth under Baseline Scenarios 278
6.4   Elements of the New Normal Baseline, 2035 279
6.5   Geopolitical Alternatives, Income 2035 281
6.6   Geopolitical Alternatives, Exports 2035 283
6.7   Cooperation Alternatives, Income 2035 286
6.8   Cooperation Alternatives, Exports 2035 288
6.9   Geopolitical Interventions: Changes in Global Value Chain 295
      Participation, 2035
6.10 Enhanced Trade Cooperation: Changes in Global Value Chain 297
      Participation, 2035
6.11 Geopolitical Interventions: Share of Value-Added Exports, 2035 298

Figures

1.1   Recent Shocks and the New Normal: Income Changes in 2035 34
1.2   Geopolitical Interventions: Real Income Changes, 2035 35
1.3   Enhancing Trade Cooperation, Change in Real Income in 2035 36
2.1   Historical Trends in Information and Communication Technology, 50
      Transport Costs, Tariff Rates, and Overall Trade Costs
2.2   Trends in Global Value Chain Participation Rate, 1990–2015 52
2.3   Intraregional Trade in ASEAN, 1990–2015 54
2.4   Volume of Global Value Chain Trade Surged in the 2000s 55
2.5   Global Value Chain Participation Varies Greatly across ASEAN 56
2.6   Global Value Chain Trade in ASEAN is Driven Mostly by 57
      Backward Participation
2.7   Origins of Foreign Value Added within ASEAN Exports 59
2.8   Share in ASEAN Global Value Chain Trade by Industry 59
2.9   ASEAN Global Value Chain Trade in Manufacturing and Services 61
      Evolve in Tandem, 1990–2015
2.10 Sectoral Global Value Chain Trade Varies Significantly across 62
      ASEAN
2.11 Growth in Global Gross Domestic Product and Trade Volume, 63
      1980–2019
2.12 Backward Global Value Chain Participation Rates in the People's 65
      Republic of China, 2000–2017
2.13 Global Economic Policy Uncertainty Index and Trade Policy 65
      Uncertainty Index, January 2000–December 2019

2.14 Global Value Chain Participation in ASEAN has a Nonlinear   67
      Relationship with per Capita GDP, 1990–2015
2.15 Average Spillovers to ASEAN of a 1% Local Output Shock to   70
      Global Value Chain Partners
2.16 Global Supply Disruption Index, January 2000–December 2021   71
2.17 Growth of Backward and Forward Global Value Chain Trade   72
      in 2020 and 2021, by ASEAN Country–Sector Pairs
2.18 ASEAN Global Value Chain Trade Slump (2020) and   73
      Recovery (2021)
2.19 Breakdown of the Growth of ASEAN Global Value Chain Trade   75
      during Major Crises
2.20 Recovery of ASEAN Global Value Chain Trade from COVID-19   75
      Shocks
2.21 Contribution to Growth of ASEAN Global Value Chain Trade,   76
      by Sector
2.22 Contribution to Growth of ASEAN Global Value Chain Trade,   77
      by Partner
2.23 COVID-19 Stringency Index across ASEAN, January 2020–   79
      December 2021
2.24 Discretionary Fiscal Response to the COVID-19 Crisis in   80
      Selected ASEAN Economies
2.25 Fully Vaccinated Individuals as of December 2021   81
2.26 Average Marginal Effects of Stringency and Vaccination Rate   83
      on Global Value Chain Participation Rate
3.1   Number and Share of Jobs in Global Value Chains, Southeast Asia   111
3.2   Share of Jobs Associated with Global Value Chains by Economy,   112
      Southeast Asia
3.3   Share of Jobs Associated with Global Value Chains by Sector,   113
      Southeast Asia
3.4   Number and Share of Jobs Associated with Intraregional Value   114
      Chains, Southeast Asia
3.5   Share of Women Employed in Global Value Chains, Southeast Asia   114
3.6   Share of Youth Workers Employed in Global Value Chains and   116
      the Total Economy, Southeast Asia
3.7   Share of Employees Employed in Global Value Chains and in   117
      the Total Economy, Southeast Asia
3.8   Share of Workers in High-Skill Occupations Employed in Global   117
      Value Chains and in the Total Economy, Southeast Asia
3.9   Working Poverty Rate in Southeast Asia and Non-Southeast Asia   122
      Economies, 2000–2021
3.10 Estimated Change in Working Poverty Associated with an   123
      Increase of One Standard Deviation in Backward and Forward
      Global Value Chain Participation in Southeast Asia by Age and Gender

3.11	Estimated Change in Labor Productivity Associated with an Increase of One Standard Deviation in Backward and Forward Global Value Chain Participation in Southeast Asia	124
3.12	Estimated Change in Employment Shares Associated with an Increase of One Standard Deviation in Global Value Chain Participation in Southeast Asia by Economic Sector	125
3.13	Number of Regional Trade Agreements Involving At Least One Southeast Asian Country	133
4.1	Internet of Things Ecosystem	151
4.2	Number of Patent Assignees Related to Electric Vehicles, 2011–2022	158
4.3	Top Assignees of Patents Related to Autonomous Vehicles	158
4.4	Destination of ASEAN Passenger Car Exports	161
4.5	ASEAN's Share in Global Car Exports	162
4.6	ASEAN's Share in World Exports of Subassemblies	162
4.7	ASEAN's Share in Parts and Component Exports	163
4.8	Sunrise and Sunset Industry Segments of Parts and Component Industry	164
4.9	Consumer Survey of Auto Engine Preference	165
4.10	ASEAN Exports of Body Systems and Drive Train Subassemblies	168
4.11	ASEAN Exports in Automotive Parts and Components	169
4.12	Share of Electric Vehicles in ASEAN Auto Exports	170
4.13	Electronics and Electrical Global Value Chain	171
4.14	Semiconductor Value Chain	172
4.15	Foreign Value Added in ASEAN Electronics and Electronics Exports	
4.16	ASEAN Electronic Components Exports to the People's Republic of China and the Rest of the World, 2002–2021	178
4.17	End-market Share in Global Semiconductor Demand, 2019	181
5.1a	Percent Change in Investment in Brunei Darussalam—Scenario 1	212
5.1b	Percent Change in Investment in Brunei Darussalam—Scenario 2	212
5.2	Percent Change in Output—Brunei Darussalam	213
5.3a	Percent Change in Investment in Cambodia—Scenario 1	216
5.3b	Percent Change in Investment in Cambodia—Scenario 2	217
5.4	Percent Change in Output—Cambodia	218
5.5a	Percent Change in Investment in Indonesia—Scenario 1	221
5.5b	Percent Change in Investment in Indonesia—Scenario 2	221
5.6	Percent Change in Output—Indonesia	222
5.7a	Percent Change in Investment of Lao People's Democratic Republic—Scenario 1	226
5.7b	Percent Change in Investment in Lao People's Democratic Republic—Scenario 2	226
5.8	Percent Change in Output—Lao People's Democratic Republic	227
5.9a	Percent Change in Investment of Malaysia—Scenario 1	230
5.9b	Percent Change in Investment in Malaysia—Scenario 2	230
5.10	Percent Change in Output—Malaysia	231

5.11a Percent Change in Investment in the Philippines—Scenario 1   234
5.11b Percent Change in Investment in the Philippines—Scenario 2   234
5.12   Percent Change in Output—Philippines   235
5.13a Percent Change in Investment in Singapore—Scenario 1   238
5.13b Percent Change in Investment in Singapore—Scenario 2   238
5.14   Percent Change in Output—Singapore   239
5.15a Percent Change in Investment in Thailand—Scenario 1   242
5.15b Percent Change in Investment in Thailand—Scenario 2   242
5.16   Percent Change in Output—Thailand   243
5.17a Percent Change in Investment in Viet Nam—Scenario 1   247
5.17b Percent Change in Investment in Viet Nam—Scenario 2   247
5.18   Percent Change in Output—Viet Nam   248
6.1   Recent Shocks and the New Normal: Income Changes   262
6.2   Geopolitical Interventions in Trade: Income Changes   263
6.3   New Cooperation Alternatives: Income Changes   263
6.4   Production Structure of the Global Trade Model   266
6.5   Structure of Global Value Chain and Regional Value Chain Analysis 267
6.6   Participation in Global Value Chains, Baseline 2021 and 2035 294

Boxes

1.1   Impact of the People's Republic of China's Zero-COVID Policy on   7
       the Region's Global Value Chains
1.2   ASEAN Global Value Chains—Robustness and Resilience   9
       of Four Machinery Groups
1.3   Global Value Chain Contribution to ASEAN Development   13
       and Poverty Reduction
1.4   Working Hours Lost in ASEAN in 2020   16
1.5   Women in Global Value Chains   18
1.6   Labor Impact of the Automotive Transformation   22
1.7   Policies That Help Control and Reduce Carbon Emissions   27
2.1   COVID-19 and Global Value Chain Trade in ASEAN   84
3.1   The COVID-19 Pandemic and Its Impact on Labor Markets   107
       in Southeast Asia
3.2   Which Jobs Are Linked to Global Value Chains?   109
3.3   Women in Sectors Highly Integrated in Global Value Chains   114
4.1   Bottlenecks in Electric Vehicle Manufacturing   153
4.2   Labor Impact of Automotive Industry Transformation   156
4.3   Artificial Intelligence and the Automotive Industry   160
4.4   People's Republic of China: Climate Change and Electric Vehicles 166
4.5   Understanding the Semiconductor Industry and Technologies   174
4.6   Viet Nam's Rapid Growth in the Electronics and Electrical   178
       Global Value Chain
4.7   Changing Skill Requirements in the Job Market   185

Foreword

Association of Southeast Asian Nations (ASEAN) economies need to urgently readjust and strengthen their positions in regional and global value chains (GVCs) to bolster resilience against the evolving challenges they face—not least the risks of future pandemics, geopolitical instability, and climate change.

The region has overcome past challenges through strong exports, sound macroeconomic policies, and strong buffers. And it has continued to do well thus far this decade. The region recovered rapidly from the pandemic's devastating impact in 2021 and 2022 despite the initial effects of the Russian invasion of Ukraine.

Yet, it would be a mistake to see ASEAN's relative strength over the past 3 years as reason for complacency. The coronavirus disease (COVID-19), the Russian invasion of Ukraine, growing tensions between the United States and the People's Republic of China, and climate risks exposed weaknesses across the GVC network. Business as usual is not an option. Ignoring these risks could upend the region's GVC participation and reduce the huge benefits it has gleaned from global trade and the resilience it continues to build.

This volume's timely collection of papers examines recent developments affecting GVC participation—particularly in the ASEAN—and could help policy makers decide the best way forward. There are many important findings. Several stand out including the following:

- GVCs proved more resilient to COVID-19 impact than expected, even as firms had to adjust, given their dependence on only a few suppliers for essential inputs and goods. The region needs to build stronger resilience in its GVC segments while expanding trade, investment, and regional integration.
- As new technology continues to upgrade GVCs, the competitive advantage of employing low-skilled labor diminishes. The region must create a "critical mass" of workers with new technological skills to work with new technologies. Governments, businesses, and public–private partnerships must work to upskill employees, increase human capital, and promote innovation.

- ASEAN economies need to go "green." The best-case scenario is that policies promoting decarbonization also strengthen ASEAN's GVCs. These policies will, among other things, design nontariff measures and set low (or zero) tariffs on climate-smart goods. They should accelerate trade digitalization and promote climate-smart trade, green transport infrastructure, and carbon pricing.
- The stakes are high. Recent global shocks and geopolitical trade protectionism could disrupt growth in ASEAN, the Indo-Pacific region, and elsewhere. The research explores the sizable policy impact and benefits of deepening Asia's trade cooperation and expanding it to include other regions.

We are confident this book will prove valuable to policy makers as they prepare the way forward. The last several years remind us that headwinds and shocks are inevitable. They also show us that by strengthening and exploiting opportunities for greater regional and global integration, we can further deepen ASEAN's economic resilience and sustainability.

Ramesh Subramaniam
Director General
Southeast Asia Department
Asian Development Bank

About the Editors

Mia Mikic is a trade economist with a keen interest in sustainable development and proven track record in academia and international civil service. She is engaged as research fellow at the University of Waikato.

Guy Sacerdoti has been a consultant for ADB for the past 20 years, working primarily as an economics editor and speechwriter on regional cooperation and integration. He has covered Southeast Asia extensively since 1975 for a variety of publications including the former Far Eastern Economic Review.

James Villafuerte leads the Association of Southeast Asian Nations (ASEAN) Policy Network at the Asian Development Bank (ADB). His areas of research include economic and regional cooperation issues in Southeast Asia, economic outlook and risk assessment, COVID-19 impact and drivers of economic recovery.

Dulce Zara is a senior regional cooperation officer at the Southeast Asia Department. Her work experience covers knowledge management, program management, strategic planning, results management, and economic analysis since she joined ADB in 2007. She works with country teams across Southeast Asia to produce quality partnership strategies and operational plans, country performance assessments, and economic publications and related events.

About the Authors

Chapter 1

Mia Mikic is advisor at large for ARTNet. She is a board member of the Friends of Multilateralism Group, Board of Advisors for the Trade Policy Research Forum, and the Advisory Board of the Center on Inclusive Trade and Development, Georgetown Law, United States.

Chapter 2

Adrian Mendoza is assistant professor at the University of the Philippines (UP) School of Economics and is currently completing his master of statistics degree in UP Diliman. His previous research covers technology and economic growth, complexity and economic diversification, innovation and internationalization in global value chain (GVC) firms; social and technological upgrading in GVCs; trade wars; and the labor and trade impact of the coronavirus disease (COVID-19), among others.

James Villafuerte is a principal economist at the Southeast Asia Department at the Asian Development Bank. He conducts research on a wide range of economic and regional cooperation issues in Southeast Asia, including trade and GVC participation, infrastructure financing, and climate change, among others.

Chapter 3

Phu Huynh is a labor economist for the International Labour Organization (ILO) in Geneva, Switzerland specializing in employment policies and issues in Southeast Asia. With 15 years of experience analyzing labor market trends, he has advised senior policy makers and leaders of employer and worker organizations throughout Asia and the Pacific. He has published studies on working conditions in Asia's garment sector, the impact of ASEAN integration on skills demand, technology and the future of jobs, and the impact of crises on employment and labor markets.

Kee Beom Kim is macroeconomic and employment policies specialist at the Employment Policy Department of the ILO in Geneva, Switzerland. His work focuses on providing technical support in the design and implementation of national economic, employment, and labor market policies; and conducts research on important macroeconomic and employment issues.

Christian Viegelahn is employment specialist of the Office for Pacific Islands Countries of the ILO in Suva, Fiji. He offers technical advice to senior policy makers and leaders of the region's employer and worker organizations on employment-related policies and issues. His research focuses on labor economics, the future of work, international trade, global value chains, and macroeconomics.

Chapter 4

Gloria Pasadilla is consultant at the Philippine Department of Trade and Industry and is currently helping implement the Creative Industry Development Act, focusing particularly on new media services. She is partner and director of the Leadership Design Studio Pte, Inc. and a member of the Advisory Board of the Trade Policy Research Forum.

Chapter 5

Sindhu Bharathi is the senior research analyst at Infinite Sum Modelling LLC and holds expertise in economic modeling, data analytics, and policy analysis. She has experience of working on a broad range of Computable General Equilibrium models including GTAP-E, GTAP-Power, GTAP-E-Power, GTAP-Value Added, among others. Bharathi is a key expert for an African Development Bank study on "Assessing the Potential Benefits and Costs of the African Continental Free Trade Area (AfCFTA) on African Economies." She is a contributor to the Global Trade Analysis Project (GTAP) database.

Sumathi Chakravarthy is managing director of Infinite Sum Modelling, United States, and has wide experience and expertise in economic modeling, trade policy analysis, technology leadership, and product management. She has worked on several research studies focusing on using a computable general equilibrium framework to analyze policy impact. Chakravarthy is team leader for an African Development Bank study on "Assessing the Potential Benefits and Costs of the African Continental Free Trade Area (AfCFTA) on African Economies." She has contributed to the building of the GTAP database from IO tables.

Badri Narayanan Gopalakrishnan serves NITI Aayog, Government of India, as a fellow, wherein he headed the verticals of Trade and Commerce, Strategic Economic Dialogue, International Cooperation and Vision India@2047. He founded Infinite Sum Modelling LLC and is an expert in trade, environmental/energy, labor, and public health policies. He has informed the process of decision making in several major economic policies such as free trade agreements, technology regulations, etc., both through his academic research and consulting/advisory projects.

Chapter 6

Peter Petri is Carl J. Shapiro professor of international finance at the Brandeis International Business School (IBS), a nonresident senior fellow of the Brookings Institution, and visiting fellow of the Peterson Institute for International Economics. He has written and consulted extensively on Asia and Pacific trade, investment, and innovation. He was founding dean of Brandeis IBS and has held visiting appointments at the ADB Institute; the Organisation for Economic Co-operation and Development; the World Bank; the World Trade Organization; and at Fudan, Keio, and Peking universities.

Michael Plummer is director of the School of Advanced International Studies (SAIS) Europe, SAIS professor of international economics, and Eni professor of economics at Johns Hopkins University. He has taught at more than a dozen universities in Asia, Europe, and North America and has advised many governments in Asia, North America, and Europe on trade policy and regional cooperation.

Acknowledgments

This publication was prepared by the Regional Cooperation and Operations Coordination Division (SERC) of the Southeast Asia Department (SERD) of the Asian Development Bank (ADB). It was financed by ADB under the Knowledge and Support Technical Assistance (TA)-9964 Policy Advice for COVID-19 Economic Recovery in Southeast Asia.

The publication was edited by Mia Mikic, Guy Sacerdoti, James Villafuerte, and Dulce Zara.

The editors would like to thank all contributors to this book, namely: Sindhu Bharathi, Sumathi Chakravarthy, Badri Narayanan Gopalakrishnan, Phu Huynh, Kee Beom Kim, Adrian Mendoza, Gloria Pasadilla, Peter Petri, Michael Plummer, Shujiro Urata, Christian Viegelahn, and James Villafuerte.

The editors are grateful to Alfredo Perdiguero, SERC director for providing support to the study.

The editors are also grateful for the valuable comments and suggestions from all peer reviewers, namely: Jayant Menon from ISEAS-Yusof Ishak Institute; Lorraine Elliott from Coral Bell School of Asia Pacific Affairs of Australian National University; Sameer Khatiwala, Jong Woo Kang, Mahinthan Mariasingham, Arief Ramayandi, and Paul Vanderberg from ADB; and Peter Morgan from ADB Institute. The editors would also like to acknowledge members of the ASEAN Policy Network who provided useful comments and suggestions, particularly: Emma Allen, Henry Ma, Teresa Mendoza, and Eve Cherry Lynn from ADB.

James Villafuerte, principal economist; and Dulce Zara, senior regional cooperation officer led the preparation of this report. Mae Hyacinth Kyocho and Joyce Marie Lagac, ADB consultants, provided research and technical support, while Melissa May Ebarvia and Camille Genevieve Salvador extended administrative assistance. Mike Cortes typeset and produced the layout as well as created the cover design. Lawrence Casiraya and Blanche Fernandez copyedited the manuscript, while Maria Guia de Guzman proofread the report. The editors likewise acknowledge the Support Division of the Department of Communications, ADB, who facilitated the publishing of this report.

Abbreviations

ACE	Association of Southeast Nations Centre for Energy
ADAS	advanced driver assistance system
ADB	Asian Development Bank
AFC	Asian financial crisis
AFTA	ASEAN Free Trade Area
AI	artificial intelligence
ALMP	active labor market policy
AMRO	ASEAN+3 Macroeconomic Research Office
APEC	Asia-Pacific Economic Cooperation
APTIR	Asia-Pacific Trade and Investment Report
ASCCR	ASEAN State of Climate Change Report
ASEAN	Association of Southeast Asian Nations
ASEAN+3	ASEAN plus Japan, the People's Republic of China, and the Republic of Korea
ASIC	application specific integrated circuits
A&T	assembly and testing
AVE	ad valorem equivalent
BAU	business-as-usual
BEV	battery electric vehicle
CBTAs	carbon border tax adjustments
CEPA	Comprehensive Economic Partnership Agreement
CES	constant elasticities of substitution
CGCC	Credit Guarantee Corporation of Cambodia
CGE	computable general equilibrium
CHIPS	Creating Helpful Incentives to Produce Semiconductors and Science
CO_2	carbon dioxide
COP	Conference of the Parties
COVID-19	coronavirus disease
CPTPP	Comprehensive and Progressive Agreement for Trans-Pacific Partnership
CPU	central processing unit
DAVAX	directly absorbed value-added exports
DRAM	dynamic random-access memory
DVA	domestic value added
E&E	electrical and electronics
EU	European Union
EV	electric vehicle
FDC	domestic double counting

FDI	foreign direct investment
FTAAP	Free Trade Area of the Asia Pacific
FTA	free trade agreement
GDP	gross domestic product
GEI	Government Efficiency Index
GFC	global financial crisis
GHG	greenhouse gas
GST	global stocktake
GTAP	global trade analysis project
GTM	global trade model
GVC	global value chain
HEV	hybrid electric vehicle
HS	harmonized system
IAVAX	indirectly absorbed value-added exports
IC	integrated circuit
ICE	internal combustion engine
ICT	information and communication technology
IDM	integrated device manufacturer
IEA	International Energy Agency
ILO	International Labour Organization
IMF	International Monetary Fund
IoT	Internet of Things
IIoT	industrial Internet of Things
IPCC	Intergovernmental Panel on Climate Change
IPEF	Indo-Pacific Framework for Economic Prosperity
IRENA	International Renewable Energy Agency
ISCO	international standard classification of occupations
ISIC	international statistical industry classification
LCOE	levelized cost of electricity
MGI	McKinsey Global Institute
MNC	multinational company
MRIO	multiregional input–output
MRIOT	multiregional input–output tables
MSME	micro, small, or medium-sized enterprise
MtCO$_2$e	metric ton of carbon dioxide equivalent
MW	megawatt
NATO	North Atlantic Treaty Organization
NATO+	North Atlantic Treaty Organization and their member allies
NDC	nationally determined contribution
NEV	new energy vehicle
NTB	nontariff barrier
OECD	Organisation for Economic Co-operation and Development
OEM	original equipment manufacturer
OLS	ordinary least squares

OSAT	outsourced semiconductor assembly and test
PCB	printed circuit boards
PHEV	plug-in hybrid electric vehicle
PPP	purchasing power parity
PV	photovoltaic
R&D	research and development
RCEP	Regional Comprehensive Economic Partnership
RESCUE	Reinforce Supply Chain Under Emergency
RTA	regional trade agreement
RVC	regional value chain
UNCTAD	United Nations Conference on Trade and Development
UNDP	United Nations Development Programme
UNFCCC	United Nations Framework Convention on Climate Change
UNIDO	United Nations Industrial Development Organization
VAX	value-added exports
WMO	World Meteorological Organization
WTO	World Trade Organization

1

Toward Future-Proofing Global Value Chains

Mia Mikic

ASEAN Is Facing an Evolving "New Normal"

Serious risks remain for the Association of Southeast Asian Nations (ASEAN) to fully use its global and regional value chains to continue its recovery and meet its sustainable development vision. The best way to mitigate these risks is to make growth more inclusive and aligned with its net-zero emission commitments.

For decades, ASEAN grew into an important supplier, stopover, and end user in global value chains (GVCs) and production networks. Its rapid economic development was predicated on an outward-oriented trade strategy based on strong GVC linkages supported by foreign direct investment and regional trade agreements (RTAs).[1] As a result, the region has become one of the most important regional hubs for GVCs. Development benefited immensely. Most ASEAN economies created a strong manufacturing and export base, generated more and better-quality jobs, fostered innovation and technology, spread knowledge, and reduced poverty. However, there were others that concentrated GVC participation in one or a few sectors with limited economy-wide social or economic benefits—and without much regard for environmental protection.[2] Nevertheless, ASEAN gross domestic product (GDP) expanded at an average annual growth rate of 5.7% from 2000 to 2019, making it the third-largest economy in Asia and the fifth-largest globally. The ASEAN Community 2025 Vision committed to "leave no one behind" as economic expansion continued—despite signs that globalization (particularly in investment and trade) was weakening as global economic uncertainties deepened. While some members were benefiting from increasing trade tensions between the United States (US) and the People's Republic of China (PRC), by and large average ASEAN GVC participation suffered.[3]

Then, in early 2020, the coronavirus disease (COVID-19) pandemic shocked the world. ASEAN GDP declined relatively less in 2020 than most other emerging economies and by end-2021 had fully offset the drop in

---

[1] ASEAN members have collectively signed 130 RTAs—as notified to the World Trade Organization (WTO) as of November 2022. Including seven ASEAN and ASEAN+1 agreements, another 60 trade agreements have been signed with various partners regionally and globally. By comparison, the European Union as a customs union has signed 46 trade agreements (WTO RTA database [assessed 28 November 2022]).

[2] For example, poor work conditions in Malaysia's palm oil industry or occupational safety issues in Cambodia's garment industry (see SWI. 2019. *Nestlé criticised over migrant palm oil workers in Malaysia*. 17 September. https://www.swissinfo.ch/eng/responsible-business_nestl%C3%A9-criticised-over-migrant-palm-oil-workers-in-malaysia/45234426.). In Myanmar, progress on poverty reduction was reversed due to the recent developments started in early 2021.

[3] Early estimates showed Viet Nam, Cambodia, and a few other ASEAN economies to benefit from geopolitical trade tensions; see more in Anukoonwattaka and Lobo (2019) or Abiad et al. (2018) .

output. GDP expanded by 5.6% in 2022 before decelerating to 4.7% in 2023 (ADB 2022b)—higher than the average for most regions in Asia. ASEAN's relative economic resilience has been linked to steady progress on policy reforms, but even more to its continued integration, both regionally and globally.[4] This comes through in the title of the first *ASEAN Development Outlook* (2021)— "ASEAN's modern economic success has been founded on its external relationship with the world, rather than its internal relationship with its own past and future."[5]

Obviously, much hinges on ASEAN's ability to maintain its place in global and regional integration through its GVC participation and regional value chains (RVCs). This book—a collection of edited papers—was motivated by the desire to understand the disruptive effects the pandemic had on ASEAN's GVC participation; and to assess its ability to address post-pandemic challenges, including climate change. Given ASEAN's dependence on GVC-linked trade and production, the book sets out to investigate how resilient GVCs have been during the first years of the pandemic. The findings can be fed into the policies that help ASEAN economies build resilience against recurring pandemics or other shocks. Importantly, it highlights three policy areas vital for building forward better—jobs, technology and decarbonization.

Before the work on the book was completed, new global challenges emerged that affected governance and evolving policies. Geopolitical tensions—already evident pre-pandemic—were aggravated by calls for reduced dependency on foreign supplies and imports, especially from physically and structurally (for example, politically) distant countries. As a result, a revival of previous industrial policies that included subsidies for favored economic sectors, for example, reappeared in economies that have long been destination markets for ASEAN exporters. The Russian invasion of Ukraine—which fueled further price increases and disrupted access to natural resource commodities and food—significantly altered how governments and the private sector evaluate risk as the global economy trended toward fragmentation once more. Regrettably, long-standing support for an open, rules-based system retreated as more discretionary, power-based approaches gained strength. Thus, we expanded our analysis

---

[4] Resilience—the ability to quickly return to equilibrium when shocked—has different meanings to different economic actors (Gereffi 2021). Firms participating in GVCs mostly see resilience as finding an adequate balance between operational efficiency and risk management. The GVCs/supply chains will see it as identifying an appropriate governance structure allowing for participating firms to flexibly reorganize and diversify suppliers where needed. And finally, a country will see national resilience through the lens of market stability; national security; and the uninterrupted pursuit of economic, social, and environmental goals. While different for each economic actor, resilience across firms, GVCs, and markets is interconnected and interdependent. They either support one another or amplify where resilience is lacking.

[5] ASEAN. 2021a. *ASEAN Development Outlook*. Jakarta: ASEAN Secretariat. p.21.

to incorporate the realities of a new—or ever-evolving—"new normal." This "new normal" must be able to adapt to pandemic-affected ecosystems, fragmentation that resorts to protectionism, and renewed confidence in state intervention, along with more frequent and destructive disasters due to climate change—all spiced by deepening geopolitical tensions. This breeds new risks and amplifies those already known to ASEAN. While they can paint a dimmer picture of ASEAN's near future, they may also provide impetus to better understand how they can affect members' long-term participation in the global economy—especially through trade, investment, and GVCs. They will help define what a full and lasting post-pandemic recovery would look like, and set a path toward moving forward on Sustainable Development Goal targets.

In today's unpredictable geopolitical environment, on top of continuing pandemic challenges, it is reasonable to identify six risks confronting internationally shared production networks and value chains and their importance to recovery and sustained, more inclusive, and "green" growth:[6]

i.   Problems accessing resources, intermediate inputs, and commodities important for both backward and forward GVC linkages—including policies and disruptions in cross-border logistics.
ii. Shortages of the new skills required along value chain segments.
iii. Difficulties in accessing sufficient, reasonably priced energy affected by both geopolitical disruptions and country commitments under the Paris Agreement.[7]
iv. Barriers to global and regional market access stemming from unilateral policies affecting trade and investment (including possible carbon taxes).
v.   Disregard for multilateral trading rules in favor of discretionary, power-based rules that create further fragmentation.
vi. Interruptions in financial flows, rising prices, and issues with debt financing.

Ignoring these risks could upend ASEAN participation in GVCs and the benefits its economies enjoy, along with creating lon-run resilience against new shocks. The chapters included here offer comprehensive, novel analyses and the evidence needed to inform policy makers on ways to respond to these risks. It provides useful background information for regional consultations involving governments, academia and the business community.

---

[6]   Obviously, ASEAN faces other risks; this list covers those that relate to ASEAN's reliance on foreign markets as future sources of prosperity.
[7]   These are given as the nationally determined contributions (NDCs).

This overview chapter summarizes the five chapters.[8] The next section details ASEAN's GVC participation in global and intraregional value chains before and during the pandemic (Chapter 2). It also identifies what could contribute to increasing ASEAN's value chain resilience. The next three sections summarize the research results of Chapters 3, 4, and 5—addressing the challenges of jobs, technology and innovation, and decarbonization. The penultimate section summarizes the main findings of the final chapter (Chapter 6) that uses the new normal as a baseline for a novel computable general equilibrium (CGE) model to analyze complex developments in the global economy and the effects on international value chains. Chapter 6 sets out seven increasingly complex policy scenarios ranging from geopolitically motivated reshoring, near-shoring, and friend-shoring of trade proposals for extending RTAs. The final section offers some takeaways for policy makers.

ASEAN Remains a Value Chain Hub with Greater Reliance on Intraregional Links

Despite a gradual decline in importance to overall trade, GVCs remain the trademark of ASEAN integration. The COVID-19 pandemic has, however, nudged ASEAN economies toward deepening intraregional value chains.

GVCs define 21st century international trade. ASEAN's participation grew roughly in step with global trends and was driven by the same forces—new technology, favorable market conditions, and the reforms that helped lower international trade costs (see chapter 2, figure 2.1).[9] Over the years, ASEAN has become one of the most important regional hubs for GVCs in manufacturing, with individual members having participation rates higher than the average GVC participation rate for the Asia and Pacific (ADB 2022).

---

[8] The final version of this chapter benefited enormously from the discussion at the Global Value Chains Project's midterm review workshop organized on 29-30 August 2022 with the chapter authors, peer reviewers, and Asian Development Bank (ADB) participants.

[9] See Chapter 2: The State of Play of ASEAN Global Value Chains. Value-added trade within GVCs refers to value added that crosses at least two borders between initiation of production and final consumption—following the methodology of Borin and Macini (2019) and Belot i, Borin, and Mancini (2020). It can flow between countries with a direct trading relationship, or indirectly through a third country (see ADB, Research Institute for Global Value Chains at the University of International Business and Economics, World Trade Organization, Institute of Developing Economies–Japan External Trade Organization, and China Development Research Foundation. 2021. *Global Value Chain Development Report 2021: Beyond Production.* Manila. https://www.adb.org/sites/default/files/publication/747966/global-value-chain-development-report-2021.pdf). It is also customary to define GVC trade as a sum of backward and forward participation shares in a country's gross exports.

After the 2008–2009 global financial crisis (GFC), however, both ASEAN GVC trade and participation rates lost momentum, even more than global trends—or "slowbalization" (*The Economist* 2019). This was due to a combination of structural and cyclical factors, some emanating from policy changes or external shocks. Three shocks in particular helped prevent further growth of ASEAN's average GVC participation rate to pre-GFC levels—(i) disasters (2011), (ii) increasing trade tensions (2018), and (iii) the COVID-19 pandemic (from 2020).

With the onset of the pandemic, ensuing lockdowns and other mobility restrictions (Box 1.1), GVCs were quickly blamed for supply shortages, market disruptions, and barriers to health responses. Indeed, the initial months of the pandemic exposed the risks of both an overreliance on few or even a single supplier (or buyer) as well as not having access to efficient logistics, including digitalized trade services.

ASEAN was seen as more vulnerable to GVC contagion effects given that its economies were moving toward deeper interdependency and co-movements of national business cycles—conditions ripe for crisis contagion. ASEAN's sensitivity to shocks from its major trading partners (the PRC, Germany, Japan, the Republic of Korea [ROK], and the US) has shifted over the last 2 decades with sensitivity to the PRC-related economic shocks increasing relative to others. Thus, it is no surprise that ASEAN's GVC trade dipped by 9% in 2020, combining the region's backward (–7.4%) and forward (–13.4%) trade contractions. What may come as a surprise is that the decline continued the downward trend already triggered by the 2018 tariff increases by the US and PRC and, in fact, was relatively weaker in terms of the trade flows contraction (Chapter 2, Figure 2.19).

Box 1.1: Impact of the People's Republic of China's Zero-COVID Policy on the Region's Global Value Chains

The People's Republic of China (PRC) imposed lockdowns in 2020 at the start of the pandemic in Wuhan and other major cities. But its rigid zero-coronavirus disease (COVID-19) strategy has resulted in more lockdowns and contributed to supply disruptions in major markets. The latest lockdown cycle, which began in April 2022, effectively prolonged global supply chain disruptions. Among the most affected cities was Shanghai, the PRC's largest city with the world's busiest port, parts of the capital Beijing, and the northern province of Jilin, where automobile factories and other manufacturers industries are located. At the time of writing, Foxconn's Apple iPhone factory in Zhengzhou, Henan appeared to be seriously affected.[a]

The lockdowns in 2022 hit both demand and supply of products involved in the value chains. National statistics reported falling retail sales, industrial production, and employment.

The effect of the lockdowns on shipping was marked by port congestion and delays. By mid-2022, it took far longer for ships to leave the PRC and arrive at other major ports than before the pandemic. Due to travel restrictions and COVID-19 testing requirements, trucks were unable to pick up containers from ports, causing further delays and reduced exports. As a result, freight costs rose dramatically—sometimes double or triple—although by late 2022 they began to drop, mainly due to falling export demand, especially on routes out of the PRC. The World Container Index is approximately one-third of its peak level during the last months of 2021.[b] Demand was affected by many factors, including a return to spending on traditional services as many countries started to reopen for travel and face-to-face contact; inflation from rising energy costs; changes in production processes; and the impact of protectionist measures, including those designed to trigger reshoring.

However, expectations that lockdowns would drive companies out of the PRC into ASEAN economies and more recently India may be unfounded.[c] While there is significant interest in relocating some manufacturing to Viet Nam, the PRC remains the center of global value chains, particularly electronics—where there is a decline in the use of foreign inputs. The PRC works continuously to reduce reliance on foreign inputs. It has also increased exports of intermediate goods, enlarging its value added in others' exports (forward linkages). Thus, the PRC is now more integrated into global and regional value chains while less dependent on the rest of the world (Natixis) (Box Figure 1.1.2). On the other hand, frequent lockdowns and the ensuing bottlenecks did slow export recovery. ASEAN exports follow the same trend, highly sensitive to the PRC's economic cycle.

continued on next page

Box 1.1 (continued)

Box Figure 1.1.1: Asymmetric Participation in Value Chains

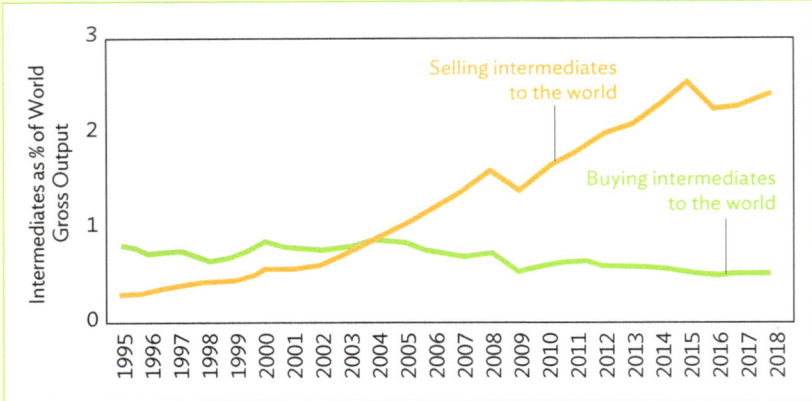

Box Figure 1.1.2: People's Republic of China Exports to the World

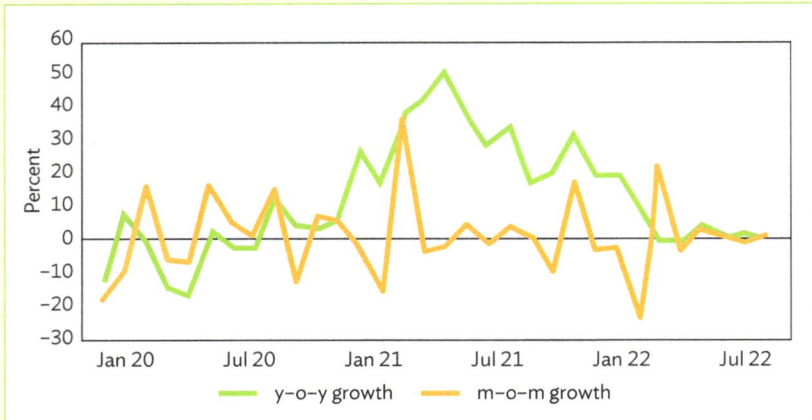

m-o-m = month-on-month, y-o-y = year-on-year.

[a] Costs to Apple in lost iPhone 14 sales could reach $1 billion a week (Bloomberg News. 2022. Violent Protests Erupt at Apple's Main IPhone Plant in China. *Bloomberg Asia*. 23 November. Bloomberg.com/news/articles/2022-11-23/violent-protests-erupt-at-apple-s-biggest-iphone-plant-in-china#xj4y7vzkg; and Liu, J. 2022. Apple has a huge problem with an iPhone factory in China. *CNN Business*. 26 November. https://edition.cnn.com/2022/11/25/tech/apple-foxconn-iphone-supply-china-covid-intl-hnk/index.html (accessed 26 November 2022).

[b] World Container Index (https://infogram.com/world-container-index-1h17493095xl4zj) (accessed 26 November 2022).

[c] It is more likely that a range of new export controls and due diligence monitoring measures will affect decoupling in future. See M. Bessler. CSIS. 2023. The Drive to Decouple. *CSIS*. 24 January. https://www.csis.org/blogs/new-perspectives-asia/drive-decouple.

Sources: R. Baldwin. 2022. The Peak Globalisation Myth: Part 1. VOX EU CEPR. 31 August. https://cepr.org/voxeu/columns/peak-globalisation-myth-part-1; Asian Development Bank.

In 2021, as increasing vaccination rates allowed for less-stringent containment measures globally, ASEAN economies enjoyed a strong recovery in GVC trade. As expected, the speed of recovery varied: highest in Indonesia (GVC trade up by 49.6%) and the Lao People's Democratic Republic (Lao PDR) (47.4%). Other members also recorded double-digit growth between 16% and 29% (Brunei Darussalam was the exception, contracting further by 7.7%) (Chapter 2, Figure 2.20). The recovery also differed markedly across sectors. Medium- and high-tech manufacturing and business services reacted most (both down in 2020 and up in 2021), as they are the most integrated into GVCs (Chapter 2, Figure 2.21). Machinery GVCs were more resilient to the pandemic shock, as they quickly returned to pre-pandemic trade levels (Box 1.2). The rebound in GVC trade was fueled by several factors—relaxed health restrictions, government stimulus for businesses and households, and strong consumer demand for durable goods, particularly as accelerated e-commerce covered for lower spending on traditional services.

Box 1.2: ASEAN Global Value Chains—Robustness and Resilience of Four Machinery Groups

To analyze the impact of the pandemic on global value chains (GVCs), monthly and yearly changes in machinery parts trade (for general, electric and electronic, transport, and precision machinery) was compared before and after the outbreak (2019–2020). Various previous studies found trade in parts closely related to GVC developments.

The analysis found that more than 90% of machinery products continued to be exported for all countries except the Philippines, for which the proportion was 80% (Box Table 1.2.1). The rate of change in exports was decomposed into changes based on the export status. The decline in exports was mostly due to a drop in the value of continuously exported products (intensive margin), not due to exported products pulled (extensive margin) from international markets. This shows that GVCs were not physically broken down—and thus robust—with the reduction caused by a pandemic-induced decline in supply due to temporary factory closures and disrupted transportation. Once the supply shock eased, trade value and volume recovered.

Econometric analysis of the pandemic impact on machinery parts trade found that the pandemic—measured by newly confirmed infections—caused a notable decline in the value of trade, but that the damage was short-lived. Trade recovered quickly, in most cases within 1 month of the shock. This shows GVC resilience, consistent with the earlier observation that GVCs were not physically broken but only temporarily disrupted because of the supply shock.

continued on next page

Box 1.2 (continued)

Box Table 1.2.1: Changes in Status of Exported Products (2019–2021)
(number of HS six-digit codes)

	Indonesia	Malaysia	Philippines	Thailand	Viet Nam
Continue	1,027	1,049	713	1,089	1,002
New	41	31	87	10	24
Exit	39	25	119	24	54

HS = Harmonized System.
Source: Baek et al. (Forthcoming). COVID-19 Pandemic and GVC Trade in ASEAN.

Box Table 1.2.2: Export Growth for 2019–2021 by Exported Product Status
(%)

Exporter	Sector	Total	Continue	New	Exit
Indonesia	General	7.7	7.7	0	0
	Electric	33.3	33.3	0	0
	Transport	25.8	25.8	0	0
	Precision	15.7	15.7		
Malaysia	General	31.2	31.3	0	0
	Electric	24.6	24.6		0
	Transport	−22.2	−22.4		0.2
	Precision	45.4	45.4	0	0
Philippines	General	3.4	3.2	−0.1	0.2
	Electric	12.2	12.2	0	0
	Transport	−14.6	−14.6	0	0
	Precision	−3.7	−3.7	0	0
Thailand	General	4.1	4.0	0	0.1
	Electric	16.4	16.4	0	
	Transport	5.0	5.0	0	
	Precision	−12.7	−12.7	0	
Viet Nam	General	152.2	152.2	0	0
	Electric	34.4	34.4	0	0
	Transport	−1.7	−1.7	0	0
	Precision	−49.5	−49.5	0	0

Note: 0 means very small change, while a blank means the product classification does not exist in the market.
Source: Baek et al. (Forthcoming). COVID-19 Pandemic and GVC Trade in ASEAN.

International trade data was used by Baek et al. (2023) to examine just how resilient GVCs are in four machinery-related industries in five ASEAN economies (Indonesia, Malaysia, the Philippines, Thailand, and Viet Nam).[10] Machinery is defined by clustering products based on the Harmonized System (HS) six-digit classification into four groups of machinery—general, electric, transport, and precision. There were three main results: (i) the pandemic damage on trade flows were limited and did not last long; (ii) GVCs were both robust and resilient, with, for example, trade in machinery parts recovering quickly; and (iii) the pandemic did not change trade patterns by either product composition or trading partner.

To better prepare ASEAN economies to withstand external shocks that combine demand and supply disruptions globally, understanding what drives the reactions to previous crises is as important as reactions from the pandemic itself. Some of these relate to operations and relationships of firms within value chains, while others are linked to policies needed to create an enabling space for businesses to operate.

As the chapters make clear, the more agile the business sector, the faster the economic and trade recovery. Firms that adequately assess the risks associated with operations and invest in contingency plans do best. Despite the cost implications and profit impact, those that have alternative supply sources and delivery routes—as well as contingency plans across the business—benefit. It boils down to business readiness (boosted with proper incentives) to complement or replace, if necessary, the "just-in-time" cost minimization model with the "just-in-case" risk exposure optimization model. Moving on from the response to the pandemic, businesses now have to pay full attention on how to move forward resiliently while using zero or as little as possible of carbon in their production and trade. They also should think of accounting for emissions produced while their products are consumed or disposed of.

The role policy makers play is fundamental, although one or more degrees removed from the actual GVC operations. A conducive business environment needs to maintain stable macroeconomic fundamentals, create a non-distortive regulatory environment, choose non-trade policies with minimal trade disruption, promote flexible yet fair labor markets, and be aware of the need for financial and social protection. In short, it builds resilience to external shocks.

---

[10] See Box 2.1: COVID-19 and the GVC Trade in ASEAN.

Unfortunately, firms are becoming ever more restricted in deciding on which products and partners to work with in GVCs, which all means increasing long-term costs in some foreign markets. While these restrictions are closely associated with the deteriorating global geopolitical outlook—with no early resolutions in sight—some are driven by decarbonization strategies now in place in many of ASEAN's destination markets. Long-term investors clearly prefer sustainability and green financing so ignoring that could deter future investment in the region. ASEAN economies will need to strategically tap the network of existing regional trade agreeements (RTAs) to circumvent any worsening in trade relations. If anything, ASEAN GVC trade is skewed toward backward linkages. ASEAN's trade with the "Plus 3" economies (the PRC, Japan, and the ROK) is roughly three times the size of intra-ASEAN trade (both GVC and non-GVC trade). Further diversification based on "open regionalism" accounting also for the need to green the supply chains continues to be the best response to the new normal.

Takeaway for policy makers

It is fair to conclude that GVCs proved more resilient to the pandemic than what many expected. And policy makers helped by boosting their countries and their firms' capability to address the challenges. However, one cannot ignore the problems faced by firms with a dependence on a few suppliers for essential goods; the reliance on manual labor (especially for essential supplies) and legacy technologies, which hampered both the production and distribution of these goods; and supply chains that severely affected both by business closures and logistical problems. Coupled with the uncertainty and turmoil in the current global economy, ASEAN can consider all measures that strengthen resilient participation in value chains without unnecessarily discouraging participation in trade, investment, and regional integration—all while honoring its carbon reduction commitments. This is motivated by the need to protect industries and segments involved with GVCs and regional value chains (RVCs), given their proven contributions to poverty reduction and prosperity in the long run.

Box 1.3: Global Value Chain Contribution to ASEAN Development and Poverty Reduction

The relationship between global value chains (GVCs) and development is not straightforward. While some results point to the positive impact GVC integration has on growth and employment, others show mixed effects on inequality, productivity, and upgrading technology (and environmental degradation). The World Bank (2020) estimates that a 1% increase in GVC participation boosts per capita income by more than 1%, roughly twice as much as the effect from conventional trade. This is consistent with evidence from developing Asia. Fujita (2019) also found a positive relationship between the growth of GVC participation and growth in Association of Southeast Asian Nations (ASEAN) per capita income. The largest growth spurt occurs when GVC participation moves out of primary activities to basic manufacturing, as in Cambodia and Viet Nam (World Bank 2020).

There is also some evidence that poverty reduction is greater when associated with an increase in GVC trade rather than standard trade. In Viet Nam, regions with more intensive GVC participation saw poverty decline more than elsewhere (World Bank 2020). As Susantono (2019) notes, a big portion of the drop in Asia's poverty rate (from 70% in 1981 to less than 10% in 2016) was due to expanding GVCs. Labor-intensive GVC segments provided employment to millions of low-wage workers, especially in labor-intensive industries such as textiles, apparel, and footwear. For low-income countries, then, increasing participation in even simple GVC activities can have a significant impact on employment, income, and welfare.

Figure: GVC Participation in ASEAN Has a Nonlinear Relationship with Per Capita GDP

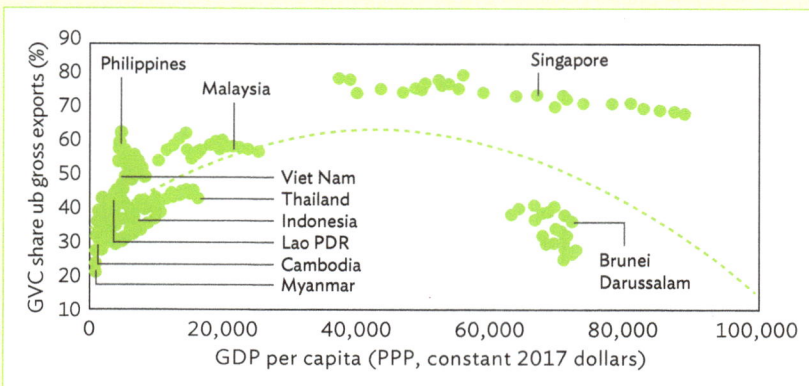

GDP = gross domestic product, GVC = global value chain, Lao PDR = Lao People's Democratic Republic, PPP = purchasing power parity.
Source: World Bank (2020), World Development Indicators.

continued on next page

Box 1.3 (continued)

The GVC participation rate has a nonlinear relationship with per capita GDP in ASEAN (Figure). At lower development levels, GVC participation has a strong positive relationship with GDP per capita. However, this begins to weaken or even reverse at higher levels, as in the case of Brunei Darussalam and Singapore. For less-developed and emerging economies, connecting to GVCs still provides an opportunity to increase income and productivity through various external channels such as trade, foreign direct investment, and productivity spillovers. First, greater GVC participation broadens the export market for domestic products. Second, GVC trade opens countries to foreign markets, standards, and regulations that may boost domestic competitiveness. Third, GVCs give access to cheaper and quality inputs and technologies that boost productivity. And fourth, inter-firm networks within GVCs may facilitate knowledge transfer through information sharing, firm-to-firm coordination, and other informal interactions.

Several studies show that GVCs in developing countries are good for labor and job creation.[a] In Viet Nam, the employment share of the population grew faster in provinces that became more GVC-intensive (World Bank 2020). They can boost job creation through the scale effects of foreign market participation as well as new investments in local production facilities. GVC participation can lead to higher wages through skills upgrading and increased productivity. They also offer greater foreign market access to micro, small, and medium sized enterprises—which employ most of the workforce. Econometric analysis covering 13 sectors in 40 countries over 15 years found that a 10% increase in GVC participation increased average productivity by 1.7% (Constantinescu, Mattoo, and Ruta 2017). De Vries et al. (2019) also found evidence of functional upgrading in several Asian economies, for example, seen by a rapid increase in research and development (R&D) employment in GVCs. In some cases, GVCs can even create better working conditions by adopting private standards governing worker health, safety, and treatment (OECD 2012; Bamber et al. 2014; Farole 2016; Hollweg 2019; World Bank 2017 and 2020; Shepherd 2021). For instance, Mendoza (2019) documented that Philippine manufacturers linked to GVCs have better labor conditions than purely domestic-oriented producers. Also, social upgrading within GVCs seems more robust when accompanied by upgraded technology.

For ASEAN, then, the use of advanced technology within GVCs, the need to adjust to changing demands of trading partners, and greater exposure to global competition contributed to increasing rates of technological adoption and learning (Felipe 2018). For example, Thailand's integration into appliance and automotive GVCs upgraded its technological skills and R&D capabilities (Abe 2013). Similarly, Viet Nam's recent success in electronics GVCs was helped by multinational investments in domestic R&D facilities. Torres de Oliveira et al. (2021) found that GVC participation in Viet Nam is associated with more process innovation.

[a]   See also Chapter 3.
Source: C. Viegelahn, P. Huynh, and K.B. Kim. (Forthcoming). *Jobs and Global Value Chains in Southeast Asia.*

Global Value Chains Can Create More and Better Jobs in ASEAN

In ASEAN, more than one-in-four jobs are linked to GVCs. They are anchors for stability across labor markets. Yet, there are wide differences across industries and economies. Increased GVC participation is associated with decreasing working poverty and increasing labor productivity at the country level—associations with other dimensions of better job quality are not universal and highly sector-dependent. To secure and spread benefits from GVCs, ASEAN economies need coherent, comprehensive, and integrated employment policy frameworks.

To help with recovery and to build forward better, GVCs need to provide more and better jobs—a steady rise in employment and decent jobs associated with value chain production and trade. Chapter 3 examines both and offers important policy recommendations.

Many ASEAN jobs are closely linked to GVCs and contribute to the production of goods and services consumed worldwide. In 2021, there were 75 million workers in nine ASEAN countries holding GVC-related jobs—more than 25% of total employment, up 2 percentage points from 2020 (or an additional 7 million jobs).[11] This brought the number of jobs linked to GVCs above the 2019 pre-crisis levels. Given the massive damage to labor from the COVID-19 pandemic, GVCs could be considered one factor driving the region's recovery in 2021 once restrictions began to ease (Box 1.4).

However, there are sharp differences in ASEAN's GVC jobs. Changes in the share of GVC jobs to total employment since 2000 show rapid increases in Viet Nam, Thailand, Cambodia, and the Lao PDR, while Malaysia, the Philippines, and to a certain extent Brunei Darussalam (since the pandemic) saw their shares fall. Singapore and Indonesia did not see much change, especially since 2010, but are at very different levels: Singapore with a 50% share while Indonesia at just over 10% (Chapter 3, Figure 3.2). The overall characteristics of ASEAN economies best explain these differences. In small less-developed economies such as the Lao PDR and to some extent Cambodia, developing agricultural value chains and growing domestic value contributed to GVC job growth. Viet Nam, by contrast,

---

[11] Estimates for Myanmar are not available. The methodology estimates the number of jobs in a particular country and sector that are dependent on the production of goods and services that cross borders (either as an input or as a final good) at least once before they reach the final consumer. Therefore, both direct and indirect jobs are counted (chapter 3, annex 1).

benefited more from foreign direct investment in manufacturing
(in garments and electronics, among others).

Box 1.4: Working Hours Lost in ASEAN in 2020

The pandemic hit labor markets hard. In 2020, aggregate working-hour losses—
both in lost jobs and declining working hours for those still employed—rose
7.4% relative to the fourth quarter of 2019. This was equivalent to the full-time
work of more than 20 million people, assuming a 48-hour work week.
The second quarter was the worst during the pandemic, with ASEAN's
working-hour losses reaching more than 17%.

New infections from virus variants, and gaps in vaccine access, distribution,
and containment continued to cause a 6.8% drop in working hours in 2021,
relative to before the pandemic. Working hours were estimated to remain below
pre-crisis levels in 2022, as the gradual recovery, geopolitical uncertainties, and
increasing food and energy prices added to the pandemic impact.[a]

[a] International Labour Organization (ILO). 2022. ILO Monitor on the World of Work, 10th Edition.
Source: ILO, ILOSTAT Database. https://ilostat.ilo.org/data/ (accessed 20 November 2022).

Manufacturing generates the highest share of jobs linked to GVCs. In 2021,
more than 60% of employment in manufacturing was linked to GVCs—
about the same as in 2000 but higher than the 50% just after the global
financial crisis. Agriculture almost doubled its share of GVC-linked
jobs—still around 20%, but a few percentage points higher than services.
The share of non-manufacturing GVC jobs has fallen since 2000, though
stabilizing in 2021 (Chapter 3, Figure 3.3). Within manufacturing, the
electronics sector, among others, has become a stabilizing factor with jobs
bouncing back due to strong consumer demand.[12]

It is also important to note that many of the manufacturing jobs are in
low- and medium-technology sectors, which tend to be associated with
higher carbon dioxide emissions. However, the highest share of jobs
in manufacturing is in consumer sectors such as electrical and optical
equipment, leather and footwear, and textiles and garments. In these
sectors, lead firms often face greater scrutiny from consumers about the
sustainability features of their products and are under increasing pressure to
ensure that carbon footprints are minimized across the entire value chains.
Estimating how many jobs are linked to intraregional value chains as

---

[12] Based on available ILOSTAT data, employment in electronics and electrical equipment manufacturing was
4.2% higher in the fourth quarter of 2021 relative to the fourth quarter of 2019 in Malaysia. In Thailand,
employment was consistently higher throughout 2020 and in the first quarter of 2021 relative to pre-
pandemic levels. In Viet Nam, employment in electronics and electrical equipment manufacturing saw
double-digit growth throughout 2020 and 2021 relative to pre-pandemic levels.

opposed to GVCs is interesting given the rising importance of ASEAN integration. Despite the higher share of ASEAN trade linked to RVCs compared to trade linked to GVCs, jobs linked to intraregional value chains remain relatively small—just 10 million jobs, or 13% of GVC jobs. With the projected rise of intraregional value chains continuing, this could be a source of new employment growth.

Who benefited in ASEAN from employment opportunities provided through GVC production and trade? The following are some detailed results of the research done related to gender, age, and skills:

- In 2021, the share of women holding GVC-related jobs (45%) was higher than their share of total employment (42%), highlighting the potential of GVCs in making labor markets more inclusive. This corresponded to almost double the number of women employed in GVC jobs in 2000. However, many of these jobs remain in sectors with lower skill requirements and lower pay, and they offer fewer leadership and promotion opportunities (Box 1.5).
- Likewise, since 2000, the share of young workers in GVC-related jobs is consistently higher than in total employment. However, both shares have declined over time, possibly because young people are staying in school longer for more education and better training.
- The share of employees in GVC-related jobs—an important measure of job quality—is also consistently higher than in total employment. In 2021, more than half of GVC jobs (54%) were held by employees, 2 percentage points more than for total employment. Especially in developing countries, employees tend to have better-quality jobs in the sense that their jobs offer on average more wage stability and better employment conditions than those self-employed.
- However, the share of workers in low- and medium-skill occupations is also higher in GVC-related jobs than in total employment. In 2021, only 11% of workers in high-skill occupations were in GVC jobs compared to 14% in total employment. This indicates that jobs created through GVCs in ASEAN are driven by sectors in which low- and medium-skill occupations are particularly prevalent such as garments, leather and footwear, and electronics, among others.

Box 1.5: Women in Global Value Chains

Sectors like garments and electronics are particularly important entry points for workers in Association of Southeast Asian Nations (ASEAN) global value chains (GVCs). And they have created important opportunities for women, including young women, to participate in the labor market.

Women in Indonesia, the Philippines, and Thailand took advantage of these opportunities at earlier stages of development. But their share in garments, for example, have fallen or stayed the same in more recent decades, as women in less-developed ASEAN economies have taken on these opportunities.[a] In Cambodia, female employment in garments tripled in a decade, rising from 256,000 in 2007 to 831,000 in 2017, with women accounting for 80% of the workforce.[b] Similarly, in Viet Nam, female employment in garments more than doubled between 2007 and 2020, rising from 1.6 million to 3.4 million—almost 75% of total employment in the sector. In Myanmar, the number of women working in garments almost doubled from 612,100 in 2015 to 1.0 million in 2019, or more than 85% of employment in the sector.

Similarly, GVCs in electronics also play an important role in hiring women, with the share of women in electronics higher than the female share of total employment in Cambodia, the Philippines, Thailand, and Viet Nam.

Figure: Female Employment in Garments, Electronics, and the Economy in Selected ASEAN countries

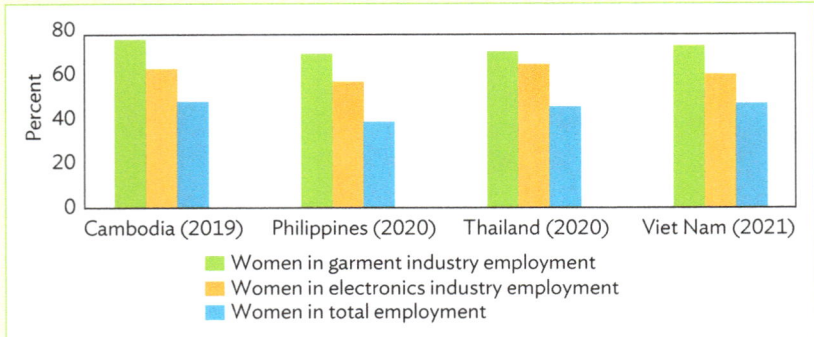

ASEAN = Association of Southeast Asian Nations.
Source: International Labour Organization (ILO) calculations based on ILO, ILOSTAT Database. https://ilostat.ilo.org/data/ (accessed 20 November 2022).

[a] The employment figures here refer to overall employment in garments and electronics in the region. A high share of jobs in these sectors is likely linked to GVCs.
[b] Garments include the manufacture of textiles (ISIC 13), wearing apparels (ISIC 14), and leather and related products (ISIC 15). All data from ILOSTAT. Male employment in garments in Cambodia increased at an even faster rate than female employment, but from a low base of 53,000 in 2007 to 212,000 in 2017.
Source: ILO. 2018. *Gender Gaps in the Garment, Textiles and Footwear Sector in Developing Asia,* ILO Asia-Pacific Garment and Footwear Sector Research Note.

Backward linkages are often described as "import to export," because they use imports to produce direct exports. In contrast, forward participation is based on supplying inputs to foreign producers for their use in exports (which becomes indirect exports, also known as "export to export").

Econometric analysis offers several important insights on the link between deeper GVC participation and jobs over the past 2 decades. Increased backward and forward GVC participation were associated with higher labor productivity and lower working poverty at the country level. However, enhanced GVC participation was not universally linked to other dimensions of better job quality, such as higher shares in wage employment and higher-skilled employment. Greater forward GVC participation in ASEAN was tied to a lower wage employment share overall—despite higher wage employment shares in manufacturing—emanating from the mostly self-employed agricultural workers in the primary sector. Higher GVC participation was also linked to greater demand for low- and medium-skilled employment at the expense of higher-skilled jobs. Nevertheless, greater backward GVC integration was correlated with some employment gains for women. However, the benefits were concentrated in the primary sector and personal and professional services, both typically less skill-intensive, less productive, and lower paid. Finally, a literature review underscored the deficiencies in GVCs in providing decent work.

Well-designed social protection and labor market policies can help cushion the shocks GVCs propagate as well as their distributional consequences. Investments in a broad range of skills are needed to move into higher value-added work within the value chain. And deeper trade agreements, which increasingly include labor provisions, can help strengthen the link between increased GVC participation and decent work. Investment in social protection will be enhanced as more companies opt to decarbonize their GVC operations as some jobs might be lost in the process.

Takeaway for policy makers

Deeper GVC participation in ASEAN over the past 2 decades is associated with some positive labor market gains. However, some important benefits— accelerated labor productivity growth, expansion in wage employment, and more and better jobs for youth and women—have yet to fully take hold. These results underline a critically important point: the link between GVCs and the creation of good jobs is not automatic. It requires comprehensive labor market policies and institutions supported by strong social dialogue between governments and organizations representing employers and workers. It is critical to have a strategy that can help transform these relationships, using employment and social protection policies that reduce gender inequalities, make the labor market more inclusive, and invest across a broad range of skills development to allow workers to shift into higher value-added jobs within the value chain. Deep trade agreements, with labor provisions, can help strengthen the link between increased GVC participation and decent work. On the other hand, some environmental provisions of these type of agreements, as well as some recent unilaterally pursued initiatives (also known as industrial policies) with objectives of tackling climate change might inadvertently cause trade and investment flows diversion and thus a loss of jobs in ASEAN.

Innovation and Technology Can Increase Participation in ASEAN Global Value Chains

New technology is at the same time an enabler of growth and resilience, and a serious disruptor of the status quo. Technology is fast transforming GVC products such as automobiles and electronics. ASEAN's competitive advantages based on cheap labor will no longer drive GVC (re)location and participation. For ASEAN to retain its role in GVCs, a comprehensive innovation policy should include developing the skills needed in an increasingly tech-driven new normal.

Technology has changed the calculus for multinational companies leading GVCs. They used to seek out places with cheap labor as a major consideration in deciding where to invest. The original ASEAN economies, wanting foremost to give their people jobs, benefited from this paradigm and became important players in multinational companies' GVCs. But the new technology transforming today's industries is changing the offshoring and outsourcing that were the bedrock of GVC production and trade in past decades. Importantly, anchor companies' new positioning is often part of their overall operations decarbonization strategies. ASEAN now needs to not only be integral part of decarbonization but crucially ramp up development of more skilled labor to continue to climb the innovative GVC ladder.

New technology creates new jobs, while others are rendered obsolete. The question is what skills do these new jobs require? Some "new" jobs today did not exist yesterday, such as big data analysts, artificial intelligence (AI) trainers, AI translators, blockchain traders, and cybersecurity specialists, among countless others. With new technologies, economic competitiveness depends on the availability of an abundant skilled workforce that can fill these new job descriptions.

Chapter 4 uses case studies in the automotive and electronics GVCs to help understand how technology-induced changes will impact those ASEAN economies that have been active in these GVCs. The chapter highlights the need for skills development to attract investments in the high-tech industries of the future (Box 1.6). It offers suggestions on how to handle innovation and skills development while balancing "new normal" risks.

The drive toward electric and autonomous cars, for example, has made ASEAN's continued role in automotive GVCs more uncertain. Incorporating new and ever-evolving technology is essential. Battery storage and energy capacity continue to rise as costs per output decrease—making electric vehicles (EVs) more affordable and desirable. Climate change and net-zero carbon emission commitments is another factor driving more EV production. With roughly 30% of carbon emissions coming from transportation, the automotive industry is under increasing government (and social) pressure to shift from internal combustion engines (ICEs) to low carbon-emitting EVs.

ASEAN demand for EVs, however, is negligible for now. This is actually good news for the ASEAN value chain because its market for finished products is largely within the region rather than global (Chapter 4, Figure 4.4). This means that the technology-induced threat to labor and employment might not be as intense in ASEAN as in developed countries (and ASEAN has some time to plan for a transforming RVC). Suppliers for the automotive industry, however, especially parts and component manufacturers, might be worse off because their products are marketed and distributed globally. To the extent that EVs use less parts and components, many suppliers may eventually find themselves out of business.

As mentioned, there is still some time before much of this happens, thankfully. First, because ICE cars are not going to disappear anytime soon. Consumer surveys show many still prefer ICE vehicles and would not buy EVs without subsidies. Second, EV production must overcome several bottlenecks—including constraints on sourcing raw materials (for batteries), the threat of supply chain disruptions in producing inputs such as silicon steel, as well as lack of well-developed charging infrastructure. Recent developments in subsidy policies of major players (the US and the European Union [EU]) will undeniably affect ASEAN prospects.

Box 1.6: Labor Impact of the Automotive Transformation

As more countries ban the sale of conventional internal combustion engine (ICE) cars in the coming decades, the shift to electric vehicle (EV) manufacturing should result in net job losses across the automotive industry. Some workers can be retrained for EV production, but the number of EV jobs will not compensate for the ICE jobs lost. There are three reasons why:

i. EVs have fewer parts to assemble as they have no emissions; they do not need parts or modules like exhaust systems, mufflers, catalytic converters, or tailpipes; they have no spark plugs, fuel tanks, or radiators. All this means less labor. The most complex part of EV production is battery manufacturing, which is largely automated and outsourced, with little manpower needed. The drop in labor demand will reverberate across traditional parts suppliers in the value chain as well as in aftermarket services.

ii. EV skills are slightly different from those used for ICEs. EVs rely on electrical, chemical, and software engineering skills, while ICEs require mechanical and materials engineering. Retraining will be needed to shift workers out of ICE to EV manufacturing.

    Sales and after-market services skills will also change. Salespeople will have to learn how to pitch EVs. For example, in addition to flaunting the latest entertainment system, salespeople must learn about batteries. Different batteries store varying amounts of energy—the popular cobalt-based lithium-ion batteries have better capacity—but cobalt itself has geopolitical and environmental issues (research on eliminating cobalt from lithium-ion batteries is well underway). Their characteristics affect EV driving ranges and recharging costs, key considerations for most EV buyers.

    Service technicians must also adapt. For example, unlike ICEs, EVs do not require periodic oil changes, tune-ups, radiator flushes, or spark plugs replacements. Thus, they need fewer auto technicians. Even EV brakes last longer because of EVs' regenerative braking system that helps reduce brake pad wear and tear. Dealerships and repair shops will transform as well.

iii. Indirect labor in the car industry will also be affected. Besides less mechanics for maintenance and repair, gas station attendants will also likely be put out of work. There will likely be fewer charging stations compared with the current number of gas stations and pumps, with charging stations requiring fewer employees as they are often unmanned (and people can charge their EVs overnight at home).

Sources: P. Eisenstein. 2019. Electric Vehicles Pose 'Real Risk' for Autoworkers, With Fewer Parts—and Jobs—Required. *NBC News*. https://www.nbcnews.com/business/autos/electric-vehicles-pose-real-risk-autoworkers- halving-number-people-required-n1060426; D. Conigliaro. 2019. Automotive, *This is How Employment in the Car Industry is Changing*. https://www.morningfuture.com/ en/2019/04/15/automotive-innovation-change-work/.

In electronics and electrical products, ASEAN covers more than 10% of global semiconductor parts and component exports.[13] Semiconductors power all electronic devices, so demand continues to rise. Malaysia, Thailand, the Philippines, and Singapore have for years been an important part of the semiconductor GVC, while Viet Nam is the fast-growing new entrant. It provides these economies with many job opportunities and contributes a fair share of GDP.

Globally, the industry continues to consolidate major producers along the semiconductor value chain. This is partly due to the high capital intensity in fabrication, and partly due to short life cycles or rapidly changing semiconductor technology, which leads to mergers or acquisitions. ASEAN's role has been in the labor-intensive stage of assembly, packaging, and testing. Countries like Malaysia tried to upgrade its position in the value chain as it attempted to attract foundries, but was not successful globally. Other ASEAN economies have had similar difficulties in climbing the value chain. Singapore alone was able to become a knowledge hub, attracting key firms in chip design.

While demand for semiconductors is constantly growing, ASEAN's continued participation depends on overcoming some significant challenges. For example, producers could get stuck in a semiconductor segment with little room for growth, either because they manufacture components that serve less-innovative markets, their existing technologies are old, or regulatory changes overseas are driven by new normal geopolitics.[14] The majority of Philippine exports, for example, are in computer-related office equipment and hard disk drives—considered "sunset products" with less room for innovation. Hard disk drives, also a key export of Thailand, are being replaced with hybrid or solid-state drives for use in data centers. This is part of the trend toward cloud computing rather than local or personal storage. In contrast, Viet Nam has joined the fast-growing market of smartphones and tablets which offer more opportunities for expansion and growth. ASEAN's challenge is to push for investments from multinational companies catering to new and innovative products, particularly those needed for Industry 4.0, AI, and the Internet of Things. The question is whether ASEAN can offer the skilled manpower required.

---

[13] The electronics and electrical industry manufactures electrical parts and components, electronic equipment, and end products that contain electronics (the so-called 3Cs—consumer electronics, communications, and computer/storage/office) (Chapter 4, Figure 4.1).

[14] The US recently passed the CHIPS and Science Act (August 2022)—also known as Creating Helpful Incentives to Produce Semiconductors for America Act. Its goal is to (i) reduce the likelihood that external shocks disrupt chip supply, (ii) boost US competitiveness and create domestic jobs, and (iii) protect semiconductors from being sabotaged during the manufacturing process (V. Kannon and J. Feldgoise. 2022. After the CHIPS Act: The limits of reshoring and Next Steps for US Semiconductor Policy. *Carnegie Endowment for International Peace.* November). The European Chips Act will likely be updated to match the US despite the EU promoting a Trade and Technology Council between the US and the EU for cooperating on and coordinating policies.

Another challenge for ASEAN is the increasing forward linkage foundry expansion ("pure play fabs") that include the assembly, testing, and packaging that was previously outsourced to third parties and third markets. These fabs have the capacity to provide 2.5D/3D packaging expertise, a packaging methodology for including multiple integrated circuits inside one package, which is required for cutting-edge chips. This push into the back-end business will compete with external outsourced semiconductor assembly and test from ASEAN economies, threatening their value-added contribution to the GVC, but also pushing companies to upgrade their technologies to become more competitive.

Several policies can help address ASEAN's human capital challenge. The skills typically required in technology are engineering, computer science, programming, and analytics (math/statistics). In the digital economy, there is a particularly acute shortage of skills that deal with complex data analytics, as well as the need for workers with problem-solving skills that can integrate applications and systems (Frederick, Bamber, and Cho 2018).

Sometimes, these skills need to be married with creativity, business-related skills, and soft skills to join the C-suite of companies. Governments need to (i) promote in-house training; (ii) encourage university and private partnerships; (iii) constantly update science and engineering curricula to keep up with technological advancements; (iv) consider having an individual learning account—akin to a portable provident fund—where individuals, companies and government contribute funds for individuals to draw on for certified training and upskilling.

Takeaway for policy makers

Technology is responding to the calls to tackle climate change risks and in the process is changing GVCs. Low-skilled labor will no longer be a competitive advantage for developing economies that want to climb the GVC ladder. The automotive and electronics and electrical case studies give examples of skills that will no longer be needed and the trends that could upend ASEAN's earlier comparative advantage in specific segments of the value chain. Improving the core determinants for investment growth—such as infrastructure and connectivity—remains key. But a critical mass of technology skills is becoming mandatory. Government and private partnerships are needed to upskill employees, bolster human capital development, and promote and sustain innovation policies. Furthermore, ASEAN needs to take a "whole of technology" approach if aiming to transform itself into a technology and knowledge hub. Digitalization and the advance of frontier technology is not reserved to selected sectors but must be mainstreamed throughout an economy. Governments urgently need comprehensive innovation and training policies to complement smart regulation, high-quality digital infrastructure, and green investment to allow firms and workers to shift to higher value-added and green GVCs.

Decarbonization in ASEAN's Global Value Chain-Driven Economies

Emission reduction targets can be met through strong investment and capacity building. But they are likely more dependent on well-thought-out strategies and policies to replace nonrenewable energy sources. ASEAN will need to determine how best to make up for the lost domestic value added contained in its energy-intensive exports to the PRC, Japan, the ROK, the US, and the EU.

ASEAN economies continue to forge and fine-tune their strategies for managing natural resources to ensure balanced prosperity and the well-being of current and future generations.[15] Asia, including ASEAN, emits more greenhouse gas (GHG) during production than anywhere in the world—in terms of consumption, advanced economies remain on top. Trade, including transport, explains the difference. The reason Asia produces so much carbon emissions is its role as "factory of the world." It has used its comparative advantages as global production and trade reorganized around GVCs to minimize overall costs related to production, transport, information, regulation, and other policies. If Asia and ASEAN want to shed this label, should they stop producing for the world and stop trading? Not necessarily, because trade and GVCs have brought a type of prosperity only dreamed about 4 decades ago. There is no reason the future cannot be both green and prosperous.

Studies on the impact of trade (and its inseparable component, transport) on the environment and climate change provide a widely accepted breakdown of the elements and channels of interactions, including the direct, scale, composition, technique, and regulatory effects.[16]

---

[15] See ASEAN State of Climate Change Report. 2021a. https://asean.org/wp-content/uploads/2021/10/ASCCR-e-publication-Final-12-Oct-2021.pdf; and ASEAN's statement to COP26. 2021b. https://asean.org/wp-content/uploads/2021/10/10.-ASEAN-Joint-Statement-to-COP26.pdf.

[16] The positive link between specialization in production and trade on one hand and transport on another is increasingly questioned due to enhancement and spread of additive manufacturing or so-called 3D printing technology.

The regulatory effect was added to show how connectivity through trade and investment affects the adoption of certain climate-friendly policies or standards. The traditional view is that increasing trade and deepening GVCs must necessarily boost emissions and damage the environment. And in most cases, it does.

However, this view is incomplete and does not reflect the complexity of positive and negative relationships. Ultimately, this complexity is a barrier to reaching general *a priori* conclusions on the impact of trade and GVCs—and points to the need for empirical analysis. Nevertheless, it is still possible to say that trade, investment, and GVCs can be climate-smart as they consist of, for example, promoting trade in environment-friendly goods and services, digitalization of trade and transport procedures, and increasing investment in renewable energy. If left exclusively to market forces, it plainly will not happen automatically. But if incorporated into comprehensive policy packages that offer the right incentives to get the private sector on board, so to speak, then trade and investments in value chains can be done with lesser effect on emissions (Box 1.7).

ASEAN already committed to reduce emissions at the 2021 United Nations Climate Change Conference (COP26). To make it happen, however, it must incorporate climate goals into all policies. Increasing resilience requires both a focus on efficiency in getting goods and services to the market and following the principles of environmental sustainability in managing value chains. Trade and investment policies cannot do this without a supportive package of complementary policies. Using technology to boost productivity and competitiveness requires the support of solid regulations, long-term improvements in trade and other infrastructure (including connectivity), and human capital development.

Environmental policies must focus on decarbonization through investment in renewable energy and in improving efficiency, both in terms of energy consumption and production. This can happen by directly substituting energy sources. But it also requires rethinking how complex value chains can be simplified and shortened to promote sustainable economic, social, and environmental development.

Box 1.7: Policies That Help Control and Reduce Carbon Emissions

Policies must promote, add to, and assist ongoing decarbonization efforts by providing effective incentives. It is possible to group policies into four categories: (i) policies that reduce and eliminate fossil fuel subsidies, (ii) policies that help set a realistic carbon price, (iii) policies that reduce carbon leakage through border carbon tax adjustments, and (iv) policies that reduce the costs of trading climate-smart and environmental goods so they filter into climate-smart consumption and production.

i.   **Eliminating fossil fuel subsidies**. Economies across Asia and the Pacific spent more than $175 billion on fossil fuel subsidies in 2019. At a time when many governments have limited fiscal space—after pandemic-related stimulus—removing subsidies should offer a welcome reprieve. Removing subsidies would also promote more efficient allocation of domestic and foreign investment and other resources. A justification for keeping subsidies to assist in poverty reduction and industrial policy has long been debunked as a losing strategy in the long run.

ii. **Carbon pricing**. Neither of the two recognized carbon pricing policies that bring the private cost of carbon in line with its social costs has gained global acceptance. The emission trading scheme, better known as cap-and-trade, count on those producing little to sell their surplus carbon quota to those who pollute more. This allows the market to keep an economy at its allowed level of carbon emissions. Carbon taxes operate more directly in closing the gap between private and social costs and, because they penalize high polluters, may create incentives for new investment into clean energy infrastructure and production.

iii. **Border tax adjustments to address carbon leakage**. Carbon leakage occurs when high-emission production moves to countries with less-stringent carbon policies (used to be called "pollution havens"). If uncontrolled, global emissions could easily increase despite efforts to reduce them. Without a single global policy that can eliminate leakages, one option is to introduce carbon border tax adjustments (CBTAs). These also address producers' concerns over losing competitiveness if domestic carbon pricing is higher than those of overseas competitors. The proposed European Union Carbon Border Adjustment Mechanism is the most advanced. CBTA and is set to be in effect in 2024. According to the Asia-Pacific Trade and Investment Report (APTIR) 2021, there are several issues pending before implementing CBTAs.[a] The first involves how to calculate the correct tax adjustment. Various methodologies have been proposed, each with advantages and drawbacks. The second is how to ensure CBTA implementation does not violate World Trade Organization rules.

continued on next page

Box 1.7 (continued)

Arguably, these allow for internal taxes to be "border adjusted," and CBTAs can be imposed or rebated on manufactured goods made using imported products (Flannery et al. [2020], as cited in APTIR 2021). CBTAs also worry developing countries, as their impact depends on how easily a country can adapt. In general, businesses in developing economies cannot respond quickly, so CBTAs will likely have greater effects, leading to greater inequality. Those affected most will have large exports in those sectors initially taxed, most likely energy and manufacturing. CBTAs placed on agricultural products exported from low-income regions could exacerbate rural poverty (Hasegawa et al. [2018], as cited in APTIR [2021], p.116). Reduced exports as a result of CBTAs could also lead to lower wages and higher unemployment, especially for women (Soprano [2021], as cited in APTIR [2021], p.116). Thus, CBTAs must be carefully designed to ensure developing countries are not disproportionately affected.

iv. **Policies that reduce trade costs for environmental goods and services.** APTIR (2021) found that tariffs and other barriers are often higher for climate-responsible and environment-friendly goods than on those that damage the climate and environment through the production process or consumption. Trade liberalization for climate-smart and environmental goods that filter into consumption and production should be a key climate change policy. Also, nontariff measures—such as energy labels on imported goods—can also help reduce carbon emissions. Trade and transport facilitation are necessary to reduce carbon emissions per transaction or on a per-shipment basis, so as not to cause any unintended consequences of a further increase in trade volume. Reforms in government procurement and infrastructure investment are also extremely important.

[a] Asia-Pacific Trade and Investment Report 2021: Accelerating Climate-Smart Trade and Investment for Sustainable Development, Economic and Social Commission for Asia and the Pacific (ESCAP), United Nations Environment Programme (UNEP), and United Nations Conference on Trade and Development (UNCTAD), 2021.
Source: APTIR. 2021. Asia-Pacific Trade and Investment Report 2021: Accelerating Climate-Smart Trade and Investment for Sustainable Development, ESCAP, UNEP and UNCTAD. https://www.unescap. org/kp/APTIR2021.

The recent surge in energy and commodity prices make decarbonization of GVCs more urgent, as if another reminder about urgency is really needed.[17] ASEAN policy makers and businesses must act.

---

[17] See for example the recently issued Intergovernmental Panel on Climate Change (IPCC) report (https://www.ipcc.ch/report/sixth-assessment-report-working-group-i/).

The study in chapter 5 measures the impact of emission targets and reductions (decarbonization) on ASEAN economic activity and GVCs. It examines how renewable energy technologies can replace emission-intensive sources aligned with a country's commitment to the Paris Agreement. The analysis is done by combining the Global Trade Analysis Project (GTAP)-E-Power and GTAP-Value Added models.[18]

To estimate the impact of the change in emissions in 2030 relative to 2020 on economic activity and ASEAN GVCs, two scenarios are modeled. The first business-as-usual (BAU) scenario assumes each country can replicate the same amount of reduced carbon emission in the decade from 2020 to 2030 as they did the previous decade (from 2010 to 2020). It turns out that only Singapore reduced emissions between 2010 and 2020 (by 19.6%), while the others increased (some substantially) emissions—so their 2030 emission levels are assumed the same as in 2020. The results show ASEAN GDP increasing by $194.3 million. There is a 5.8% increase in investment into renewable power and a 1.7% decline in investments made in nonrenewable power. This increases ASEAN's renewable power output up by 11.2%, with nonrenewable sources dropping by 1.7%. Beyond electricity, there is a 0.32% decline in coal, oil, and gas. The increase in renewables is enough to meet the energy requirements for countries to maintain the same level of emissions between 2020 and 2030, and include the expected drop in renewable energy. In other words, if ASEAN members increase investments in renewables by 5.8%, their output will increase by 11.2% with carbon emissions unchanged between 2020 and 2030.

The second scenario uses nationally determined contributions (NDCs) to estimate the economic and value chain impact of decarbonization assuming NDC targets are met.[19] The estimated cost is $50.1 billion. The obvious follow-up is whether ASEAN economies can afford the investment.

The answer is easiest by asking yet another question—what will the total cost be if the NDCs are not met? Following Rennert et al. (2022), the social cost of carbon is estimated to be $185 per metric ton of carbon dioxide equivalent ($MtCO_2e$). With ASEAN emissions at 1,651.89 $MtCO_2e$ in 2020, the aggregate social cost from carbon emissions is $306 billion, six times the cost of meeting the targets. Can ASEAN afford the huge cost? Obviously not. But, by achieving the NDC targets, it could save $256 billion in potential social costs, five times the estimated GDP losses.

---

[18] Both models are extensions of the standard GTAP framework.

[19] See chapter 5 for details on constructing the baseline and description of the methodology used.

Clearly, the focus should switch from "if" to "how" to achieve the NDCs. One necessary step is accelerating the shift to renewables. One option is to "deprive" polluting sectors of investment. By increasing investments in renewables, countries end up reducing investments available for others, particularly energy-intensive sectors. This certainly helps drive the overall decline. The next option is to look at changing trade patterns, especially GVCs. Meeting NDCs will help drive the changes in current production networks, if climate finance can support building new green production facilities convert them into green value chains.[20]

It is also important to understand the impacts over time. Though the capital costs of moving into renewable energy might seem high, the long-term benefits of these technologies are greater, especially as they mature and improve efficiency. Capital costs drop while the social costs saved are much bigger.

Because one of the major emissions sources is energy sector itself, it is important to consider how fast nonrenewable energy will be replaced by renewables. Despite the significant increase in ASEAN's renewable power capacity, growing populations and industrial development mean the aggregate power demand remains far greater than the increase in renewables. So to meet emission reduction targets, well-thought-out strategies and policies are needed to make the replacement attractive. This has already been a concern in many countries with good renewable infrastructure in hand. Also, carbon leakage, which happens in countries with lower NDC targets, must be considered to achieve a green economy.

Coal remains the dominant energy source for ASEAN economies. Electricity generation and power sources should be the priority for carbon mitigation policies and emission reduction plans. Differentiating generation sources and investments needed to migrate to high-efficiency, low-emission, renewable power generation—and fuel sources like solar, wind, and hydro—is key to satisfying the increased demand while reducing emissions to NDC levels. Removing subsidies on fossil fuel consumption to support the shift to renewables would enable more efficient allocation of scarce resources. With ASEAN supply chains entangled with several developed and developing countries across the globe, any disruption could cause a ripple effect across value chains and affect entire GVC operations.

---

[20] The results of the GTAP-Value Added model show that when ASEAN emissions are reduced to the levels prescribed in NDC targets, it would cost $165.2 billion in domestic value-added components, with a $1.7 billion decline in foreign value added.

Domestic value added would fall in energy-intensive sectors like coal, gas, manufacturing, and oil products, all of which contribute a sizable share of global exports—coal (31.7%), oil (6.5%), gas (17.25%), light manufacturing (4.93%), and textiles and apparel (8.2%). This could impact exports to the PRC, Japan, the ROK, the US, and the EU as they hold the most domestic value-added content among ASEAN economies. These countries could shift imports from other countries with lower NDCs, thus leading to global carbon leakage.

Foreign value-added components increase in textiles, light manufacturing, coal, oil, processed food, and heavy manufacturing, among others. There is an increase in both domestic and foreign value-added components in grain and other agricultural exports like meat. Thus, in energy-intensive sectors, ASEAN members may become more dependent on foreign value-added components.

Some countries like Brunei Darussalam and Indonesia are highly dependent on fossil fuel trade. These could lose out as other countries reduce fossil fuel imports as they try to meet NDC targets. So, by investing in renewables, ASEAN economies can meet both their NDC targets and weaken their dependence on fossil fuels. And, as the capital cost of renewable technologies is expected to decline as they mature, estimated GDP losses would decrease further.

Takeaway for policy makers

Future-proofing ASEAN economies and value chains includes making them think "green." They must become climate- and environment-responsible. The relationship between trade, investment, GVCs, and decarbonization is complex and multifaceted. In the best-case scenario, policies that promote decarbonization also strengthen ASEAN GVCs' long-term competitiveness and resilience. This involves a careful balancing act—maximizing potential benefits of ASEAN GVCs and RVCs while minimizing the risks and costs of decarbonization. Policies that help offset the costs—reducing the impact of other components in trade costs—include adopting climate-smart nontariff measures and low or zero tariffs on climate-smart goods; accelerating trade digitalization; adopting climate-smart trade and transport infrastructure; and preparing for carbon pricing, including carbon border tax adjustments (CBTAs). ASEAN economies have a much better chance of meeting their NDCs targets while staying competitive and attractive GVC locations if they cooperate with one another rather than approaching these challenges individually.

Deepening Regional Integration and Cooperation under an Evolving "New Normal"

The post-pandemic "new normal" creates new challenges for ASEAN economies and their value chains. Deepening economic integration is one way to approach emerging risks. Regional integration has certainly helped ease the trade impact, especially when GVCs are involved. An ASEAN fully integrated in "mega-RTAs" will raise its long-term growth trajectory.

The foundation of ASEAN economic development is an outward-oriented production, trade, and investment strategy that embraces "open regionalism." It has led to its economies being considered some of the most open, dynamic, and resilient in the world.[21] They benefited from a confluence of factors—most notably lower trade costs and market openness—which allowed ASEAN industries to join international production networks and value chains. However, recent geopolitical tensions and the string of external shocks since the COVID-19 outbreak may end up limiting ASEAN's role in global production networks. In any case, the new normal continues to evolve. New risks come with new opportunities. And ASEAN may need to modernize its outward-oriented development model to balance both while continuing to build a sustainable, inclusive, and green future.

Chapter 6 provides a comprehensive and quantitative review of the evolving outlook for growth and economic cooperation in trade-oriented economies—such as those in ASEAN.[22] It focuses on several policy scenarios, some of which analyze and quantify the impact of policies that address geopolitical risks with some offering new proposals for expanding existing RTAs. The research methodology uses a new medium-term simulation model to analyze effects on GVCs.[23]

The findings are based on three sets of simulations of global economic development from 2021 to 2035. The first set provides a new normal baseline incorporating the most recent shocks from the Russian invasion of Ukraine and the surge in natural resource prices. The second assesses the consequences of proposed "geopolitical interventions" in trade flows and patterns that reflect political and national security interests, along with concerns over supply chain disruptions throughout the pandemic.

---

[21] See, for example, Viet Nam's surge to the top in trade to GDP ratio among large developing economies (chapter 6).

[22] Chapter 6 "Scenarios for a Global 'New Normal' and ASEAN GVCs" authored by Peter Petri and Michael Plummer.

[23] See the methodology section in chapter 6.

Three new approaches to reconfiguring GVCs are considered: reshoring, near-shoring, and friend-shoring. The third set then optimistically analyses the economic and trade impact for "new enhanced economic cooperation," a group of four scenarios that examine the Regional Comprehensive Economic Partnership (RCEP), two possible expansions of the Comprehensive and Progressive Trans-Pacific Partnership (CPTPP)—adding seven economies at different stages—and a "Great Reach" wave of agreements that adds the PRC; the US; the EU; and Taipei,China to the CPTPP; and India to the RCEP. This admittedly unrealistic option defines a benchmark for renewed global cooperation (although it leaves out Africa and Latin America).

It is important to treat these results as insights on quantitative change—rather than exact findings—due to the high policy uncertainty and volatility. Caution is needed when interpreting stylized policy scenarios, such as friend-shoring, which currently lack details like, for example, tariff schedules for tariff rates used to model RTAs.

The empirical results strongly suggest that recent shocks to the global economy, as well as proposed restrictions on global trade patterns (in part a response to recent shocks), will likely disrupt ASEAN trade and growth. It does not make judgements on the effects these policies might have on other non-economic goals. While these developments are essentially exogenous to ASEAN, the estimates do show that deepening and widening economic cooperation can materially offset some of the emerging risks (Figures 1.1, 1.2, and 1.3).[24]

Figure 1.1 shows the new normal baseline reflecting the cumulative, long-term effects of the Russian invasion of Ukraine with higher resource prices and their macroeconomic consequences. Global GDP would fall by 2.2% below the baseline trajectory in 2035, with the resource price surge having the greatest negative impact, especially for the resource-importing economies of ASEAN and RCEP. RCEP members will be hurt most given the large increase in import prices and deterioration in terms of trade. In sum, the new normal shock, while depressing medium-term incomes for most regions, has modest effects (except for the Russian Federation).

---

[24] For the list of economies under each group, see the appendix to chapter 6.

Figure 1.1: Recent Shocks and the New Normal: Income Changes in 2035 (%)

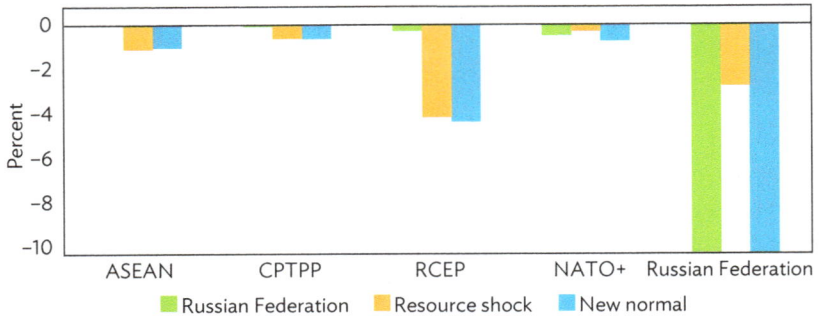

ASEAN = Association of Southeast Asian Nations, CPTPP = Comprehensive and Progressive Trans-Pacific Partnership, NATO+ = North Atlantic Treaty Organization members and their allies, RCEP = Regional Comprehensive Economic Partnership.
Note: Results are not fully shown for the Russian Federaiton and new normal; their values are −22.4% and −23.4%, respectively. Global GDP is −2.2%.
Source: Authors' simulation as cited in Chapter 6, Figure 6.1.

Figure 1.2 reports modeling results for the geopolitical intervention scenarios.[25] As mentioned, three approaches to managing trade are stylized: (i) reshoring (a new name for what used to be known as "made-at-home" protection of domestic industry); (ii) near-shoring (which assumes trade risks rise with distance and provides incentives for firms/traders to keep trade within a region); and (iii) friend-shoring (intending to replace a substantial part [or all] of trade with geopolitical adversaries with trade among friendly partners).[26]

All three approaches would generate significantly negative global results. Near-shoring leads to the largest global income losses of 1.2% (−$1.6 trillion), but reshoring 0.9% (−$1.2 trillion) and friend-shoring 0.6% (−$0.8 trillion) are also costly. In these scenarios, income changes are driven by large declines in global trade, ranging from 11.1% (−$4.0 trillion) for near-shoring, 9.2% (−$3.3 trillion) for reshoring, and 5.0% (−$1.8 trillion) for friend-shoring. ASEAN and RCEP economies, especially the PRC, fare worst. Scenarios that reinforce already strong trade relationships cause the least harm.

---

[25] See section II, chapter 6.

[26] Chapter 6 correctly posits that friend-shoring is just a new name for already existing and frequently used practices. However, it goes on to note an important difference between these old practices and the new proposal. The old examples involved lowering barriers among friends (as in, for example, signing free trade agreements with selected partners) rather than raising them against unfriendly outsiders.

Figure 1.2: Geopolitical Interventions: Real Income Changes, 2035 (%)

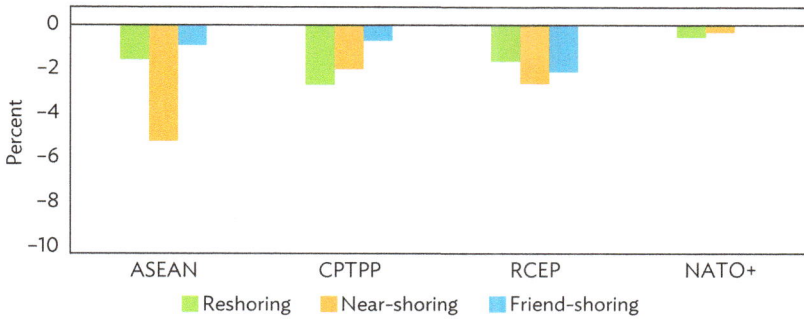

ASEAN = Association of Southeast Asian Nations, CPTPP = Comprehensive and Progressive Trans-Pacific Partnership, NATO+ = North Atlantic Treaty Organization members and their allies, RCEP = Regional Comprehensive Economic Partnership.
Source: Authors' simulations as cited in Figure 6.2, chapter 6.

Figure 1.3 shows results of modeling new enhanced trade cooperation. Not surprisingly, all results are positive as increasing the coverage of trade agreements (adding members) is expected to generate larger gains (the bigger the agreement, the better the outcomes). RCEP increases member incomes by $245 billion (0.6%), although its diversionary effects reduce global gains to about two-thirds of the amount. ASEAN economies fare especially well under RCEP, with income gains of 1.3% despite free trade agreements (FTAs) already in place with other members. The two CPTPP enlargements likewise generate benefits (the first raises global incomes by $101 billion, while the second adds $57 billion, for a total of $158 billion increase relative to the baseline). Of the seven prospective CPTPP members, four are ASEAN members. But clearly the "Global Reach" scenario offers the largest gains, raising incomes by 1.1% ($1.4 trillion) worldwide, including by 4.0% ($0.2 trillion) in ASEAN.

Unique features of the model used in chapter 6 allow to explore how different geopolitical interventions and other policies might affect GVCs. A severe disruption of GVCs arises from such policies fragmenting production and increasing its costs, reducing global average GVC participation rate by 4.5% (reshoring), 7.3% (near-shoring), and 9% (friend-shoring) by 2035. The countries most affected would be small, open, manufacturing economies like those in ASEAN. It is noteworthy that friend-shoring causes the biggest damage when this metric is used (compared to earlier use of income change). A likley explanation is that friend-shoring eliminates flows of trade between NATO+ and countries not considered "friends" (e.g., the PRC) where currently most of the GVC trade is sourced from. On the positive side, enhanced economic cooperation lowers trade costs thus increase GVC participation. In sum, GVCs play a key role in determining the effects of trade policies and geopolitical strategies, especially in regions like ASEAN.

Figure 1.3: Enhancing Trade Cooperation, Change in Real Income in 2035

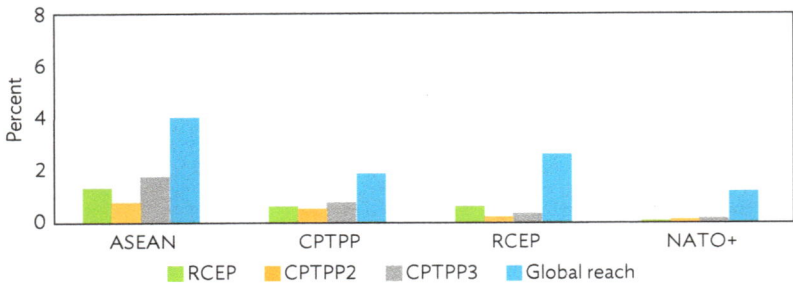

ASEAN = Association of Southeast Asian Nations, CPTPP = Comprehensive and Progressive Trans-Pacific Partnership, NATO+ = North Atlantic Treaty Organization members and their allies, RCEP = Regional Comprehensive Economic Partnership.
Source: Authors' simulations; Macro tables (accessed 23 August 2022) as cited in Chapter 6, Figure 6.3.

Takeaway for policy makers

Recent global shocks and potential geopolitical trade interventions, developments mostly beyond ASEAN's control, could sharply disrupt ASEAN growth, the Asia and Pacific region, and similar economies elsewhere. At the same time, the research finds that impacts of policy choices—principally for deepening trade cooperation in Asia and expanding it into other regions—are sizeable and could also affect long-term global prospects. Net outcomes are not preordained, and the stakes are high, especially for ASEAN, a group of unusually open economies.

Future-Proofing ASEAN Participation in Global Value Chains

ASEAN successfully conquered several regional and global crises over the years by taking the needed national responses, and also by working together to strengthen resilience against the inevitable "next one." The pandemic was really something new. It was a genuine global crisis that affected every aspect of daily life. It required political, social, and economic responses that grew increasingly coordinated within and across countries. As the region prepared to cautiously open its borders to international travel and tourism—while recharging trade and investment flows and keeping GVCs functioning—new geopolitical and economic challenges emerged. They shaped an ever-evolving "new normal" in the face of heightened uncertainty and fears of recession, dashing hopes for a quick post-pandemic rebound throughout much of the region. One of the many new risks involved just how ASEAN members would react to the changing parameters defining global and regional trade, investment, and value chains. This book offers a comprehensive and novel analysis backed by the evidence needed to help policy makers respond to these challenges.

No country or region was immune to the pandemic's health, social and economic impact—and the scarring it left behind. ASEAN was no different.[27] As the pandemic unfolded, ASEAN used some of the resilience it had built over the years to ease the effects from demand and supply shocks. Looking back, there were several groups of factors contributing to this resilience: (i) solid macroeconomic positions, (ii) reasonable government and ASEAN-wide resistance against the global trend toward restrictive trade policies and practices, (iii) measures to control rising costs affecting trade and production, and (iv) flexible and accommodating policies to help business continue value chain production and trade.

There is a solid body of empirical evidence cited here that emphasizes the importance of government and private sector cooperation in building resilience to shocks, from the pandemic to the impact of extreme weather. Businesses that rely on international transactions, such as GVCs, are adapting to deal with the external shocks and disruptions caused by events such as the pandemic. Many firms have shown their capacity to internalize risks and shift their business model from "just-in-time" production and distribution to one that incorporates the redundancy needed to adjust to outside pressure. That allowed ASEAN trade and investment to continue to flow with fewer and less severe disruptions than the rest of the world—another aspect of ASEAN's overall resilience.

---

[27]   See ADB (2022a) for an excellent ASEAN-wide and member-focused analysis.

This process of reinforcing both agility and resilience must continue to help business become better prepared. During the pandemic, some businesses did not know just how their value chain structures were vulnerable. Firms should invest in thoroughly mapping their value chains to understand the risks and how they are linked—whether they are lead firms or suppliers, as well as vulnerabilities of logistics providers, and the role the public sector plays in stockpiling and financing. Looking forward, they will need to be able to track sources of energy, emissions, and waste in all of their operations. The firms themselves are best positioned to decide on the level of diversification in engaging multiple suppliers and linkages along the value chain. This is the key to increasing resilience. These decisions, however, must be made given the existing business environment defined by government policies.

So what is the government's role? It also needs to invest in preparing for new and more frequent risks from disruptions—including access to a steady supply of essential goods and services. Data collected during the pandemic shows that countries did better with more trade and stable, predictable trade policies than otherwise. Evidence shows that firms with access to more affordable and higher-quality digital infrastructure were more resilient. Therefore, in addition to solid macroeconomic fundamentals, the minimal help needed from governments is to keep borders open for trade and investment and allow for hard and soft infrastructure required to digitalize business and trade processes. It is necessary to understand that global decarbonization cannot materialize without global trade and investment flows contributing to it. One of the major drivers of net zero is adoption of renewable energy-generating technologies and fuels and this implies that they have to be accessible to all through trade because they will not be produced everywhere where needed. And thus, the cost of production and trade will remain important and will still be a factor in GVC resilience.

But as ASEAN knows, resilience also means securing the resource base through human skills development, decarbonizing GVCs, and making available technology more inclusive:

- Human skills development requires comprehensive labor market policies and institutions supported by strong social dialogue—between governments and organizations representing employers and workers. It is critical to have a strategy that can help transform these relationships, using employment and social protection policies that reduce gender inequality, make the labor market more inclusive, and invest across a broad range of skills development—to allow workers to move into higher value-added jobs within the value chain. Deep trade agreements with labor provisions can help strengthen the link between increased GVC participation and decent work.

- The relationship between trade, investment, GVCs, and decarbonization is complex and multifaceted. In the best-case scenario, policies that promote decarbonization also strengthen long-term GVC competitiveness and resilience. This requires a careful balancing act—maximizing the potential benefits of ASEAN GVCs and RVCs while minimizing the risks and costs of decarbonization. Policies that help offset the costs—reducing the impact of other trade cost components—include (i) adopting climate-smart nontariff measures and low or zero tariffs on climate-smart goods; (ii) accelerating trade digitalization; (iii) adopting climate-smart trade and transport infrastructure; and (iv) preparing for carbon pricing, such as CBTAs.
- Technology continues to change GVCs, making low-skilled work less relevant for maintaining the competitive advantage needed to climb the GVC ladder. The automotive, electronics, and electrical case studies presented here are examples of skills that will no longer be needed, and the trends that reduce ASEAN's earlier comparative advantage in specific value chain segments. Improving the core determinants for investment to grow—such as infrastructure and connectivity—remains prerequisite. But a critical mass of technology skills is increasingly mandatory. Government and private partnerships are needed to upskill employees, bolster human capital development, and promote and sustain innovation policies.

ASEAN benefited greatly by joining the global economy as its trade and investment patterns expanded. It did this primarily for clear economic reasons. Unfortunately, recent geopolitical changes mean decisions must be made based on more than economic criteria alone. Today, national security priorities are changing—sometimes drastically—both the type and tone of the trade and investment policies of ASEAN's major trading partners. As demonstrated in chapter 6, some of these constraints on choosing a trading partner may be damaging the welfare and trade of ASEAN members and other economies. National security issues often weaken trading partners' economic and social prosperity. The way forward is through a return to strengthening international cooperation—a particularly strong feature of ASEAN. Keeping borders open for trade and investment is the only proven way of allowing firms to promote diversification and substitution of products, services, and partners to build more resilient value chains. Diversified value chains are a much more powerful source of resilience than vulnerability. And, as it has done successfully over the years, ASEAN should continue to leverage intra-ASEAN cooperation as a buffer against heightened risk. It should be taken as an opportunity to future-proof ASEAN and ease its path toward a sustainable, inclusive, and green economy.

References

Abe, M. 2013. Expansion of Global Value Chains in Asian Developing Countries: Automotive Case Study in the Mekong Subregion. In D. Elms and P. Low, eds. *Global Value Chains in a Changing World*. Geneva: WTO Publications. pp. 385-406.

Abiad, A. et al. 2018. The Impact of Trade Conflict on developing Asia. *ADB Working Paper Series*. No. 566. https://www.adb.org/sites/default/files/publication/471496/ewp-566-impact-trade-conflict-asia.pdf.

Asian Development Bank. 2022. *Asian Economies Integration Report 2022*. Manila. https://www.adb.org/sites/default/files/publication/770436/asian-economic-integration-report-2022.pdf.
———. 2022a. *Southeast Asia: Rising from the Pandemic*. Manila. https://www.adb.org/sites/default/files/publication/779416/southeast-asia-rising-pandemic.pdf.
———. 2022b. *Asian Development Outlook 2022 Supplement*. Manila. https://www.adb.org/sites/default/files/publication/844296/ado-supplement-december-2022.pdf.

Anukoonwattaka, W. and R. S. Lobo. 2019. Trade wars: Risks and opportunities for Asia-Pacific economies from US tariffs. *Trade, Investment and Innovation Working Paper* No. 01/19. 22 May. ESCAP Trade, Investment and Innovation Division. https://repository.unescap.org/bitstream/handle/20.500.12870/1171/ESCAP-2019-WP-Trade-wars-risks-and-opportunities.pdf?sequence=1&isAllowed=y.

ASEAN Secretariat. 2021a. ASEAN Development Outlook 2021 – Inclusive and Sustainable Development. https://asean.org/wp-content/uploads/2021/07/ASEAN-Development-Outlook-ADO_FINAL.pdf.
———. 2021b. ASEAN State of Climate Change Report 2021. https://asean.org/wp-content/uploads/2021/10/ASCCR-e-publication-Correction_8-June.pdf.
———. 2021c. ASEAN Joint Statement On Climate Change to the 26th Session Of the UNFCCC COP26. https://asean.org/wp-content/uploads/2021/10/10.-ASEAN-Joint-Statement-to-COP26.pdf.

Baldwin, R. 2022. The peak globalisation myth: Part 1. 31 August. https://cepr.org/voxeu/columns/peak-globalisation-myth-part-1.

Bamber, P. K. Fernandez-Stark, G. Gereffi, and A. Guinn. 2014. Connecting Local Producers in Developing Countries to Regional and Global Value Chains: Update. *OECD Trade Policy Papers* No. 160. Paris: OECD Publishing. http://dx.doi.org/10.1787/5jzb95f1885l-en.

Belotti, F., A. Borin, and M. Mancini. 2020. Economic Analysis with Inter-Country Input-Output Tables in Stata. *Policy Research Working Paper* No. 9156. Washington, DC: World Bank.

Borin, A. and M. Mancini. 2019. Measuring What Matters in Global Value Chains and Value-Added Trade. *Policy Research Working Paper* No. 8804. Washington, DC: World Bank. http://hdl.handle.net/10986/31533.

Conigliaro, D. 2019. Automotive- this is how employment in the car industry is changing. *Morning Future*. 15 April. https://www.morningfuture.com/en/2019/04/15/automotive-innovation-change-work/.

Constantinescu, C., A. Mattoo, and M. Ruta. 2017. Does vertical specialization increase productivity? *Policy Research Working Paper* No. 7978. Washington, DC: World Bank. http://hdl.handle.net/10986/26145.

de Vries, G., Q. Chen, R. Hasan, and Z. Li. 2019. Do Asian Countries Upgrade in Global Value Chains? A Novel Approach and Empirical Evidence. *Asian Economic Journal* 33(1): 13-37. https://doi.org/10.1111/asej.12166.

Eisenstein, P. 2019. Electric vehicles pose 'real risk' for autoworkers, with fewer parts – and jobs – required. NBC News. 3 October. https://www.nbcnews.com/business/autos/electric-vehicles-pose-real-risk-autoworkershalving-number-people-required-n1060426.

Farole. T. 2016. Do Global Value Chains Create Jobs? Impacts of GVCs Depend on Lead Firms, Specialization, Skills, and Institutions. *IZA World of Labor* 2016: 291. 10.15185/izawol.291

Felipe, J. 2018. Asia's Industrial Transformation: The Role of Manufacturing and Global Value Chains (Part 2). *ADB Economics Working Paper Series*. No. 550. Manila. Asian Development Bank.

Frederick, S., P. Bamber, and J. Cho. 2018. *The Digital Economy, Global Value Chains, and Asia*. Korea: Korea Institute for Industrial Economics and Trade and Duke University Global Value Chains Center.

Fujita, M. 2019. *Global Value Chains in ASEAN: A Regional Perspective.* Tokyo: ASEAN-Japan Centre.

Gereffi, G. 2021. Keys to Building Resilient Global Value Chains. Presentation at the USITC GVC Virtual Symposium, United States International Trade Commission, Washington, DC. December. (mimeographed).

Hollweg, C. 2019. Global Value Chains and Employment in Developing Economies. In *The Global Value Chain Development Report 2019: Technological Innovation, Supply Chain Trade and Workers in a Globalized World*. Washington, DC: World Bank. pp.63-81.

International Labour Organization (ILO). 2018. Gender Gaps in the Garment, Textiles and Footwear Sector in Developing Asia, ILO Asia-Pacific Garment and Footwear Sector Research Note.

_____. 2022. ILO Monitor on the World of Work, 10th Edition. Multiple crises threaten the global labour market recovery. https://www.ilo.org/wcmsp5/groups/public/---dgreports/---dcomm/---publ/documents/briefingnote/wcms_859255.pdf.

International Monetary Fund. 2022. World Economic Outlook – Countering the Cost-of-Living Crisis, October, Output Growth Projections. https://www.imf.org/en/Publications/WEO/Issues/2022/10/11/world-economic-outlook-october-2022 (accessed November 2022).

Intergovernmental Panel on Climate Change (IPCC). 2021. *Climate Change 2021: The Physical Science Basis*. https://report.ipcc.ch/ar6/wg1/IPCC_AR6_WGI_FullReport.pdf.

Kannon, V. and J. Feldgoise. 2022. After the CHIPS Act: The limits of reshoring and Next Steps for US Semiconductor Policy. Carnegie Endowment for International Peace. November.

Mendoza, A. 2019. Economic and Social Upgrading in Global Value Chains: Insights From *Philippine Manufacturing Firms. Philippine Journal of Public Policy: Interdisciplinary Development Perspectives* 2018:25–65. doi.org/10.54096/YDYB1094.

Organisation for Economic Co-operation and Development (OECD). 2012. *Global Production Networks and Employment: A Developing Country Perspective*. Paris: OECD. https://www.oecd.org/dac/aft/GlobalProductionNetworks_Web_USB.pdf.

Rennert, K., F. Errickson, and B.C. Prest. 2022. Comprehensive evidence implies a higher social cost of CO2. *Nature* 610, 687–692. https://doi.org/10.1038/s41586-022-05224-9.

Shepherd, B. 2021. The Post-COVID-19 Future for Global Value Chains. *UNDP Policy Brief*. New York. https://www.undp.org/sites/g/files/zskgke326/files/migration/asia_pacific_rbap/GVC-policy-brief-FINAL.pdf.

Susantono, B. 2019. Strengthening the Chains That Helped Pull Asia Out of Poverty. *Asian Development Blog*. 2 October. https://blogs.adb.org/blog/strengthening-chains-helped-pull-asia-out-poverty.

The Economist. 2019. *The steam has gone out of globalization*. 24 January. https://www.economist.com/leaders/2019/01/24/the-steam-has-gone-out-of-globalisation?gclid=EAIaIQobChMI0o_TsZP2_QIVM4JLBR1ZsAgpEAAYASAAEgK-uPD_BwE&gclsrc=aw.ds.

Torres de Oliveira, R., et al. 2021. Exporting to Escape and Learn: Vietnamese Manufacturers in Global Value Chains. *Journal of World Business* 56(4). https://doi.org/10.1016/j.jwb.2021.101227.

United Nations. 2021. *Asia-Pacific Trade and Investment Report 2021: Accelerating Climate-Smart Trade and Investment for Sustainable Development*. https://www.unescap.org/kp/APTIR2021.

Viegelahn, C., P. Huynh, and K.B. Kim. (Forthcoming). Jobs and Global Value Chains in Southeast Asia. ILO Working Paper.

World Bank. 2017. Jobs in Global Value Chains. *Jobs Notes* No. 1. Washington, DC: World Bank. https://openknowledge.worldbank. org/bitstream/handle/10986/27263/116316-BRI-WB-GVC-JobsNote-FinalWeb-PUBLIC.pdf?sequence=1&isAllowed=y.

_____. 2020. World Development Report 2020: Trading for Development in the Age of Global Value Chains. https://www.worldbank.org/en/ publication/wdr2020.

World Trade Organization. Regional Trade Agreements Database. http://rtais.wto.org/UI/PublicMaintainRTAHome.aspx.

2

The State of Play of ASEAN
Global Value Chains

Adrian Mendoza and James Villafuerte

Introduction

Global value chains (GVCs) drive the growth and complexity of international trade. The World Bank (2020) estimates that around half of global trade in the 2010s was transacted through GVCs, substantially higher than the 40% during the 1980s. In Asia, GVCs also account for more than 40% of gross exports. This makes Asia the second most GVC-integrated region in the world, next to Europe.[1] This key position is mainly traced to the rise of East Asia and the Association of Southeast Asian Nations (ASEAN) as important manufacturing hubs in increasingly fragmented global production networks. Popularly referred to as Factory Asia, the region covers closely interconnected production networks: Japan and the Republic of Korea (ROK) serve as major offshoring countries, with the People's Republic of China (PRC) and ASEAN supplying inputs and assembling parts and components (Choi and Rhee 2014). The diverse economic profiles of these countries helped the region participate in a wide range of GVC activities, from resource-intensive upstream processing to manufacturing, marketing, and logistics.

ASEAN's rise in GVCs is remarkable. Over the last 3 decades, ASEAN has positioned itself in important segments of many global production networks. This fueled the region's continuing, impressive transition from commodity-based to higher-end manufactured exports. While figures vary depending on the data and methodology used, historical trends show that ASEAN's GVC-related trade has grown in importance, accounting for around 40%–50% of the region's total trade during the 2010s. At present, the region has the highest GVC participation rate among major economic blocs worldwide, next only to the European Union (Fujita 2019). This strong GVC participation is supported by globally integrated regional supply chains in various sectors, from food and garments manufacturing to smart phones and automobiles. The region is also growing in services GVCs, particularly logistics and financial services.

Strong inflows of foreign direct investment (FDI) have helped deepen GVC integration, with ASEAN already accounting for 20% of total developing country FDI stocks before the Asian financial crisis (AFC) (OECD and UNIDO 2019). As multinational companies (MNCs) use FDI to coordinate globally dispersed supply chains, trade and investment in GVCs also become increasingly intertwined. For instance, Efogo, Wonyra, and Osabuohien (2022) found strong empirical support for the FDI–GVC nexus based on data from 43 developing countries from 2010 to 2019. As of 2016,

---

[1] Based on the United Nations Conference on Trade and Development-Eora Multiregional Input–Output (UNCTAD-Eora MRIO), the GVC participation rates of Asia and Europe in 2015 were 43% and 56%, respectively. The global GVC participation rate reached 48% (World Bank 2020).

ASEAN accounted for 21% of the total FDI stock in developing countries, with 90 of the top 100 MNC having commercial presence in the region (ASEAN 2017). From 2017 to 2019, ASEAN received more FDI inflows than the PRC. The bulk of the region's FDI is in GVC-enabling services such as finance, logistics, and sales. Investment also flows into GVC-intensive manufacturing such as garments, chemicals, the automotive industry, and electronics. These investments are important sources of physical capital, foreign skills and technologies, and productivity spillovers (Uttama and Peridy 2010).

Evidence indicates that GVCs contribute to ASEAN's economic dynamism. Participation in GVCs played a key role in transforming predominantly agricultural economies in ASEAN into industrial success stories. Felipe (2018) suggests that much of the region's industrial progress, export growth, and expanding production capabilities occurred within the context of deepening GVC integration. This can be seen, for example, as more local value added goes into GVC trade (Zhong and Su 2021). Some firm-level studies also provide support for the learning effects of GVCs, as in the case of Indonesia (Urata and Baek 2021). This is consistent with recent econometric evidence showing that GVC participation has a positive impact on long-run domestic productivity growth in most East and Southeast Asian countries (Mallick and Zhang 2022).

Numerous studies show that deeper integration into international production networks boosts export and output growth, expands employment opportunities, facilitates knowledge spillovers, increases income and productivity, and reduces poverty (see next section). These results, however, vary greatly across firms, sectors, and countries, with the relevant impact channels also changing on a case-by-case basis. In ASEAN, the rate of upgrading has been uneven, with GVC-related activities in the Lao People's Democratic Republic (Lao PDR) and Myanmar mainly concentrated in primary sectors, while other members moved into either limited manufacturing or advanced manufacturing and services (World Bank 2020). This is partly due to a diversity of skills, technological capabilities, physical and virtual connectivity, and policy support.

There are very few studies documenting ASEAN's collective GVC experience on the one hand, and the relative performance of individual economies on the other. Yet, these baseline facts are needed to deepen our understanding of ASEAN's unique position in regional and global production networks. It is also important to understand the evolution of ASEAN GVCs within the broader context of Factory Asia's phenomenal rise as global manufacturing hub. What are the economic and institutional conditions underlying the emergence of ASEAN as an important host of GVC activities? What drove the evolution of the region's GVC participation over the years? What is the impact of past global crises on ASEAN's GVC trade? What is the current status of GVCs in the region in the aftermath of COVID-19? How does regional integration impact ASEAN's GVC trade? And what are the main opportunities and risks ASEAN faces as it upgrades within GVCs?

This chapter provides an overview of the evolution of ASEAN's GVC participation over the last 30 years against the background of a dynamic economic landscape, both globally and across ASEAN+3 (ASEAN plus Japan, the PRC, and the ROK). It also discusses the state of play and future direction of ASEAN GVCs more than 2 years into the COVID-19 pandemic. Here, GVC trade is defined as transactions that cross borders more than once—following Borin and Macini (2019) and Belotti, Borin, and Mancini (2020). This methodology decomposes gross exports into: (i) value-added exports (VAX) directly absorbed in the immediate destination (DAVAX), (ii) VAX indirectly reexported to third countries (IAVAX), (iii) reflection or the portion of VAX that is ultimately reabsorbed by the source country itself (REF), (iv) domestic double counting (DDC), (v) foreign value added, and (vi) foreign double counting (FDC). The sum of DAVAX, IAVAX, and REF is collectively referred to as the domestic value added (DVA) not counted as part of total GVC trade.

The rest of the chapter is organized as follows: Next section presents some stylized facts on the evolution of GVCs in ASEAN prior to the pandemic, using data derived from multi-region input–output tables (MRIOT) such as the United Nations Conference on Trade and Development-Eora Multiregional Input–Output (UNCTAD-Eora MRIO) from 1990 to 2015 and the ADB MRIOT from 2007 to 2021. Due to data limitations, the evolution of ASEAN GVCs during the 1990s and 2000s will be analyzed using the UNCTAD-Eora MRIO, while recent experience during the pandemic will be assessed based on ADB's updated MRIOT. Given the primary focus on broad trends, harmonizing the two tables is beyond the scope of this chapter. The penultimate section analyzes the impact of the pandemic on ASEAN's GVC performance, with special focus on the role GVCs play in propagating shocks as well as in fostering recovery. The last section concludes by identifying the major trends likely to affect ASEAN's future participation in GVCs.

Global Value Chains Prior to the COVID-19 Pandemic: Global Trends and ASEAN's Experience

The 1980s and 1990s saw a dramatic rise in GVCs as an important channel for international trade flows. Transactions within GVCs are characterized by several distinct features:

- The production process is geographically fragmented—meaning, suppliers perform highly specialized functions in scattered locations. These firms are linked to international production networks via FDI and trade, which facilitate the flow of resources within GVCs. But they can also serve as channels that propagate systemic shocks to supply chains.
- GVCs involve more trade in intermediate goods and auxiliary services than trade in final goods. This makes firms and countries more sensitive to adjustments or disruptions in any segment of the production network.
- MNCs typically coordinate GVC activities by using different organizational arrangements. Their business decisions are driven by strategies to improve efficiency, find new markets, and explore untapped resources (Dunning and Lundan 2008). MNCs' investment, offshoring, and trading activities are motivated by these objectives.

Several factors contributed to the increased fragmentation of global production during the 1990s. First, better transport infrastructure and logistics reduced the "iceberg costs" of trade and improved overall cargo handling. For instance, the use of the global positioning system and modern container vessels significantly cut delivery times and minimized cargo losses or damage. More seaports, airports, and inland road networks improved the connectivity of GVC suppliers between and within countries. And a stronger emphasis on trade facilitation like modernizing customs and simplifying importing and exporting procedures further lowered the costs of cross-border trade transactions.

Second, new technology and policy reforms significantly reduced communication and coordination costs, leading to the so-called "second unbundling" or geographic disintegration of production processes (Baldwin 2014). While falling transport costs allowed for the "first unbundling"—or the physical separation of production and consumption— the combination of lower transport and communication costs allowed for a finer segmentation of production stages. Greater access to information and communication technology (ICT) led MNCs to offshore certain functions without losing quality or efficiency. The ICT revolution opened a new era of fast and safe exchange of information, allowing suppliers in developing countries to connect with large MNCs. This meant that instructions, product specifications, orders, and market intelligence could be easily shared among distant producers within the supply chain.

Third, parallel reforms in trade and investment policy further liberalized global transactions, encouraging firms to expand their international operations. Ruta (2017) documented that deep preferential trade agreements boosted value-added trade and trade in parts and components. This grew out of tariff cuts and the relaxation of border controls, along with broad cooperation in investment, technology, infrastructure, competition policy, and the regulatory environment. In addition, unilateral and nondiscriminatory liberalization (as in the case of East Asia during the 1980s), regional trade agreements, and the resulting decline in trade barriers helped feed the continued growth of fragmentation, offshoring, FDI, and GVC trade over the last 3 decades (Figure 2.1). This created a "reverse magnification effect," where the benefits of lower trade costs spread across customs borders. For example, Anderson and Mohs (2011) suggest that the take-off of the electronics GVC coincided with the removal of tariffs on key technology and telecommunication products under the World Trade Organization's (WTO) 1997 Information Technology Agreement.

The liberalized global environment led to rapid, undisrupted growth of GVC trade prior to the 2008–2009 global financial crisis (GFC) (Figure 2.2). GVC trade as a share of global trade increased from 41% in 1980 to 52% in 2008—driven by increased fragmentation of production in advanced economies on the one hand, and greater GVC participation by emerging economies, especially ASEAN+3, on the other (World Bank 2020). This period was also characterized by (i) intensive unbundling in high-tech manufacturing, such as electronics, transport equipment, and machinery; (ii) deeper GVC integration in financial and business services; and (iii) integration in primary sectors like mining, quarrying, and petroleum. This "hyperglobalization" was aided by a liberalizing trading system under the WTO and by favorable technological advances that allowed broader access of countries to international markets.

Figure 2.1: Historical Trends in Information and Communication Technology, Transport Costs, Tariff Rates, and Overall Trade Costs

Internet and Mobile Use, 1990–2020

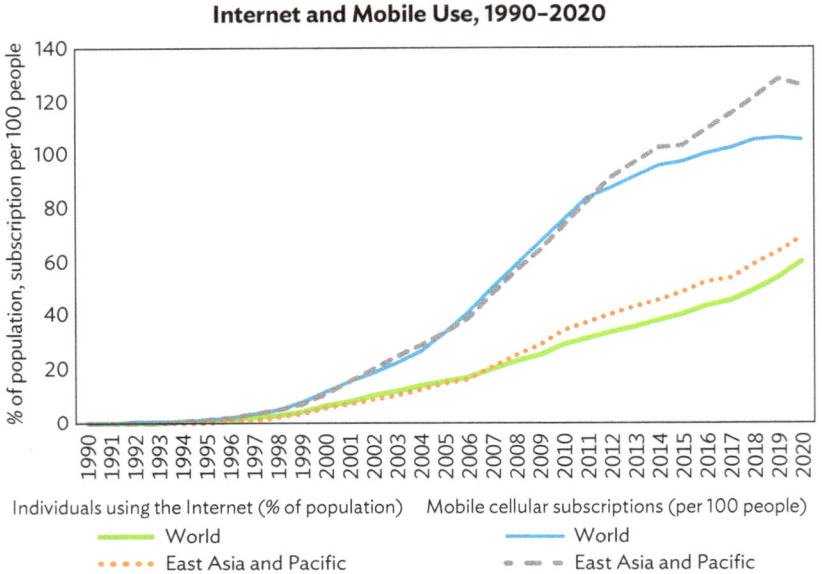

Individuals using the Internet (% of population)

— World

····· East Asia and Pacific

Mobile cellular subscriptions (per 100 people)

— World

– – – East Asia and Pacific

Transport Cost Indices, 1930–2005 (1930 =100)

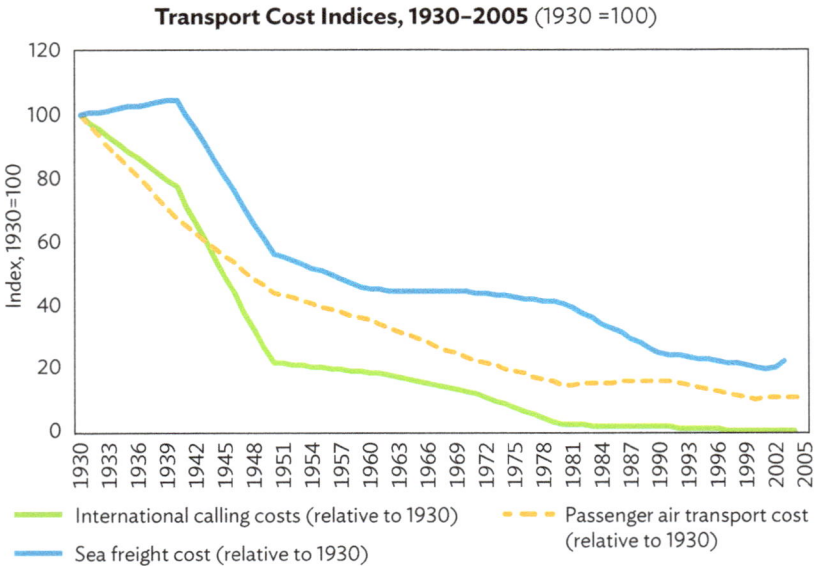

— International calling costs (relative to 1930)

— Sea freight cost (relative to 1930)

– – – Passenger air transport cost (relative to 1930)

continued on next page

Figure 2.1 (continued)

Average Applied Tariff Rates, 1988–2017

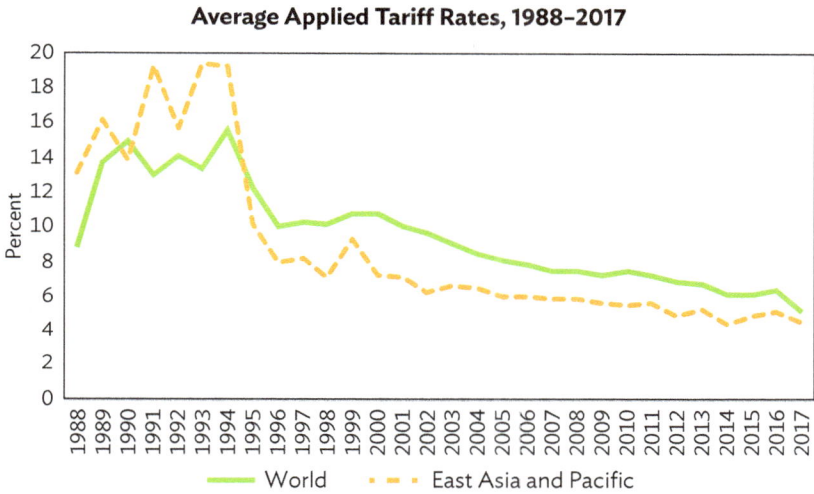

Legend: —— World   - - - East Asia and Pacific

Trade Cost Indices, 2000–2018

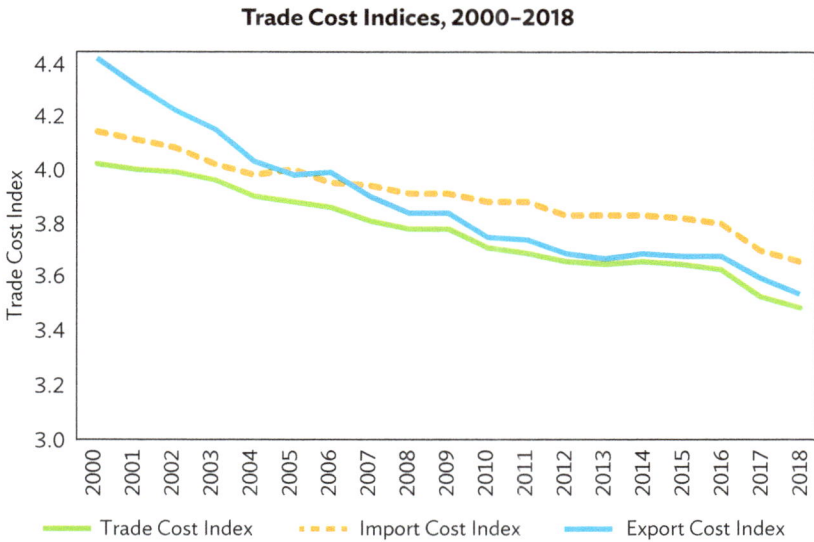

Legend: —— Trade Cost Index   - - - Import Cost Index   —— Export Cost Index

Note: The global trade cost indices are simple averages of available country–sector data provided by the World Trade Organization. They incorporate transport and travel costs, information and transaction costs, information and communication technology connectedness, trade policy and regulatory differences, and governance quality.
Sources: Our World in Data. https://ourworldindata.org/ (accessed 12 February 2022); World Bank. https://data.worldbank.org/ (accessed 12 February 2022); World Trade Organization (2020).

Figure 2.2: Trends in Global Value Chain Participation Rate, 1990–2015

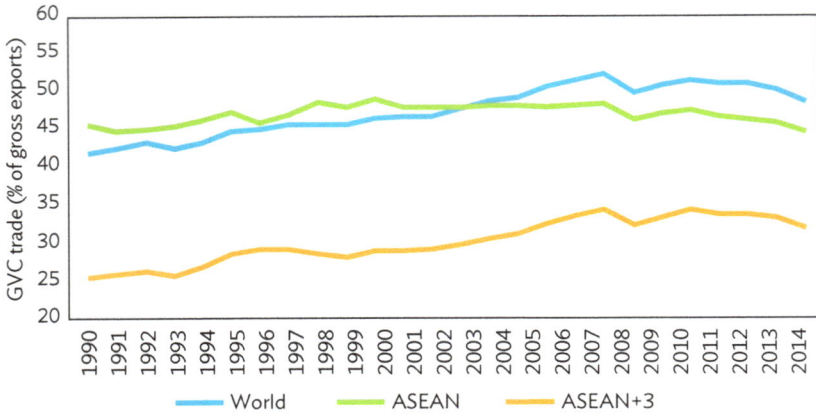

GVC = global value chain.
Note: ASEAN+3 refers to the 10 members of the Association of Southeast Asian Nations (ASEAN) plus Japan, the People's Republic of China, and the Republic of Korea.
Sources: Authors' calculation using the United Nations Conference on Trade and Development Eora Multi-region Input–Output (UNCTAD-Eora MRIO) Database. https://worldmrio.com/eora/ (accessed 12 February 2022); World Bank (2020).

In East Asia and ASEAN, several decades of economic transformation set the stage for the region's emergence as a global manufacturing powerhouse by the end of the 20th century. In parallel with the first and second unbundling, the growing economic interconnectedness in what was to become ASEAN+3 in 1999 helped build a viable model of cross-border production networks that exploit regional variations in resources, wages, and comparative advantages. This was evident, for example, after the Plaza Accord in 1985, when Japanese exports lost competitiveness due to the yen appreciation (Thorbecke and Salike 2011). To minimize costs, Japanese firms relocated labor-intensive functions to ASEAN, the PRC, and the ROK where wages were lower. Japan-based factories instead focused on producing technology-intensive components which were ultimately exported to plants in low-wage locations like the PRC for final assembly.

ASEAN was at the forefront of hyperglobalization and rapid GVC growth between 1990 and 2008. The foundation for this was laid when members began to adopt critical enabling policies:

i.   export-led industrialization in the 1970s and 1980s helped in their successful entry in key GVC sectors such as garments, the automotive industry, and electronics;

ii.   proactive labor market policies helped leverage relatively cheap and diverse labor resources;

iii. strategic investments in ICT and trade infrastructure helped reduce transport and communication costs—overcoming the physical and virtual distances from headquarters and manufacturing hubs;

iv.   increasingly liberal investment policies and an improved overall business climate helped attract FDI to support export-led development; and

v.   lower tariff and nontariff barriers freed up companies from depending on limited local inputs and facilitated greater trade in intermediate goods in the region.

Importantly, the 1993 ASEAN Free Trade Agreement (AFTA) helped cement the region's status as global production hub and major FDI destination. The latter part of the 1990s saw AFTA expand to include new ASEAN members—Viet Nam (1995), the Lao PDR and Myanmar (1997), and Cambodia (1999). AFTA supported stronger regional connectivity through the freer movement of people and capital, coordinated industrial policies, and cooperation in infrastructure development. In general, data suggest that ASEAN members with more free trade agreements (FTAs) have higher GVC participation rates.

ASEAN's GVC participation broadly tracked the global trend during the 1990s. But the region's GVC-related trade grew faster (10% average annual growth) than the global rate during the decade (Figure 2.2). ASEAN thus globalized much faster than the rest of the world during the 1990s. However, its GVC participation rate seems to have peaked in the opening years of the 2000s, followed by 2 decades of slow decline. This was a significant deviation from the continuing upward trend in the global GVC participation rate until the GFC. Results by Zhong and Su (2021) support this, concluding that international fragmentation in ASEAN decreased while production localization increased after 2007. Baldwin (2022) observes the same trend for the PRC, where "peak globalization" happened before the GFC. Some studies also argue that by the 2000s, the expansionary effect of trade liberalization in the 1990s may have started to taper off, leaving limited room for further growth (Yamashita 2021). Others suggest that intra-ASEAN regional value chain (RVC) transactions gained more importance in recent decades. Improving regional production capacity and interconnectedness contributed to this regionalization trend, especially in electronics (Korwatanasakul and Intarakumnerd 2021).

Intraregional trade in ASEAN increased significantly in the 1990s, peaking at around 24% in 1996, just before the AFC (Figure 2.3). The rise of intra-ASEAN trade during the 1990s was driven by the growing importance of intraregional RVC trade—whose share of gross ASEAN exports increased from 9.6% in 1990 to 15.7% in 1996, but fell to 14.5% in 1998 in the aftermath of the AFC. Intra-ASEAN RVC trade gradually recovered the decade after the crisis, before being disrupted again by the GFC. Historically, interregional RVC trade accounts for about two-thirds of total ASEAN intraregional trade. This means a large portion of trade within ASEAN is connected to the operations of regional production networks. Nevertheless, there is a noticeable increase in the share of non-GVC intra-ASEAN trade in recent decades, reflecting the rising income and consumption of the region's large domestic market. Fujita (2019) documented that intra-ASEAN RVCs are most prevalent in finance, electricity, gas and water, mining, petroleum, transport services, and electrical, electronic equipment and machinery.

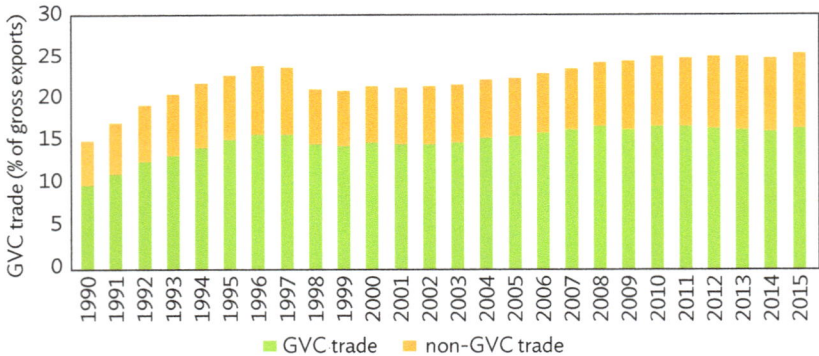

Figure 2.3: Intraregional Trade in ASEAN, 1990–2015

ASEAN = Association of Southeast Asian Nations, GVC = global value chain.
Source: Authors' calculation using United Nations Conference on Trade and Development-Eora Multiregional Input–Output.

The GVC participation rate in ASEAN+3 also closely tracked the global trend. This highlights the major role East Asia played in driving the overall GVC trade, especially with the PRC as a global manufacturing powerhouse. However, the ASEAN+3 GVC participation rate is significantly lower than ASEAN's (Figure 2.2). This implies ASEAN exports are more GVC-oriented than in East Asia. It also suggests a greater portion of East Asia's exports is consumed at the immediate destination instead of reexported to a third country. In the PRC's case, it is likely that imported inputs are already absorbed by local producers that serve the large domestic market—consistent with the PRC's economic rebalancing toward greater domestic orientation and less reliance on export-led growth strategies.

There was a surge in the size of ASEAN's GVC transactions after the 1990s (Figure 2.4). The same can be said for ASEAN+3. In the short span of 1 decade, the volume of trade via production networks in these regions more than doubled. This was driven by the confluence of technological breakthroughs, favorable market conditions, and policy reforms that accelerated production fragmentation and GVC trade during the 2000s. The digital revolution intensified during the decade, which brought faster internet, powerful computers, and modern electronic gadgets. The e-ASEAN Framework Agreement was formally adopted in 2000 to support the liberalization and growth of ICT and e-commerce. The 2000s was also the start of stronger economic cooperation across the region. After ASEAN+3 was formalized in 1999, trade agreements with Japan, the PRC, and the ROK were signed. In 2001, the PRC accession to the WTO further strengthened the role of Factory Asia as a global production hub.

Figure 2.4: Volume of Global Value Chain Trade Surged in the 2000s

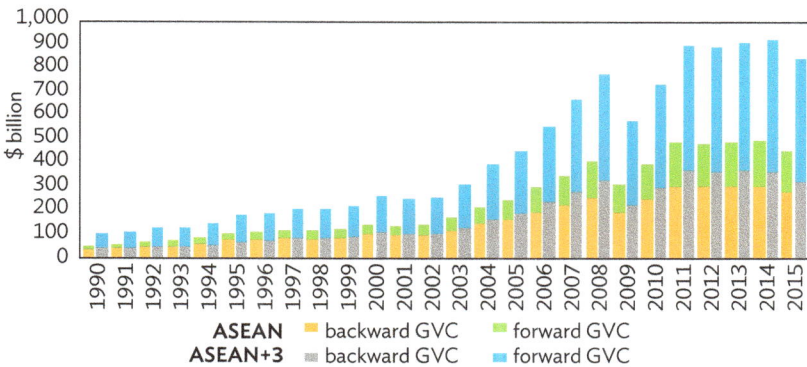

ASEAN = Association of Southeast Asian Nations; ASEAN+3 = ASEAN plus Japan, the People's Republic of China, and the Republic of Korea; GVC = global value chain.
Source: Authors' calculation using United Nations Conference on Trade and Development-Eora Multiregional Input–Output.

GVC-linked ASEAN firms generally import inputs, process, manufacture and assemble them, and then reexport. This explains why the surge in ASEAN's GVC trade was driven mainly by higher backward transactions or importing inputs used in exports. Over the years, however, this has matured somewhat, as forward transactions in ASEAN's overall GVC trade increased in relative importance. In ASEAN + 3, forward GVC trade was historically larger, with Japan and the ROK supplying technology-intensive parts and components, as well as FDI, capital goods, skills, and headquarter services. The PRC, on the other hand, exported large value added in metal and mineral products, as well as downstream services such as wholesale and retail trade, financial services, and logistics.

Individual ASEAN members' experience with GVCs were broadly consistent with the regional trend. Except for the Philippines and Singapore, GVC participation intensified between 1990 and 2008, with Brunei Darussalam, Indonesia, Myanmar, Thailand, and Viet Nam expanding their GVC trade significantly (Figure 2.5). Across the region, the pre-GFC years were characterized by double-digit average growth of GVC trade. Cambodia had the highest average increase of 25%, following major liberalization in the 1990s that brought in more FDI and greater GVC participation in manufacturing and services.

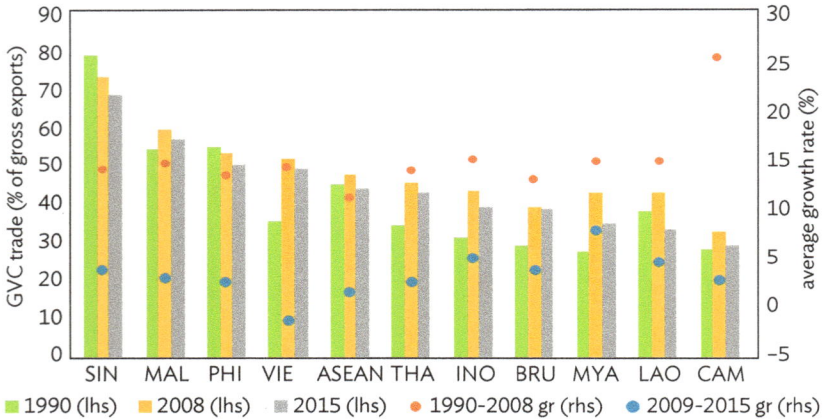

Figure 2.5: Global Value Chain Participation Varies Greatly across ASEAN

ASEAN = Association of Southeast Asian Nations, BRU = Brunei Darussalam, CAM = Cambodia, gr = growth rate, GVC = global value chain, INO = Indonesia, LAO = Lao People's Democratic Republic, lhs = left-hand scale, MAL = Malaysia, MYA = Myanmar, PHI = Philippines, rhs = right-hand scale, SIN = Singapore, THA = Thailand, VIE = Viet Nam.
Source: Authors' calculation using United Nations Conference on Trade and Development–Eora Multiregional Input–Output.

The heterogeneity in GVC participation across ASEAN reflects various levels of development, resources, and degree of liberalization. As shown empirically by López-González and Kowalski (2017), the structural characteristics of a country (such as economic size, share of manufacturing and geographic location) are important determinants of GVC participation. Singapore remains the most GVC-connected economy in ASEAN, due to its unique position as one of the world's busiest ports and financial centers—a major entrepot for goods traded between Asia, Europe, and the US. It also serves as a regional center, where different GVC segments scattered around ASEAN are coordinated. In contrast, Cambodia, the Lao PDR, and Myanmar have the weakest GVC linkages. The integration of these countries in regional production networks remains incomplete, as they joined ASEAN only in the late 1990s. Despite Cambodia's strong position in the textile and garment value chains, it has relatively weaker GVC participation compared to the Lao PDR and Myanmar which have broader-based participation in agriculture and other industrial sectors (Figure 2.6).

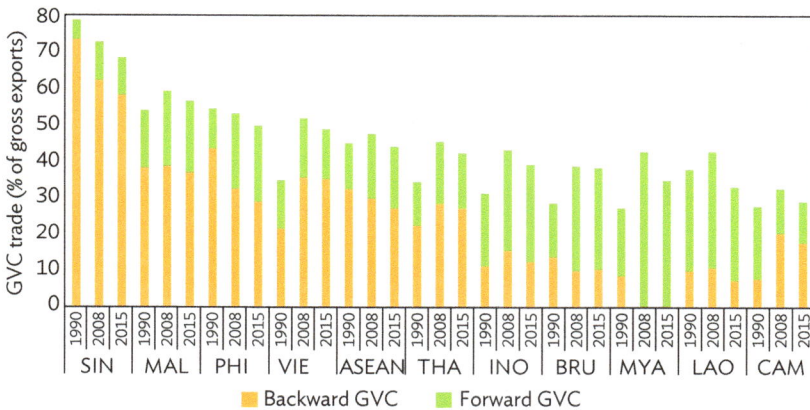

Figure 2.6: Global Value Chain Trade in ASEAN is Driven Mostly by Backward Participation

ASEAN = Association of Southeast Asian Nations, BRU = Brunei Darussalam, CAM = Cambodia, GVC = global value chain, INO = Indonesia, LAO = Lao People's Democratic Republic, MAL = Malaysia, MYA = Myanmar, PHI = Philippines, SIN = Singapore, THA = Thailand, VIE = Viet Nam.
Source: Authors' calculation using United Nations Conference on Trade and Development-Eora Multiregional Input–Output.

As a whole, most GVC trade in the region happens via backward participation or foreign value added embedded in a country's exports. This is true for highly GVC-integrated ASEAN economies such as Malaysia, the Philippines, Singapore, Thailand, and Viet Nam. GVC transactions in these countries mainly involve exports of goods and services with large amounts of imported value added. For Singapore, this is not surprising given its reliance on foreign inputs against limited domestic resources. For Malaysia, the Philippines, Thailand, and Viet Nam, their midstream position in GVCs means that semi-processed inputs are usually sourced from other parts of the value chain. In contrast, forward transactions are more important in resource-rich Brunei Darussalam, Indonesia, the Lao PDR, and Myanmar. In other words, the bulk of GVC trade in these economies came from domestic value added incorporated in other countries' exports. For example, Myanmar's GVC transactions were almost entirely forward. Myanmar, the Philippines, and Singapore saw huge declines in backward GVC participation rates from 1990 and 2008, while Cambodia, Indonesia, Thailand, and Viet Nam had sizeable increases. In general, the broad historical pattern from 1990 to 2008 was that forward participation remained relatively stable compared to the varying share of backward trade over the years.

Japan, the US, and the European Union (EU) were historically the most important sources of imported value added to ASEAN exports, especially during the 1990s (Figure 2.7). One interesting trend is the progressive decline of the US as a major source of value added to ASEAN. In contrast, backward GVC trade of ASEAN with East Asia remained relatively stable over the years, implying that East Asia solidified its position as ASEAN's most important GVC partner. Among East Asian countries, the 2000s saw Japan and the PRC gradually switching places, with the PRC becoming a more important supplier of inputs to ASEAN exporters. This reflects the structural change in East Asia's regional production networks. Japan declined as a major supplier of inputs as it upgraded to other nonmanufacturing GVC functions such as research and development (R&D), product design, marketing, and other headquarter services. By contrast, Baldwin (2022) notes that the PRC became a major global supplier of industrial inputs, with PRC-made inputs accounting for around 3% of world output in 2018. The PRC's move toward greater openness in the 2000s attracted MNC investments which helped expand its production capabilities—both for serving the domestic market and supplying GVCs. The extensive MNC presence in the PRC further strengthened its GVC linkages, especially with ASEAN where some segments of the multinational supply chains were located. For instance, Antràs (2014) traces the supply chain of Apple's iPad in ASEAN+3, with parts originating in Japan, the PRC, the ROK, and Viet Nam.

ASEAN's GVC participation is mainly concentrated in manufacturing, followed by services. The contribution of agriculture to the region's GVC trade remains marginal. From 1990 to 2008, manufacturing accounted for around three-quarters of the region's GVC trade, with more than half of that from electrical and machinery equipment (Figure 2.8). Other important sectors include petroleum, minerals and non-metallic products, metal products, and textiles and wearing apparel. Interestingly, transport

Figure 2.7: Origins of Foreign Value Added within ASEAN Exports

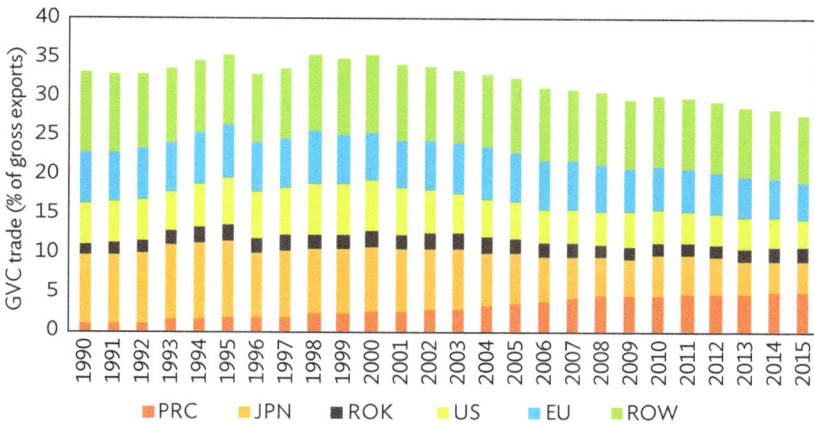

ASEAN = Association of Southeast Asian Nations, EU = European Union, GVC = global value chain, JPN = Japan, ROK = Republic of Korea, PRC = People's Republic of China, ROW = Rest of the World, US = United States.
Note: EU does not include Romania due to lack of data.
Source: Authors' calculation using United Nations Conference on Trade and Development-Eora Multiregional Input–Output.

Figure 2.8: Share in ASEAN Global Value Chain Trade by Industry

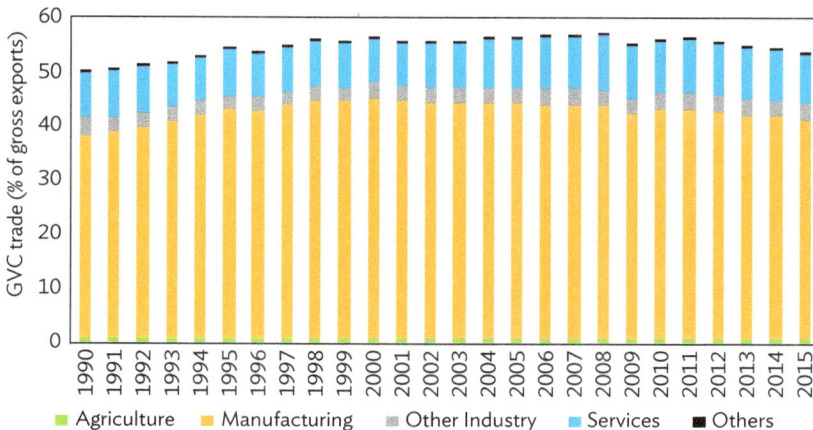

ASEAN = Association of Southeast Asian Nations, GVC = global value chain.
Source: Authors' calculation using United Nations Conference on Trade and Development-Eora Multiregional Input–Output.

equipment has a very small share of ASEAN's GVC trade in manufacturing, despite the strong linkages to East Asia's automotive supply chains. After peaking in 2000, the relative importance of manufacturing in ASEAN GVCs decreased slightly. One possible explanation is that local producers have been using more domestic value added in their exports, instead of relying on imported inputs.

By contrast, the share of ASEAN services trade has been slowly expanding, due to the growth of GVC trade in financial intermediation, business services, and transport. While the traditional notion of GVC fragmentation applies to manufacturing, the rising importance of services highlights two points: (i) fragmentation leaves distant production stages relying on auxiliary services such as communication, finance, transport, marketing, and back-office support for efficient cross-border coordination; and (ii) new technology and liberalization allowed virtual collaboration to produce professional (legal, business, and medical), educational (online), and recreational (streaming) tradable "final services."

Manufacturing and services GVC trade in ASEAN are intertwined (Figure 2.9). Services support manufacturing GVCs by linking geographically distant factories. Due to fragmentation, services such as logistics, finance, marketing, and back-office support become the glue that binds physically separated stages in manufacturing. Services move inputs, people, and information from one production stage to another. Moreover, marketing and distribution, wholesale and retail trade, and after-sales services deliver final products to consumers. Moving forward, digitalization and further liberalization of services will provide more options for countries to increase GVC participation.

Intertwined manufacturing and services is the result of "servicification," where manufacturing increasingly incorporates services inputs or sells products that bundle physical goods and services. For GVCs, servicification is a counterexample of the usual assumption that firms in fragmented production networks are hyperspecialized in narrowly defined tasks or activities. Instead, producers seem to perform a bundle of activities with tangible and intangible components. Advances in technology and liberalization created new ways for services to be incorporated into the production process. For example, manufacturers of machinery and transport equipment can also offer installation, maintenance, and repair as part of their sales package.

Figure 2.9: ASEAN Global Value Chain Trade in Manufacturing and Services Evolve in Tandem, 1990–2015

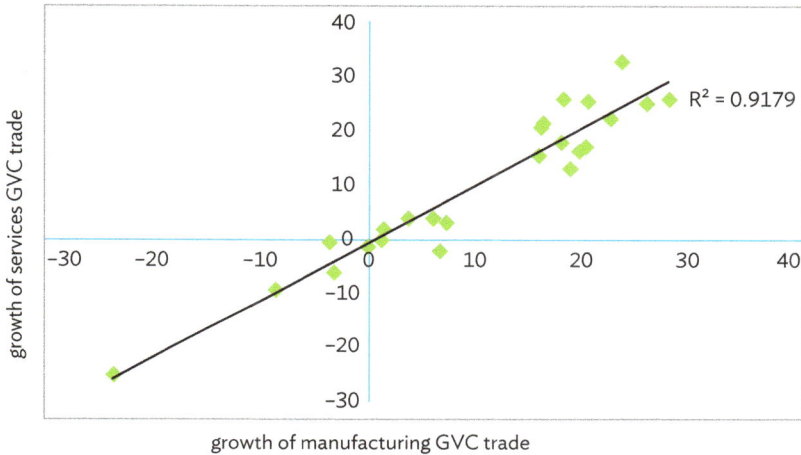

ASEAN = Association of Southeast Asian Nations, GVC = global value chain.
Source: Authors' calculation using United Nations Conference on Trade and Development-Eora Multiregional Input–Output.

GVC trade across ASEAN is quite diverse (Figure 2.10). Countries with moderate to high GVC participation rates—Indonesia, Malaysia, the Philippines, Singapore, Thailand, and Viet Nam—are linked to GVCs primarily through manufacturing, followed by services. Except for Viet Nam, the share of agriculture GVCs is small. In fact, modular and high-tech manufacturing dominate GVC trade in these countries. ASEAN has become an important hub for automotive and electronics value chains—from labor-intensive assembly and testing in the Philippines, Thailand, and Viet Nam to more capital-intensive R&D and design in Malaysia and Singapore (Korwatanasakul and Intarakumnerd 2021). Between 1990 and 2008, Cambodia, Indonesia, the Lao PDR, Thailand, and Viet Nam saw a huge jump in manufacturing GVC share. GVC composition in Myanmar, the Lao PDR, and Cambodia was more mixed (Figure 2.10). The GVC participation rate in agriculture was higher in these countries—not surprising given the relative importance of the primary sector compared to the small manufacturing industry. Brunei Darussalam is a special case, as GVC trade is mainly resource-based, dominated by mining and quarrying (Fujita 2019). Indonesia, Myanmar, and Viet Nam also have relatively significant nonmanufacturing GVC participation, specifically in mining and quarrying. This heterogeneity in ASEAN's GVC participation has the potential for complementarities among different country specializations to better integrate production networks and accelerate economic convergence. For example, more advanced ASEAN economies may move some resource- or labor-intensive manufacturing to Cambodia, the Lao PDR, or Myanmar. This boosts their participation in GVCs, while allowing more advanced ASEAN economies to develop new comparative advantages in technology-intensive and sophisticated functions.

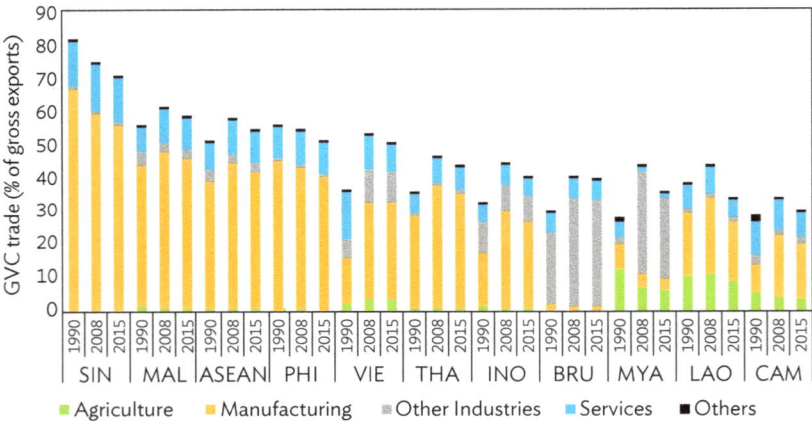

Figure 2.10: Sectoral Global Value Chain Trade Varies Significantly across ASEAN

ASEAN = Association of Southeast Asian Nations, BRU = Brunei Darussalam, CAM = Cambodia, GVC = global value chain, INO = Indonesia, LAO = Lao People's Democratic Republic, MAL = Malaysia, MYA = Myanmar, PHI = Philippines, SIN = Singapore, THA = Thailand, VIE = Viet Nam.
Source: Authors' calculation using United Nations Conference on Trade and Development-Eora Multiregional Input–Output.

ASEAN Global Value Chains after the Global Financial Crisis

The financial crisis in 2007–2008 ushered in "slowbalization" or receding globalization and slower trade growth. From 9% average annual growth during the 2000s, merchandise exports grew by an average of just 4.7% the following decade. From 2009 to 2015, GVC trade grew by an average 1.4%, given the anemic recovery from the GFC. In ASEAN, GVC trade fell by 24% in 2009, with the GVC participation rate dropping from 48% to 46%. GVC trade rebounded sharply in 2010 and 2011, as the worst effects of the GFC began to subside with renewed global demand for goods and services, including those produced in Factory Asia (Figures 2.2 and 2.4).

The recovery, however, was short-lived. In 2011, the earthquake and tsunami in Japan and flooding in Thailand severely interrupted supply chains across the region. Automotive and electronics GVCs were particularly paralyzed, causing several months of negative export growth. While this supply shock was temporary, the volume of ASEAN's GVC trade has stagnated since 2012 (Figure 2.4). Moreover, ASEAN's GVC participation rate began to decline, falling from 46.4% in 2012 to 44.3% in 2015 (Figure 2.2).

The slowdown in GVC trade came from a confluence of factors:

Slower world economic growth. Although global gross domestic product (GDP), trade flows, and FDI bounced back within 2 years of the GFC, global growth remained anemic and below pre-GFC levels. This loss of momentum was particularly stark in the case of global trade. Between 2000 and 2007, global trade volume grew at an annual average rate of about 7.4%, outpacing the average GDP growth of roughly 3.3% a year. By 2012, trade volume was growing the same rate as GDP (Figure 2.11). Ferrantino and Taglioni (2014) argue that, because weak demand for final goods creates multiple shocks to various parts and components, the effect of negative demand shocks may be larger in regions such as ASEAN+3, where GVCs are more important. Due to a bullwhip effect, a reduction in final demand can lead to an even bigger drop in intermediate trade given the magnification of shocks in complex GVC linkages (Altomonte et al. 2012).

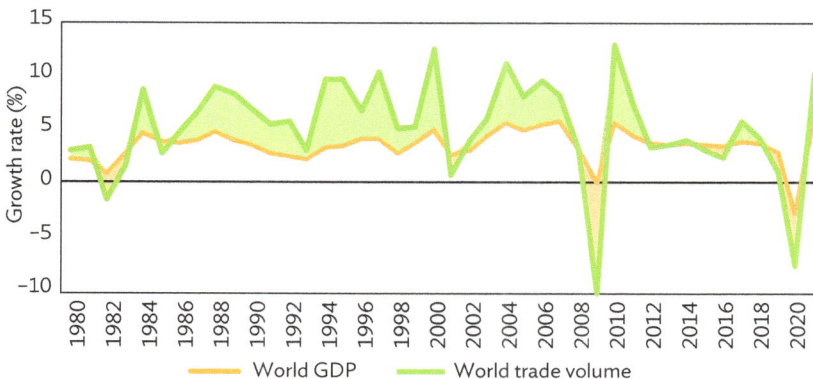

Figure 2.11: Growth in Global Gross Domestic Product and Trade Volume, 1980–2019

GDP = gross domestic product.
Source: International Monetary Fund. 2022. *World Economic Outlook.* https://www.imf.org/en/Publications/WEO/Issues/2022/10/11/world-economic-outlook-october-2022.

Reconfigured GVCs. The GFC exposed the risk of excessive fragmentation, forcing countries and multinationals to reorganize global production. The alternative—more consolidation and less fragmentation—shortens value chains (Xing, Gentile, and Dollar 2021; World Bank 2020; Constantinescu, Mattoo, and Ruta 2017). There are at least two important reasons for this. First, companies wanted more robust and resilient value chains better able to withstand global shocks. For example, Delis, Driffield, and Temouri (2019) found that the wave of "reshoring" over the past decade was triggered by the GFC. Recent anti-globalization movements also intensified calls for "backshoring," "nearshoring," and "renationalization" of GVCs— shortening value chains by moving offshore functions closer to home. And second, stronger domestic production capability means less dependence on foreign supply chains. For example, ASEAN members were particularly affected by the PRC's import substitution policies—causing its backward GVC participation rates to decline beginning in 2011 (Figure 2.12). While the world became more connected to the PRC, the country itself seemed to move toward greater domestic vertical integration (Garcia-Herrero and Nguyen 2019). Baldwin (2022) highlights this asymmetry, with global output becoming more dependent on inputs from the PRC. By contrast, the PRC has increasingly sourced intermediates from its own industrial base, with imported inputs accounting only for 1% of global output in 2018. The PRC's domestic rebalancing and better local production capacities mean less demand for imported value added and lost GVC transactions with ASEAN. The same principle can be applied to increasing automation in advanced economies, where robotization in manufacturing can trigger reshoring of GVC functions currently done in low-wage locations in developing countries.

Slower liberalization and greater policy uncertainty. After the GFC, there were no major multilateral liberalization initiatives, while protectionism even increased in many economies. This not only slowed globalization but contributed to heightened volatility in global governance. Continuing trade tensions between the PRC and the US—which broke out in 2018—further increases the uncertainty in global trade policy (Figure 2.13). Trade conflicts expose the dangers of abandoning a rules-based trading system toward more "power-based" bargaining. World trade becomes far less predictable with distortions amplified through GVC linkages. With ASEAN strongly connected to the PRC and the US production networks, the tariffs imposed by these two trading giants disrupt the region's intermediate goods trade. Those directly targeted by the tariff hikes—like agriculture and electronics—are hardest hit. Thus, restoring stability in global trade policy is needed to renew confidence in the world trading system and reduce the lingering costs of uncertainty due to trade conflicts.

Figure 2.12: Backward Global Value Chain Participation Rates in the People's Republic of China, 2000–2017

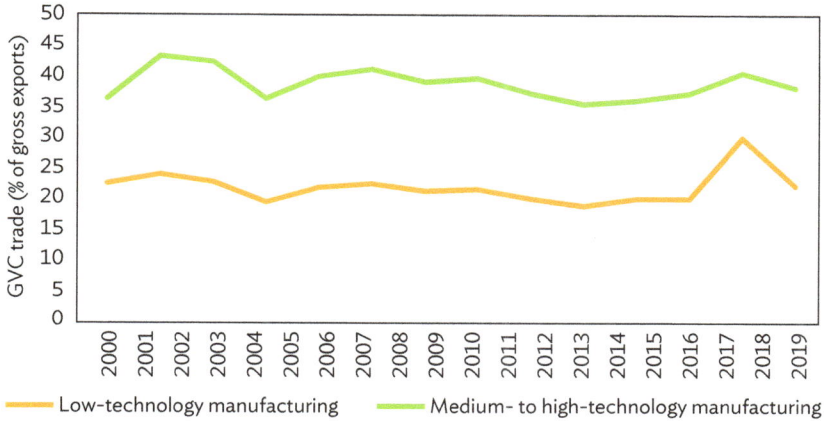

GVC = global value chain.
Source: Asian Development Bank (ADB) calculations using data from the ADB multiregional input–output tables.

Figure 2.13: Global Economic Policy Uncertainty Index and Trade Policy Uncertainty Index, January 2000–December 2019

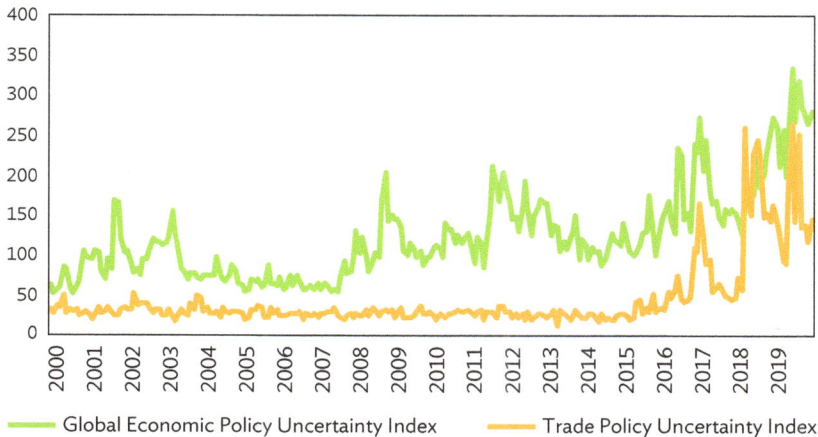

Sources: Economic Policy Uncertainty. https://www.policyuncertainty.com/ (accessed 20 February 2022); Baker, Bloom, and Davis (2016); Caldara et al. (2020).

Structural issues. Globalization lost steam after the GFC partly due to a lack of new drivers for finer fragmentation and more GVC trade. What led to the first and second unbundling—falling transport and communication costs and reduced tariff rates—have already reached historic lows (Figure 2.1). So, a new wave of technological breakthroughs and policy reforms may be needed to stimulate GVC trade. For example, innovations and policy support that accelerate a third unbundling—enabling virtual separation of labor providers and their services—may boost trade across a wide range of services (for example, business consulting, telemedicine, R&D, information technology, and animation).

The Development Impact of Global Value Chains on ASEAN

The relationship between GVCs and economic development is not straightforward. While some results point to the positive impact of GVC integration on growth and employment, others show mixed effects on inequality, productivity, and upgrading technology (World Bank 2020). The World Bank (2020) estimates that a 1% increase in GVC participation boosts per capita income by more than 1%, roughly twice as much as the effect from conventional trade. This is consistent with existing evidence from developing Asia. Sawada and Khan (2017) show that from 1990 to 2010, Asian economies with the fastest-growing GVC participation had GDP per capita growth rates two percentage points above the global average. Fujita (2019) also found a positive relationship between the growth of GVC participation and growth in ASEAN per capita income.

According to the World Bank (2020), the largest growth spurt happens when GVC participation transitions from primary activities to basic manufacturing, as in Cambodia and Viet Nam.

There is also some evidence that poverty reduction due to GVC trade tends to be greater than standard trade. In Viet Nam, for instance, regions with more intensive GVC participation saw greater poverty reduction (World Bank 2020). As Susantono (2019) noted, a big portion of the drop in Asia's poverty rate (from 70% in 1981 to less than 10% in 2016) was due to expanding GVCs across the region. Labor-intensive GVC segments provided employment to millions of low-wage workers, especially in industries such as textiles, wearing apparel, and footwear. For low-income countries, then, increasing participation in even simple GVC activities can have a significant impact on employment, income, and welfare.

The GVC participation rate has a nonlinear relationship with per capita GDP in ASEAN (Figure 2.14). At lower development levels, GVC participation has a strong positive relationship with GDP per capita. However, this begins to weaken or even reverse at higher levels of per capita GDP, as in the case of Brunei Darussalam and Singapore. For less developed and emerging economies, connecting to GVCs still provides an opportunity to increase income and productivity through various external channels such as trade, FDI, and productivity spillovers. First, greater GVC participation broadens the export market for domestic products. Second, GVC trade opens countries to foreign markets, standards, and regulations that may boost domestic competitiveness. Third, GVCs give access to cheaper and quality inputs and technologies that increase productivity. And fourth, inter-firm networks within GVCs may facilitate knowledge transfer through information sharing, firm-to-firm coordination, and other informal interactions.

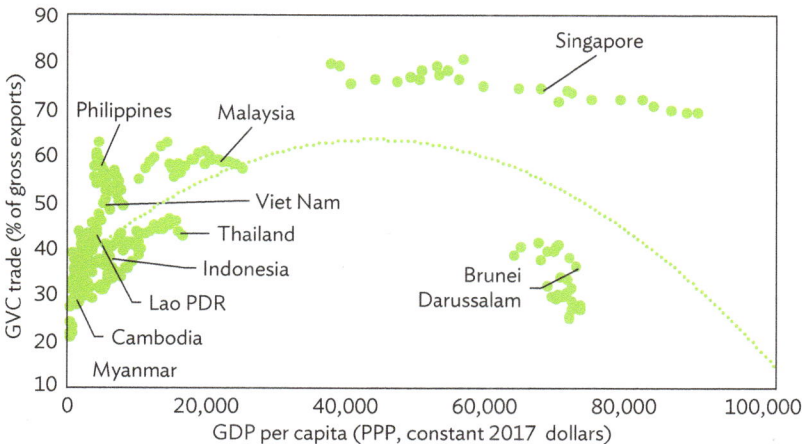

Figure 2.14: Global Value Chain Participation in ASEAN has a Nonlinear Relationship with per Capita GDP, 1990–2015

ASEAN = Association of Southeast Asian Nations, GDP = gross domestic product, GVC = global value chain, Lao PDR = Lao People's Democratic Republic, PPP = purchasing power parity.
Source: World Bank. 2020. *World Development Indicators*. https://databank.worldbank.org/source/world-development-indicators (accessed 20 February 2022).

Several studies show that GVCs help create jobs and improve labor conditions in developing countries. In Viet Nam, for instance, the employment share of the population grew faster in provinces that became more GVC-intensive (World Bank 2020). GVC participation can boost job creation through the scale effects of foreign market participation as well as of new investments in local production facilities. They can lead to higher wages through skills upgrading and increased productivity. GVCs also offer greater foreign market access to small and medium-sized enterprises where most workers in an economy are employed. A study by Constantinescu, Mattoo, and Ruta (2017) covering 13 sectors in 40 countries over 15 years found that a 10% increase in GVC participation increased average productivity by 1.7%. De Vries et al. (2019) also documented functional upgrading in several Asian countries, seen by the rapid increase in R&D employment in GVCs. In some cases, GVCs can even create better working conditions by adopting private standards governing workers' health, safety, and rights (OECD 2012; Bamber et al. 2014; Farole 2016; Hollweg 2019; World Bank 2017 and 2020; Shepherd 2021). For instance, Mendoza (2019) documented that Philippine manufacturers linked to GVCs have better labor conditions than purely domestic-oriented producers. Also, improving the quality of employment within GVCs seems more robust when accompanied by technological upgrading.

For ASEAN, then, the use of advanced technology within GVCs, the need to adjust to changing demands of trading partners, and greater exposure to global competition contributed to increasing rates of technological adoption and learning (Felipe 2018). For example, Thailand's integration into appliance and automotive GVCs upgraded the country's technological skills and R&D capabilities (Abe 2013). Similarly, Viet Nam's recent success in electronics GVCs was helped by multinational investments in domestic R&D facilities. Torres de Oliveira et al. (2021) found that GVC participation in Viet Nam is associated with more process innovation.

The Impact of COVID-19 on ASEAN Global Value Chains

Globalization links big and small countries through a complex network of economic, geopolitical, technological, and cultural ties. This fueled an unprecedented era of liberalization; rapid growth in output, trade, and productivity; and impressive development through higher incomes and reduced poverty. However, one of the major consequences of globalization has been the greater co-movement of national businesses cycles due to increased sensitivity to global shocks, whether positive or negative. An example was the synchronous collapse of world trade in 2008 and 2009 at the height of the Great Recession. Similarly, the systemic disruption of regional supply chains in ASEAN+3 in 2011 resulted from the interdependence of production networks in the region. Recent geopolitical trade tensions also slowed global trade and increased instability within GVCs due to higher trade costs and interrupted flows of inputs. These examples show that remote shocks can quickly intensify into a full-blown global crisis in an age of interconnected economies (Mendoza 2021a). Initially, minor risks can have ripple effects through various international transmission channels such as trade, investment, and financial systems. The interdependence of producers across countries can amplify seemingly trivial glitches into global disruptions. Prior to the emergence of GVCs, one would expect global shocks to spread slowly due to weaker trade linkages.

The ADB Multiregional Input–Output Tables (MRIOT) was used to calculate the static economic spillovers to ASEAN from shocks coming from its major GVC partners (Figure 2.15).[2] Globalized production amplified the spillovers because of the interdependence of various countries and industries directly through bilateral trade and indirectly via complex input–output linkages. Shocks to major economies can generate direct and indirect effects depending on how strongly they are connected to ASEAN. Three important trends are worth noting. First, the sensitivity of ASEAN to shocks from the US declined during the 2000s, although it increased slightly in recent years. Second, ASEAN has become more exposed to spillovers from East Asia mainly due to the growing influence of the PRC. A 1% positive shock on the PRC output would produce a weighted average impact of just 1.7% on ASEAN output in 2000. But that tripled to 4.9% by 2010 and quadrupled to 6.3% in 2020. Thus, over the years ASEAN has grown more sensitive to shocks to the PRC economy. Also, the PRC overtook the US and Japan in the early 2000s as the biggest source of potential shocks to ASEAN. Spillovers from the EU remained relatively small, as suggested by the size of German shocks. And third, sensitivity to global shocks tends to decrease during a deep trade crisis (as in 2008). As expected, trade activities shrink during global downturns, which means transmission channels for international shocks also weaken.

---

[2]   The spillovers are calculated as follows:

$$s = V(I - A)^{-1}d$$

where s is the vector of spillovers, V is the diagonal matrix containing the value-added share in output per country, $(I - A)^{-1}$ is the Leontief inverse, and d is the vector of demand shocks.

Figure 2.15: Average Spillovers to ASEAN of a 1% Local Output Shock to Global Value Chain Partners

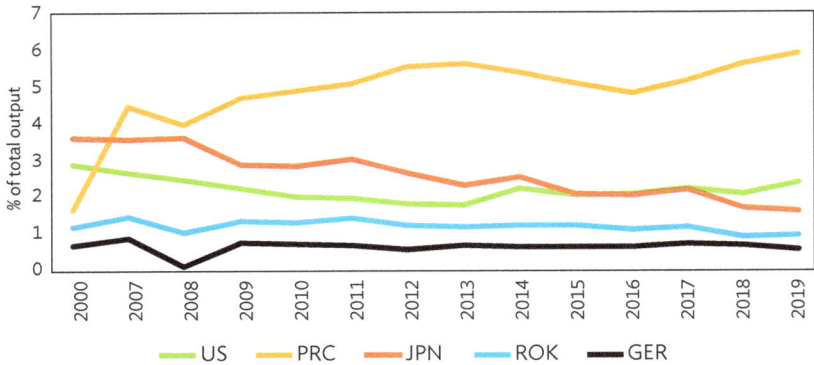

ASEAN = Association of Southeast Asian Nations, GER = Germany, JPN = Japan, PRC = People's Republic of China, ROK = Republic of Korea, US = United States.
Source: Authors' calculations using ADB MRIOT.

By extension, negative shocks to ASEAN's major GVC partners, especially the PRC, have the potential to disrupt regional production networks. The COVID-19 pandemic is a case in point. Its exponential spread across national boundaries led to the so-called "Great Lockdown" that disrupted economic activities over a wide range of sectors. The spike in global supply chain disruptions in 2020 particularly hit production hubs in East Asia and ASEAN, where many industries were temporarily paralyzed by strict containment measures, factory closures, and logistics challenges (Figure 2.16). Cigna and Quaglietti (2020) estimated that GVC linkages could amplify the effect of negative shocks on world trade by an additional 25% of the losses from direct bilateral trade. This magnification effect happens precisely due to the interconnected production activities across national boundaries. According to Baldwin and Freeman (2020), there are three main channels through which the economic contagion caused by the pandemic were magnified by the current structure of GVCs. First, the major outbreaks happened in key GVC hubs in Asia, Europe, and North America, causing disruptions to producers directly connected to global industrial centers. Second, the supply disruptions in hard-hit countries generated a chain reaction that affected the operations of domestic producers and their local and foreign suppliers (and the suppliers' suppliers). And third, lower production and heightened global uncertainty reduced output, employment, and income, which, via the bullwhip effect, exacerbated the strain on GVC activities and further dragged down consumer and business spending.

Figure 2.16: Global Supply Disruption Index, January 2000–December 2021

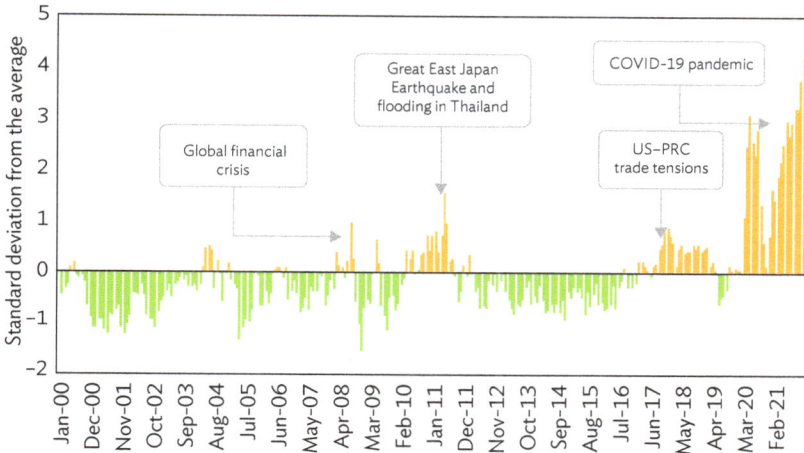

COVID-19 = coronavirus disease, PRC = People's Republic of China, US = United States.
Source: New York Federal Reserve.

The interconnected operations of countries and sectors in GVCs can be seen by the simultaneous drop in backward and forward GVC trade across ASEAN country–sector pairs in 2020 (Figure 2.17). Shocks propagated via GVCs affect a sector or country through interweaving production and consumption channels. What started as a supply shock (such as difficulty in importing inputs)—which disrupted domestic and foreign supply chain operations—eventually evolved into employment, income, and consumption shocks (Mendoza 2021a). Guerrieri et al. (2020) argued that the initial pandemic supply shocks changed aggregate demand more than the original shocks. The magnification is due to the circular nature of transactions in GVCs, which allow initial shocks to generate second-round effects through intricate input–output linkages. This explains why a negative productivity shock—such as the initial lockdowns in a limited number of sectors or locations—generated chain reactions that transcended industries and countries (Mendoza 2021a).

Figure 2.17: Growth of Backward and Forward Global Value Chain Trade in 2020 and 2021, by ASEAN Country–Sector Pairs

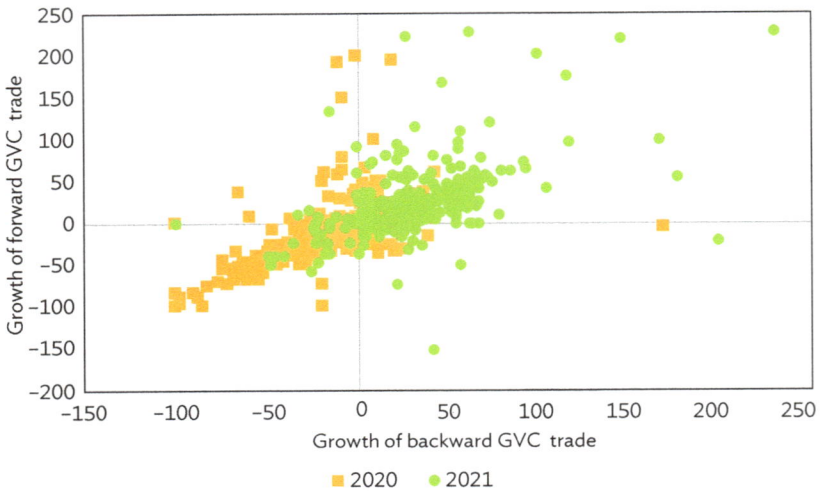

ASEAN = Association of Southeast Asian Nations, GVC = global value chain.
Note: Some country–sector pairs with outlying growth rates were excluded to show the pattern more clearly.
Source: Authors' calculation using ADB MRIOT.

The "scattered" green dots in Figure 2.17 show that growth in 2021 was highly uneven, but the majority of country–sector pairs in ASEAN rebounded strongly. This highlights an important feature of GVC interconnectedness, and trade openness in general—sectors or countries more integrated with the global economy tend to have more flexibility during periods of heightened volatility. While economies with stronger GVC linkages have higher exposure to the adverse effects of negative global shocks, they also tend to recover faster after a crisis (Altomonte et al. 2012). By their very nature, GVCs are dynamic structures and very responsive to internal and external changes (such as input costs, the policy environment, and new technology). An important implication is that exposure to supply chain risk is not necessarily bad, especially when firms and countries have contingency measures to deal with uncertainty (Arriola et al. 2020). Therefore, building robust supply chains does not mean cutting off global linkages, but learning how to ride the waves during global economic storms. Borin, Mancini, and Taglioni (2021) highlighted the role of GVC participation in building resilience by diversifying a country's trade portfolio and reducing exposure to risks from a few important partners.

ASEAN as a whole was not spared from the disruptive effects of the pandemic, with GVC trade dropping by 9% in 2020 (Figure 2.18). This was driven by synchronous contractions in the region's backward and forward GVC trade, which fell by 7.4% and 13.4%, respectively. However, the decline in ASEAN's GVC trade in 2020 was just a continuation of the downward trend caused by the US–PRC trade tensions in 2018. In fact, GVC transactions in the region already fell by 16.6% in 2019, driven by the 8.2% and 32.2% decline in backward and forward GVC trade, respectively. The drastic impact of the trade conflict on ASEAN's GVC trade can be explained by the region's close connection with the US and the PRC, both as suppliers and buyers of inputs and as destinations of final exports. Given the strong linkages between ASEAN and PRC GVCs, the higher US tariffs on key PRC exports had rippling effects on ASEAN suppliers to the PRC, especially in agriculture, mining, metal, machinery, and transport equipment. Similarly, higher PRC tariffs hurt US production and income, which pulled down demand for inputs and consumption goods, including those from ASEAN.

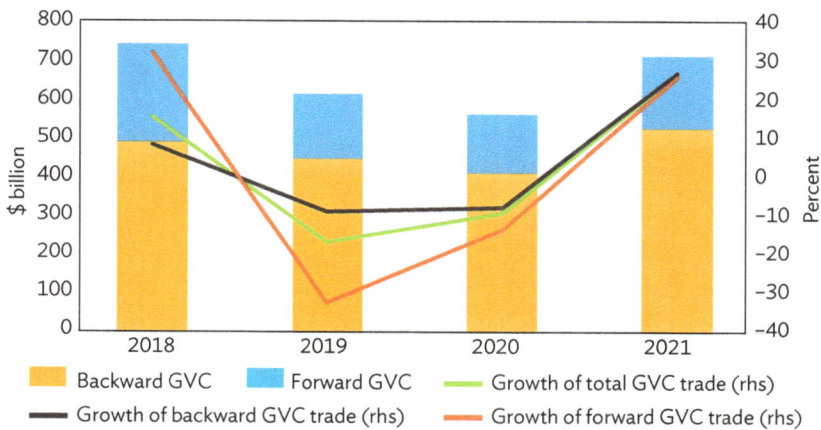

Figure 2.18: ASEAN Global Value Chain Trade Slump (2020) and Recovery (2021)

ASEAN = Association of Southeast Asian Nations, GVC = global value chain, rhs = right-hand scale.
Source: Authors' calculations using ADB MRIOT.

ASEAN's GVC transactions bounced back quickly in 2021, surpassing pre-pandemic levels. Again, this underscores the benefits of inherent GVC flexibility in adjusting to shocks. ASEAN's GVC trade surged by 27.8% in 2021, while the GVC participation rate increased to 48.7% from 46.2% in 2020. This was partly traced to higher demand due to East Asia's quick recovery, especially the PRC. In 2020, GVC trade in East Asia surged by a whopping 38.9%, while the GVC participation rate rose from 31.7% to 34.1%. Nevertheless, ASEAN's strong rebound may also be attributed to its own resilience and pro-active emergency responses at the height of lockdowns and supply chain disruptions. While many MNCs reorganized their regional supply chains and moved disrupted functions across locations, some ASEAN firms were quick to take over (for example, Samsung and Hyundai moving some activities to Viet Nam during lockdowns in the PRC and the ROK). Others scaled up production to make up for factory closures (as with Malaysia's rubber glove manufacturers [Gereffi, Pananond, and Pedersen 2022]). Others redirected operations to take advantage of emerging opportunities, especially in manufacturing hygiene kits and personal protective equipment. In general, building GVC resilience and flexibility necessarily involves improving the readiness of workers, firms, and governments to manage supply chain risks during and after disruptions (Miroudot 2020). This requires skills upgrading; technological and organizational innovation; and capacity-building for effective surveillance, monitoring, contingency planning, and international policy coordination.

Figure 2.19 breaks down the contribution of backward and forward transactions to the negative growth of ASEAN's GVC trade in major crisis periods since 2009. Despite the steeper decline in forward GVC trade in 2019 and 2020 (Figure 2.18), its contribution to the overall drop of ASEAN's GVC transactions was smaller compared to what was traced to backward GVC trade (Figure 2.19). This was due to the smaller share of forward transactions in ASEAN's GVC trade. Compared with previous crisis periods, ASEAN's GVC trade contraction due to COVID-19 was less severe than either the 2009 GFC impact or the US–PRC trade tensions in 2019. One explanation is that the contraction due to COVID-19 merely exacerbated the lingering disruptions caused by the trade tensions. ASEAN production networks were already distressed prior to the pandemic, so the COVID-19 shock only caused incremental disruptions. In fact, in the hypothetical scenario where US–PRC trade tensions did not escalate in 2018 and ASEAN's GVC transactions did not grow in 2019, the likely decline of ASEAN's GVC trade in 2020 due to the pandemic would have been similar to the plunge in 2009. This suggests that the trade impact of GVC disruptions vary depending on the type, origin, magnitude, duration, and propagation channel of the shock. Systemic shocks that affect a large portion of GVCs, especially in production hubs, will significantly lower production. By contrast, the effect of local and temporary shocks such as in 2011 will more likely be limited and short-lived.

In 2021, ASEAN economies enjoyed a strong recovery in GVC trade as lockdowns and supply constraints receded due to vaccinations and better containment measures. Indonesia and the Lao PDR gained most, as GVC trade surged by 49.6% and 47.4%, respectively. The others also enjoyed double digit growth—between 16% to 29%. The only exception was Brunei Darussalam, where GVC trade fell by 7.7%.

Figure 2.19: Breakdown of the Growth of ASEAN Global Value Chain Trade during Major Crises

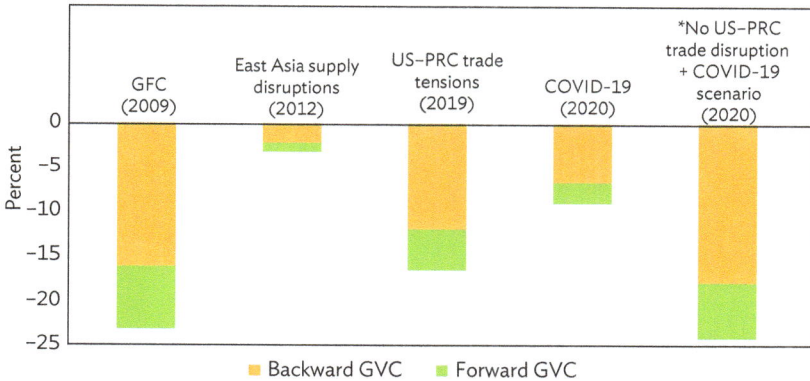

ASEAN = Association of Southeast Asian Nations, COVID-19 = coronavirus disease, GFC = global financial crisis, GVC = global value chain, PRC = People's Republic of China, US = United States.
Source: Authors' calculation using ADB MRIOT.

Figure 2.20: Recovery of ASEAN Global Value Chain Trade from COVID-19 Shocks

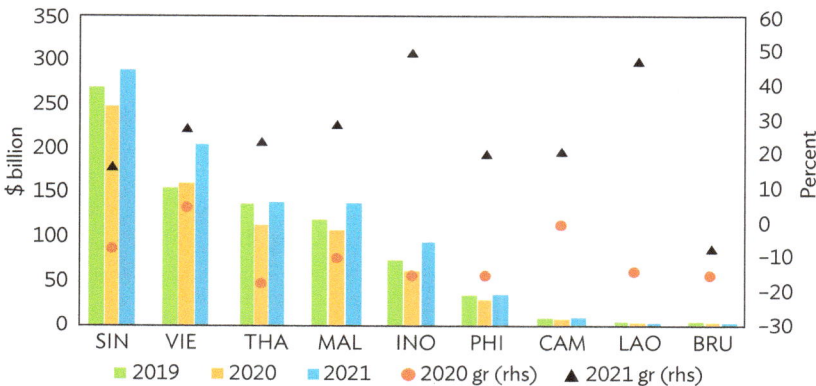

ASEAN = Association of Southeast Asian Nations, BRU = Brunei Darussalam, CAM = Cambodia, COVID-19 = coronavirus disease, gr = growth, INO = Indonesia, LAO = Lao People's Democratic Republic, MAL = Malaysia, PHI = Philippines, rhs = right-hand scale, SIN = Singapore, THA = Thailand, VIE = Viet Nam.
Source: Authors' calculations using ADB MRIOT.

Manufacturing and services are most integrated to GVCs, and were thus hardest hit in 2020. ASEAN's GVC trade declined in 2020 mainly due to the weak performance of medium- to high-tech manufacturing and business services. More specifically, electrical and optical equipment, the region's biggest GVC sector, fell by 5.3%—equivalent to about one-fifth of the overall reduction in ASEAN's GVC trade. For manufacturing, production was hit first by local and foreign supply chain disruptions which cut the flow of inputs across borders (Mendoza 2021a). In addition, the slump in backward GVC transactions in manufacturing was exacerbated by final demand shocks which reduced the consumption of exports, and by extension, the demand for imported inputs to these exports. In services, lost consumption in contact-intensive industries due to mobility restrictions and weak demand for transport and logistics were culprits. However, manufacturing and services bounced back in 2021, showing that resilient GVCs can easily recover from disruptions so long as there are built-in mechanisms (like diversified portfolios and business continuity plans) that allow suppliers to internalize risks and adjust to shocks.

Some sectors are more robust and resilient than others (Figure 2.21). Ando and Hayakawa (2021), for instance, find that machinery GVCs were resilient to both demand shocks (such as the 1997–1998 AFC and the 2007–2008 GFC), as well as supply shocks (such as the 2011 Great East Japan Earthquake and Thailand's floods). During the pandemic, they find that although general and electric machinery, precision machinery, and transport equipment were hurt, exports from all three machinery sectors recovered quickly and returned to their pre-pandemic levels by September 2020.

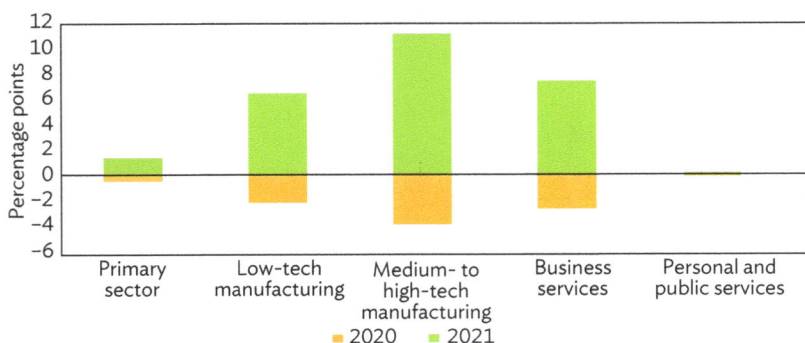

Figure 2.21: Contribution to Growth of ASEAN Global Value Chain Trade, by Sector

ASEAN = Association of Southeast Asian Nations, GVC = global value chain.
Source: Authors' calculations using ADB MRIOT.

Several studies show that while GVCs expose producers to external risks, they also help them recover quickly after shocks hit. For instance, Todo, Nakajima, and Matous (2015) found that Japanese firms with more extensive networks outside the tsunami-affected areas in 2011 were able to resume production faster than others. This implies that diversified input sources and export markets add flexibility to production, especially during supply chain disruptions. More recent analysis by Brenton, Ferrantino, and Maliszewska (2022) shows that GVCs can be a conduit for recovery through financial and technical assistance from lead firms to their suppliers. There is a tendency for lead firms to preserve existing network relationships given the costs of finding substitute or new suppliers (Simola 2021).

The biggest shocks to ASEAN's GVC trade during the pandemic came from the PRC, the US, and other major East Asian economies such as Japan; the ROK; and Taipei,China. The bulk of these shocks affected backward GVC trade. There are three main transmission channels: (i) production networks within ASEAN struggled through local disruptions, lockdowns, and factory closures which reduced demand for imported inputs; (ii) input suppliers also suffered internal disruptions, making them unable to produce for GVCs; and (iii) reduced consumption moderated demand for GVC exports and their inputs.

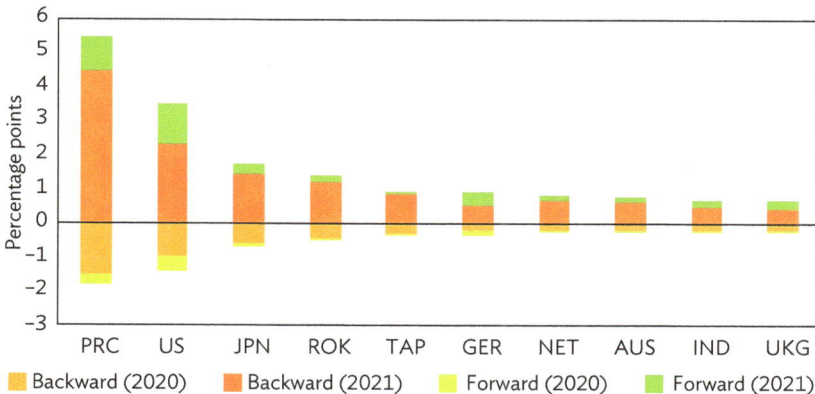

Figure 2.22: Contribution to Growth of ASEAN Global Value Chain Trade, by Partner

ASEAN = Association of Southeast Asian Nations; AUS = Australia; GER = Germany; GVC = global value chain; IND = India; JPN = Japan; ROK = Republic of Korea; NET = The Netherlands; PRC = People's Republic of China; TAP = Taipei,China; UKG = United Kingdom; US = United States.
Source: Authors' calculations using ADB MRIOT.

However, these constraints partly relaxed in 2021, leading to a recovery of ASEAN's transactions with its major GVC partners. Importantly, this strong rebound is closely aligned with the quick recovery in East Asia. The combination of solid policy support and business agility buoyed GVC operations in the region. For instance, the PRC acted aggressively to contain COVID-19 outbreaks—enforcing lockdowns, building new health facilities, and developing several vaccine brands—which helped restore business activities and investor confidence just months after the pandemic broke out. The country's previous experience dealing with severe acute respiratory syndrome may have also helped. Japan and the ROK offered incentives to help diversify the supply chains of their multinationals, many of which relocated some production activities to ASEAN. Lessons learned from the Great East Japan Earthquake in 2011 also helped firms and governments deal with the pandemic disruptions.

How did policy contribute to the strong rebound of ASEAN's GVC trade in 2021? The pandemic's impact on GVCs has been shaped by both the public health crisis and measures taken by governments and businesses. Early studies on the initial trade impact of COVID-19 find that both the disease itself and containment measures significantly affected GVC trade (Baldwin and Tomiura 2020; Baldwin and Freeman 2020; Guan et al. 2020; OECD 2021; Hayakawa and Mukunoki 2021; Zhang 2021). For example, Mendoza (2021a) found that the combined effects of stringent containment measures and severe COVID-19 outbreaks significantly reduced the probability of growth in backward and forward GVC trade in 2020. In the early stages of the pandemic, the containment measures halted factory operations and disrupted transport and trade in services, leading to supply shortages and logistical bottlenecks (Dickinson and Zemaityte 2021; WTO 2020). Supply disruptions worsened as countries imposed temporary trade restrictions to secure domestic supplies of food and medical goods.

The COVID-19 Stringency Index across ASEAN increased sharply during the early months of the pandemic (Figure 2.23). But trends diverged as the pandemic progressed, with countries calibrating containment responses by the severity of infections and deaths. Interestingly, index values have not returned to zero even with the introduction of vaccines and the overall reduced number and severity of infections.

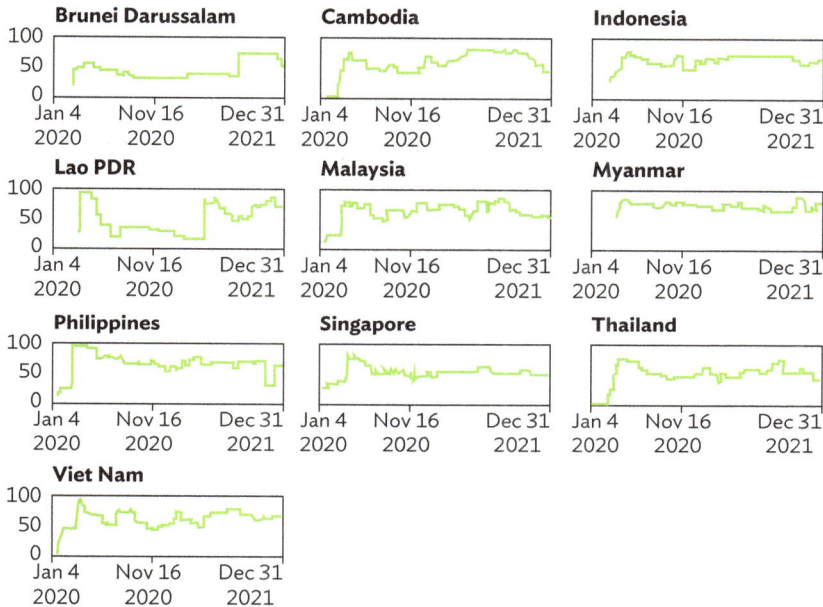

Figure 2.23: COVID-19 Stringency Index across ASEAN, January 2020–December 2021

ASEAN = Association of Southeast Asian Nations, COVID-19 = coronavirus disease, Lao PDR = Lao People's Democratic Republic.
Note: The index consolidates various containment indicators such as school, workplace and public transport closure, restriction on mass gathering and public events, restriction of internal movement and international travel, and stay-at-home requirements (Hale et al. 2021).
Source: Our World in Data.

Governments across the region also used monetary and fiscal stimulus packages to support the economy during lockdowns. Financial aid of varying scope and magnitude were given to frontline workers, vulnerable households, and struggling firms to partially make up for welfare losses caused by escalated health risks, factory closures, massive unemployment, and income erosion. In ASEAN, Singapore had the largest fiscal response to COVID-19—additional spending and foregone revenues reached 18.4% of GDP in 2020, while equity, loans, and guarantees equaled 4.7% of GDP (Figure 2.24). Other countries such as Thailand, Indonesia, and the Philippines also allocated significant fiscal support to their own economies at the height of the pandemic.

Figure 2.24: Discretionary Fiscal Response to the COVID-19 Crisis in Selected ASEAN Economies

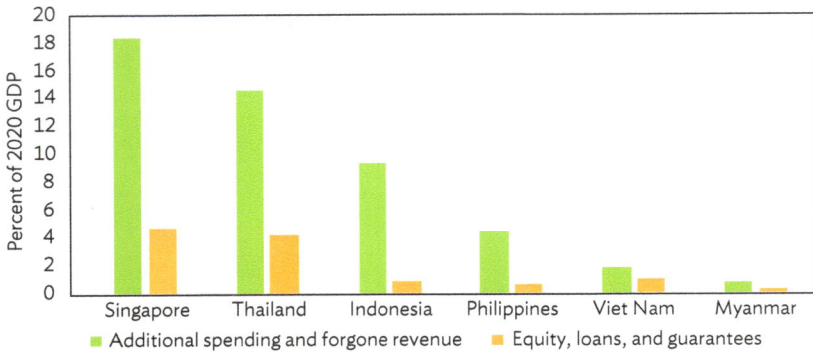

ASEAN = Association of Southeast Asian Nations, COVID-19 = coronavirus disease, GDP = gross domestic product.
Source: International Monetary Fund.

The size of the fiscal response alone was insufficient to either stop the spread of the virus or buoy trade and the overall economy. For example, Viet Nam did quite well initially in limiting infections and keeping the economy active despite relatively small fiscal stimulus. In addition to fiscal support, Pitterle and Niermann (2021) found that good governance, strong macroeconomic fundamentals, and economic diversification also helped soften the economic damage from the virus and containment measures.

The rapid development and availability of several effective vaccines was a game changer in both controlling the number and severity of infections and in stimulating economic and GVC recovery. Prior to the vaccines, resuming economic activities heightened the risk of fresh surges and new virus variants, especially in countries with weak health systems and inefficient pandemic responses. New outbreaks in vaccine-deficient countries led to continued strict containment measures. Extended lockdowns and social distancing resulted in more supply chain disruptions with spillovers propagated worldwide through international input–output linkages.

The resurgence of ASEAN's GVC trade in 2021 was accompanied by a steep rise in the number of fully vaccinated people in the region (Figure 2.25). Yet, there is a marked divergence in vaccination rates across countries. Higher income countries with small populations such as Brunei Darussalam, Malaysia, and Singapore are way ahead of their regional neighbors. In contrast, vaccination rates in Myanmar, Indonesia, the Lao PDR, and the Philippines were lagging as of December 2021.

Figure 2.25: Fully Vaccinated Individuals as of December 2021
(% of population)

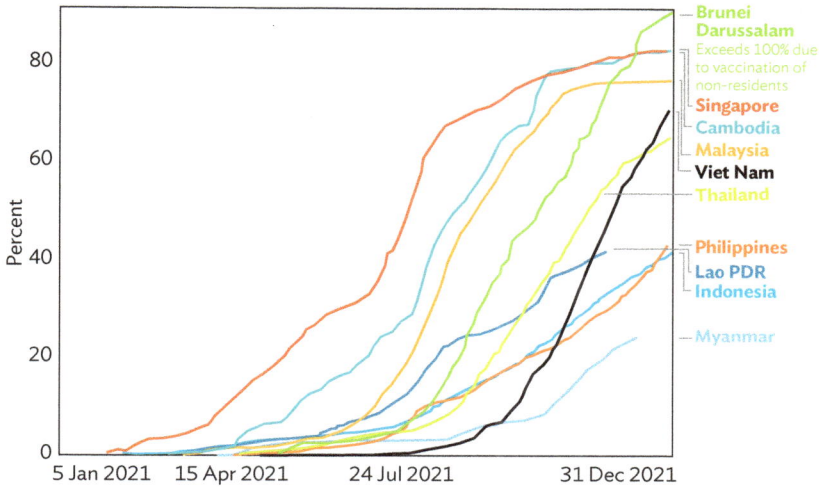

Lao PDR = Lao People's Democratic Republic.
Source: Our World in Data.

The rest of this section estimates a simple econometric model that identifies the effect of COVID-19 policies on a country's GVC participation rate. We used fractional logit regressions given that the dependent variable (the GVC participation rate in 2021) is a value between zero and one. The regression results confirm that more stringent containment measures have a negative effect on the GVC participation rate, mainly through its disruptive impact on backward transactions (columns 3 and 4 of Table 2.1). The stringency index captures the closure of factories and transport services, restrictions on domestic and international travel, and social distancing. Stricter policies limited the mobility of people and inputs, and thus the ability of local suppliers to produce. Greater stringency translates into more serious interruptions in local and foreign supply chains, so GVC-related production and exports contracted as a result of temporary shocks to operations. In terms of vaccination rate, the regressions generate positive and significant results only for overall and backward GVC participation rates. As mentioned, the positive impact of a wider vaccination coverage on GVC activities is intuitive—higher vaccination rates increase productivity at individual, firm, and aggregate levels as vaccines reduce the probability and severity of infections. This results in less absences due to sickness, reduced precautionary factory shutdowns, fewer supply chain disruptions, higher capacity utilization, and higher GVC-related production and consumption.

Table 2.1: Impact of COVID-19 Policies on Global Value Chain Participation Rate in 2021, Marginal Effects

	Overall GVC participation rate			Backward GVC participation rate	Forward GVC participation rate
COVID-19 Stringency Index (2021)	−0.004***	−0.004***	−0.005***	−0.003**	−0.001
	(0.001)	(0.001)	(0.001)	(0.002)	(0.001)
COVID-19 vaccination rate (2021)		0.001	0.002*	0.003**	−0.001
		(0.001)	(0.001)	(0.001)	(0.001)
GEI (2020)			0.137**	0.104	0.051
			(0.066)	(0.091)	(0.047)
Vaccination rate* GEI			−0.003**	−0.002*	−0.001
			(0.001)	(0.001)	(0.001)
GDP per capita, PPP (2020)	0.002***	0.001*	0.002***	0.002**	0.000
	(0.002)	(0.001)	(0.001)	(0.001)	(0.001)
ASEAN (dummy)	0.032	0.024	0.035	0.027	0.009
	(0.035)	(0.033)	(0.029)	(0.045)	(0.024)
East Asia (dummy)	−0.070**	−0.084***	−0.065**	−0.067**	0.000
	(0.027)	(0.027)	(0.028)	(0.032)	(0.016)
Number of observations	61	61	61	61	61
Pseudo R-squared	0.011	0.012	0.015	0.016	0.002
Wald statistic	34.29***	39.37***	55.50***	26.10***	9.30

ASEAN = Association of Southeast Asian Nations, COVID-19 = coronavirus disease, GDP = gross domestic product, GEI = Government Efficiency Index, GVC = global value chain, PPP = purchasing power parity.
Notes:
(i)   Data in parentheses are robust standard errors.
(ii)   * $p < 0.10$, ** $p < 0.05$, *** $p < 0.001$
(iii)   GDP per capita (in thousands) is measured in constant 2017 international dollars.
Source: Authors' calculation using data from ADB MRIOT, International Monetary Fund, Our World in Data, and World Bank.

The negative impact of stringency on GVC participation rates does not significantly change with and without vaccination rates in the model. This suggests that as of 2021, the stringency measures had not fully adjusted to the growing share of the population with vaccine shots. Moving forward, to eliminate lingering disruptions that affect supply chain operations, countries should consider further relaxing containment measures as vaccination coverage expands.

In addition to the stringency index and vaccination rates, we also control for the efficiency of the public sector in planning and implementing policies. We used the World Bank's Government Efficiency Index which measures perceptions about "quality of public services, the quality of the civil service and the degree of its independence from political pressures, the quality of policy formulation and implementation, and the credibility of the government's commitment to such policies." The overall GVC participation rate is positively affected by good perceptions about government efficiency. This highlights the role of the public sector in building an enabling business and policy environment for GVC suppliers, especially during periods of crisis and supply disruptions.

The negative effect of stringency on GVC participation rates tends to dissipate at higher levels of perceived government efficiency (Figure 2.26). Yet, government efficiency tends to moderate the positive effect of the vaccination rate on the GVC participation rate. This crowding out effect may be explained by the fact that at higher levels of public sector efficiency, the government may support GVC operations through policy interventions other than stringent containment measures, while the impact of immunization becomes secondary as the vaccination rate approaches 100%.

Figure 2.26: Average Marginal Effects of Stringency and Vaccination Rate on Global Value Chain Participation Rate

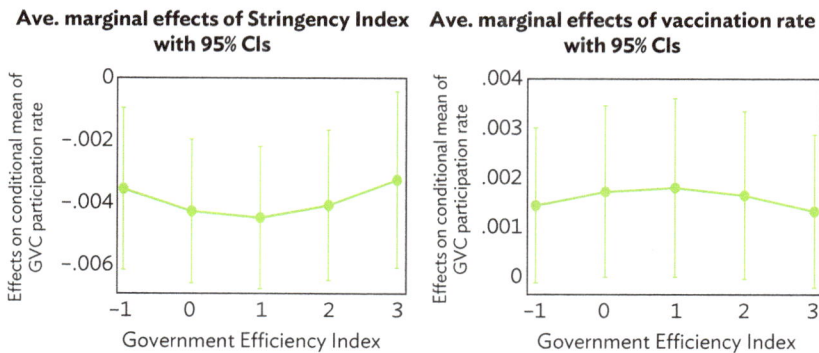

Ave. marginal effects of Stringency Index with 95% CIs

Ave. marginal effects of vaccination rate with 95% CIs

CI = confidence interval, GVC = global value chain.
Source: Authors' calculation.

Box 2.1: COVID-19 and Global Value Chain Trade in ASEAN

Global value chains (GVCs) that have contributed substantially to economic growth in Association of Southeast Asian Nations (ASEAN) economies in the region are generally integrated into the global movements of goods and services and are involved in regional value chains and GVCs. Machinery is an important component of trade in the region with the share of the ASEAN region comprising approximately 10% of world exports and imports of machinery parts.

The spread of the coronavirus disease (COVID-19) and the implementation of strict emergency measures resulted in a slowdown of economic activities. Quarantine measures and lockdown restrictions disrupted production, putting pressure on manufacturing activities. Unemployment and reduced working hours dampened consumer spending, affecting demand for exports in ASEAN. While the economy has started to recover in 2021, concerns have been raised on the impact of the pandemic on GVCs.

Trade disruptions

Based on the findings of a study by Baek et al. (Forthcoming), the negative impacts of the pandemic were limited, indicating the robustness of GVCs in ASEAN. From 2019 to 2021, more than 90% of the products continued to be exported in Indonesia, Malaysia, Thailand, and Viet Nam; while the proportion for the Philippines is at 80%.

Using monthly trade data (Box Figure 2.1A) for four machinery industries (general, electric, transport, and precision), the findings show that 80%–90% of the products were continuously imported from January 2020 to December 2021, indicating that imports of machinery parts were very robust. Exports were not as robust as the proportion of exports that were continuously exported ranged between 45.2% for the Philippines and 81.2% for Thailand. However, data on exports suggest resiliency as the products that stopped being exported came to be exported again a few months later.

Box Figure 2.1A: Monthly Trade Status in Parts

(a) Indonesia

	Export			Import	
Freq.	%	January 2020 > December 2021	Freq.	%	January 2020 > December 2021
274	63.72	●●●●●●●●●●●●●●●●●●●●●●●●●	396	90.83	●●●●●●●●●●●●●●●●●●●●●●●●●
4	0.93	●●●○●●●●●●●●●●●●●●●●●●●●●	1	0.23	○○○○○○○○●○●●○○○○○●●○○○○○
4	0.93	●●●●●●●●○●●●●●●●●●●●●●●●●	1	0.23	○○○○○○○●●●●○●○○○○○●○●●○○
3	0.7	●●●●○○●●●●●●●●●●●●●●●●●●●	1	0.23	○○○●○○○●○○○●●●●●○●○○○○●○○
3	0.7	●●●●●●●●●●●●●●●●●●○●●●●●●	1	0.23	○○○●○○○●○○○●●○○●●●●●○○○○○
2	0.47	○○○○○○○○○○○○○○○○○○○○○○○●	1	0.23	○○●○○○○○○○○●○○○○○●○○○●●○
2	0.47	○○○○○○○○○○○○○○○○○○○○○○●○	1	0.23	○●○○○○○○○○○○○○●●○○○●○○●○
2	0.47	●●○○●●●●●●●●●●●●●●●●●●●●●	1	0.23	○●○●●○●○●●○○○○○●●○○○●●○●
2	0.47	●●●○○●●●●●●●●●●●●●●●●●●●●	1	0.23	○●●○●●●●●●●●●●●●●●●●○○●●●
2	0.47	●●●●●○○●●●●●●●●●●●●●●●●●●	1	0.23	●○○○○○○○○○●○○○○○○○○○○○○○
132	30.7	(other patterns)	31	7.21	(other patterns)

continued on next page

Box 2.1 (continued)

(b) Malaysia

	Export			Import	
Freq.	%	January 2020 > December 2021	Freq.	%	January 2020 > December 2021
313	73.13		393	90.34	
14	3.27		1	0.23	
4	0.93		1	0.23	
2	0.47		1	0.23	
2	0.47		1	0.23	
1	0.23		1	0.23	
1	0.23		1	0.23	
1	0.23		1	0.23	
1	0.23		1	0.23	
1	0.23		1	0.23	
58	20.56	(other patterns)	33	7.59	(other patterns)

(c) Philippines

	Export			Import	
Freq.	%	January 2020 > December 2021	Freq.	%	January 2020 > December 2021
171	45.24		349	80.97	
7	1.85		14	3.25	
3	0.79		4	0.93	
2	0.53		3	0.70	
2	0.53		2	0.46	
2	0.53		2	0.46	
2	0.53		1	0.23	
1	0.26		1	0.23	
1	0.26		1	0.23	
1	0.26		1	0.23	
186	49.21	(other patterns)	53	12.3	(other patterns)

(d) Thailand

	Export			Import	
Freq.	%	January 2020 > December 2021	Freq.	%	January 2020 > December 2021
350	81.21		399	91.72	
2	0.46		2	0.46	
2	0.46		1	0.23	
1	0.23		1	0.23	
1	0.23		1	0.23	
1	0.23		1	0.23	
1	0.23		1	0.23	
1	0.23		1	0.23	
1	0.23		1	0.23	
1	0.23		1	0.23	
70	16.24	(other patterns)	26	5.98	(other patterns)

continued on next page

Box 2.1 (continued)

(e) Viet Nam

Export			Import		
Freq.	%	January 2020 > December 2021	Freq.	%	January 2020 > December 2021
295	69.74	●●●●●●●●●●●●●●●●●●●●●●●●	378	86.9	●●●●●●●●●●●●●●●●●●●●●●●●
3	0.71	○○○○○○○○○○○○○○○●○○○○○○○○	3	0.69	●●●●●●●●●●●●●●●●●●●●●●○●
3	0.71	●●●●●●●●●●●●●●●●●●●●●●●	2	0.46	○○○○○○○○○○○○○○●○○○○○○○●
2	0.47	●●●●○○○○○○○○○○○○○○○○○○	1	0.23	○○○○○○○○○○○○●○○○○○○●○○○
2	0.47	●●●●●●●●●●●○○●○●●○●●●●	1	0.23	○○○○○○○○○○○○○●○○○○●●●○○○
2	0.47	●●●●●●●●●●●●●●●●●●●●●○●	1	0.23	○○○○○○○○○○●○○○○○○○○○○○●
2	0.47	●●●●●●●●●●●●●●●●●○●●●●	1	0.23	○○○○○●○●○●●○●●●○○○○●●●
1	0.24	○○○○○○○○○○○○○○○○○○○○●●	1	0.23	○○○○○●●○○○○○○●●○●○○○○○○
1	0.24	○○○○○○○○○○○○○○○○○○○●●○	1	0.23	○○○○●○○○○●●●●○○○○●○○○●○
1	0.24	○○○○○○○○○○○○○○○○○○○○●○	1	0.23	○○○○●○○●●●●○○○○○●○○○○●○
111	26.24	(other patterns)	45	10.34	(other patterns)

Notes: The figures report the existence of parts trade at a monthly-level. We count the number of HS six-digit codes according to the trade patterns. O and ● indicate the non-existence and existence of trade in a concerned month.
Source: Baek et al. (Forthcoming). COVID-19 Pandemic and GVC Trade in ASEAN.

Trade growth

During the first half of 2020, both imports and exports in machinery parts declined across all regions, but the negative impact is less severe in East Asia with ASEAN showing robustness in terms of exports of general and electric machinery parts and imports of electric machinery (Box Figure 2.1B).

Box Figure 2.1B: Monthly Changes in Machinery Parts Trade in the World (January 2019 = 1)

continued on next page

Box 2.1 (continued)

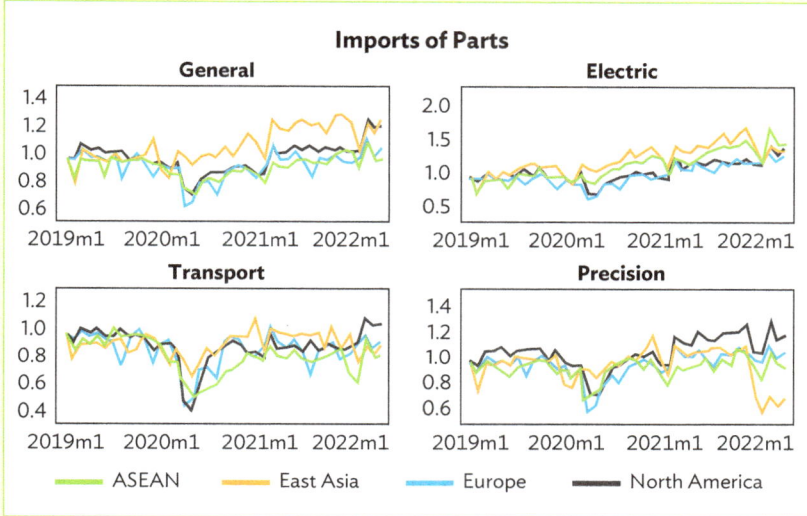

Imports of Parts

Source: Baek et al. (Forthcoming). COVID-19 Pandemic and GVC Trade in ASEAN.

The magnitude of the decline and recovery differs among ASEAN economies and industries (Figure). Viet Nam's exports and imports in general and electric machinery parts continued to grow significantly during the period but its exports of precision parts did not show a sign of recovery. In terms of industry, the exports of transport machinery parts have decreased by more than half for all ASEAN-5 economies with Philippine exports declining to one-quarter of the January 2019 level. There were some exceptions: the value of exports more than doubled from 2019 to 2020, for general and electric machinery parts for Viet Nam and precision machinery parts for Malaysia.

Patterns for the overall share of machinery in exports and imports in Southeast Asia remain stable from 2019 (pre-COVID-19) to 2021 (with-COVID-19). Electric machinery remains the industry with the largest share for both exports and imports followed by general machinery. Malaysia, the Philippines, Singapore, Thailand, and Viet Nam have shares of machinery in overall exports at 80% and imports at 40%. This finding suggests that these countries are actively engaged in exporting and importing of machinery parts and are likely to be more involved in GVCs in the machinery industries. Brunei Darussalam, Cambodia, Indonesia, the Lao People's Democratic Republic, and Myanmar have shares of machinery in overall exports at less than 10% and 20% for imports.

continued on next page

Box 2.1 (continued)

Box Figure 2.1C: Monthly Changes in Machinery Parts Trade in ASEAN
(January 2019 = 1)

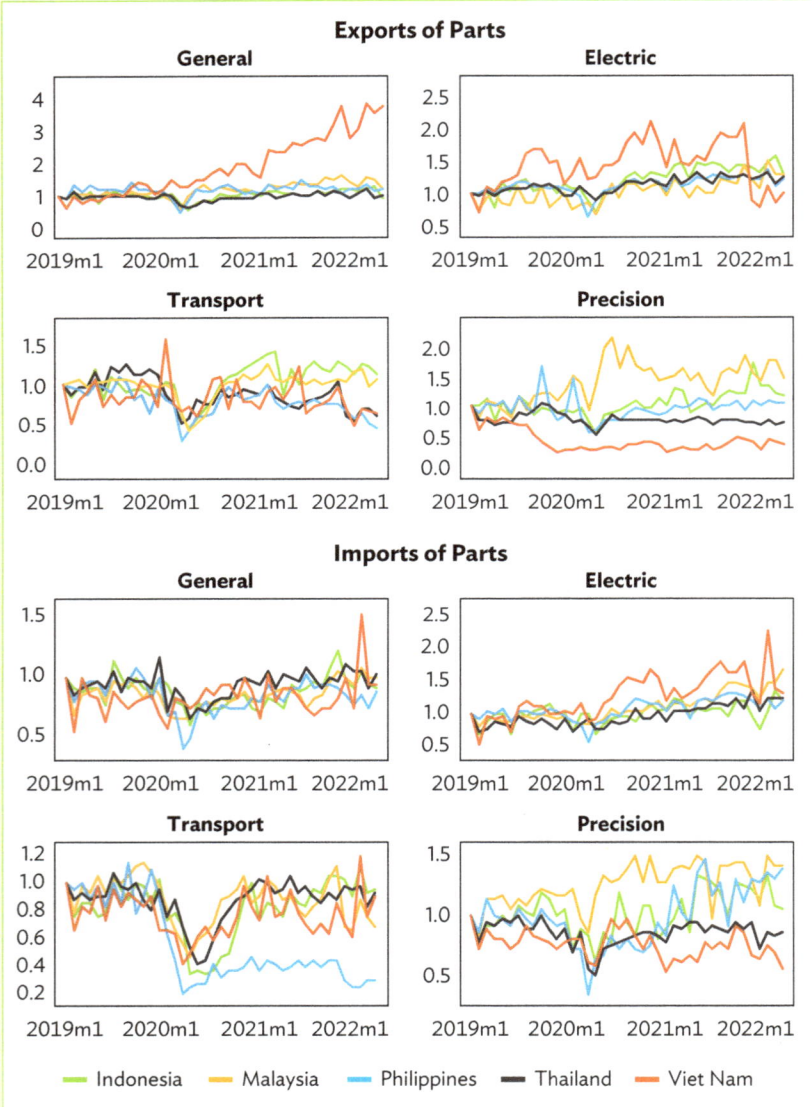

Source: Baek et al. (Forthcoming). COVID-19 Pandemic and GVC Trade in ASEAN.

continued on next page

Box 2.1 (continued)

The composition of machinery exports and imports are also consistent from 2019 to 2021. For Malaysia, the Philippines, and Singapore, trade in parts accounts for 75% of total exports while only 40% for Indonesia, Thailand, and Viet Nam. For imports, the share of trade in parts for Malaysia, Singapore, and Viet Nam is around 75% to 80% while slightly lower at 60% for Indonesia, the Philippines, and Thailand. Both Malaysia and Singapore are heavily involved in production and trade in parts, but Indonesia, Thailand, and Viet Nam are engaged in assembling final goods for exports.

ASEAN-5 countries are integrated in both regional value chains and GVCs. East Asia remains a major partner of ASEAN economies for GVCs. Viet Nam has strong ties with the Republic of Korea due to the presence of Samsung in the country, which imports machinery parts to produce smartphones. Thailand relies on Japan as an important import source of machinery parts reflecting the presence of Japanese automobile companies in the country. Many Southeast Asian economies have strong ties with the People's Republic of China through GVCs. Outside the region, the European Union and the United States remain as the region's notable export destinations.

Competitiveness and quality

Using the ratio between exports to the world and imports from the world for four different types of machinery parts, Baek et al. (Forthcoming) found that ASEAN-5 countries generally do not have competitiveness in machinery parts production but there are industries in which ASEAN-5 countries are competitive. Malaysia, the Philippines, and Thailand are competitive in machinery parts. Thailand also has competitiveness in electric machinery and transport machinery parts. While there are changes in the ratio between exports and imports from 2019 to 2021, this could reflect changes in the level of production because the competitiveness of production machinery parts does not seem to change in 2 years. An increase in the ratio from 2019 to 2021 may reflect sustained production while a decrease in the ratio may reflect an increase in imports to fulfill domestic demand. Interpreting the ratio this way, the findings suggest that ASEAN-5 countries were successful in continuing and maintaining production of machinery part and indicate the robustness and resilience of GVCs involving ASEAN-5 countries.

In terms of quality, ASEAN-5 countries mostly produce low-quality machinery parts. The figure shows the export values of machinery parts according to level of quality with group 1 being the lowest and group 5 with the highest quantity. Singapore shows a relatively large value for group 5 machinery parts reflecting the technical capability of its machinery parts industry. For Thailand and Viet Nam, group 1 machinery parts has the largest value while for Malaysia, the Philippines, and Singapore, group 2 machinery parts has the

continued on next page

Box 2.1 (continued)

highest value. These findings indicate that for ASEAN-5 to achieve a higher level of industrialization, they must upgrade the quality of its machinery parts production in their GVCs.

Box Figure 2.1D: Quality of Machinery Parts Produced by Selected ASEAN Countries ($ billion)

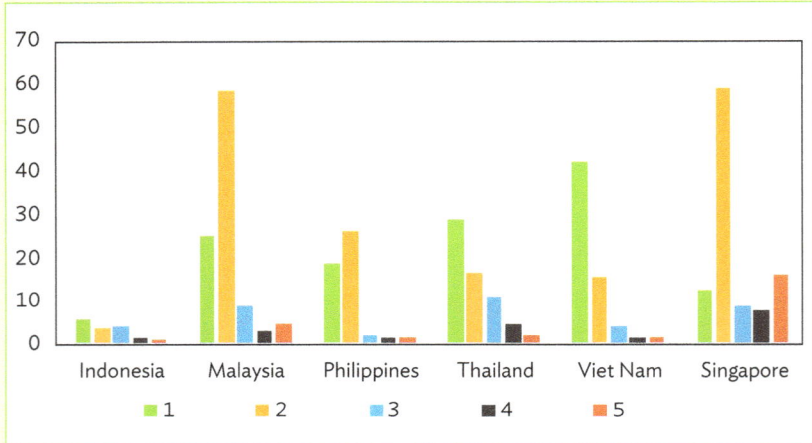

ASEAN = Association of Southeast Asian Nations.
Source: Baek et al. (Forthcoming). COVID-19 Pandemic and GVC Trade in ASEAN.

Note: This box is based on Baek, Y., Hayakawa, K., Mukonoki, H., and Urata, S. Forthcoming. COVID-19 Pandemic and GVC Trade in ASEAN.

The Future of ASEAN Global Value Chains

While ASEAN's GVC trade recovered quickly from the disruptions caused by the pandemic, governments should consider further relaxing containment measures as vaccination rates continue to rise. This will boost the GVC recovery by minimizing, if not eliminating, remaining supply chain constraints. Calibrated containment measures and vaccination programs should remain key short-run strategies to insulate ASEAN GVCs from any recurring shocks from new outbreaks. This is particularly important given the disruptions from the continuing US–PRC trade tension and geopolitical friction in Europe. In addition, supply chains are still strained by input shortages, increased freight costs, cargo delays, and port congestion that could protract disruptions in some countries. The overall volatility of the global economy also adds pressure to already fragile GVCs. Governments should continue working on improving public sector efficiency to ease the business and regulatory environment for GVC suppliers. Government support through fiscal stimulus packages, financial aid, and regulatory adjustments should be carried out quickly yet effectively given the rapid transmission of shocks in GVCs.

Given that production networks are interconnected across the region, governments need coordinated strategies in supporting a robust post-pandemic recovery of ASEAN GVCs. This requires a firm commitment to existing plans—such as the Hanoi Plan of Action on Strengthening ASEAN Economic Cooperation and Supply Chain Connectivity in Response to the COVID-19 Pandemic—which identifies major resources that can be leveraged to promote supply chain connectivity and robustness amid production and logistics constraints.[3] For example, the Hanoi Plan aptly recognizes the importance of (i) avoiding new tariff and nontariff barriers that hamper the flow of raw materials and essential goods, (ii) upholding trade facilitation measures such as the ASEAN Single Window, and (iii) building stronger physical and digital infrastructure as detailed in the e-ASEAN Framework Agreement[4] and the Master Plan on ASEAN Connectivity 2025.[5]

The pandemic showed just how important e-commerce will become in future GVCs. The sudden shift to "work-from-home" arrangements and the e-commerce boom increased demand for digital ICT and innovation. However, the Fourth Industrial Revolution or 4IR technologies are eroding ASEAN's advantage in cheap labor: first, as machines replace workers involved with production in GVCs; and second, as automation technologies reduce the share of labor cost to total costs, meaning demand for cheap labor will decrease (De Backer et al. 2016). Also, 4IR technologies are biased toward workers with higher skills, shifting demand away from lower-skilled workers. These could lead to reshoring or nearshoring production back to home countries. Developing economies competitive in low- to medium-skill tasks could experience a shortage of high-skilled workers and a surplus of medium- and low-skilled workers (Bertulfo, Gentile, and de Vries 2019). The risk is apparent in labor-intensive industries such as textiles, which employ a significant share of labor in ASEAN GVCs. Governments and businesses can prepare by investing more in training and re-skilling. They should also consider horizontal upgrading

---

[3]   ASEAN. Hanoi Plan of Action on Strengthening ASEAN Economic Cooperation and Supply Chain Connectivity in Response to the COVID-19 Pandemic. https://asean.org/wp-content/uploads/2020/06/Hanoi-POA.pdf.

[4]   e-ASEAN Framework Agreement. https://agreement.asean.org/media/download/20140119121135.pdf.

[5]   ASEAN. 2017. Master Plan on ASEAN Connectivity 2025. Jakarta. https://asean.org/wp-content/uploads/2018/01/47.-December-2017-MPAC2025-2nd-Reprint-.pdf.

to broaden the scope of their GVC participation where labor and technology requirements match their current capabilities. While technological upgrading is ideal for moving to more sophisticated value chain activities, scaling participation in both low- and high-tech sectors may provide inclusive opportunities for suppliers and workers with varying skills and capabilities.

In the medium term, governments and businesses should cooperate on building GVCs that are resilient and robust. Miroudot (2020) distinguished between the two—resilience is the ability to return to normal operations after disruptions, while robustness is the ability to remain in operation during disruptions. Robustness comes from minimizing the sources of uncertainty in supply, logistics, and policies. It includes diversifying suppliers and locations, allowing certain redundancies, shock-proofing logistics networks, investing in state-of-the art technologies for risk assessment, contingency planning, and supply chain monitoring. Lead firms can also offer financial and technical support to vulnerable suppliers to prevent potential breakdowns along the supply chain. Governments should contribute by maintaining a stable and predictable policy environment, identifying and supporting essential sectors prone to disruptions, setting up early warning systems and information-sharing platforms, and investing in trade facilitation and ICT infrastructure.

According to a survey by the World Economic Forum in 2012, supply chain managers have a pretty good idea of the most likely sources of disruptions—from environmental (for example, disasters, extreme weather, health) to geopolitical (conflicts, trade restrictions, terrorism) to economic (demand shocks, commodity price shocks, border delays, currency fluctuations, energy shortages) to technological (ICT disruptions, logistics bottlenecks) (Doherty and Botwright 2020). Governments and businesses should prepare broadly outlined strategies to regularly assess the likelihood of each—as well as how to manage a particular shock if it occurs. Comprehensive mapping of production networks will help, especially in marking vulnerable areas and identifying segments where "circuit breakers" can be installed to prevent the transmission of shocks throughout the value chain system. For example, Toyota created a Reinforce Supply Chain Under Emergency (RESCUE) database after the 2011 earthquake and tsunami. The database contains information on alternative suppliers the company can tap during disruptions (Toyota 2016). However, systems like these require powerful computers that can monitor real-time events across supply chains. Thus, firms and regulators should build additional capacity in ICT and machine learning.

While robustness is needed for continuity, it is also important in building GVC resilience, especially during severe shocks such as the pandemic, which caused the sudden stop of multiple activities. Resilient GVCs require agility and flexibility by both firms and policy makers. Government support may be needed to keep highly vulnerable suppliers afloat. Information sharing during and after a crisis is critical—so producers and regulators can incorporate best practices and lessons from the mistakes of others within their own recovery plans. For example, knowing what firm strategies and government policies worked and what did not during a crisis can help suppliers formulate effective recovery plans after a shock. Governments should construct an information-sharing platform, especially for small and medium-sized enterprises with limited resources and surveillance capacities. Most importantly, they should avoid policies and regulations that can add to the disruption. For instance, new trade barriers or convoluted customs procedures could hamper the smooth flow of intermediate inputs and essential goods.

Some strategies that build robustness also help improve resilience. For example, diversifying suppliers and locations provide alternative sources of inputs when usual partners have yet to recover from a shock. Increasing the flexibility of both facilities and workers also helps firms shift to new products and services as new demand emerges during crises.

The US and the PRC will most likely remain the biggest sources of external shocks to ASEAN over the medium term. But the US–PRC trade decoupling is leading to a bifurcation in trade, particularly technology-related products. By January 2021, average US tariffs on imports from the PRC was 19.3%, more than six times higher than in 2018. The tariffs affected 66.4% of the US imports of PRC products. Likewise, the PRC retaliatory tariffs on US imports also remained high at 20.7% and covered 58.3% of the PRC imports of the US products (Bown 2021). ASEAN could become the epicenter for this techno-competition, with significant consequences for the smooth flow of electronics trade in the region. ASEAN governments and industries need to carefully calibrate their strategies given their significant exposure and vulnerability to US–PRC trade. The region should also be ready to grab opportunities arising from the ongoing reorganization of East Asia's GVCs. Instead of reshoring or nearshoring, many MNCs with production facilities in the PRC are looking to ASEAN as the most viable alternative location (Viet Nam, for example, benefited from the relocation of some PRC production). Governments and suppliers, individually and collectively, should continue strengthening their capacities to attract new investment. Policy makers may have to revisit their investment incentives and domestic regulations to make the business climate compatible with emerging opportunities in ICT products, e-commerce, and logistics, among others.

In advanced economies, regulatory and industrial policy changes, such as due diligence legislation to mitigate environmental, human, social, and labor impacts of trade, will affect the current structure of GVCs. The focus on deep decarbonization and green growth is particularly relevant given the commitments made under the Paris Agreement. Countries trying to attract FDI must also consider the increasing importance of green technology and green innovation in MNC investment and offshoring decisions.

Despite various threats to ASEAN's participation in GVCs, the region's growing economic integration can be a buffer against external shocks. Stronger linkages between the region's production networks can ease the flow of inputs and labor across ASEAN members; provide information sharing, knowledge, and technology spillovers; and reduce dependence on value added from outside the region. ASEAN's linkages with East Asian GVCs further broadens available resources and markets. This can make ASEAN RVCs less vulnerable to global shocks from the EU and the US, for example. Still, diversification outside ASEAN+3 remains useful, as the region has a history of internal shocks that can disrupt regional and global economies.

ASEAN's commitment to open regionalism continues to make it attractive for trade and investment. As a pillar of the ASEAN Economic Community, open regionalism uses FTAs toward further liberalization. ASEAN has been the most active subregion in forging FTAs, which will continue to be the main drivers of liberalization in the absence of any progress on the multilateral front. Since most ASEAN FTAs are intraregional, interlinkages through RVCs will become even stronger.

Currently, the biggest intraregional ASEAN FTA is the Regional Comprehensive Economic Partnership (RCEP), which offers several improvements over ASEAN + 1 FTAs: (i) it increases market access for services trade, allowing foreign participation in many sectors; (ii) its investment provisions lock in investment liberalization and prevents backtracking on commitments, and includes a work program covering investor–state dispute settlements; (iii) it establishes single rule of origin criteria and provides ample scope for rule of origin cumulation; and (iv) it includes comprehensive trade facilitation measures to strengthen goods clearance procedures and reduce nontariff barriers to trade.

RCEP could provide massive opportunities for participating countries. A small change in cost competitiveness can have a huge impact on the entry or exit of firms within production networks, depending on the industry. By harmonizing rules and promoting regulatory convergence, RCEP can play a major role in consolidating and expanding RVCs. Also, the US–PRC trade tension should emphasize RCEP's importance (Petri and Plummer 2020), adding to the pivot toward further regionalization of trade in Asia.

ASEAN will retain many of its existing comparative advantages, but needs to address the gaps exposed by the pandemic. Countries must respond to other emerging trends such as recurring disruptions, automation, and climate change. Succeeding chapters examine future opportunities and risks to the growth and upgrading of ASEAN GVCs.

References

Abe, M. 2013. Expansion of Global Value Chains in Asian Developing
    Countries: Automotive Case Study in the Mekong Subregion.
    In D. Elms and P. Low, eds. *Global Value Chains in a Changing World*.
    Geneva: WTO Publications. pp. 385–406.

Altomonte, C., F. Di Mauro, G. Ottaviano, A. Rungi, and V. Vicard. 2012.
    Global Value Chains During the Great Trade Collapse: A Bullwhip
    Effect? *CEP Discussion Paper*. No. 1131. London: Centre for
    Economic Performance, London School of Economics and Political
    Science.

Anderson, M., and J. Mohs. 2011. The Information Technology Agreement:
    An Assessment of World Trade in Information Technology
    Products. *Journal of International Commerce and Economics*. 3(1):
    109-156.

Ando, M., and K. Hayakawa. 2021. Global Value Chains and COVID-19:
    An Update On Machinery Production Networks in East Asia. *ERIA
    Policy Brief*. No. 2021-04. Jakarta: Economic Research Institute for
    ASEAN and East Asia.

Antràs, P. 2014. Grossman–Hart (1986) Goes Global: Incomplete Contracts,
    Property Rights, and the International Organization of Production.
    Journal of Law, Economics, and Organization. 30(1): 118-175.
    https://doi.org/10.1093/acprof:oso/9780199826223.003.0021.

Arriola, C., S. Guilloux-Nefussi, S.H. Koh, P. Kowalski, E. Rusticelli, and
    F. van Tongeren. 2020. Efficiency and Risks in Global Value Chains
    in the Context of COVID-19. *OECD Economics Department Working
    Paper*. No. 1637. Paris: OECD Publishing.

Asian Development Bank (ADB). 2022. *Asian Economic Integration Report
    2022: Advancing Digital Services Trade in Asia and the Pacific*.
    Manila: ADB. https://aric.adb.org/pdf/aeir/AEIR2022_complete.
    pdf.

———. n.d. Asian Development Bank Multiregional Input–Output Tables.
    https://mrio.adbx.online/adb-gvc-indicators/.

Association of Southeast Asian Nations (ASEAN). 2017. *ASEAN Investment
    Report 2017: Foreign Direct Investment and Economic Zones
    in ASEAN*. Jakarta: ASEAN. https://asean.org/wp-content/
    uploads/2017/11/ASEAN-Investment-Report-2017-1.pdf.

Baek, Y., K. Hayakawa, H. Mukonoki, and S. Urata. 2023. COVID-19
    Pandemic and GVC Trade in ASEAN.

Baker S., N. Bloom, and S. J. Davis. 2016. Measuring Economic Policy
    Uncertainty. *The Quarterly Journal of Economics*. 131(4): 1593–1636.
    https://doi.org/10.1093/qje/qjw024.

Baldwin, R. 2014. Trade and Industrialization After Globalization's 2nd Unbundling: How Building and Joining a Supply Chain are Different and Why it Matters. In R. Feenstra and A. Taylor, eds. *Globalization in an Age of Crisis: Multilateral Economic Cooperation in the Twenty-first Century*. Chicago: University of Chicago Press.

_____. 2022. The Peak of the Globalisation Myth: Part 1. *VoxEU*. August 31. https://cepr.org/voxeu/columns/peak-globalisation-myth-part-2-why-goods-trade-ratio-declined.

Baldwin, R., and R. Freeman. 2020. Supply Chain Contagion Waves: Thinking Ahead on Manufacturing 'Contagion and Reinfection' from the COVID Concussion. *VoxEu*. 1 April. https://voxeu.org/article/covid-concussion-and-supply-chain-contagion-waves.

Baldwin, R., and E. Tomiura. 2020. Thinking Ahead About the Trade Impact of COVID-19. In R. Baldwin and B. Weder di Mauro, eds. *Economics in the Time of COVID-19*. Washington, DC: CEPR Press. pp. 59–71. https://voxeu.org/content/economics-time-covid-19.

Bamber, P. K. Fernandez-Stark, G. Gereffi, and A. Guinn. 2014. Connecting Local Producers in Developing Countries to Regional and Global Value Chains: Update. *OECD Trade Policy Papers*. No. 160. Paris: OECD Publishing. http://dx.doi.org/10.1787/5jzb95f1885l-en.

Belotti, F., A. Borin, and M. Mancini. 2020. icio: Economic Analysis with Inter-Country Input-Output Tables in Stata. *Policy Research Working Paper*. No. 9156; Washington, DC: World Bank.

Bertulfo, D., E. Gentile, and G. de Vries. 2019. The Employment Effects of Technological Innovation, Consumption, And Participation in Global Value Chains: Evidence from Developing Asia. *ADB Economics Working Paper* Series. No. 572. Manila: ADB. http://dx.doi.org/10.2139/ssrn.3343998.

Borin, A., and M. Mancini. 2019. Measuring What Matters in Global Value Chains and Value-Added Trade. *Policy Research Working Paper*. No. 8804. Washington, DC: World Bank. http://hdl.handle.net/10986/31533.

Borin, A., M. Mancini, and D. Taglioni. 2021. Measuring Exposure to Risk in Global Value Chains. *Policy Research Working Paper*. No. 9785. Washington, DC: World Bank. http://hdl.handle.net/10986/36314.

Bown, C.P. 2021. US–China Trade War Tariffs: An Up-to-date Chart. *Peterson Institute for International Economics*. 16 March. https://www.piie.com/research/piie-charts/us-china-trade-war-tariffs-date-chart.

Brenton, P. M. Ferrantino, and M. Maliszewska. 2022. *Reshaping Global Value Chains in Light of COVID-19: Implications for Trade and Poverty Reduction in Developing Countries*. Washington, DC: World Bank. http://hdl.handle.net/10986/37032.

Caldara, D., M. Iacoviello, P. Molligo, A. Prestipino, and A. Raffo. 2020. The Economic Effects of Trade Policy Uncertainty. *Journal of Monetary Economics.* 109 (January 2020): 38-59. https://doi.org/10.1016/j.jmoneco.2019.11.002.

Casella, B., R. Bolwijn, D. Moran, and K. Kanemoto. 2019. Improving the Analysis of Global Value Chains: The UNCTAD-Eora Database. *Transnational Corporations.* 26(3). https://unctad.org/system/files/official-document/diaeia2019d3a5_en.pdf.

Choi, B., and C. Rhee, eds. 2014. *Future of Factory Asia.* Seoul: Korea Economic Research Institute.

Cigna, S., and L. Quaglietti. 2020. The Great Trade Collapse of 2020 and the Amplification Role of Global Value Chains. *ECB Economic Bulletin.* 5/2020. Brussels: European Central Bank. https://www.ecb.europa.eu/pub/economic-bulletin/focus/2020/html/ecb.ebbox202005_02~da476a5273.en.html.

Constantinescu, C., A. Mattoo, and M. Ruta. 2017. Does Vertical Specialization Increase Productivity? *Policy Research Working Paper.* No. 7978: Washington, DC: World Bank. http://hdl.handle.net/10986/26145.

De Backer, K., C. Menon, I. Desnoyers-James, and L. Moussiegt. 2016. Reshoring: Myth or Reality? OECD Science, *Technology and Industry Policy Papers.* No. 27. Paris.. http://dx.doi.org/10.1787/5jm56frbm38s-en.

Delis, A., N. Driffield, and Y. Temouri. 2019. The Global Recession and the Shift to Re-shoring: Myth or Reality? *Journal of Business Research.* 103 (October): 632–43. https://doi.org/10.1016/j.jbusres.2017.09.054.

de Vries, G., Q. Chen, R. Hasan, and Z. Li. 2019. Do Asian Countries Upgrade in Global Value Chains? A Novel Approach and Empirical Evidence. *Asian Economic Journal.* 33(1): 13-37. https://doi.org/10.1111/asej.12166.

Dickinson, R., and G. Zemaityte. 2021. How Has the COVID-19 Pandemic Affected Global Trade? World Economic Forum. 8 August. https://www.weforum.org/agenda/2021/08/covid19-pandemic-trade-services-goods/.

Doherty, S., and K. Botwright. 2020. What Past Disruptions Can Teach Us About COVID-19. *World Economic Forum.* 27 March. https://www.weforum.org/agenda/2020/03/covid-19-coronavirus-lessons-past-supply-chain-disruptions/.

Dunning, J., and S. Lundan. 2008. *Multinational Enterprises and the Global Economy, second edition.* UK: Edward Elgar Publishing Limited.

Economic Policy Uncertainty. Economic Policy Uncertainty Index. https://www.policyuncertainty.com/.

Efogo, F., K. O. Wonyra, and E. Osabuohien. 2022. Foreign Direct Investment and Participation of Developing Countries in Global Value Chains: Lessons from the Last Decade. *International Review of Applied Economics*. 36(2): 264-284. 10.1080/02692171.2021.1962255.

Farole. T. 2016. Do Global Value Chains Create Jobs? Impacts of GVCs Depend on Lead Firms, Specialization, Skills, and Institutions. *IZA World of Labor* 2016: 291. 10.15185/izawol.291.

Federal Reserve Bank of New York. Global Supply Chain Pressure Index. https://www.newyorkfed.org/research/policy/gscpi#/overview.

Felipe, J. 2018. Asia's Industrial Transformation: The Role of Manufacturing and Global Value Chains (Part 2). *ADB Economics Working Paper Series*. No. 550. Manila: ADB.

Ferrantino, M., and D. Taglioni. 2014. Global Value Chains in the Current Trade Slowdown. *VoxEU*. 6 April. https://voxeu.org/article/global-value-chains-current-trade-slowdown.

Fujita, M. 2019. *Global Value Chains in ASEAN: A Regional Perspective*. Tokyo: ASEAN-Japan Centre.

Garcia-Herrero, A., and T. Nguyen. 2019. *Supply Chain Transformation: The World is More Linked to China While China Becomes More Vertically Integrated*. Paris: Natixis Research. https://www.research.natixis.com/Site/en/publication/-_JQUR-0gdezsHpW3oZJLosBM Lm42dNjkaNv7SfiCFY%3D?from=email.

Gereffi, G., P. Pananond, and T. Pedersen. 2022. Resilience Decoded: The Role of Firms, Global Value Chains, and the State in COVID-19 Medical Supplies. *California Management Review*. 64 (2). https://doi.org/10.1177/00081256211069420.

Guan, D. et al. 2020. Global Supply-Chain Effects of COVID-19 Control Measures. *Nature Human Behaviour*. 4:577–587. https://doi.org/10.1038/s41562-020-0896-8.

Guerrieri, V., G. Lorenzoni, L. Straub, and I. Werning. 2020. Macroeconomic Implications of COVID-19: Can Negative Supply Shocks Cause Demand Shortages? *NBER Working Paper*. No. 26918. Cambridge, Massachusetts: National Bureau of Economic Research.

Hale, T., N. Angrist, R. Goldszmidt, B. Kira, A. Petherick, T. Phillips, S. Webster, E. Cameron-Blake, L. Hallas, S. Majumdar, and H. Tatlow. 2021. A Global Panel Database of Pandemic Policies (Oxford COVID-19 Government Response Tracker). *Nature Human Behaviour*. https://doi.org/10.1038/s41562-021-01079-8.

Hayakawa, K., and H. Mukunoki. 2021. Impacts of COVID-19 on International Trade: Evidence From the First Shock. *Journal of the Japanese and International Economies*. 60: 101–135. https://doi.org/10.1016/j.jjie.2021.101135.

Hollweg, C. 2019. Global Value Chains and Employment in Developing Economies. In *The Global Value Chain Development Report 2019: Technological Innovation, Supply Chain Trade and Workers in a Globalized World*. Washington, DC: World Bank. pp. 63–81.

International Monetary Fund (IMF). 2021a. Fiscal Policy Response Database. https://www.imf.org/en/Topics/imf-and-covid19/Fiscal-Policies-Database-in-Response-to-COVID-19.

_____. 2021b. *World Economic Outlook*, October 2021. Washington, DC: IMF. https://www.imf.org/en/Publications/WEO/Issues/2021/10/12/world-economic-outlook-october-2021.

_____. 2022. *World Economic Outlook*, October 2022. Washington, DC: IMF. https://www.imf.org/en/Publications/WEO/Issues/2022/10/11/world-economic-outlook-october-2022.

Korwatanasakul, U., and P. Intarakumnerd. 2021. *Global Value Chains in ASEAN: Electronics*. Tokyo: ASEAN-Japan Centre.

Lenzen, M., D. Moran, K. Kanemoto, and A. Geschke. 2013. Building EORA: A Global Multi-Region Input–Output Database at High Country and Sector Resolution. *Economic Systems Research*. 25(1): 20-49. https://doi.org/10.1080/09535314.2013.769938.

López-González, J., and P. Kowalski. 2017. Global Value Chain Participation in Southeast Asia: Trade and Related Policy Implications. In L. Y. Ing and F. Kimura, eds. *Production Networks in Southeast Asia*. London: Routledge.

Mallick, J., and A. Zhang. 2022. Global Value Chains (GVCs) Participation Patterns and Impacts on Productivity Growth in the Asian Economies. *Journal of the Asia Pacific Economy*. 10.1080/13547860.2022.2080428.

Mendoza, A. 2019. Economic and Social Upgrading in Global Value Chains: Insights From Philippine Manufacturing Firms. *Philippine Journal of Public Policy*: *Interdisciplinary Development Perspectives* 2018: 25–65. doi.org/10.54096/YDYB1094.

_____. 2021a. Disruptions in Global Value Chains Due to COVID-19: Stylized Facts and Policy Lessons. *Philippine Review of Economics*. 58(1-2): 214-240. doi.org/10.37907/9ERP1202JD.

_____. 2021b. Restructuring Global Value Chains in the Post-Pandemic World: China's Evolving Role and What it Means for the Philippines. *Discussion Paper*. 2021-04. Quezon City, Philippines: UP Center for Integrative and Development Studies.

Miroudot, S. 2020. Reshaping the Policy Debate on the Implications of COVID-19 for Global Supply Chains. *Journal of International Business Policy*. 3(4): 430–42. https://link.springer.com/article/10.1057/s42214-020-00074-6.

Organisation for Economic Co-operation and Development (OECD). 2012. *Global Production Networks and Employment: A Developing Country Perspective.* Paris: OECD. https://www.oecd.org/dac/aft/GlobalProductionNetworks_Web_USB.pdf.

_____. 2021. Global Value Chains: Efficiency and Risks in the Context of COVID-19. *OECD Policy Responses to Coronavirus (COVID-19)*, 11 February. https://www.oecd.org/coronavirus/policy-responses/global-value-chains-efficiency-and-risks-in-the-context-of-covid-19-67c75fdc/.

OECD and UNIDO. 2019. *Integrating Southeast Asian SMEs in Global Value Chains: Enabling Linkages with Foreign Investors.* Paris: OECD and UNIDO. www.oecd.org/investment/Integrating-Southeast-Asian-SMEs-in-global-value-chains.pdf.

Our World in Data. https://ourworldindata.org/.

Petri, P., and M. Plummer. 2020. RCEP: A New Trade Agreement That Will Shape Global Economics and Politics. Order From Chaos Blog, Brookings. 16 November. https://www.brookings.edu/blog/order-from-chaos/2020/11/16/rcep-a-new-trade-agreement-that-will-shape-global-economics-and-politics/.

Pitterle, I., and L. Niermann. 2021. The COVID-19 Crisis: What Explains Cross-CountryDifferences in the Pandemic's Short-Term Economic Impact? *DESA Working Paper.* No. 174. New York: United Nations Department of Economic and Social Welfare. https://desapublications.un.org/working-papers/covid-19-crisis-what-explains-cross-country-differences-pandemics-short-term.

Ruta, M. 2017. Preferential Trade Agreements and Global Value Chains: Theory, Evidence, and Open Questions. In D. Dollar, J. G. Reis, and Z. Wang, eds. *Global Value Chain Development Report 2017: Measuring and Analyzing the Impact of GVCs on Economic Development.* Washington, DC: World Bank. https://www.wto.org/english/res_e/booksp_e/gvcs_report_2017_chapter8_appendix.pdf.

Sawada, Y., and F. Khan. 2017. Doubling Down on GVC-Linked FDI. *Asian Development Blog,* 2 August. https://blogs.adb.org/blog/doubling-down-gvc-linked-fdi.

Shepherd, B. 2021. The Post-COVID-19 Future for Global Value Chains. *UNDP Policy Brief.* New York, United States. https://www.asia-pacific.undp.org/content/rbap/en/home/library/sustainable-development/the-post-covid-19-future-for-global-value-chains.html.

Simola, H. 2021. The Impact of COVID-19 on Global Value Chains. *BOFIT Policy Briefs.* 2/2021. Helsinki: Bank of Finland Institute for Emerging Economies (BOFIT). https://nbn-resolving.de/urn:nbn:fi:bof-202101141046.

Susantono, B. 2019. Strengthening the Chains That Helped Pull Asia Out of Poverty. *Asian Development Blog.* 2 October. https://blogs.adb.org/blog/strengthening-chains-helped-pull-asia-out-poverty.

Thorbecke, W., and N. Salike. 2011. Understanding Foreign Direct Investment in East Asia. *ADBI Working Paper Series.* No. 290. Tokyo: Asian Development Bank Institute. https://www.adb.org/sites/default/files/publication/156145/adbi-wp290.pdf.

Todo Y., K. Nakajima, and P. Matous. 2015. How Do Supply Chain Networks Affect the Resilience of Firms to Natural Disasters? Evidence from the Great East Japan Earthquake. *Journal of Regional Science.* 55(2): 209–229. https://doi.org/10.1111/jors.12119.

Torres de Oliveira, R., T. Nguyen, P. Liesch, M.L. Verreynne, and M. Indulska. 2021. Exporting to Escape and Learn: Vietnamese Manufacturers in Global Value Chains. *Journal of World Business.* 56(4). https://doi.org/10.1016/j.jwb.2021.101227.

Toyota. 2016. *Five Years On: Toyota's Efforts to Build a Disaster Resilient Future.* https://global.toyota/en/detail/11373994.

United Nations Conference on Trade and Development (UNCTAD). UNCTAD-Eora Multi-Region Input–Output Tables. https://worldmrio.com/eora/.

_____. UNCTADStat. https://unctadstat.unctad.org/EN/.

Urata, S., and Y. Baek. 2021. Does GVC Participation Improve Firm Productivity? A Study of Three Developing Asian Countries. *ADBI Working Paper Series.* No. 1245. Tokyo: Asian Development Bank Institute. https://www.adb.org/publications/does-gvcparticipation-improve-firm-productivity.

Uttama, N. P., and N. Peridy. 2010. Foreign Direct Investment and Productivity Spillovers: The Experience of ASEAN Countries. *Journal of Economic Integration.* 25(2): 298–323. http://www.jstor.org/stable/23000978.

World Bank. 2017. Jobs in Global Value Chains. *Jobs Notes* No. 1. Washington, DC. https://openknowledge.worldbank.org/bitstream/handle/10986/27263/116316-BRI-WB-GVC-JobsNote-FinalWeb-PUBLIC.pdf?sequence=1&isAllowed=y.

_____. 2020. *World Development Report 2020: Trading for Development in the Age of Global Value Chains.* https://www.worldbank.org/en/publication/wdr2020.

World Bank Open Data. https://data.worldbank.org/.

World Trade Organization. 2020. Trade Costs in the Time of Global Pandemic. Information Note. 12 August. https://www.wto.org/english/tratop_e/covid19_e/trade_costs_report_e.pdf.

Xing, Y., E. Gentile, and D. Dollar, eds. 2021. *Global Value Chain Development Report 2021: Beyond Production.* Manila: Asian Development Bank, Research Institute for Global Value Chains at the University of International Business and Economics, World Trade Organization, Institute of Developing Economies – Japan External Trade Organization, and China Development Research Foundation.

Yamashita, N. 2021. East Asian Trade Integration in the Era of Global Value Chains: Prospects and Challenges. *ARTNeT Working Paper Series.* No. 205. February. Bangkok: UN Economic and Social Commission for Asia and the Pacific.

Zhang, H. 2021. The Impact of COVID-19 on Global Production Networks: Evidence from Japanese Multinational Firms. *RIETI Discussion Paper.* 21-E-014. Tokyo: Research Institute of Economy, Trade and Industry (REITI). https://www.rieti.go.jp/en/publications/summary/21030004.html.

Zhong, S., and B. Su. 2021. Investigating ASEAN's Participation in Global Value Chains: Production Fragmentation and Regional Integration. *Asian Development Review.* 38(2): 159–188. 10.1142/S0116110521500025.

3

Jobs and Global Value Chains in Southeast Asia

Christian Viegelahn, Phu Huynh, and Kee Beom Kim

The chapter will also be published as an International Labour Organization (ILO) working paper. The authors are grateful for the valuable comments and inputs provided by David Bescond, Sotiris Blanas, Marva Corley-Coulibaly, Sukti Dasgupta, Sara Elder, Sajid Ghani, Stefan Kühn, Elina Scheja, and Paul Vandenberg.

Introduction

Globalization is one of the key drivers of "transformative change in the world of work, with profound impacts on the nature and future of work, and on the place and dignity of people in it."[1] One way globalization manifests itself is through the proliferation of global value chains (GVCs).[2]

Governments and social partners—including trade unions and employer associations—find it important to "foster more resilient supply chains that contribute to decent work."[3] Southeast Asia has become a key player in GVCs over recent decades, with the region's GVC participation having a profound effect on labor markets, creating jobs for millions of workers.[4] Southeast Asia is an economically very diverse region—including high-income, upper middle, and lower middle-income economies, with varying degrees of GVC participation. The type of GVC economic activity also varies greatly, from low-cost, labor-intensive to high-value-added, technology-intensive sectors.

Increased integration of the region's economy into GVCs also affects job quality. For example, GVCs help some workers join the formal labor market.[5] Also, women are often delegated into lower-wage or lower-status employment, within and across sectors highly integrated into GVCs. In some cases, decent work deficits within GVCs remain severe, with evidence and reports of poor working conditions in GVC sectors. There are also important distributional implications of advanced and developing country participation in GVCs by way of increased wage inequality (Goldbert and Pavcnik 2007; Choi, Kim, and Seo 2019). GVC participation has been associated with higher productivity gains in firms than gains in wages, raising concerns over these gains from GVC participation being shared fairly (ILO 2017).

GVC employment in the region is deeply related to the broad macroeconomic context and other transformative dynamics. Southeast Asia's labor markets were heavily affected by the coronavirus disease (COVID-19) pandemic (Box 3.1). The current global economic environment—characterized by high inflation and geopolitical tension—will likely further hurt employment.

---

[1]   International Labour Organization (ILO) Centenary Declaration for the Future of Work.

[2]   This chapter uses "global value chains," while the ILO typically refers to "global supply chains." In this chapter, one is used as a synonym for the other.

[3]   ILO call to action for a human-centred recovery from the coronavirus disease (COVID-19) crisis that is inclusive, sustainable, and resilient.

[4]   Unless otherwise noted, Southeast Asia refers to Brunei Darussalam, Cambodia, Indonesia, the Lao People's Democratic Republic (Lao PDR), Malaysia, Myanmar, the Philippines, Singapore, Thailand, Timor-Leste, and Viet Nam.

[5]   In Viet Nam, for example, the number of formal employees in the apparel industry reached 2.3 million in 2014, more than four times the level in 2000. See Kucera and Bárcia de Mattos (2020).

Spiking commodity prices and tightening financial conditions, as well as exit strategies from the unprecedented stimulus taken in some advanced economies, will particularly affect economies in Southeast Asia through the GVC channel. At the same time, major GVC transformations—including boosting their resilience and the longer-term efforts to decarbonize supply chains—are expected to impact Southeast Asia's labor markets.[6] While not necessarily having led yet to job losses at a large scale, technology is continuing to reshape GVCs—driving production processes, logistics, and trade financing—affecting both jobs and tasks involved (Bárcia de Mattos, et al. 2020).

Integration into GVCs can exacerbate and compound geopolitical, environmental, and pandemic shocks, but they can also reduce vulnerability by diversifying suppliers and clients (Solingen, Meng and Xu 2021). What can policy makers do to leverage the large potential of GVCs for decent job creation, while at the same time addressing risks related to GVCs and their potential impact on labor markets? This chapter contributes to a better understanding of the nexus between GVC integration and labor market outcomes in Southeast Asia. It identifies several policy options that can increase resilience to shocks and ensure GVC integration leads to more inclusive, sustainable, and resilient outcomes.[7]

The purpose of this chapter is threefold. First, it assesses trends and patterns in the number of GVC jobs located in Southeast Asia, offering new estimates and analyzing how these jobs have shifted between 2000 and 2021 by sector and country, also looking at these trends during the COVID-19 pandemic. To get a better idea of the diversity of the types of jobs and workers employed in GVCs, the chapter presents jobs disaggregated by gender, age group, employment status, and occupational skill level. Second, the chapter presents results of an econometric analysis which investigates the empirical relationship between forward and backward GVC participation on one hand, and a range of labor market indicators on the other, relative to economies outside Southeast Asia. Labor market indicators include working poverty, labor productivity, and the shares of wage employment, high-skill employment, and female employment to total employment.[8] Third, the chapter identifies and discusses policies that increase resilience and support inclusive, sustainable, and job-rich outcomes for women and men from participation in GVCs, during the pandemic recovery and beyond.

---

[6]   See chapter 5 for a comprehensive discussion on decarbonizing global value chains.

[7]   This chapter complements some of the earlier work done on trade integration and its contribution to sustainable and inclusive economic growth and decent job creation: ADB and ILO, 2014, ASEAN Community 2015: Managing Integration for Better Jobs and Shared Prosperity.

[8]   The choice of indicators was inspired by ILO (2021a).

Box 3.1: The COVID-19 Pandemic and Its Impact on Labor Markets in Southeast Asia

Labor markets in Southeast Asia were hit hard by the pandemic. In 2020, aggregate working-hour losses—reflecting both contractions in employment and declining working hours for those still employed—were at 7.4% relative to the fourth quarter of 2019. These working-hour losses are equivalent to more than 20 million full-time jobs, assuming a 48-hour work week. The second quarter of 2020 had the highest working-hour losses in Southeast Asia, more than 17% (Box Figure).

Box Figure: Working Hours Lost since Fourth Quarter 2019
(%)

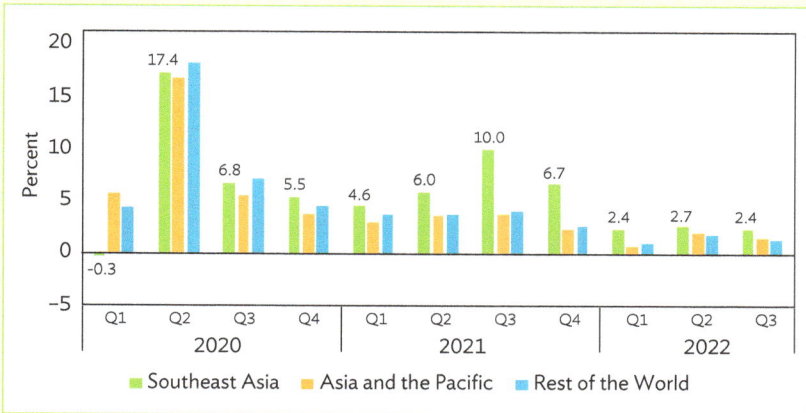

Q = quarter.
Source: ILO, ILOSTAT Database. https://ilostat.ilo.org/data/ (accessed 20 November 2022).

Due to various surges in virus infections, gaps in vaccine access and distribution, and containment policies, decreases in working hours in Southeast Asia remained high in 2021 at 6.8%. Working hours are estimated to have remained below pre-crisis levels in 2022 as well, with a slower recovery in Southeast Asia than elsewhere, as geopolitical uncertainties and increasing food and energy prices add to the pandemic impact.

Source: ILO, ILOSTAT Database. https://ilostat.ilo.org/data/ (accessed 20 November 2022).
ILO, 2022a, ILO Monitor on the World of Work, 10th Edition.

The chapter is organized as follows: the next section provides a detailed picture of the jobs in Southeast Asia linked to GVCs, presenting and discussing new estimates and trends. The penultimate section discusses the results of an empirical analysis, investigating the links between GVC integration and Southeast Asia's labor market. The final section concludes by providing some policy considerations moving forward.

How Many Jobs in Southeast Asia Are Linked to Global Value Chains?

To understand the role GVCs play in creating jobs in Southeast Asia, this section presents new estimates of the number of jobs linked to GVCs and located in Southeast Asia using data available for 2000 and 2007–2021. The analysis shows that in 2021, 75 million workers—or around one in four workers—had a job linked to GVCs, with large differences between economies and sectors. Also, the share of workers in GVCs has been increasing over time, despite some short periods of sharp volatility and setbacks—such as during the first year of the COVID-19 pandemic in 2020. In addition, women, youth, wage workers, and low- or medium-skilled workers are part of the GVC-linked workforce and are generally particularly well represented in sectors highly integrated in GVCs.

The estimation methodology builds on International Labour Organization (ILO) (2015) and Kizu, Kühn, and Viegelahn (2019), combining data from international input–output tables with detailed data on employment by sector (Appendix A) (ILO 2015; Kizu, Kühn and Viegelahn 2019). The methodology estimates the number of jobs in a particular country and sector that are dependent on the production of goods and services that—either as an intermediate input or final good—cross borders at least once before reaching the final consumer. The estimates consider both direct and indirect GVC linkages between economies and sectors (Box 3.2). Estimates of the number of GVC jobs are available for 62 economies, accounting for more than 75% of the global workforce. The estimates include nine Southeast Asian economies—Brunei Darussalam, Cambodia, Indonesia, the Lao People's Democratic Republic (Lao PDR), Malaysia, the Philippines, Singapore, Thailand, and Viet Nam—which collectively cover nearly 93% of Southeast Asia's workforce. Estimates for Myanmar and Timor-Leste are not available.

Box 3.2: Which Jobs Are Linked to Global Value Chains?

Jobs in global value chains (GVCs) include both those with direct and indirect GVC linkages (Appendix A). For example, workers employed by a cosmetics manufacturer in Malaysia, which sells cosmetics to the United States (US) or Thailand, would be counted in the estimate, as they produce final goods that cross borders at least once (Box Figure). Similarly, jobs in the Thai chemicals industry, related to the production of chemicals that are used as intermediate inputs and further processed in Malaysia by the cosmetics manufacturer, would also count as jobs in GVCs, regardless of whether the final cosmetics product is sold in Malaysia, Thailand, or the US; this is because these inputs cross the border from Thailand into Malaysia. Finally, also those jobs in the Malaysian palm oil sector which produce palm oil that ends up as an input for cosmetics sold in the Thailand or the US would be counted as jobs in GVCs; palm oil—after being processed into a cosmetics product within Malaysia—in this case, ends up crossing the border into Thailand and the US in order to reach the final consumer.

Box Figure: Jobs in Global Value Chains—Illustrating the Methodology

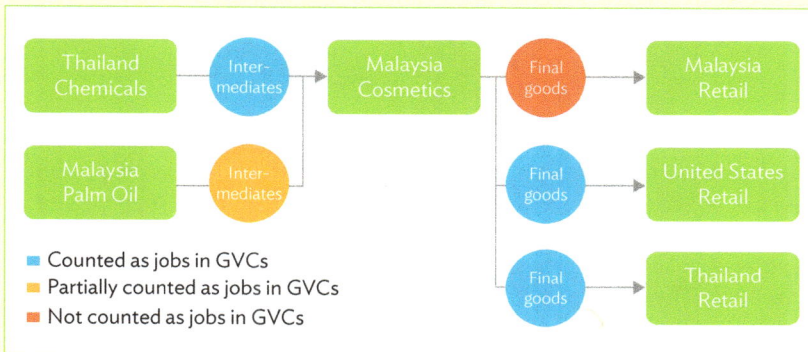

- Counted as jobs in GVCs
- Partially counted as jobs in GVCs
- Not counted as jobs in GVCs

GVC = global value chain.
Note: The circles represent the jobs linked to the production of intermediates or final goods in the given value chain, which are located in the country and sector specified in the blue box to the left.

GVC jobs are not limited to manufacturing. They include jobs in manufacturing, agriculture, services, and the nonmanufacturing industrial sector. For example, cotton and palm oil are agricultural products that require labor before entering GVCs. Rare earth elements are examples of mining products that enter GVCs, thus some mining jobs are counted as GVC jobs. Tourism-related services are exported, thereby a part of GVCs. The common denominator is that they are either directly exported—as a final or intermediate for further processing—or they enter as an intermediate input into domestically produced goods or

continued on next page

Box 3.2 (continued)

services that end up being exported. Using the methodology used here, all jobs related to these activities are counted as GVC jobs.

To estimate the number of jobs in GVCs, an assumption is made on labor productivity in GVC-related and non-GVC-related economic activities. Earlier International Labour Organization (ILO) estimates and those of other institutions assume equal labor productivity, regardless of whether the economic activity within a sector is related to GVCs or not (Horvát, Webb, and Yamano 2020; ILO 2015; Kizu, Kühn, and Viegelahn 2019). However, the literature shows that total factor productivity and labor productivity is typically higher in GVC-related activities than those not related to GVCs in a particular sector. For example, enterprises that contribute to GVCs through exports are more productive than non-exporting enterprises (Wagner 2007). As these differences are particularly stark in agriculture, the methodology makes some assumptions on productivity differentials in agriculture (Appendix A).

Sources: P. Horvát, C. Webb, and N. Yamano. 2020. Measuring Employment in Global Value Chains. *OECD Science, Technology and Industry Working Papers*. No. 2020/01. Paris: OECD; ILO. 2015. *World Employment and Social Outlook: The Changing Nature of Jobs*; T. Kizu, S. Kühn, and C. Viegelahn. 2019. Linking Jobs in Global Supply Chains to Demand. *International Labour Review*. 158(2). pp. 213–244; and J. Wagner. 2007. Exports and Productivity: A Survey of the Evidence from Firm–level data. World Economy. 30(1). pp. 60-82.

Using this methodology, 75 million workers in Southeast Asia had GVC-related jobs in 2021, accounting for more than 25% of total employment (Figure 3.1). This was nearly 7 million jobs more than in 2020, bringing the number of jobs linked to GVCs above 2019 pre-pandemic levels—compensating for the more than 4 million jobs not linked to GVCs that were lost in 2021. The share of GVC-linked jobs to total employment rose by more than 2 percentage points between 2020 and 2021. Given the harmful impact the pandemic had on the Southeast Asian labor markets in 2021, GVCs helped enhance the recovery in Southeast Asia.

In 2015–2019, the number of GVC-related jobs grew by 19 million, its share increasing by more than 5 percentage points. In 2019, both the number of GVC workers and their share of total employment peaked, driven to a large extent by the trade conflict between the United States (US) and the People's Republic of China (PRC), and subsequent relocation of some production and jobs to Southeast Asia (UNESCAP 2018; Anukoonwattaka, Romao, and Lobo 2021). In 2020, the COVID-19 pandemic disrupted the rising trend in the number and share of GVC-related jobs in Southeast Asia.[9] Especially during the initial months of the pandemic, the sharp fall in global consumer

[9]   For evidence on the impact on enterprises and workers in the garment industry, see ILO, (2020a).

demand hurt GVC-related jobs in the region (ILO 2020b; ILO 2021b). Workplace closures inside and outside Southeast Asia disrupted production and in many cases prevented the normal supply of inputs within and across borders, thereby affecting related jobs (ILO 2020c).

Figure 3.1: Number and Share of Jobs in Global Value Chains, Southeast Asia

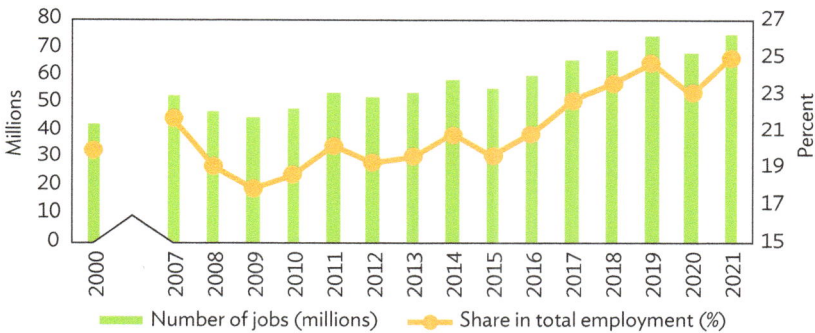

Source: ILO estimates.

There are major differences in the number of GVC jobs in each country (Figure 3.2). Economies that rapidly increased their share of GVC jobs over the past decades include Viet Nam, Thailand, Cambodia, and the Lao PDR. In particular, the Lao PDR and Cambodia saw their share of agricultural jobs linked to GVCs expand, with a growing portion of domestic value added contributing to agricultural value chains (ASEAN-Japan Centre 2019; ASEAN-Japan Centre 2021). The expansion in Viet Nam was driven by garment manufacturers producing for global brands, as well as by the foreign direct investments in electronics and semiconductors that helped create new jobs. The Philippines and Indonesia have relatively small shares of GVC jobs, largely due to the vast size of their domestic markets and demand which favors domestic trade over external trade.

Figure 3.2: Share of Jobs Associated with Global Value Chains by Economy, Southeast Asia

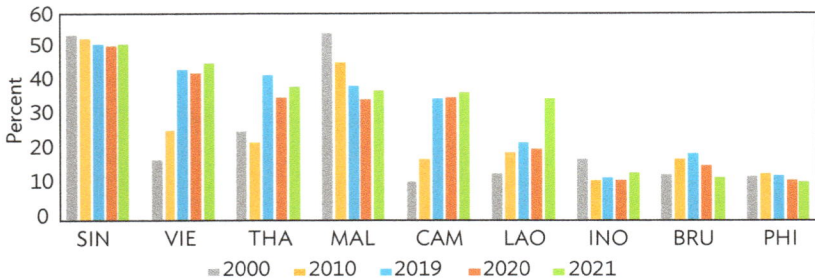

BRU = Brunei Darussalam, CAM = Cambodia, INO = Indonesia, LAO = Lao People's Democratic Republic, MAL = Malaysia, PHI = Philippines, SIN = Singapore, THA = Thailand, VIE = Viet Nam.
Note: Economies are sorted from the highest to the lowest share of global value chain jobs in total employment in 2021.
Source: ILO estimates.

Manufacturing holds the highest share of jobs in Southeast Asia's GVCs. In 2021, more than 60% of manufacturing employment was linked to GVCs, a substantial increase over 2020—emphasizing the strong role GVCs in manufacturing play in helping the labor market recover (Figure 3.3). Within manufacturing, the highest share of GVC-related jobs was in leather and footwear, followed by electrical and optical equipment and machinery. Production in these sectors is organized through highly complex GVCs, with inputs processed and shipped across borders multiple times to produce the final output. Some segments of the agriculture sector in Southeast Asia also link to GVCs, with 24% of all agricultural employment linked to GVCs in 2021. Over the past decade, agriculture has played an increasingly important role in GVC integration, doubling the share of agricultural jobs in GVCs since 2010. Also, in 2021, nearly 18% of jobs in services were GVC-related, with tourism an important contributor. More than 9% of other nonmanufacturing industrial sector jobs—including mining, construction, and utilities—were linked to GVCs.

Only about 10 million jobs, or 13% of total GVC jobs, were linked to intraregional GVCs (Figure 3.4). These jobs include those linked to final goods exports for consumption within Southeast Asia, as well as jobs linked to intermediate goods exports for further processing in Southeast Asia. This relatively low number shows the large potential for Southeast Asia to enhance intraregional integration, as well as the important role played by the region as a supplier to economies outside Southeast Asia. The share of GVC jobs linked to intraregional GVCs increased significantly from 2000 to 2007, but has stagnated since.

Figure 3.3: Share of Jobs Associated with Global Value Chains by Sector, Southeast Asia

a. By broad sector, 2021

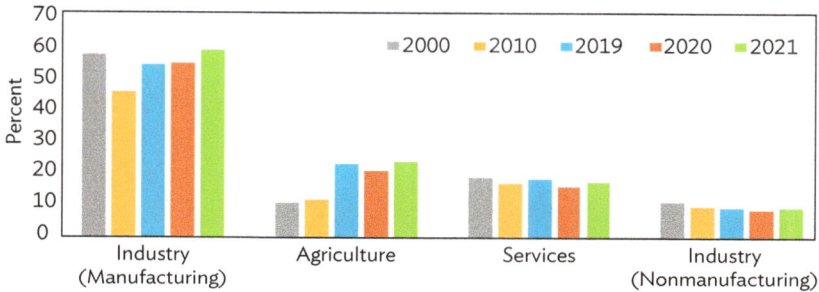

Legend: 2000, 2010, 2019, 2020, 2021

Categories: Industry (Manufacturing), Agriculture, Services, Industry (Nonmanufacturing)

b. By manufacturing subsector, 2021

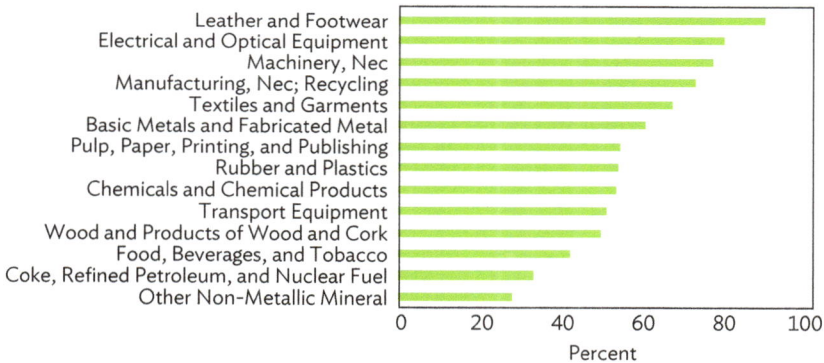

Leather and Footwear
Electrical and Optical Equipment
Machinery, Nec
Manufacturing, Nec; Recycling
Textiles and Garments
Basic Metals and Fabricated Metal
Pulp, Paper, Printing, and Publishing
Rubber and Plastics
Chemicals and Chemical Products
Transport Equipment
Wood and Products of Wood and Cork
Food, Beverages, and Tobacco
Coke, Refined Petroleum, and Nuclear Fuel
Other Non-Metallic Mineral

Percent

Source: ILO estimates.

GVCs provide jobs for millions of women across Southeast Asia. In 2021, about 34 million women worked in GVCs, accounting for 45% of all GVC jobs, which is slightly higher than the share of women in total employment in Southeast Asia (42%) (Figure 3.5). In 2000, 18 million women worked in GVCs. As the estimates assume that the share of women in non-GVC and GVC activities within a sector are identical, differences arise from a composition effect, as sectors more integrated in GVCs on average employ more women—garment and electronics are two prominent examples (Box 3.3). In general, trade helps foster gender equality and better working conditions for women under certain circumstances (World Bank and World Trade Organization 2020). However, while GVCs have undoubtedly offered opportunities for more women to find jobs, many are still found in sectors that tend to require lower skills and offer lower pay.

Figure 3.4: Number and Share of Jobs Associated with Intraregional Value Chains, Southeast Asia

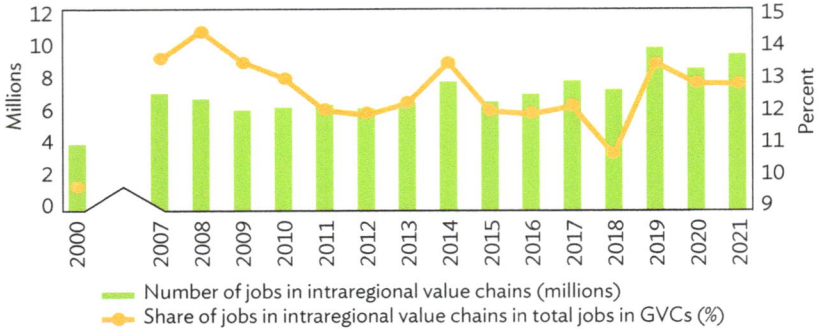

Number of jobs in intraregional value chains (millions)
Share of jobs in intraregional value chains in total jobs in GVCs (%)

Notes: Jobs in intraregional value chains include those linked to final goods exports for consumption within Southeast Asia, as well as jobs linked to intermediate goods exports for further processing in Southeast Asia
Source: ILO estimates.

Figure 3.5: Share of Women Employed in Global Value Chains, Southeast Asia

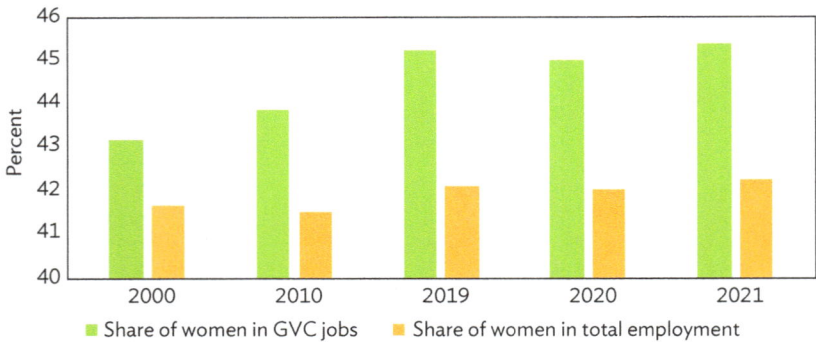

Share of women in GVC jobs   Share of women in total employment

Source: ILO estimates.

Box 3.3: Women in Sectors Highly Integrated in Global Value Chains

Garment and electronics are particularly important entry points for integrating into global value chains (GVCs) for some Southeast Asian economies. They have also created important opportunities for women, including young women, to join the labor market.

continued on next page

Box 3.3 (continued)

Women in Indonesia, the Philippines, and Thailand took advantage of this some decades ago—at earlier stages of development—while female employment in garments has fallen or remained stable more recently. By contrast, women in less-developed economies in the region have only found work in these sectors in recent years.[a] In Cambodia, female employment in the garment industry tripled in a decade, rising from 256,000 in 2007 to 831,000 in 2017, with women accounting for 80%.[b] Similarly, in Viet Nam, female garment workers more than doubled between 2007 and 2020, rising from 1.6 million to 3.4 million, with women accounting for almost 75% of all workers. In Myanmar, female employment in garments almost doubled over 4 years, rising from 612,100 in 2015 to 1.0 million in 2019, accounting for more than 85% of garment workers.

Similarly, electronics GVCs in Southeast Asia also played an important role in absorbing women labor, with the share of women in electronics higher than the female share of total employment in Cambodia, the Philippines, Thailand, and Viet Nam (Box Figure). While the number of women working in sectors such as electronics or garments expanded sharply over the past decades in some economies, it is important to stress that—at least in some of these sectors— female jobs are disproportionately low-wage and lower skilled (ILO 2018).

Box Figure: Female Employment in Garments, Electronics, and Overall in Selected Southeast Asian Economies

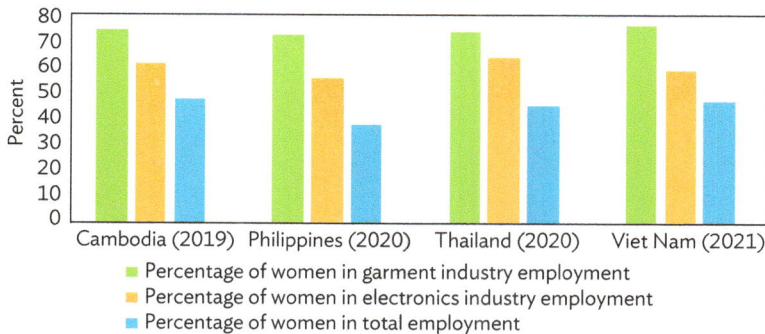

Source: ILO calculations based on ILO, ILOSTAT Database. https://ilostat.ilo.org/data/ (accessed 20 November 2022).

Notes:
[a] The employment figures here refer to overall employment in garments and electronics in Southeast Asia. A high share of jobs in these sectors is likely linked to global value chains.
[b] Garments include the manufacture of textiles (ISIC 13), wearing apparel (ISIC 14) and leather and related products (ISIC 15). All data from ILOSTAT. Male employment in garments in Cambodia increased at an even faster rate than female employment, but from a low base of 53,000 in 2007 to 212,000 in 2017.
Source: ILO. 2018. *Gender Gaps in the Garment, Textiles and Footwear Sector in Developing Asia*, ILO Asia-Pacific Garment and Footwear Sector Research Note.

Sectors that integrate into GVCs offer a disproportionately large number of jobs to youth, indicating the importance of GVCs in providing labor market opportunities for young people (Figure 3.6). However, the share of youth in GVC-related jobs, as well as their share in total employment, has decreased over time as more young people spend more years in education and training. In 2021, about 10 million young workers in Southeast Asia were estimated to have jobs linked to GVCs, accounting for 13% of all GVC employment. These estimates by age group assume that the share of young workers in non-GVC and GVC activities within a sector are identical.

Figure 3.6: Share of Youth Workers Employed in Global Value Chains and the Total Economy, Southeast Asia

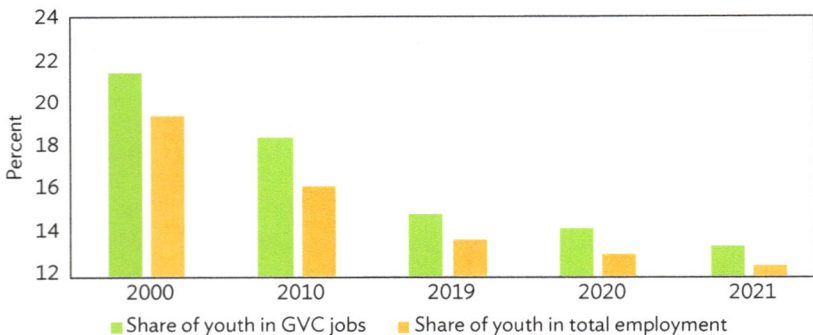

Source: ILO estimates.

GVCs offer jobs for employees as well as the self-employed. In Southeast Asia, the share of employees among GVC jobs has been consistently higher than their share in total employment, but the difference in shares has been declining (Figure 3.7). In 2021, 53% of GVC jobs were held by employees. Over time, the share of employees has been going up, reflecting rising development levels—self-employment and contributing family work are less and less important. These estimates by employment status assume that the shares of employees in non-GVC and GVC activities within a sector are identical, which in turn implies that differences are entirely driven by a sectoral composition effect, as those sectors that do show higher GVC integration on average employ a higher share of employees.

Employment can also be classified by skill level, where high-skilled employment includes managers, professionals, along with technicians and associate professionals—following the International Standard Classification of Occupations (ISCO). In 2021, 11% of those in high-skill occupations were in GVCs, compared to a 15% share of high-skill occupations to total employment (Figure 3.8). The share in high-skill occupations has consistently been lower in GVC-related jobs than in total employment.

Figure 3.7: Share of Employees Employed in Global Value Chains and in the Total Economy, Southeast Asia

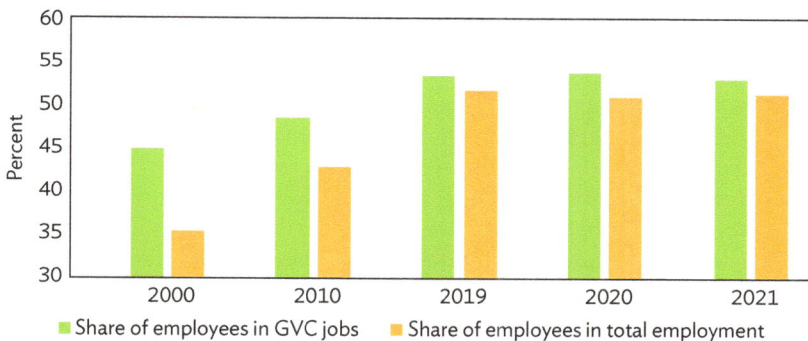

■ Share of employees in GVC jobs   ■ Share of employees in total employment

Source: ILO estimates.

Figure 3.8: Share of Workers in High-Skill Occupations Employed in Global Value Chains and in the Total Economy, Southeast Asia

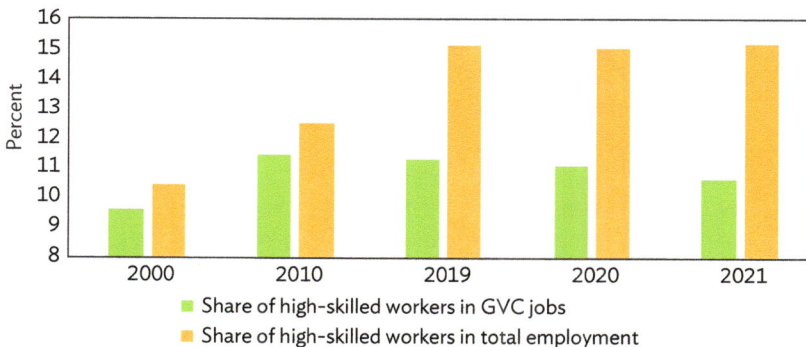

■ Share of high-skilled workers in GVC jobs

■ Share of high-skilled workers in total employment

Source: ILO estimates.

This indicates that GVCs in Southeast Asia continue to create jobs mostly in low- and medium-skill occupations. For example, most workers in garments or electronics are medium-skilled, working as plant and machine operators.

How Is Backward and Forward Participation Linked to Jobs in Southeast Asia?

Impact on the Labor Market: A Literature Review

This section describes empirical relationships based on regression analyses examining the association between forward and backward GVC participation with Southeast Asian labor markets after controlling for a variety of factors. Forward GVC participation refers to the participation of a country or a sector in GVCs as a supplier of inputs to other economies, while backward GVC participation refers to the participation in GVCs as a foreign input user.

One important motivation for policy makers to help enterprises join GVCs is to create more and better jobs. Deeper GVC participation is indeed linked to employment and higher income for some workers and enhanced working conditions overall (Shingal 2015). This is critical as better employment conditions, higher productivity, and more pay are fundamental to raising living standards sustainably. Also, more GVC participation in labor-intensive industries can help create employment opportunities and overcome barriers to decent work for certain groups, such as women (World Bank 2017). Evidence shows that increased GVC linkages have helped expand paid wage employment of women in formal firms (Shepherd and Stone 2013). Still, GVC participation does not automatically mean there is gender equality. Persistent inequalities in GVCs, for example, are evident through gender segregation both across and within sectors, lower pay for women compared to men, and a higher concentration of women in lower skilled and lower value-added GVC segments (Hollweg 2019).

The employment and labor market effects of GVC integration vary widely across economies, depending on factors such as the type of sector and position within the GVC, strategies used by lead firms, domestic skills base, and institutional environment (Farole 2016). Through backward GVC participation, for example, the positive employment and wage effects have been biased toward more skilled workers in developing economies, although less than in high-income economies (Hollweg 2019). This could be a factor in aggravating wage inequality (Shepherd and Stone 2013). The sizeable barriers to GVC participation can also exacerbate inequality, particularly given the constraints faced by smaller firms (Korwatanasakul and Paweenawat 2020).

There are myriad ways deeper GVC integration affects jobs with spill over to the labor market. For instance, backward GVC participation suggests that enterprises use and benefit from foreign inputs. This gives companies better access to a wider choice of higher-quality inputs with better technology. This can have positive effects through learning and knowledge transfer as access to information and open markets improves and technology and expertise flow between buyers and sellers across the value chain (Shepherd and Stone 2013). Firms can become more competitive and profitable, which strengthens the factors that lead to better working conditions. Also, in some cases, deeper GVC involvement can contribute to a higher skilled workforce. Deeper forward GVC linkages can attract investments in training from GVC-linked firms—helping increase overall skill levels in the labor market—to meet the higher product standards and service quality buyers require (Hollweg 2019). On the other hand, having a skilled workforce supported by strong, responsive education and training is often a precondition for successful GVC participation (OECD 2017).

GVC linkages can spur growth in aggregate productivity through different mechanisms. Investments in forward GVC segments that export final products or produce inputs for further upstream processing can speed structural transformation and the shift into higher value added, relatively less labor-intensive and more productive GVC sectors. In numerous Southeast Asian economies, for example, rising labor productivity has been linked to the shift in labor demand from agricultural production for domestic consumption toward textile and garment manufacturing for external markets (ADB and ILO 2014). Enhanced productivity can also come from deepening GVC integration as core tasks are specialized. This helps firms (i) become more efficient, (ii) find new ways to acquire higher-technology foreign inputs, (iii) absorb knowledge from innovative GVC-linked firms, and (iv) provide incentives for upscaling that results in higher productivity (Criscuolo, Timmis, and Johnstone 2015). However, this can also lead to job losses as labor-saving technologies can help meet the quality standards required by upstream markets (Pahl and Timmer 2019).

Deeper GVC participation, given its positive impact on productivity, has been associated with a reduction in poverty in some cases, especially where GVC-linked firms provide wages to attract economically inactive women and men into the labor market—or appeal to workers from lower-paid sectors. This can happen through several indirect channels: productivity gains in supplier industries can generate sharp labor demand because of input–output linkages, productivity growth can stimulate final demand, and associated structural shifts in the economy could expand labor-intensive sectors (World Bank 2020). For the rural poor, agriculture value chains in principle can reduce poverty by integrating smallholder farmers and rural households to supply chains, expanding their access to domestic and international markets, and inducing a shift to higher-value agricultural exports (World Bank 2020). Empirical evidence, however, points to a different reality in many cases. Smallholder farmers in developing economies typically face insurmountable barriers—including higher agricultural product standards, limited technical and financial capacity, and gaps in monitoring and compliance, among others—that prevent linking to forward GVCs, thus slowing the reduction in working poverty (Montalbano and Nenci 2020).

Enhanced GVC participation can theoretically lead to better working conditions from both gains in productivity, wages, and skills and through improved governance—as governments and GVC-linked firms strive to ensure compliance with buyer standards. Oftentimes driven by pressure from international consumers concerned about worker welfare, there is increasing concern over labor standards, fair wages, employment conditions, and workplace safety and health (Distelhorst and Fu 2017), although in many cases compliance remains limited to larger first-tier suppliers (Lee 2016). Nevertheless, evidence points to the prevalence of informality and poor working conditions in GVCs, especially in small-scale enterprises and subcontractors in lower-tier segments (Aked 2021; Harvey 2019). Related to this, there is also persistent child labor and forced labor in GVCs, which can be traced back to the interaction of three critical dimensions (ILO, OECD, IOM, and UNICEF 2019; Caspersz et al. 2022). These include (i) gaps in statutory legislation, enforcement, and systems of justice that allow noncompliance; (ii) poverty and other socioeconomic pressures faced by individuals and workers; and (iii) a lack of awareness, capacity, and policies on the part of businesses of their responsibility to uphold fundamental principles and labor rights.

While strengthening labor provisions in bilateral and regional trade agreements can have positive impacts (see next section), empirical evidence remains limited, given the longer-term nature of the expected impacts (ILO 2016). Nonetheless, there are concrete results in terms of ratifying international labor standards. For example, in 2020, Viet Nam ratified the ILO Convention 105 on the Abolition of Forced Labor to conclude the European Union (EU)–Viet Nam free trade agreement (FTA), which required Viet Nam to continue working toward ratifying all fundamental conventions. Viet Nam has ratified nine of the 10 fundamental conventions, the exception being ILO Convention 87 on the Freedom of Association and Protection of the Right to Organize (ILO 2020d).

The Link Between Backward and Forward Participation in Global Value Chains and Jobs in Southeast Asia

This section discusses the labor market implications of deeper GVC integration, based on the econometric analysis by Blanas, Huynh, and Viegelahn (forthcoming), which covers 62 economies and 35 industries (Appendix A). It includes detailed findings for nine Southeast Asian economies—Brunei Darussalam, Cambodia, Indonesia, the Lao PDR, Malaysia, the Philippines, Singapore, Thailand, and Viet Nam—for 2000 and 2007–2020. It provides empirical evidence from novel econometric analysis of different measures of GVC participation from ADB's Multiregional Input–Output Tables as well as real and estimated labor market data from the ILO's global repository of harmonized household survey microdata.

The econometric analysis gives some insights into the link between deeper GVC involvement in Southeast Asia and jobs over the past 2 decades. First, improvements in employment quality—approximated specifically by reductions in working poverty and increases in labor productivity— were positively associated with increased backward and forward GVC participation. Second, the results show that, on the contrary, enhanced GVC participation was not universally linked to other important dimensions of better job quality, such as higher shares in wage employment and high-skilled employment. Greater forward GVC engagement in Southeast Asia was tied to a lower wage employment share overall—notwithstanding higher wage employment shares in manufacturing—coming from the intense demand for self-employment in the agriculture-driven primary sector. Enhanced GVC participation was also linked to greater demand for low- and medium-skill employment at the expense of high-skill jobs. Third, greater backward GVC integration was correlated with some employment gains for women. However, the benefits were concentrated in the primary sector and personal and professional services, both were typically less skill-intensive, less productive, and lower paid.

GVC participation has intensified in Southeast Asia over the past couple of decades. During this period, the region made progress in the labor market by expanding productive employment and enhancing job quality. The share of workers living in extreme poverty decreased considerably from 29% in 2000 to just above 2% in 2021 (Figure 3.9). The 27 percentage point drop far outpaced progress in the world excluding Southeast Asia, where it declined by 18 percentage points since 2000. The reduction occurred across segments of the labor market, including women and young workers. Similarly, the region made remarkable strides in boosting labor

productivity—critical for a sustained increase in wages and labor income—
as a structural transformation led workers into higher value-added sectors.
Between 2000 and 2021, labor productivity—measured as output per
worker—increased by an annual average of 3% in Southeast Asia.
By comparison, labor productivity globally grew by 2.1% annually during
the same period.[10]

**Figure 3.9: Working Poverty Rate in Southeast Asia
and Non-Southeast Asia Economies, 2000–2021**
(%)

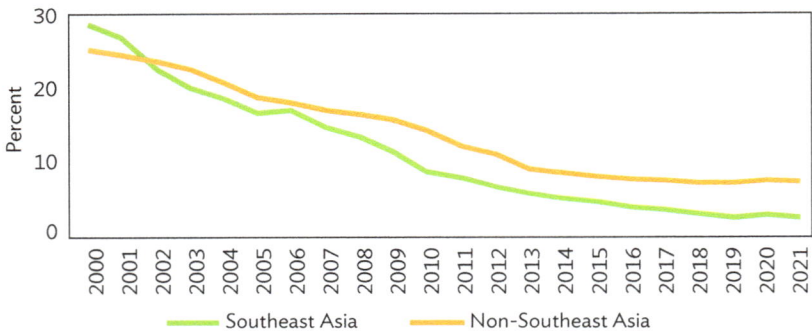

Note: Working poverty is measured as the percentage of employed persons living in poverty, defined using
the international poverty line of $1.90 per day in purchasing power parity.
Source: Authors' calculations based on ILO, ILOSTAT Database. https://ilostat.ilo.org/data/ (accessed 20
November 2022).

The better labor market coincided with deeper GVC participation over the
past 2 decades. In many cases, they may be linked. First, the expansion of
backward GVC participation by one standard deviation can be associated
with a decline in the total working poverty rate of 4 percentage points,
using data for 2000 and 2007–2019 (Figure 3.10). Similarly, the expansion
of forward GVC participation is associated with a decline in the total
working poverty rate by 5.8 percentage points. While the result on
backward GVC participation is not significantly different from the result for
economies outside Southeast Asia, the result on forward GVC participation
is specific to Southeast Asia and not found in economies outside the region.
Importantly, the robust, inverse relationship also holds for the fall in
working poverty across subgroups—male and female workers and working
youth and adults—and by comparable magnitude.

---

[10] Authors' calculations based on ILO, ILOSTAT Database. Labour productivity is measured as output (GDP in
constant 2017 international $ at purchasing power parity) per worker. https://ilostat.ilo.org/data/ (accessed
20 November 2022).

Figure 3.10: Estimated Change in Working Poverty Associated with an Increase of One Standard Deviation in Backward and Forward Global Value Chain Participation in Southeast Asia by Age and Gender
(percentage points)

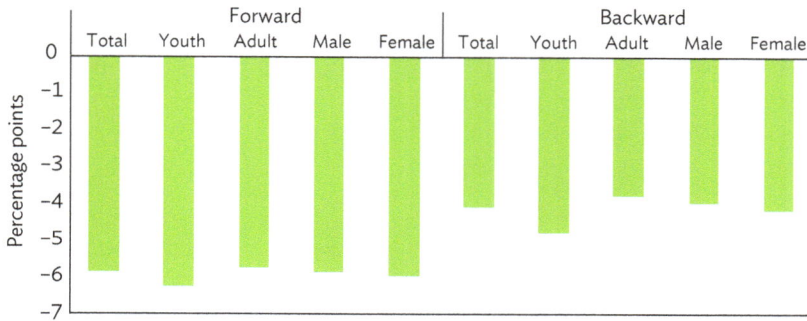

Note: All estimates are statistically significant at the 5% level. Estimates are based on ordinary least squares regressions at the country level, with country and year fixed effects. Working poverty is measured as the percentage of employed persons living in poverty, defined using the international poverty line of $1.90 per day in purchasing power parity. Youth is defined as those aged 15–24 years and adults aged 25+ years. Regression results are based on a sample that includes 2000 and 2007–2020.
Source: Authors' calculations based on Blanas, Huynh, and Viegelahn (forthcoming).

The link between GVC participation and increased labor productivity has also been quite stark, and—based on the results of Blanas, Huynh, and Viegelahn (forthcoming)—significantly more than economies outside the region under analysis. The level of labor productivity is positively associated with forward GVC participation in the Southeast Asian economies (Figure 3.11). An increase in forward GVC participation by one standard deviation is associated with an increase in real labor productivity of 9.6%. Even though the overall link between backward GVC participation and real labor productivity is statistically not significant, economies in the region are still found to perform better than those economies under analysis outside Southeast Asia when translating higher backward GVC participation into higher real labor productivity. These findings corroborate the literature on the beneficial link between GVCs and labor productivity and align with Southeast Asia's recent economic diversification, structural transformation, and skills upgrading.

Another labor market trend in Southeast Asia is the considerable progress made in expanding the portion of paid employees in total employment—a suggestive, although imperfect, measure of job security and stability. From 2000 to 2021, the wage employment share grew from 34% to

50.1%—or by 16.2 percentage points, nearly double the rate for the rest
of the world (8.6 percentage points).[11] The region also recorded some
moderate gains for employment in high-skill occupations—jobs as
managers, professionals, and associate professionals typically requiring
higher qualifications, skills, and experience. Between 2000 and 2020, the
share of employment in high-skill occupations in the region increased by
4.6 percentage points, from 9.9% to 14.5%. Although this slightly outpaced
progress in the rest of the world (4.2 percentage points), employment
outside the region remained more reliant on high-skill employment overall
(21.8% in 2020) (ILO, ILOSTATA Database).

Figure 3.11: Estimated Change in Labor Productivity Associated
with an Increase of One Standard Deviation in Backward and
Forward Global Value Chain Participation in Southeast Asia
(%)

Note: The solid bar indicates that the estimate is statistically significant at the 1% level. The diagonally
striped bar indicates that the estimate is statistically not significantly different from zero. Estimates are
based on ordinary least squares regressions at the country level, with country and year fixed effects.
Labor productivity is defined as the log of the total volume of output (measured in terms of gross
domestic product in constant prices) produced per employed persons. Regression results are based on
a sample that includes 2000 and 2007–2020.
Source: Authors' calculations based on Blanas, Huynh and Viegelahn (forthcoming).

For wage employment and high-skill employment growth, however, the
region's enhanced forward GVC participation, especially in certain sectors,
may have actually slowed these trends. Deeper forward GVC engagement
is associated with a quantitatively small decrease in the wage employment
share, or conversely an increase in the share of self-employed workers
(Figure 3.12.a). This finding is specific to Southeast Asia, but the dynamic
is heavily influenced by the agriculture-driven primary sector, where
self-employed, own-account workers and contributing family workers
are prevalent, and to a lesser degree in business services, which includes

[11]   Authors' calculations based on ILO, ILOSTAT Database. https://ilostat.ilo.org/data/ (accessed 20 November
2022).

considerable shares of self-employment in retail trade. By comparison, greater forward GVC participation in manufacturing as well as personal and professional services is associated with positive gains in the wage employment share, suggesting an expansion of opportunities for wage employment in these sectors.

Figure 3.12: Estimated Change in Employment Shares Associated with an Increase of One Standard Deviation in Global Value Chain Participation in Southeast Asia by Economic Sector
(percentage points)

a. Wage Employment, Forward Global Value Chain Participation

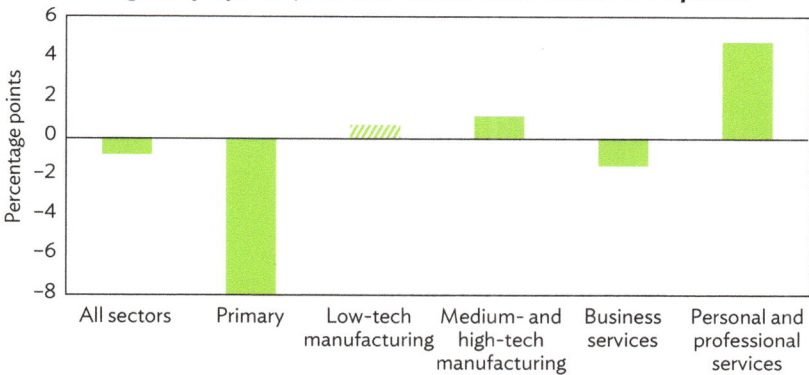

b. Employment in High-skill Occupations, Backward and Forward Global Value Chain Participation

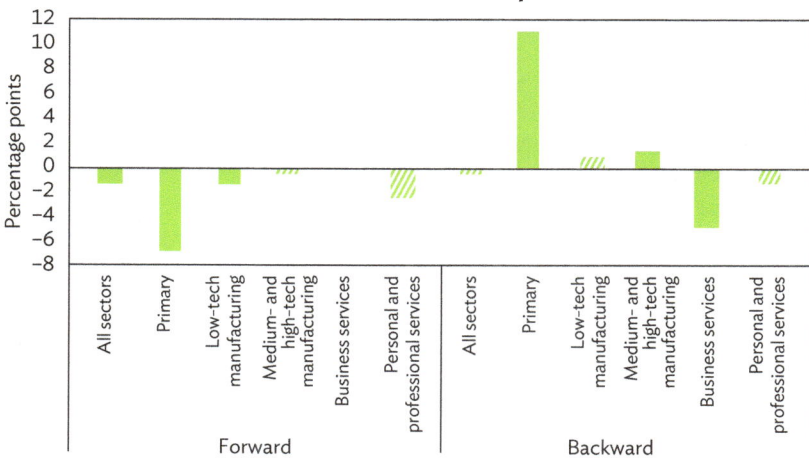

continued on next page

Figure 3.12 (continued)

c. Female Employment, Backward GVC Participation

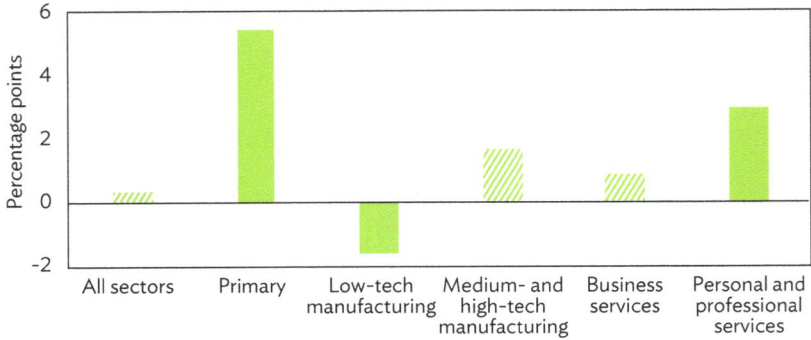

GVC = global value chain.
Note: Solid bars indicate that the estimate is statistically significant at least at the 10% level. Diagonally striped bars indicate that the estimate is statistically not significantly different from zero. Estimates are based on country–industry ordinary least squares regressions with robust standard errors and country—industry and country-year fixed effects. Employment shares are constructed so that each dimension totals 1—(a) employment status: wage employment and self-employment; b) skill: high and low/medium; and (c) gender: male and female. Employment in high-skill occupations includes managers, professionals, technicians, and associate professionals. See Appendix B for list of subsectors under broad sector headings. Regression results are based on a sample that includes 2000 and 2007–2020.
Source: Authors' calculations based on Blanas, Huynh, and Viegelahn (forthcoming).

Similarly, the results show a heterogeneous relationship between greater GVC participation and the share of employment in high-skill occupations based on economic sector (Figure 3.12.b). Greater forward GVC participation is associated with a lower share of employment in high-skill occupations overall. This pattern is specific to Southeast Asia and driven by the primary sector (with a heavy concentration of low-skilled agricultural employment) and low-technology manufacturing such as garments (which is largely reliant on medium-skill employment of plant and machine operators). The relationship between backward GVC participation and the share of employment in high-skill occupations is statistically insignificant overall. However, business services are negatively associated with the share of workers in high-skill occupations; subsectors such as retail trade and hotel and restaurants are dominated by medium-skill occupations in clerical support, services, and sales. Conversely, deeper backward GVC linkages in agriculture and medium- and high-technology manufacturing are both associated with robust gains in high-skill employment, which suggests increased demand for high-skilled workers. The increased use of foreign inputs in these sectors often require special skill requirements, which can only be met by increasing high-skill occupations such as professionals and technicians.

For women workers, the sector results also show that employment gains from backward GVC engagement are shaped by the primary sector and personal and professional services. An increase in backward GVC linkages is significantly associated with a positive expansion in the share of female employment, and particularly positive in Southeast Asian economies when compared to other economies worldwide (Figure 3.12.c). Nevertheless, both sectors in general tend to be less skill-intensive and provide comparatively fewer productive jobs with lower remuneration, meaning that gains from deeper GVC participation for female employment in Southeast Asia have been mixed. Increased GVC backward participation in low-tech manufacturing is associated with a lower female employment share; the increased sourcing of foreign inputs from other economies may in many cases make jobs currently held by women obsolete.[12] For example, an apparel factory might have previously produced textiles as an input for garment production using female labor—increased sourcing of textiles abroad would make some of those jobs obsolete.

The association of forward GVC participation and female employment shares is not statistically significant. While GVCs do create jobs for millions of women in the region, it appears that these jobs are created mainly because women are well represented in more integrated GVC sectors (see earlier section) and not because a sector increases its forward GVC participation over time. In other words, the garment industry is more integrated in GVCs than many other sectors and employs a high share of women. But if the garment industry further increases forward GVC participation, there appears to be no impact on female employment share.

Young women and men have increased their time in school and delayed joining the workforce, as seen in the declining employment share of youth generally. The proportion of youth in total employment in the region decreased from 21.2% in 2000 to 13.5% in 2021, a 7.8 percentage-point contraction.[13] In the rest of the world, the decrease in the youth employment share was also significant, although slightly lower at 6.2 percentage points. The progressively lower (higher) share of jobs taken up by youth (adults) follows trends in GVC engagement. Deeper forward GVC participation in Southeast Asia is associated with relatively greater adult employment. This likely shows the heightened demand for older workers with more experience and expertise in industries with more forward GVC engagement.

---

[12] For the Asia-Pacific region, the employment of women in the manufacturing of textiles, wearing apparel and leather declined overall between 1991 and 2021. See: ILO, forthcoming, Asia-Pacific Employment and Social Outlook 2022.

[13] Authors' calculations based on ILO, ILOSTAT Database. https://ilostat.ilo.org/data/ (accessed 20 November 2022).

In sum, deeper GVC participation during the past 2 decades is linked to some positive gains in Southeast Asia's labor market—most notably the drop in working poverty and increase in labor productivity. However, some important benefits—expanding wage employment, high-skill employment, and more and better jobs for women and youth—happened only in certain economic sectors. These results underline a critically important dynamic: the link between GVCs and the creation of higher-quality and more inclusive jobs is not automatic.

Conclusion and Way Forward

This chapter analyzed GVCs and employment in Southeast Asia over the past 2 decades. First, since 2000, the region as a whole has become increasingly dependent on GVCs for employment despite some short periods of volatility and setbacks. In 2021, an estimated 76 million workers had GVC-related jobs, or more than a quarter of total employment. Second, regional trends mask country- and sector-specific trends. Some economies—such as Singapore, Thailand, and Viet Nam—were more dependent on GVC employment than others like Indonesia, the Lao PDR, or the Philippines. Manufacturing accounted for the largest share of GVC employment, while an increasing share of agricultural jobs were linked to GVCs. Third, increased GVC participation was associated with some important, albeit mixed, progress in improving job quality. While deeper GVC integration was associated with rapid declines in working poverty and to gains in labor productivity, the relationship between increased GVC participation and greater wage employment and high-skill employment was negative in several sectors, and positive in a few. Fourth, while GVCs provide millions of jobs for women—in sectors highly integrated into GVCs—some results indicate the employment gains were associated with enhanced GVC engagement only in sectors where jobs are typically less skill-intensive and lower paid. Finally, a review of the literature highlighted that deficits in decent work in GVCs persist.

In this context, policy makers must navigate through a complex landscape.[14] Even prior to the COVID-19 pandemic, the confluence of technological change, growing economic nationalism, and the need for sustainability was expected to reshape several GVCs trajectories—including reshoring, diversification, regionalization, and replication (UNCTAD 2020).

[14]   ILO constituents established a Tripartite Working Group on Options to Ensure Decent Work in Supply Chains, which subsequently adopted a set of building blocks for a comprehensive strategy for decent work in GVCs—highlighting the importance of analyzing the challenges, best practices, root causes, and drivers of decent work deficits in developing and developed economies. See ILO Tripartite Working Group on Options to Ensure Decent Work in Supply Chains, 2022, Building Blocks for a Comprehensive Strategy on Achieving Decent Work in Supply Chains.

The pandemic—and the Russian invasion of Ukraine, which led to a variety of export restrictions—has further amplified questions over the future trajectory of GVCs in the region. What policies can contribute to inclusive, sustainable, and job-rich development from GVC participation during the recovery phase? What policies can help GVCs move up from low productivity to higher productive activities? To help navigate the way forward, several policy areas stand out as important for future policy making.

First, well-designed social protection and labor market policies are essential to cushion the shocks that GVCs propagate as well as dealing with distributional consequences. The number of workers engaged in GVCs continues to increase, and job dependence on GVCs makes them vulnerable to external shocks. Growth in GVC jobs has hardly been smooth, with both the 2008–2009 global financial crisis and the more recent COVID-19 pandemic leading to large fluctuations in the number and share of GVC workers across the region. It is also well understood that trade and GVC participation require structural transformation, which in turn requires workers to move across jobs and sectors. Social protection can provide worker support during these structural shifts and transitions. Unemployment insurance, for example, ensures income security and allows for smoothing household consumption. This allows jobseekers the time to find a new job that matches their skills, increasing labor market efficiency (ILO 2014). In addition to these passive labor market policies that provide income replacement, active labor market policies (ALMPs) that facilitate the finding of jobs and the matching between workers and vacancies are important to support workers affected by shocks, and are particularly relevant for informal workers. These policies can also slow the transmission of external shocks from urban to rural areas when rural migrant workers face retrenchment (Hagemejer and Kim 2010). As GVCs are reshaped in response to the evolving "new normal" (see the overview chapter), workers, firms, and labor markets will be affected. Social protection and labor market policies are critical not only to cushion any adverse impact from the transformation, but also in building a foundation that promotes innovation and risk-taking (Ravallion 2006). This is critical in particular for upgrading to higher productivity segments within GVCs.

Despite considerable progress in strengthening social protection systems and ALMPs, particularly on the heels of the 1997–1998 Asian financial crisis and the global financial crisis, the majority of workers in Southeast Asia do not have access to unemployment protection—with only a small portion with access to ALMPs (ILO 2019a). The COVID-19 pandemic also led economies to experiment with different policies that can be leveraged to further extend social protection and access to ALMPs. In the

Philippines, for example, the COVID-19 Adjustment Measures Program provided a one-time cash transfer to affected workers of establishments with flexible working arrangements or had to suspend operations due to the pandemic (ADB 2021). It was implemented together with the Tulong Panghanapbuhay sa Ating Disadvantaged/Displaced Workers (Tupad) Program, which offered community-based temporary employment to workers in the informal economy.

In Cambodia, a wage subsidy program for garment workers with temporarily suspended contracts provided $70 per month for each worker, with $40 provided by the government and the remaining $30 by the employer (ILO n.d.). To protect informal workers, the government also expanded its cash transfer program, providing monthly average payments of $30–$50 depending on household size and vulnerability. At the same time, a first-ever state-owned Credit Guarantee Corporation of Cambodia Plc was set up in 2020 to support micro, small, and medium-sized enterprises (MSMEs) access formal loans and stay afloat. More comprehensively, Indonesia recently introduced its first unemployment benefit package—the Job Loss Guarantee program (Jaminan Kehilangan Pekerjaan, or JKP), which in addition to cash transfers to the unemployed, provides access to labor market information and job training so affected workers can find new employment opportunities (Indonesia G20 Presidency 2022). The program provides 45% of monthly wages for the first 3 months and 25% of wages for the subsequent 3 months. Regionally, the Association of Southeast Nations (ASEAN) Comprehensive Recovery Framework secured a political commitment to expand social protection, including informal workers, protecting employment in pandemic-affected sectors, and preparing labor policies through social dialogue (ILO 2021c).

For economies without a comprehensive social protection system and vulnerable to GVC trade shocks (for example Cambodia and the Lao PDR), consideration could be given to pivoting one-time pandemic-related policies providing targeted assistance to those directly affected by trade. Several economies around the world, mostly advanced economies, have trade adjustment assistance program. While there are certainly concerns whether those suffering from trade liberalization should be treated differently than those affected by other shocks (Francois, Jansen and Peters 2011), experience in the Republic of Korea and the US indicate these programs can be useful in fostering greater public support for trade reforms (Aho and Bayard 1984; Heo 2013). For less-developed economies in the region, budgetary constraints will likely require financing though international cooperation, including aid for trade.

As mentioned earlier, there is growing evidence that the international fragmentation of production increases wage inequality in developing economies. Timmer et al. (2014) find that the share of value-added accruing to capital and higher-skilled workers increased while the corresponding share declined for low-skilled workers in developing economies between 1995 and 2008 (Timmer, Erumban, Los, Stehrer, and de Vries 2014). There is also growing concern that further GVC automation and robotics—in addition to raising anxieties in developing countries that jobs will be re-shored or near-shored—will further exacerbate wage inequalities. Social transfers and employment policies need to address these inequalities.

Second, the heterogenous relationship between GVC participation and skills development suggests that investments in a broad range of skills are needed to move into higher value-added GVC segments. These are particularly important for women, who, as the results in this chapter highlight, are concentrated in the primary sector and low-technology manufacturing. National development plans indeed place strong emphasis on skills development to apply upgraded technology; with skills road maps designed for specific sectors in some economies. Governments also promote vocational education for skilling, reskilling, and upskilling. Overall, economies tend to focus on the development of high-skilled human resources to bring the country to the technological frontier of Industry 4.0 and the digital economy. While this is important, it is equally critical to recognize that the future of work is not just high skilled. Skills development policies and program often focus on the highly educated or high-skilled workers—at the expense of the large number of workers in low- or medium-skilled occupations. Some national development plans are unrealistic and overly simplified, given the difficulty of predicting the skills required for the future. Reskilling has its limitations. For example, garment workers will not easily transform themselves into data scientists.[15] Well-designed and realistic skills development policies and programs as part of a human-centered pandemic recovery will help Southeast Asian economies move into higher GVC segments.[16]

A few countries in the region also have policies and programs that form and deepen linkages between domestic MSMEs and foreign investors, in part to encourage skill diffusion. These programs exist in Malaysia, the Philippines, Singapore, and Thailand—other ASEAN economies lack these programs or they are not well funded (OECD AND UNIDO 2019). Singapore's Pioneer Certificate Incentive and Development and Expansion Incentive programs provide tax incentives to foreign investors that

[15] The information in this paragraph is based on ILO (2019b).

[16] For more information and guidance on designing relevant skills development in a sector to support the effective participation in international trade and export diversification, see for example ILO (2020e)

introduce more advanced technology, skills, and knowledge, or that carry out new or pioneering activities (Singapore Economic Development Board 2022). In the Philippines, the Corporate Recovery and Tax Incentives for Enterprises (CREATE) Act of 2021 extends incentives to enterprises providing technical training and undertaking R&D. In Thailand, tax incentives are provided to investors doing research and development and advanced technology training. Also, they apply to investors that donate to technology and personnel development funds, educational institutions and specialized training centers in science and technology (Thailand Board of Investment 2021). In designing tax incentives, however, while they can make investing more attractive, they cannot compensate for institutional or physical infrastructure shortcomings, including deficiencies in labor market institutions (United Nations and CIAT 2018).

Third, as the link between increased GVC participation and decent work is not automatic, as highlighted in the findings of this chapter, deep trade agreements—which increasingly cover labor provisions—is one tool to strengthen the link. Labor provisions also provide an entry point for stakeholders, in particular social partners, to discuss issues related to decent jobs in GVCs (Viegelahn 2017).

Trade agreements have evolved from simply targeting tariffs to covering a broad range of provisions, including those relating to intellectual property protection, anticorruption, and environmental and social issues—often termed as deep trade agreements. For example, trade agreements in the 1950s covered eight policy areas, whereas trade agreements recently average 15 areas (Fernandes, Rocha, and Ruta (eds.) 2021). As mentioned, trade agreements now increasingly cover labor, to ensure a certain minimum level of labor standards. More specifically, these can be defined as "(i) any principle or standard (including international labor standards) or rule, which addresses labor relations, minimum working conditions, terms of employment, and/or other labor issues; (ii) any framework to promote compliance with standards through cooperative activities, dialogue and/or monitoring of labor issues; and/or (iii) any mechanism to ensure compliance with standards, either set under national law or in the trade agreement" (Corley-Coulibaly, Postolachi, and Tesfay 2022). With a safe and healthy working environment now recognized as a fundamental principle and right at work, trade provisions, which among labor issues tend to reference fundamental principles and rights at work the most will likely become increasingly standard within trade agreements. For garment factories that had questionable occupational safety and heathy records, this could help economies in the region ensure a safer and healthier work environment (Dasgupta, Poutiainen, and Williams 2011).

Around half of the trade agreements concluded worldwide between 2011 and 2020 contained labor provisions, compared to around a quarter between 2001 and 2010. At the same time the content of more recent labor provisions has become more comprehensive, including in content, application, and enforceability (Corley-Coulibaly, Postolachi, and Tesfay 2022). Longer-term trends in Southeast Asia (Figure 3.13) are less clear. But in the years leading up to the COVID-19 pandemic, labor provisions appeared in almost half of concluded FTAs. These include the Comprehensive and Progressive Agreement for Trans-Pacific Partnership—with Brunei Darussalam, Malaysia, Singapore, and Viet Nam as members—which contains provisions on cooperation for job creation and productive, quality employment. Other recent agreements with labor provisions include the EU–Viet Nam FTA (2020), the Chile–Indonesia Comprehensive Economic Partnership Agreement (CEPA) (2019), the EU–Singapore FTA (2019), and the agreement between the Philippines and the European Free Trade Association (EFTA) States (2018).

Figure 3.13: Number of Regional Trade Agreements Involving At Least One Southeast Asian Country

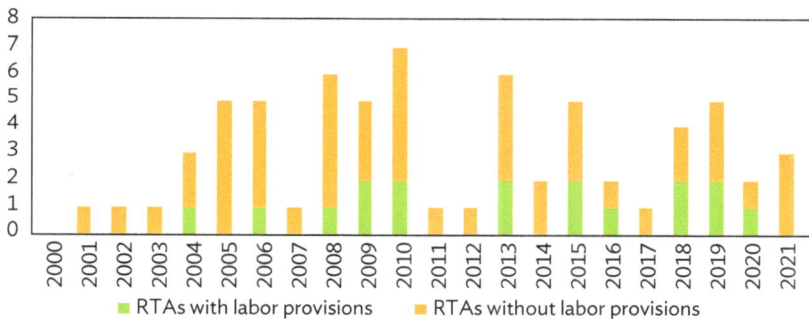

RTA = regional trade agreement.
Source: Authors' calculations based on ILO. 2022d. ILO Labor Provisions in Trade Agreements Hub (LP Hub). https://www.ilo.org/LPhub/ (accessed 18 February 2022).

A growing body of literature finds that deep trade agreements have a positive effect on trade and welfare, beyond that provided by shallow trade agreements (Fernandes, Rocha, and Ruta (eds.) 2021). In Cambodia, the gender pay gap in garments is estimated to have been reduced from 32% prior to the Cambodia–US Bilateral Textile Agreement, which included labor provisions, to 6% after implementation. By comparison, the gender wage gap in other manufacturing sectors remained unchanged (ILO 2016). Labor provisions in trade agreements neither appreciably divert nor decrease trade flows. Taken together, the findings suggest opportunities for economies in the region to benefit from increasingly deeper FTAs with labor provisions, while at the same time using them to engage with social partners and other stakeholders on more elusive benefits, including growth in higher-skilled jobs and wage employment.

Appendixes

Appendix A: Estimates of Jobs in Global Value Chains

This appendix describes the data and methodology used to produce estimates of the number of jobs in global value chains (GVCs).

Data

Estimates of the number of jobs in GVCs are constructed based on a combination of two data sources: The first consists of international input–output tables, which are available for 62 economies worldwide for 2000 and 2007–2021 from the Asian Development Bank (ADB) Multiregional Input–Output (MRIO) Database. These cover 35 sectors and provide information on economy sector level linkages in production. They are combined with a novel balanced panel database of International Labour Organization (ILO) estimates of employment by detailed sector for 1991–2021, developed specifically for this project.

Besides the estimate of total employment in a sector, the ILO database also includes for each sector an estimate of employment by gender (male and female), by age group (youth and adult), by employment status (employees and self-employed), and by occupational skill level (high-skilled and low-/medium-skilled). The ILO's harmonized microdata repository, which is the world's largest repository of national labor force survey data set, is the primary source of those labor market indicators. Some additional data were taken from other national sources. These data are cleaned, adjusted for breaks in the data series, as well as for the lack of reliability in case of data points based on less than 30 observations in the labor force survey. All missing data points are estimated using information such as gross domestic product, sector value added and employment data from other data sources such as the United Nations Industrial Development Organization (UNIDO) or the Organisation for Economic Co-operation and Development (OECD). The estimation approach followed ILO's standard methods to estimate labor market data.

Methodology

The methodology applied to estimate the number of jobs in GVCs consists of three main steps.

First, the gross output is calculated for each economy and sector that is required to produce one unit of final good demanded in any economy and sector. The Leontief inverse matrix allows to determine these technical coefficients and is computed based on international input–output tables from the ADB MRIO Database following standard input–output modeling procedures.

Second, gross output for each sector within an economy is translated into a corresponding number of jobs. By dividing employment in a sector by its gross output, the employment input per unit of gross output can be computed. In line with estimation approaches also used by other international organizations, the assumption is made that labor productivity in agriculture of high-income economies, in industry of all economies, as well as in services of all economies, does not differ between GVC-related and non-GVC-related economic activity within a sector. For the agriculture sector of upper-middle-income and lower-middle-income economies, it is assumed that only two-thirds or one-third of workers are needed in GVC-related activities relative to non-GVC-related economic activities. This assumption aims to reflect that the agriculture sector in these economies[1] is often characterized by a large segment with relatively low labor productivity levels, serving mainly local markets, and a small but highly productive segment that is integrated into GVCs serving international markets.[2]

Third, a demand vector needs to be defined that captures output produced for GVCs. The methodology used defines the latter to include any type of supply relationship that crosses borders. This includes exports of final goods and services consumed elsewhere, exports of intermediates for the production of final goods or services consumed globally, or the production of intermediates that are processed further domestically but end up as exported intermediates or final goods or services. When combining the data sources in this way, the methodology produces estimates of GVC jobs for 35 sectors in 62 economies for 2000 and 2007–2021 (Tables A3.1 and A3.2).

---

[1]   There are no low-income economies in the sample.

[2]   Future research aims to develop a methodology that estimates labor productivity differences between GVC-related and non-GVC-related activities within sectors for different groups of economies, which would allow further refinement of estimates.

Table A3.1: Jobs in Global Value Chains—Sectors

Section/Division Code	Industry
A–B	Agriculture, Hunting, Forestry and Fishing
C	Mining and Quarrying
15–16	Food, Beverages, and Tobacco
17–18	Textiles and Textile Products
19	Leather, Leather, and Footwear
20	Wood and Products of Wood and Cork
21–22	Pulp, Paper, Paper, Printing, and Publishing
23	Coke, Refined Petroleum, and Nuclear Fuel
24	Chemicals and Chemical Products
25	Rubber and Plastics
26	Other Non-Metallic Mineral
27–28	Basic Metals, and Fabricated Metal
29	Machinery, n.e.c.
30–33	Electrical and Optical Equipment
34–35	Transport Equipment
36–37	Manufacturing, n.e.c.; Recycling
E	Electricity, Gas, and Water Supply
F	Construction
50	Sale, Maintenance, and Repair of Motor Vehicles and Motorcycles; Retail Sale of Fuel
51	Wholesale Trade and Commission Trade, Except of Motor Vehicles, and Motorcycles
52	Retail Trade, Except of Motor Vehicles, and Motorcycles
H	Repair of Household Goods
60	Hotels and Restaurants
61	Inland Transport
62	Water Transport
63	Air Transport
64	Other Supporting and Auxiliary Transport Activities
J	Activities of Travel Agencies
70	Post and Telecommunications
71–74	Financial Intermediation
L	Real Estate Activities
M	Renting of Machinery and Equipment and Other Business Activities
N	Public Administration and Defense; Compulsory Social Security
O	Education
P	Health and Social Work
	Other Community, Social and Personal Services
	Private Households with Employed Persons

Notes: Based on ISIC Rev. 3.1.
Source: ADB MRIO.

Table A3.2: Jobs in Global Value Chains—Economies

ISO Code	Economy Name
AUS	Australia
AUT	Austria
BGD	Bangladesh
BEL	Belgium
BTN	Bhutan
BRA	Brazil
BRN	Brunei Darussalam*
BGR	Bulgaria
KHM	Cambodia*
CAN	Canada
HRV	Croatia
CYP	Cyprus
CZE	Czechia
DNK	Denmark
EST	Estonia
FJI	Fiji
FIN	Finland
FRA	France
DEU	Germany
GRC	Greece
HKG	Hong Kong, China
HUN	Hungary
IND	India
IDN	Indonesia*
IRL	Ireland
ITA	Italy
JPN	Japan
KAZ	Kazakhstan
KOR	Korea, Republic of
KGZ	Kyrgyz Republic
LAO	Lao People's Democratic Republic*
LVA	Latvia
LTU	Lithuania
LUX	Luxembourg
MYS	Malaysia*
MDV	Maldives
MLT	Malta
MEX	Mexico
MNG	Mongolia
NPL	Nepal
NLD	Netherlands, The

continued on next page

Table A3.2 (continued)

ISO Code	Economy Name
NOR	Norway
PAK	Pakistan
PHL	Philippines *
POL	Poland
PRC	China, People's Republic of
PRT	Portugal
ROU	Romania
RUS	Russian Federation
SGP	Singapore*
SVK	Slovakia
SVN	Slovenia
ESP	Spain
LKA	Sri Lanka
SWE	Sweden
CHE	Switzerland
TAP	Taipei,China
THA	Thailand*
TUR	Türkiye
UKG	United Kingdom
USA	United States
VNM	Viet Nam*

Note: * indicates economies of Southeast Asia.
Source: ADB MRIO.

Appendix B: Methodology for Linking Global Value Chains to Labor Market Indicators

The analysis and findings presented in this study are based on the empirical results of the forthcoming International Labour Organization (ILO) working paper *Global Value Chains and Labour Markets in South-East Asia from a Global Comparative Perspective* by Blanas et al. The paper employs various econometric techniques to measure the relationship between forward and backward participation in global value chains (GVCs) and different labor market outcomes in Southeast Asia relative to the rest of the world.

The methodology includes analysis at the economy–industry level, studying the relationship of GVC participation with the employment shares of workers in Southeast Asian economies across different dimensions— including age group, gender, occupational skill level, and employment status, among others—and identifying differences in that relationship relative to non-Southeast Asian economies. To account for nuances at the industry level, relationships are identified separately for the primary sector, low-technology manufacturing, medium- and high-technology manufacturing, business services, and personal and professional services (Table A3.3). Moreover, the analysis at the economy–industry level is supplemented with an investigation of the relationship between GVC participation and different economic and labor market indicators at the economy level such as real labor productivity and working poverty rate.[3] The measures of GVC participation include indicators for both backward and forward linkages.[4]

The analysis covers all economic activities of economies, disaggregated into 35 industries and are aligned with the International Standard Industrial Classification of All Economic Activities (ISIC) Revision 3.1 (Table A3.1). It makes use of data from a total of 62 economies worldwide, including nine Southeast Asian economies, covering the year 2000 and 2007–2020 (Table A3.2). The analysis relies on various underlying data sources. The economy–industry-level data include indicators on industry-level participation in GVCs through backward and forward linkages drawn from the Asian Development Bank Multiregional Input–Output (ADB MRIO) Tables. GVC participation measures have been constructed following primarily the methodology of Wang et al. (2013).[5] These data are combined with economy–industry-level information on employment shares of different groups of workers, calculated by the ILO from the ILO Harmonized Microdata collection of national labor force surveys. The ILO Harmonized Microdata collection is the world's largest global repository of labor force survey micro data sets, with detailed individual-and-household level information, used to produce official national statistics. The economy–level data includes GVC measures that are aggregated up to the economy level and then matched to time-varying data on economy–level economic and labor market indicators. The latter set of indicators, such as real labor productivity and the working poverty rate, are sourced from the World Bank's World Development Indicators and the ILO's ILOSTAT Database, respectively.

To examine the empirical relationships between GVC participation and labor market and economic outcomes, the methodology employs ordinary least squares (OLS) regressions in which the key explanatory variables

---

[3]   Labour productivity is measured as output (GDP in constant 2017 international $ at PPP) per worker. Working poverty rate is defined as the share of employed persons residing in a household whose members live on less than 1.90 USD per person per day (2011 PPP).

[4]   Backward linkages imply that an industry imports inputs, which are processed further, and then distributes the new inputs or final output domestically and internationally. Forward linkages imply that an industry produces inputs or final output for exporting.

[5]   Wang, Wei, and Zhu (2013).

are the backward and forward GVC participation measures of Wang et al. (2013) and the dependent variable are various labor market indicators. Specifically, the employment shares by age, gender, occupational skill level, and employment status, among others, are utilized as outcome variables in the regressions. Worth noting is that the measures of employment shares are constructed so that each dimension—skill: high and low/medium; age: youth aged 15–24 years and adults aged 25+ years; gender: male and female; and employment status: wage employment and self-employment—always totals 1.[6]

In estimations using country-level data, the specifications include dummy variables for country and year so that unobserved heterogeneity across these two dimensions is accounted for. Likewise, in estimations on country–industry-level data, the specifications account for unobserved heterogeneity across country–industry and country–year pairs with the inclusion of the relevant dummy variables. In both types of analysis, the regression controls for the output of a country or industry by including independent variables for country-level or country–industry-level data on the log of value added, which is taken from the ADB MRIO. In the country-level analysis, the regressions also control for aggregate capital intensity, calculated as the ratio of gross fixed capital formation to value added. Given the sets of dummy variables included in the different specifications, it is important to stress that the conditional correlations for Southeast Asian economies are determined and, in turn, interpreted relative to the conditional correlations for non-Southeast Asian economies, rather than in absolute terms.

---

[6]   High-skill employment includes skill levels 3 and 4, or namely occupations as managers, professionals, technicians and associate professionals.

Table A3.3: Jobs in Global Value Chains—Aggregate Sectors

Section/Division Code	Additional Industry Aggregation
A–B	Primary sector
C	Primary sector
15–16	Low-technology manufacturing
17–18	Low-technology manufacturing
19	Low-technology manufacturing
20	Low-technology manufacturing
21–22	Low-technology manufacturing
23	Medium- and high-technology manufacturing
24	Low-technology manufacturing
25	Medium- and high-technology manufacturing
26	Medium- and high-technology manufacturing
27–28	Medium- and high-technology manufacturing
29	Medium- and high-technology manufacturing
30–33	Medium- and high-technology manufacturing
34–35	Medium- and high-technology manufacturing
36–37	Low-technology manufacturing
50	Business services
51	Business services
52	Business services
H	Business services
60	Business services
61	Business services
62	Business services
63	Business services
64	Business services
J	Business services
70	Business services
71–74	Business services
L	Personal and professional services
M	Personal and professional services
N	Personal and professional services
O	Personal and professional services
P	Personal and professional services

Note: Based on ISIC Rev. 3.1. Manufacturing industries are classified as medium- and high-technology (higher-technology) or low-technology based on their research and development (R&D) intensities, as measured by the ratio of R&D expenditure to value added, following the approach of Eurostat.
Source: Blanas et al. (forthcoming) based on ADB MRIO.

References

Aho, C., and T. Bayard. 1984. Cost and Benefits of Trade Adjustment Assistance. In R.E. Baldwin and A.O. Krueger, eds. *The Structure and Evolution of Recent US Trade Policy*. Chicago: University of Chicago Press

Aked, J. 2021. Supply Chains, the Informal Economy, and the Worst Forms of Child Labour. *Child Labour Action Research Innovation in South & South-Eastern Asia (CLARISSA) Working Paper*. No. 8. Brighton: Institute of Development Studies.

Anukoonwattaka, W., P. Romao, and R. Lobo. If the US-China Trade War is Here to Stay, What are the Risks and Opportunities for Other GVC Economies Outside the War Zone? *ARTNeT Working Paper Series*. No. 209. UNESCAP.

Asian Development Bank (ADB). 2021. *COVID-19 and Labor Markets in Southeast Asia: Impacts on Indonesia, Malaysia, the Philippines, Thailand, and Viet Nam*. Manila.

ADB and International Labour Organization (ILO). 2014. *ASEAN Community 2015: Managing Integration for Better Jobs and Shared Prosperity*.

ASEAN-Japan Centre. 2019. Global Value Chains in ASEAN: Cambodia. *Paper* No. 3.

_____. 2021. Global Value Chains in ASEAN: Lao People's Democratic Republic. Paper No. 5

Bárcia de Mattos, F., S. Dasgupta, X. Jiang, D. Kucera, and A. F. Schiavone. 2020. *Robotics and Reshoring: Employment Implications for Developing Countries*, Geneva: ILO.

Blanas, S., P. Huynh, and C. Viegelahn. Forthcoming. Global Value Chains and Labour Markets in South-East Asia from a Global Comparative Perspective. *ILO Working Paper*.

Caspersz, D., H. Cullen, M. Davis, D. Jog, F. McGaughey, D. Singhal, M. Sumner, and H. Voss. 2022. Modern Slavery in Global Value Chains: A Global Factory and Governance Perspective. *Journal of Industrial Relations*. Vol. 64, No. 2. pp. 177–199.

Choi, P., K. Kim, and J. Seo. 2019. Did Capital Replace Labor? New Evidence From Offshoring. *The B.E. Journal of Macroeconomics*. Vol. 19, No. 1. pp. 1–22.

Corley-Coulibaly, M., I. Postolachi, and N. Tesfa. 2022. *A Multi-faceted Typology of Labour Provisions in Trade Agreements: Overview, Methodology and Trends*. Geneva: ILO.

Criscuolo, C., J. Timmis, and N. Johnstone. 2015. The Relationship Between GVCs and Productivity. *Background Paper*. Paris: OECD.

Dasgupta, S., T. Poutiainen, and D. Williams. 2011. *From Downturn to Recovery: Cambodia's Garment Sector in Transition*. Bangkok: ILO.

Distelhorst, G., and D. Fu. 2017. Wages and Working Conditions in and out of Global Supply Chains: A Comparative Empirical Review. *ILO ACT/ EMP Research Note.*

Farole, T. 2016. Do Global Value Chains Create Jobs? Impacts of GVCs Depend on Lead Firms, Specialization, Skills, And Institutions. *IZA World of Labour,* 2016: 291.

Fernandes, A., N. Rocha, and M. Ruta, eds. 2021. *The Economics of Deep Trade Agreements.* CEPR Press and World Bank.

Francois, J., M. Jansen, and R. Peters. 2011. Trade Adjustment Costs and Assistance: The Labour Market Dynamics. In M. Jansen, R. Peters, and J. Salazar Xirinachs, eds. *Trade and Employment: From Myths to Facts.* Geneva: ILO.

Goldberg, P., and N. Pavcnik. 2007. Distributional Effects of Globalization in Developing Countries. *Journal of Economic Literature.* Vol. 45, No. 1. pp. 39–82.

Hagemejer, K., and K. Kim. 2010. Challenges to Social Security in Asia and the Pacific: Crisis and Beyond. In S.W. Handayani and C. Burkley, eds. *Social Assistance and Conditional Cash Transfers: Proceedings of the Regional Workshop.* Manila: ADB.

Harvey, J. 2019. Homeworkers in Global Supply Chains: A Review of Literature. *WIEGO Resource Document* No. 11.

Heo, Y. 2013. Assisting Trade Adjustment in Korea: Is it a Facilitating Device for FTA Implementation? *Journal of International Logistics and Trade.* Vol. 11, No. 1. April. pp. 87–98.

Hollweg, C. 2019. Global Value Chains and Employment in Developing Economies. *Global Value Chain Development Report 2019: Technological Innovation, Supply Chain Trade, and Workers in a Globalized World.* pp. 63-82.

Horvát, P., C. Webb, and N. Yamano. 2020. Measuring Employment in Global Value Chains. *OECD Science, Technology and Industry Working Papers.* No. 2020/01. Paris: OECD.

Indonesia G20 Presidency. 2022. G20 Presidency Note on Policy Setting on Exit Strategy to Support Recovery and Addressing Scarring Effect to Secure Future Growth. https://www.g20.org/wp-content/uploads/2022/10/G20-Presidency-Note_Executive-Summary.pdf.

International Labour Organization (ILO). n.d. COVID-19 and the World of Work: Country Policy Responses. https://www.ilo.org/global/topics/coronavirus/regional-country/country-responses/lang--en/index.htm#KH.

_____. 2014. *World of Work 2014: Developing with Jobs.* Geneva.

_____. 2015. *World Employment and Social Outlook: The Changing Nature of Jobs.*

_____. 2016. *Assessment of Labour Provisions in Trade and Investment Arrangements. Studies on Growth with Equity.*

_____. 2017. *World Employment and Social Outlook 2017: Sustainable Enterprises and Jobs - Formal Enterprises and Decent Work.*

_____. 2018. *Gender Gaps in the Garment, Textiles and Footwear Sector in Developing Asia*, ILO Asia-Pacific Garment and Footwear Sector Research Note.

_____. 2019a. *Extension of Social Security in Informal Employment in the ASEAN Region.*

_____. 2019b. *Preparing for the Future of Work: National Policy Responses in ASEAN+6.*

_____. 2020a. *The Supply Chain Ripple Effect: How COVID-19 is Affecting Garment Workers and Enterprises in Asia and the Pacific*, ILO Research Brief.

_____. 2020b. *COVID-19 and Global Supply Chains: How the Jobs Crisis Propagates Across Borders.*

_____. 2020c. *The Effects of COVID-19 on Trade and Global Supply Chains*, ILO Research Brief.

_____. 2020d. ILO Welcomes Milestone to End Forced Labour in Viet Nam. Press release. 8 June. https://ilo.org/hanoi/ Informationresources/Publicinformation/Pressreleases/ WCMS_747233/lang--en/.

_____. 2020e. *Rapid STED: A Practical Guide.*

_____. 2021a. *Trade and Decent Work: Indicator Guide.*

_____. 2021b. *COVID-19, Vaccinations and Consumer Demand: How Jobs are Affected Through Global Supply Chains.*

_____. 2021c. *COVID-19 and the ASEAN Labour Market: Impact and Policy Response*, ILO Brief.

_____. 2022a. *ILO Monitor on the World of Work, 10th Edition.*

_____. 2022b. *Global Employment Trends for Youth 2022: Investing in Transforming Futures for Young People.*

_____. 2022c. *Asia-Pacific Employment and Social Outlook 2022.*

_____. 2022d. ILO Labor Provisions in Trade Agreements Hub (LP Hub). https://www.ilo.org/LPhub/.

ILO, Organisation for Economic Co-operation and Development (OECD), International Organization for Migration (IOM), and United Nations Children's Fund (UNICEF). 2019. *Ending Child Labour, Forced Labour and Human Trafficking in Global Supply Chains.*

Kizu, T., S. Kühn, and C. Viegelahn. 2019. Linking Jobs in Global Supply Chains to Demand. *International Labour Review.* Vol. 158, No. 2. pp. 213–244.

Korwatanasakul, U., and S. Paweenawat. 2020. Trade, Global Value Chains, and Small and Medium-Sized Enterprises in Thailand: A Firm-Level Panel Analysis. *ADBI Working Paper Series.* No. 1130. Tokyo: ADB Institute.

Kucera, D., and F. Bárcia de Mattos. 2020. Automation, Employment, and Reshoring: Case Studies of the Apparel and Electronics Industries. *Comparative Labor Law & Policy Journal*. 41 (1): 101–128.

Lee, J. 2016. Global Supply Chain Dynamics and Labour Governance: Implications for Social Upgrading. *ILO Research Paper* No. 14.

Montalbano, P., and S. Nenci. 2020. The Effects of Global Value Chain (GVC) Participation on the Economic Growth of the Agricultural and Food Sectors. *Background paper for The State of Agricultural Commodity Markets (SOCO) 2020.*

Organisation for Economic Co-operation and Development (OECD). 2017. *OECD Skills Outlook 2017: Skills and Global Value Chains.*

OECD and UNIDO. 2019. *Integrating Southeast Asian SMEs in Global Value Chains: Enabling Linkages with Foreign Investors*. Paris.

Pahl, S., and M. Timmer. 2019. Do Global Value Chains Enhance Economic Upgrading? A Long View. *Journal of Development Studies*. Vol. 56, No. 9. pp. 1683–1705.

Ravallion, M. 2006. Transfers and Safety Nets in Poor Countries: Revisiting the Trade-offs and Policy Options. In A. Banerjee, R. Benabou, and D. Mookerjee, eds. *Understanding Poverty*. New York: Oxford University Press.

Shepherd, B., and S. Stone. 2013. Global Production Networks and Employment: A Developing Country Perspective. *OECD Trade Policy Papers*. No. 154.

Shingal, A. 2015. Labour Market Effects of Integration into GVCs: Review of Literature. *R4D Working Paper* 2015/10. World Trade Institute, University Bern.

Singapore Economic Development Board. 2022. Pioneer Certificate Incentive and Development and Expansion Incentive. https://www.edb.gov.sg/content/dam/edb-en/how-we-help/incentive-and-schemes/PC%20and%20DEI%20Brochure.pdf.

Solingen, E., B. Meng, and A. Xu. 2021. Rising Risks to Global Value Chains. In *Global Value Chain Development Report 2021: Beyond Production*. Asian Development Bank, Research Institute for Global Value Chains at the University of International Business and Economics, the World Trade Organization, the Institute of Developing Economies—Japan External Trade Organization, and the China Development Research Foundation.

Thailand Board of Investment. 2021. A Guide to the Board of Investment 2021. https://www.boi.go.th/upload/content/BOI-A%20Guide_EN.pdf.

Timmer, M., A. Erumban, B. Los, R. Stehrer, and G. de Vries. 2014. Slicing Up Global Value Chains. *Journal of Economic Perspectives*. Vol. 28, No. 2. pp. 99–118.

Wang, Z., S. Wei, and K. Zhu. 2013. Quantifying International Production Sharing at the Bilateral and Sector Levels. *NBER Working Paper*. No. 19677.

UNCTAD. 2020. *World Investment Report 2020: International Production Beyond the Pandemic*. New York and Geneva: United Nations.

UNESCAP. 2018. *Asia-Pacific Trade and Investment Report 2018: Recent Trends and Developments*.

United Nations and CIAT. 2018. *Design and Assessment of Tax Incentives in Developing Countries*.

Viegelahn, C. 2017. How Trade Policy Affects Firms and Workers in Global Supply Chains: An Overview. In *ILO: Handbook on Assessment of Labour Provisions in Trade and Investment Arrangements*. Geneva.

Wagner, J. 2007. Exports and Productivity: A Survey of the Evidence From Firm-Level Data. *The World Economy*. Vol. 30, No. 1. pp. 60–82.

World Bank. 2017. Jobs in Global Value Chains. *Jobs Notes* No. 1.

_____. 2020. *World Development Report 2020: Trading for Development in the Age of Global Value Chains*.

World Bank and World Trade Organization. 2020. *Women and Trade: The Role of Trade in Promoting Gender Equality*.

4

Technology, Global Value Chains, and Jobs: Continuing ASEAN's Role in Transformed Global Value Chains

Gloria Pasadilla

Introduction

For decades, multinational companies (MNCs) sought out low-cost manufacturing locations to improve their bottom lines and remain competitive. But technology is changing their calculus. Countries in the Association of Southeast Asian Nations (ASEAN), with abundant cheap labor, benefited from this paradigm and became important players in MNC global value chains (GVCs). Technological transformation affects all industries, however, and is changing the old pattern of offshoring and outsourcing—the bedrock of GVCs. Cheap labor, for new and emerging industries, is no longer a major selling point that attracts MNC investment. Technology that modularizes tasks and de-verticalizes production— and made outsourcing/offshoring possible—is now making production reshoring or near-shoring more attractive.

Technology's impact on the old paradigm and its disruption of the decades-old GVC model will affect jobs and employment across Asia, especially in countries that still rely on relatively less-skilled labor as a source of comparative advantage. Automation, artificial intelligence (AI), and 3D printing are examples of technologies that use less cheap labor. Certainly, political considerations of some reshoring were part of the reckoning in industries like semiconductors; likewise, not all industries will likely reshore *en masse*. But wise governments are heeding the winds of change and adjusting their strategies to attract investments. Skills and manpower development should be a major plank of those strategies.

This chapter considers case studies of automotive and electronics GVCs. It tries to understand the technology-induced changes in these industry value chains and their potential impact on ASEAN members that have been actively involved in these GVCs. The chapter concludes by suggesting policy responses—especially on skills development for the technology-dominated industries of the future—as an important part of overall innovation policies. The next section discusses how the new technology skills bias is a threat to developing countries GVC participation. Industry discussions of automotive and electronics transformations follow. The paper concludes with a summary of policy considerations on skills development and innovation policy.

Technology and Value Chains

Technology facilitated the growth of GVCs. First, it allowed MNCs to shift from vertically integrated production systems into modular production, which made outsourcing and offshoring to developing countries possible. Advances in information and communication technology (ICT) helped coordinate the various nodes of GVCs, from research to logistics and shipment, across different parts of the globe. Smart components built into products allowed both satellite guidance and live data monitoring of product shipments. It also made it possible to track product use throughout its lifecycle.

Newer technologies are also aiding manufacturing processes. 3D printing shortens lead times on producing spare parts. It also minimizes the need to keep a large inventory of parts and components, provided their digital blueprint remains available. Cloud-based solutions generate insights from data for efficiency monitoring or predictive maintenance. Cloud platforms allow collaboration among members of the GVC network. Augmented or virtual reality helps improve field service efficiency, allowing technical expertise to help solve specific problems elsewhere without requiring them to travel to do onsite repairs.

But technology is also disrupting many industries at seemingly breakneck speed. Some technologies are by themselves also creating their own GVCs. The Internet of Things (IoT) ecosystem, for example, is like a triangle where many connected smart devices—from mobile phones to fitness bands to cars, from consumer electronics to smart homes, smart buildings, factories and cities—define the base (Figure 4.1).

In between is the infrastructure—such as the cloud, network and connectivity, and data flows management—that facilitate the interconnection of smart devices. At the top of the triangle are platforms, apps and other services. The top portion—mostly services—is expected to be the fastest growing part of the ecosystem's value (MGI 2015). This simple illustration highlights the increasing importance of services in a technology-dominated economy.

Figure 4.1: Internet of Things Ecosystem

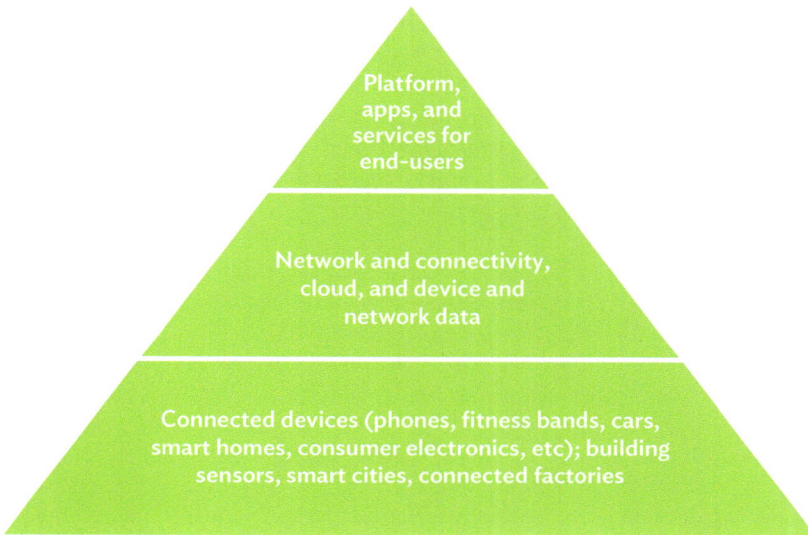

Platform, apps, and services for end-users

Network and connectivity, cloud, and device and network data

Connected devices (phones, fitness bands, cars, smart homes, consumer electronics, etc); building sensors, smart cities, connected factories

Source: Author based on MGI (2015).

Skills Bias in New Technologies

New technologies create new jobs and make others obsolete. A 2020 World Economic Forum study said that while 75 million jobs can disappear, 133 million new jobs will be created. The question is, what skills do these new jobs require? The descriptions of some "new" jobs now did not exist before, such as big data analysts, AI trainers, AI translators, blockchain traders, and cybersecurity specialists. In an era of new technologies, country competitiveness depends upon the availability of an abundant skilled workforce that can meet these new job descriptions.

Understandably, for developing countries, worries over a technology's impact on competitiveness lies in its bias toward skilled labor, where developed countries have the advantage. Robotics, data analytics, and automation all require skilled labor, threatening to displace some jobs that used to require less-skilled manpower. Some technologies may be heralding the demise of traditional labor-intensive manufacturing where developing countries hold comparative advantage. To the extent developed economies are considered endowed with more skilled labor, reshoring many GVCs in developed countries becomes more attractive.

The study by Autor, Mindell, and Reynolds (2020) foretell what can happen to jobs as technology develops further. In 1940, more than 25% of employment was in production and more than 15% in farming and mining. By 2018, less than 10% was in production and only about 1% in farming and mining, with those working as professionals close to 25%, and managers 15%. Interestingly, of the jobs in production, 48% were in categories that did not exist in 1940; 75% as professionals and 43% as managers. This shows that as technology increasingly dominates the workspace, some current jobs will disappear while new categories of workers emerge.

Technology's impact on less developed and developing countries is likewise not reassuring. Rodrik (2018) postulates that as the technological frontier shifts further out, fewer firms from developing and less developed countries would be able to join GVCs. Because new technologies are associated with stringent demands on precision and quality standards, they create new rules for participating in GVCs. Consequently, unless small companies (in developed but especially developing countries) have niche products or services or possess coveted technology, they will find it more difficult to join new value chains, particularly if they are knowledge- and innovation-driven. Thus, from the standpoint of employment and GVC participation, new technologies will likely benefit rich economies endowed with skilled labor, more than less developed or developing countries.

For developing countries to continue participating as GVCs evolve and new ones emerge, investments in human capital must be stepped up. Global firms will continue to look for good infrastructures, open trade policies, a stable economic policy environment, and other economic indicators as important factors for locating their foreign investments. But compared with previous periods, the availability of skilled human resources has now become a more important determinant in MNC decisions.

Transformation of the Automotive Manufacturing Global Value Chain

ASEAN members continue as important contributors to the automotive GVC. But profound changes in the industry, especially electrification and autonomous cars, have made its future role uncertain. Factors driving the transformation are mostly technology-related. For example, battery storage and capacity continue to improve, increasing driving range and the attraction of going electric. Climate change and net-zero commitments are also factors behind the momentum for more electric vehicle production. With roughly 30% of carbon emissions emanating from transportation, the automotive industry is under increasing pressure from governments to shift from internal combustion to electric-powered vehicles, which emit little carbon, if at all. Consumers are increasingly sympathetic to environmental protection, which also fuels demand for electric vehicles. Given these technological and environmental trends, many see the future of automobiles going electric.

Except for the People's Republic of China (PRC), most of the growth in electric vehicle (EV) production is strongest in developed countries across the European Union (EU), the United States (US), Japan and the Republic of Korea. However, developing countries will eventually catch up on the demand side, with many already promoting electric three-wheeled, short-distance public transport. But for now, the high price of EVs relative to internal combustion vehicles, the cost and availability of electric charging infrastructure, and limited driving range have kept demand low. On the production side, EV manufacturing also faces supply bottlenecks, including sourcing raw materials for batteries, electrical steel, and semiconductors (Box 4.1).

Box 4.1: Bottlenecks in Electric Vehicle Manufacturing

The future of the automotive industry is electric. By 2030, as more countries ban internal combustion vehicles, and top original equipment manufacturers (OEMs) increase their electric vehicle (EV) models, the EV market share is expected to reach 40%. However, there are many constraints: sourcing raw materials for car batteries, supply chain issues for other critical inputs like electrical steel and semiconductors, and the lack of a robust support infrastructure such as battery charging stations and stable electrical grids.

Battery constraints

The battery is the most valuable part of the EV, roughly 40% of its value. But with increasing demand, it faces supply chain issues. First, extracting and processing raw materials such as aluminum or manganese, nickel and cobalt—mostly used for lithium-ion batteries—face criticism from environmental and human rights groups for mining activities and poor working conditions, including child labor. Second, the raw materials and battery manufacturing are concentrated in a few countries in Asia or Africa. For instance, 70% of the world's cobalt reserves are in the Democratic Republic of Congo; thus, political instability could reverberate across the entire battery supply chain. Battery manufacturers are concentrated in Asia,

continued on next page

Box 4.1 (continued)

especially in the People's Republic of China (PRC), Japan, and the Republic
of Korea which, together, produce 97% of the global supply. The PRC alone
had 93 battery factories in 2020 compared to four in the United States.
Geopolitical issues loom large and can become a pivotal supply chain pain
point that could disrupt EV production worldwide.

Innovations in lithium mining, extraction, and battery chemistry are underway,
however. For example, one technology company is experimenting using
nanotech membranes for more rapid and efficient lithium separation during
the metal refining process. Others are also working on battery recycling
technology to minimize increased mining. OEMs are also responding through
strategic alliances with battery makers or vertically integrating to control the
supply of key components.

Silicon steel

Another critical EV input is electrical or silicon steel, an iron-silicon alloy
that has superior magnetic properties, especially the so-called xEV grade
non-oriented electrical steel (xEV NOES). xEV NOES is produced by a very
limited number of manufacturers and are concentrated in Japan, the PRC, and
the Republic of Korea. It requires huge capital investments. Projections show
the specialized steel mills cannot meet market demand between 2023 and
2025 without additional investments, which will take 2–8 years to provide the
additional capacity required.

The projected shortage in electrical steel affects OEMs electrification plans,
and the most vulnerable are those with a higher mix of EVs or hybrid vehicles
in their model portfolio.

Semiconductors

A typical vehicle, whether internal combustion, hybrid, or EV, uses thousands
of microchips. This crippled automobile production during the coronavirus
disease pandemic when semiconductor manufacturers could not supply the
chips needed. The cause was a demand surge in consumer electronics during
the pandemic which clashed with the just-in-time manufacturing strategy
of automakers. Semiconductor suppliers prioritized chips supply for mobile
phones and laptops. Demand from the auto industry is only a small share of
total demand so it lacked clout with semiconductor manufacturers (Priddle
2021). Toyota was the only OEM that kept a large stock of semiconductors

continued on next page

Box 4.1 (continued)

in inventory and so was saved from factory stoppages. A large chunk of auto industry demand is for lower quality and cheaper chips (legacy chips) used for everything from door locks to window controls. Cutting-edge chips are used for brakes and advanced driver assistance systems. This lack of semiconductors cost the global auto industry about $210 billion in lost sales and lost production of 11.3 million vehicles (AlixPartners 2021).

The car industry is rethinking its lean inventory management system, having more direct collaboration with traditional tier-2 (or lower) semiconductor suppliers, and using less multiple chips. Instead of having a chip for each module, automakers are considering switching to a centralized architecture that uses more advanced but fewer chips. OEMs are also building direct partnerships or long-term supply contracts with semiconductor companies.

Inadequate charging and electricity grid infrastructure

EV batteries need to recharge. Accessibility and interoperability of public charging infrastructure—affordable and fast—is prerequisite for the sustainable growth of EV demand. Yet, while this infrastructure has grown across developed countries, developing countries will need an aggressive strategy to build the necessary stations.

A robust power grid must also be in place to cater to the increased demand for electricity and high-speed charging requirements (Deloitte 2021). The increase in peak load of electricity demand due to uncoordinated and high-speed charging can undermine power grid stability and result in quicker infrastructure deterioration. In some places, high-speed charging caused a breakdown and burnout of medium voltage distribution transformers. Thus, the charging network infrastructure must account for the available capacity of grids to mitigate the impact of a sudden surge in demand. Some solutions include the use of smart charging infrastructure, and incentives for consumers to shift loads.

Sources: Burkacky, Lingemann, and Pototzky (2021); Vittori, Evans, and Fini (2021).

Along with electrification, autonomous cars—although not yet commonplace—will also revolutionize the transport industry. Autonomous car infotainment and connectivity, together with other vehicle software, will be important differentiating factors defining industry dominance. Value creation in the industry will increasingly be driven by data and service rather than hardware (Deloitte 2019). Advances in robotics and automation will continue to affect production processes and, consequently, profoundly change labor requirements throughout the automotive value chain (Box 4.2).

Box 4.2: Labor Impact of Automotive Industry Transformation

As more countries ban the sale of conventional cars in the coming decades, the shift from internal combustion vehicles to electric vehicles (EVs) is expected to result in net job losses. Some workers can be retrained for EVs but the number of new jobs will not compensate for the number of jobs lost. First, EVs have fewer parts to assemble: they have no carbon dioxide emissions; they do not need parts or modules like exhaust systems, mufflers, catalytic converters, or tailpipes; they require fewer parts and components—no spark plugs, fuel tanks, or radiators. All this means they require less labor. The more complex part of EV production are the batteries, but that is largely automated, with little manpower needed. Overall labor demand in the industry will thus decrease throughout the value chain as well as in aftermarket services.

New skills requirement

The skills needed for EVs are slightly different from those used for traditional vehicles. EVs rely on electrical, chemical, and software engineering skills, while internal combustion uses mechanical and materials engineering capabilities.

Sales and after-market service skills will also change. Salespeople will have to learn how to pitch to potential EV buyers. For example, a crucial differentiator for EVs will be battery qualities. Different batteries can store various amounts of energy—phosphate batteries, for example, have lower energy storage capacity than those made with cobalt. Battery characteristics affect driving range, a key consideration for many EV buyers.

Service technicians also need to know how to handle EVs. For example, unlike before, EVs do not require technicians to periodically change oil, perform engine tune ups, flush radiators, or change spark plugs. EVs also require less maintenance because they use fewer parts. Even EV brakes last longer as they use regenerative braking systems that help reduce wear-and-tear on brake pads. The result is lost income for car dealers/service firms and repair shops over the ownership cycle of a vehicle.

Other indirect labor

Indirect labor in the car industry will also be affected. Along with mechanics, workers in gas stations will be out of commission. There will likely be fewer charging stations than the current number of gas stations and pumps, which again translates into fewer jobs.

Sources: Eisenstein (2019); Conigliaro (2019).

These trends have seen the industry reinventing all aspects of its business: changing product/car portfolios, transforming business models and establishing strategic collaboration and partnerships, and revising manufacturing processes to improve customer experience.

Top original equipment manufacturers (OEMs) in the car industry are working strategically to protect their lead positions in both EV manufacturing and in producing connected and autonomous cars. All of the strongest OEMs now include EVs in their car lineups for competitive and regulatory reasons.

Partnerships with competitors, suppliers, booking platforms, technology companies, and even delivery services have sprouted for strategic and pragmatic reasons. One is to share the cost of capital and investment risks from research and development (R&D), accelerate vehicle development, and join the race for market dominance. Another is to exploit a strategic partner's intellectual property and knowledge advantage where car manufacturers hold less competitive advantage. A search of patent databases for EVs and autonomous cars, for example, shows OEMs and technology companies accumulating intellectual property useful for electric and autonomous car production. For example, Toyota, Hyundai, Honda, Nissan, and Ford hold the most EV-related patents, while Daimler, Toyota, Ford, BMW, and General Motors have the most for autonomous vehicles (Figure 4.2). Technology firms like Qualcomm, Baidu, Waymo, Google, and Apple hold patents important for self-driving vehicles with other major patent owners/suppliers like Denso and Bosch (Figure 4.3). Knowledge cross-fertilization between manufacturers and technology firms should produce eye-catching innovation.

Cross-industry linkages are also heralding a more complex automotive supply chain with a different combination of players. It promises to transform the automotive value chain from the OEM-dominated linear model—from raw material sourcing to suppliers to final product—to a web where multiple companies contribute both hardware and software to an ecosystem of connected systems inside the vehicle (Deloitte 2019). Examples of reported horizontal and vertical partnerships, joint ventures, and acquisitions show that OEMs are not the only ones taking partnership, consolidation, and restructuring initiatives, but also major tier 1 suppliers like Delphi Automotive (Table 4.1). AI is also increasingly used in new-era automobiles and in their manufacturing (Box 4.3).

Figure 4.2: Number of Patent Assignees Related to Electric Vehicles, 2011–2022

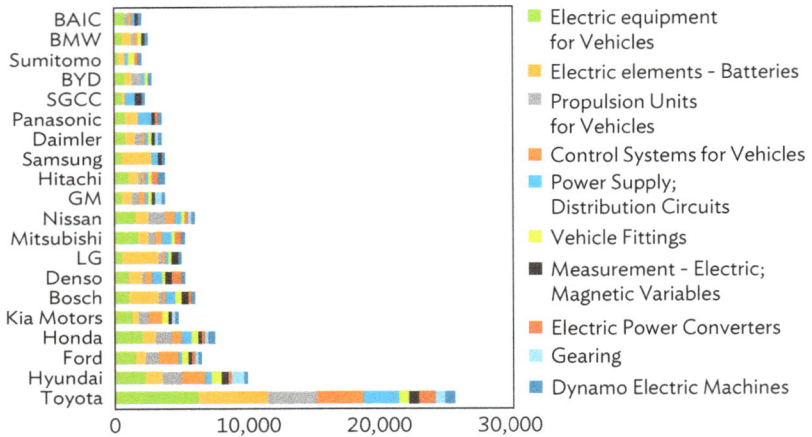

BAIC = Beijing Automotive Industry Holding, BYD = Build Your Dreams, GM = General Motors, SGCC = State Grid Corporation of China.
Source: Author based on Relecura database (accessed 12 February 2022).

Figure 4.3: Top Assignees of Patents Related to Autonomous Vehicles

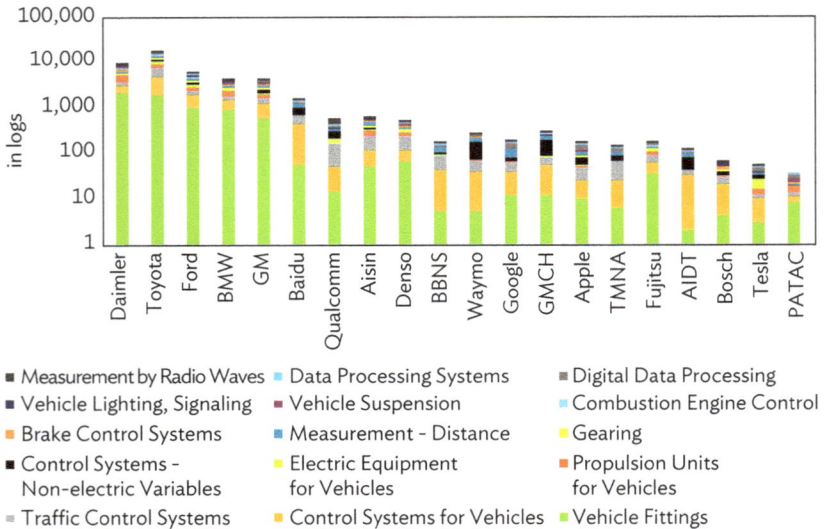

AIDT = Apollo Intelligent Driving Technology (Beijing), BBNS = Beijing Baidu Netcom Science Technology Co Ltd, GMCH = GM Cruise Holdings Llc, PATAC = Pan Asia Technical Automotive Center, TMNA = Toyota Motor North America Inc.
Source: Author. Based on Relecura database.https://relecura.com/ (accessed 12 February 2022).

Table 4.1: Automotive Industry Transformation: Partnership, Acquisition, Joint Venture Highlights

Original Equipment Manufacturers	Target	Notes
Toyota	Suzuki	Investment. $900 million, approximately 4.9% stake
	Softbank	Form Monet Technologies to develop autonomous cars
	Subaru	Increase stake to 20% from 17%
Ford	Mahindra and Mahindra (Mumbai)	$275 million joint venture
Honda	Hitachi	Combine car parts businesses to create a components company worth $17 billion
Jaguar, General Motors	Lyft*	Partnership
General Motors	Cruise Automation	Acquisition
Daimler	BMW, Audi	Partnership
Daimler–BMW–Audi	HERE (mapping services)	Acquisition by Daimler–BMW–Audi consortium
Renault–Nissan–Mitsubishi	Various startups	Consortium investment in startups
General Motors	LG Chemical (battery manufacturing)	Joint venture
General Motors	General Electric	Create a regional supply chain for materials like electrical steel to expand electric vehicle range
Fiat–Chrysler–French Peugeot S.A. Group		Merger
Hyundai	Aptiv	Joint venture for autonomous vehicle
Volkswagen	Ford	Invest $2.6 billion in Ford's Argo artificial intelligence
Ford–Amazon	Rivian	Joint investment in Rivian (electric vehicle startup)
Delphi Automotive		Split to Aptiv and Delphi Technologies
Tenneco	Federal–Mogul	Acquisition, then split new company into aftermarket or ride performance and powertrain technology
Continental		Divest powertrain business to invest in software capabilities

Source: Author, based on Wayland (2019); Campbell, Waldmeir, and Inagaki (2018); Deloitte (2019).

Box 4.3: Artificial Intelligence and the Automotive Industry

Many autonomous cars will heavily rely on artificial intelligence (AI). Much remains under development. But the use of AI is already pervasive in today's automotive design. It is used not only for self-driving but also for security and safety, detection of traffic and road objects, rideshare reservations, or for driver assistance systems such as driver drowsiness detection, automatic steering, braking or accelerating, lane changing, or parking.

Some technology firms or startups are developing software that provide intelligence capabilities (speech recognition, natural language understanding, speech synthesis) that have many applications, including in automotive. Other AI analyze driving behavior, alert drivers of possible danger, and help fleet companies track their vehicles and driver performance to cut insurance premiums for safer drivers.

AI is also changing how cars are built and/or repaired. Although robots have been present for years, they have not worked side by side with humans. Now they are embedded in production chains together with labor, handling materials, doing tests, and packing. Automotive machine data are collected and analyzed using AI software which provide data for insurers and networked repair facilities. Data analytics can also help determine how to make vehicles safer and longer-lasting.

AI is also used for self-driving delivery solutions for restaurants, grocery stores, or pharmacies catering to online buyers.

Source: Schroer (2022).

ASEAN in the New Automotive Value Chain

ASEAN as parts supplier for electric vehicles

Several features of ASEAN's automotive industry can help evaluate the impact of the global shift to EVs. First, ASEAN's car trade is geared more to the regional market (Figure 4.4). One-third of its exports go to other ASEAN countries and rise to more than 50% (in 2020) if exports to the Plus 3 countries—the PRC, Japan, and Republic of Korea—are included. In 2020, ASEAN's regional exports totaled $4 trillion of its $12 trillion global exports. Its exports to the Plus 3 add another $2 trillion. ASEAN's automotive industry export share is approximated at less than 5% of total exports, meaning its value added in automotive manufacturing is small relative to developed countries that are home to big automobile MNCs.

Figure 4.4: Destination of ASEAN Passenger Car Exports
($ million)

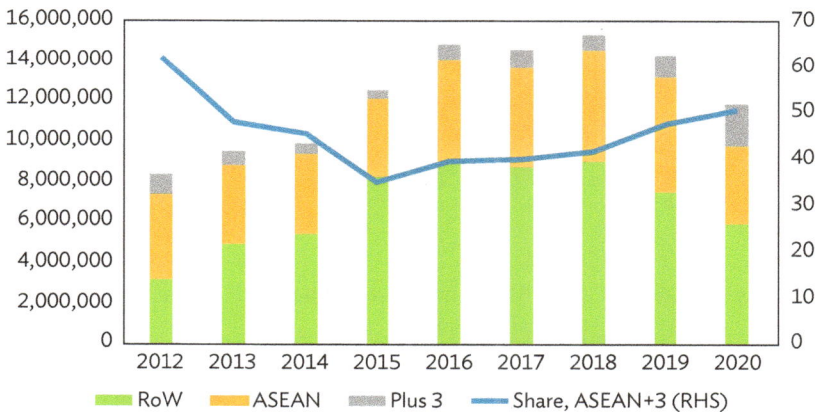

ASEAN = Association of Southeast Asian Nations; ASEAN+3 = ASEAN plus Japan, the People's Republic of China, and the Republic of Korea; RHS = right-hand side; RoW = Rest of the World.
Source: World Bank, World Integrated Trade Solution database using HS2002 (HS87032, 87033, 87039) (accessed 8 February 2022).

Second, ASEAN's role in the automotive value chain is stronger as part of the supplier network of OEMs. ASEAN hosts OEM subsidiaries that do final assembly, but finished cars are mostly for the domestic market with a few for regional distribution. While ASEAN's share in the global finished car exports is less than 1% (Figure 4.5), its share in the production of subassemblies and parts and components is more significant. ASEAN exports of body system subassemblies grew rapidly beginning in 2015, although most went to the Plus 3 countries, particularly Japan. Its share in global exports of drive trains is less than body system subassembly but its value is 10 times higher. For parts and components, ASEAN's share in global exports of components for body systems, drive trains, and electrical systems are even larger. In particular, pre-pandemic ASEAN exports of electrical system components reached 9% of global exports and at its peak in 2019 was valued close to $14 billion (Figures 4.6 and 4.7).

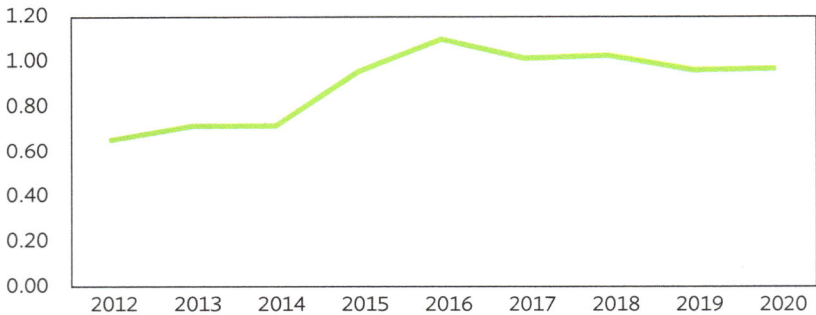

Figure 4.5: ASEAN's Share in Global Car Exports
(%)

ASEAN = Association of Southeast Asian Nations.
Notes: Passenger vehicles: HS 87032, 87033.
Source: Author. Based on World Bank. https://wits.worldbank.org/ (accessed 10 February 2022).

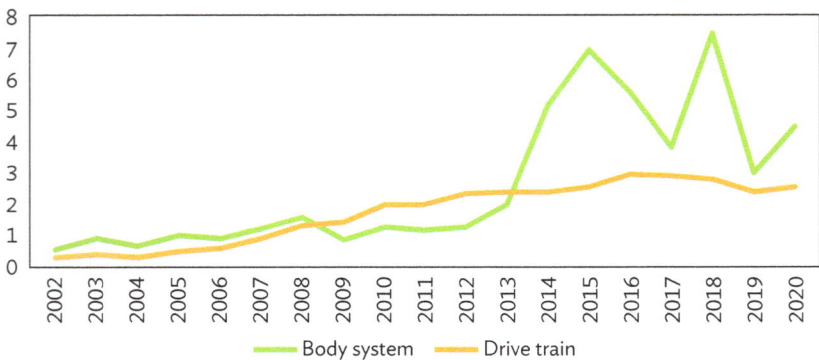

Figure 4.6: ASEAN's Share in World Exports of Subassemblies
(%)

ASEAN = Association of Southeast Asian Nations.
Notes: Body system subassembly—HS 870600; drive train subassembly—HS 840733, 840734, 840820.
Source: Author. Based on World Bank. https://wits.worldbank.org/ (accessed 10 February 2022).

Figure 4.7: ASEAN's Share in Parts and Component Exports (%)

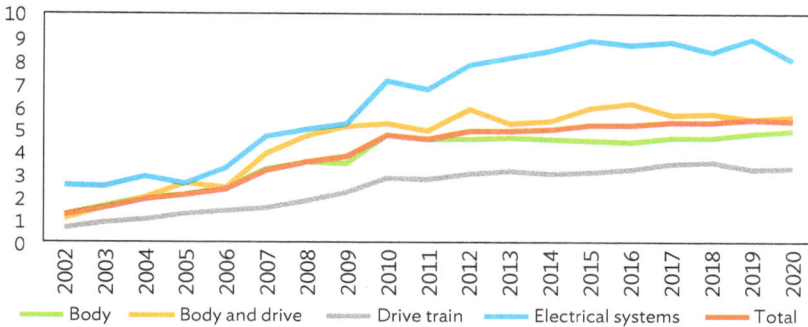

ASEAN: Association of Southeast Asian Nations.
Notes: Body parts and components—22 HS categories based on classifications from Sturgeon, et.al (2016); Drive train parts—HS 840991, 840999, 870840, 870850, 870860, 870893; Body/drivetrain—HS 870899; Electrical—HS8507, 8511, 854430, 851220, 851230, 851240, 851290
Source: Author based on wits.worldbank.org (accessed 10 February 2022).

Because ASEAN'S role in the GVC has been as supplier, what will happen as less parts and components are needed for EVs? As traditional cars disappear, some parts and components will no longer be needed (Table 4.2). Based on the World Integrated Trade Solution trade data, these parts and component exports were worth $274.5 million in 2020. Yet, some part segments, such as electric drive trains, battery manufacturing, advanced driver assistance systems (ADAs), and other software systems (Figure 4.8) will see high growth.

Table 4.2: Examples of Parts of Traditional Cars Not Needed in Electric Vehicles

Modules/Subassembly	Parts and Components
Body system (suspension)	Mounted brake linings; suspension systems and parts (including shock absorbers)
Body system (front and rear end modules)	Radiators; silencers and exhaust pipes; filtering or purifying machinery and apparatus for gases
Drive train	Parts suitable for use in internal combustion engines; gear boxes; drive-axles with differentials, whether provided with other transmission components or not; non-driving axles and parts
Electrical system	Electrical ignition or starting equipment used for spark ignition or compression-ignition for internal combustion engines (e.g., ignition magnetos, magneto-dynamos, ignition coils, spark plugs, glow plugs, starter motors): generators and cutouts of a kind used in conjunction with such engines

Source: Author

Figure 4.8: Sunrise and Sunset Industry Segments of Parts and Component Industry

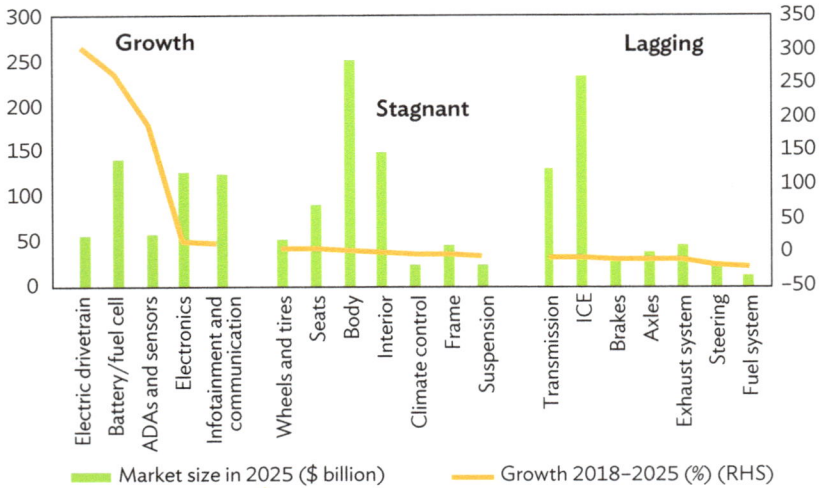

ADA = advanced driver assistance system, ICE = internal combustion engine, RHS = right-hand side.
Source: Adapted by Author from Figure 2 in Deloitte (2019).

ASEAN has time to adjust and adapt

With the expected frenzied transformation of the global automotive industry, ASEAN auto parts and component suppliers will see reduced demand over time. But it has time to adapt to the new GVC. This is because demand for EVs in and outside the region will not drastically swing from internal combustion to electric any time soon. First, a survey of consumer preferences for their next vehicle purchase shows the majority in Southeast Asia still prefers gas-fueled cars (Figure 4.9). Even consumers favoring EVs still prefer hybrid cars, a combination of internal combustion and battery; hybrid production does not have a major effect on demand for parts and components and thus on labor and employment.

Second, places with lower electricity costs will more likely see faster EV demand growth. However, even if average electricity prices are relatively lower in ASEAN compared to the global average, not all countries have well-developed power infrastructure. If oil prices plummet, ASEAN consumers have, additionally, less incentive to shift to EVs, unless governments adopt regulatory disincentives for buying internal combustion engines to mitigate environmental warming.

Figure 4.9: Consumer Survey of Auto Engine Preference

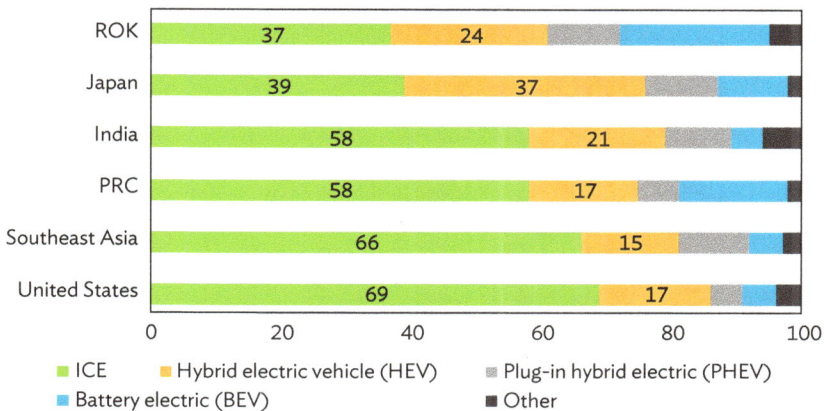

ICE = internal combustion engine, PRC = People's Republic of China, ROK = Republic of Korea.
Note: Survey question: What type of engine would you prefer in your next vehicle?
Source: Deloitte (2022).

Unlike developed countries, the region's developing economies do not yet have focused policies to promote the transition toward EVs. For example, in California in the US, high fuel taxes nudge more consumers to opt for EVs. In the PRC, restrictions introduced on internal combustion vehicles registered in major cities in 2014 "forced" more consumers to buy EVs (Box 4.4). In ASEAN, countries have varying explicit policies to incentivize EV production and consumption (Table 4.3). Indonesia, the Philippines, and Thailand provide some fiscal benefits for foreign investors to produce EVs locally; Singapore has a consumer purchase subsidy; Thailand has a government purchase quantity commitment that can help increase EV market penetration.

High unit prices are another factor that stymie demand. EVs still command a high premium over internal combustion engine vehicles, which prohibits large scale EV use, especially in countries with low purchasing power. Again, the lack of accompanying infrastructure like charging station networks—a key consideration for EV buyers—also dampens demand. Singapore and Thailand are the only countries with a significant number of public charging stations.

In sum, the lackluster EV demand in ASEAN means that the market for parts and components will remain robust at least over the medium term.

Box 4.4: People's Republic of China: Climate Change and Electric Vehicles

The People's Republic of China (PRC) is the world's biggest carbon dioxide emitter. Having New Energy Vehicles (NEVs) as a designated "pillar" industry in the "Made in China 2025" plan, the PRC achieves a double goal—to reduce its high dependence on oil and reduce its carbon footprint. At the same time, under this strategy, local manufacturers will have government support in supplying electric vehicles (EVs) to the domestic market and perhaps, eventually, become one of the dominant global players in a transformed future auto industry.

As with the PRC's previous strategies, it experiments on various policies that can work, removing policies not beneficial and improving those that are (Carnell and Pang, 2021). These policy experiments include:

- Direct research and development grants; consumer purchase tax rebates and sales subsidies
- Special (premium) license plates
- 10% of original equipment manufacturer (OEM) internal combustion sales credit equivalents satisfied through EV sales
- Removed "white list" of domestic battery makers for OEMs to benefit from NEV subsidies
- Removed requirement to form joint ventures with PRC partners for NEVs for sale domestically (in 2018), facilitating the entry of Tesla's self-owned operation in Shanghai, the People's Republic of China

In 2020, 1.4 million EVs were sold, equivalent to 6% of the PRC vehicle market (Dyer, 2021). NEV sales are targeted to reach 20% of new car sales by 2025—equivalent to 5.4 million units, or a five-fold increase within 5 years.

EV players use different strategies. Battery EV (BEV) startups only supply electric car models, developing high technology batteries with extended driving ranges. Others produce both internal combustion engine vehicles and NEVs (hybrids and BEVs). Others manufacture hybrid EVs which qualify as NEVs, although their electric range is limited and run almost like an internal combustion car. These hybrid vehicles are used only to minimally qualify for government subsidies. As in advanced economies, PRC EV car manufacturers will need to partner with technology companies like Baidu, Alibaba, Huawei, or Xiaomi to develop both software and hardware expertise.

Source: Dyer (2021); Carnell and Pang (2021)

Table 4.3: Policy Support for Electric Vehicle Development in ASEAN

	Tariff reduction or tax cuts	Purchase subsidies / Usage incentives	Battery swapping or charging station program	R&D subsidy or grant to adapt EV to local context	Others
Indonesia	Proposal to offer tax cuts to foreign OEMs		Battery swapping trials*		
Malaysia	High import tariff for cars to support domestic production		Plan to build 25,000 public charging point by 2030; 100,000 private		
Philippines	EVs exempted from excise tax		200 charging stations (for fleets)*		Plan to replace old public utility vehicles with green-friendly vehicles
Singapore		Tax rebate of 45% for the additional registration fee, capped at S$20,000	EV promotion includes increasing chargers at private properties		
Thailand	Reduction of excise tax from 10%–30% ICEVs to 2%–10% for domestically produced EVs; Corporate tax exemption		About 1,000 charging stations installed throughout the country within 200 kms of one another	Financial incentives for investments in R&D, innovation, human resources development	Government commitment to purchase EVs out of the fiscal budget
Viet Nam	High import tariff for cars to support domestic production				

ASEAN = Association of Southeast Asian Nations, EV = electric vehicle, R&D = research and development, OEM = original equipment manufacturer, ICEV = internal combustion engine vehicle.
Note: * Private sector initiatives.
Source: Author's adaptation of information from Deloitte (2021).

Impact on Global Parts and Component Exports

Even as regional demand for EVs will not soar any time soon, the shift in global demand toward EVs is a threat for ASEAN subassemblies, parts and component manufacturers. This is because most of their exports are destined for global rather than regional markets. ASEAN's external exports of body systems and drive trains are significant and rising (Figure 4.10).

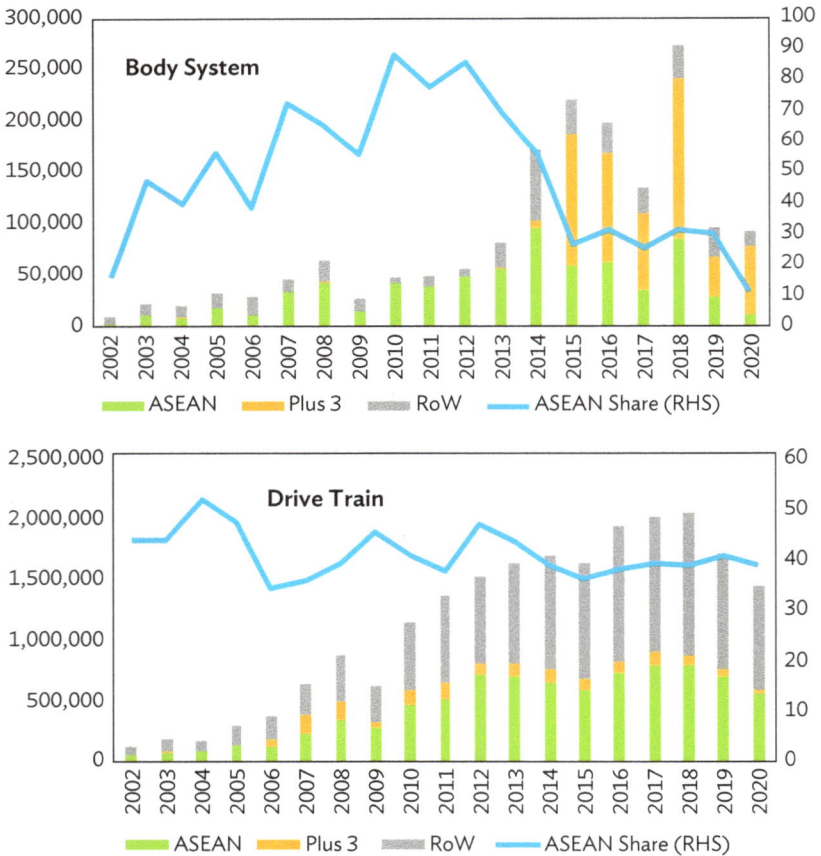

Figure 4.10: ASEAN Exports of Body Systems and Drive Train Subassemblies

($ million)

ASEAN = Association of Southeast Asian Nations, RHS = right-hand side, RoW = rest of the world.
Source: Author based on data from wits.wordlbank.org (accessed 12 February 2022).

Even more than subassemblies, car parts and component exports are more global than regional (Figure 4.11). Two of ASEAN's biggest exports by value are electrical systems and components and parts for body system modules. Regional exports of these two sectors are less than 20% of ASEAN exports, while more than 80% go outside the region. Thus, despite a stable demand forecast for traditional cars in ASEAN over the next few decades, the global rise in EV demand—including in the Plus 3 countries—where EV sales have surged since 2017, will affect demand for parts and components (Figure 4.12). If so, employment will also be affected, meaning ASEAN's suppliers must start adapting to the EV era now. Strategies could include consolidating and restructuring along with major global parts suppliers, a shift in business strategies, and inevitably, labor adjustment in the car parts and component segment, including retraining and upskilling.

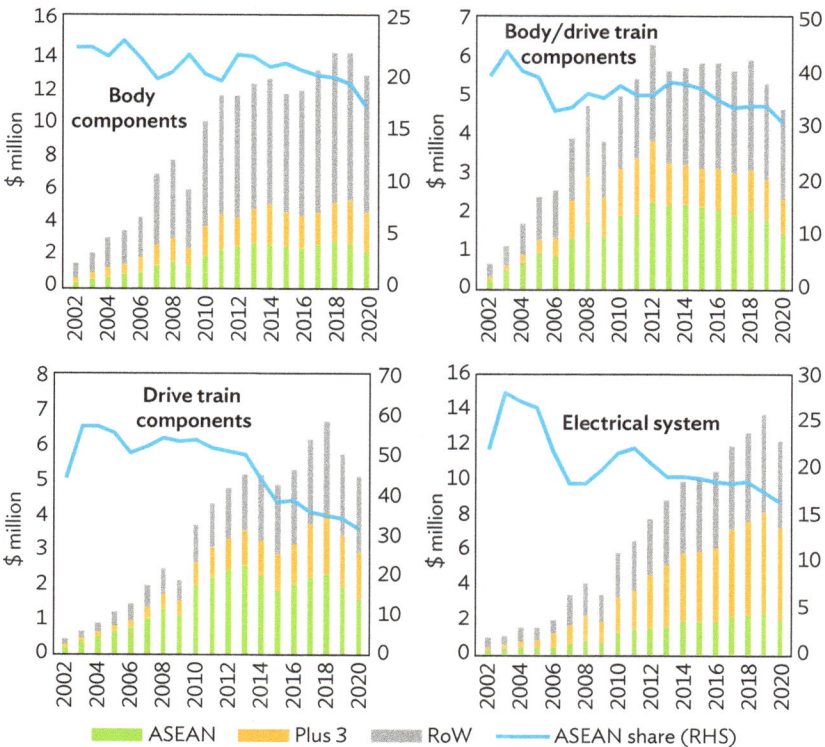

Figure 4.11: ASEAN Exports in Automotive Parts and Components
($ million)

ASEAN = Association of Southeast Asian Nations, RHS = right-hand side, RoW = rest of the world.
Source: Author based on wits.worldbank.org (accessed 12 February 2022).

Figure 4.12: Share of Electric Vehicles in ASEAN Auto Exports
(%)

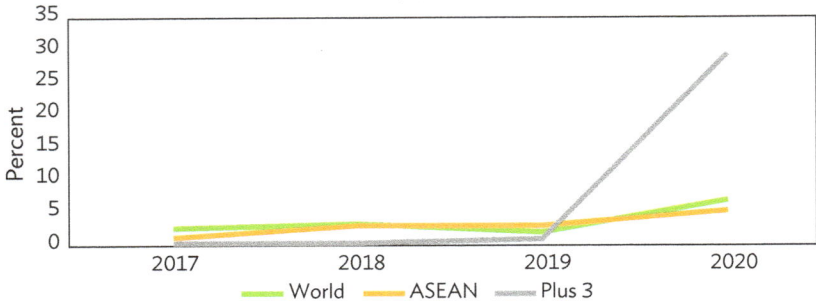

ASEAN = Association of Southeast Asian Nations, HS = Harmonized System.
Note: Electric car is based on HS2017, HS code 87034 to 87038.
Source: Author. Based on World Bank. https://wits.worldbank.org/ (accessed 8 February 2022).

Electronics and Electrical Industry

The electronics and electrical (E&E) industry involves the manufacture of electrical parts and components, electronic equipment, and end-products that intensively use electronics or the so-called 3Cs—consumer electronics, communications, and computers/storage/office (Figure 4.13). With IoT, autonomous cars, and other digital revolutions, the end-product segment of the industry using electronics has become more elastic. End-products can include anything from refrigerators to medical equipment to industrial equipment (industrial IoT products) to EVs.

Electronics include semiconductor wafers assembled into integrated circuits (ICs) or active discrete (standalone), passive ICs or bare circuit boards. These are then pieced together into subassemblies like printed circuit boards (PCBs) or product-specific parts. Electrical components include wires and cables, switchgear, and transformers.

Distribution and sales methods for electronic components vary. Customized products are sold directly to specific buyers, while standard products usually go through distributors. Semiconductor and PCB companies are likely to sell their products directly to electronic product manufacturers, while passive electronic components sell most of its products to distributors. The components or subassemblies are shipped from an assembly and testing (A&T) facility to either a main distribution center (primarily in Singapore; Hong Kong, China; and Taipei,China) or to tier 1 electronics manufacturing services (EMS) companies in the region (Duke CGCC 2016).

Figure 4.13: Electronics and Electrical Global Value Chain

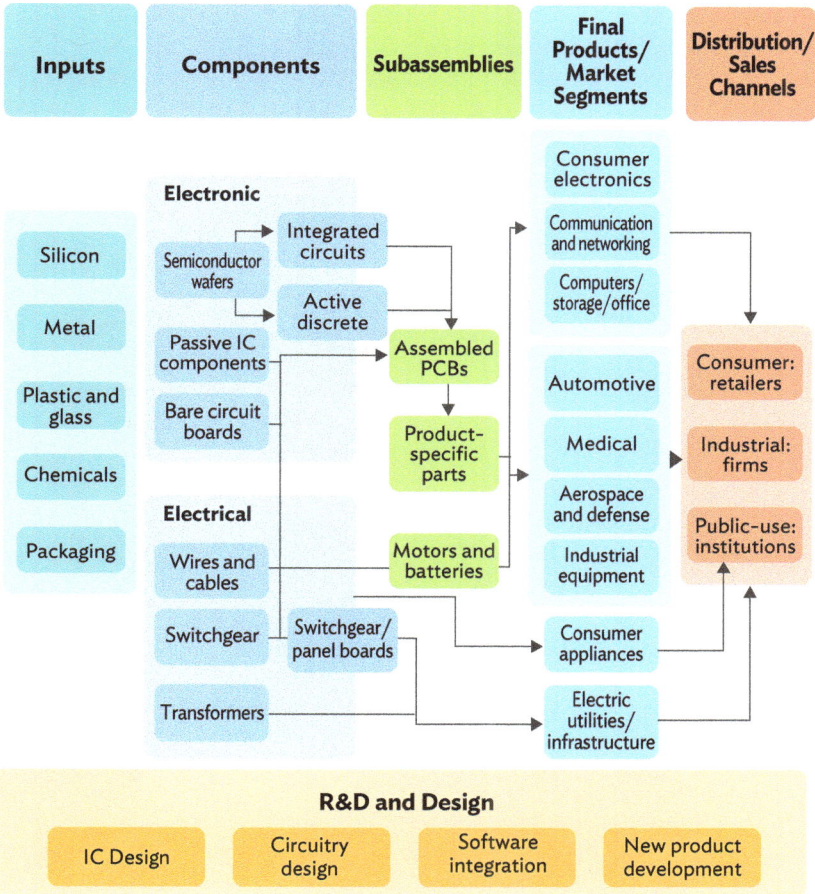

| Inputs | Components | Subassemblies | Final Products/ Market Segments | Distribution/ Sales Channels |

Electronic

- Silicon
- Metal
- Plastic and glass
- Chemicals
- Packaging

Semiconductor wafers → Integrated circuits / Active discrete

Passive IC components

Bare circuit boards

Assembled PCBs

Product-specific parts

Electrical

- Wires and cables
- Switchgear → Switchgear/ panel boards
- Transformers

Motors and batteries

Consumer electronics
Communication and networking
Computers/ storage/office
Automotive
Medical
Aerospace and defense
Industrial equipment
Consumer appliances
Electric utilities/ infrastructure

Consumer: retailers
Industrial: firms
Public-use: institutions

R&D and Design

| IC Design | Circuitry design | Software integration | New product development |

IC= integrated circuit, PCB = printed circuit board, PCBA = printed circuit board assembly, R&D = research and development.
Source: Duke CGCC (2016).

The semiconductor value chain sits within the E&E industry. It is characterized by deep interdependencies between countries and nodes of the chain. No country is autonomous in semiconductor production, which starts with design, followed by fabrication and assembly (Figure 4.14; Box 4.5). Each step is specialized and has its own specific characteristics. Fabless companies (many known brands from the US or EU such as Apple) design chips without manufacturing capability. The few that have both design and manufacturing capabilities are called integrated device manufacturers (IDMs). Specially designed chips by fabless companies are sent to foundries for fabrication. The dominant foundries are based in Taipei,China and the Republic of Korea. The foundries, in turn, rely on equipment, chemicals, and silicon wafers from the US, EU, and Japan. The final phase of semiconductor production is assembly and testing (A&T), a labor-intensive activity and thus mostly outsourced to low-cost locations such as ASEAN economies and the PRC.

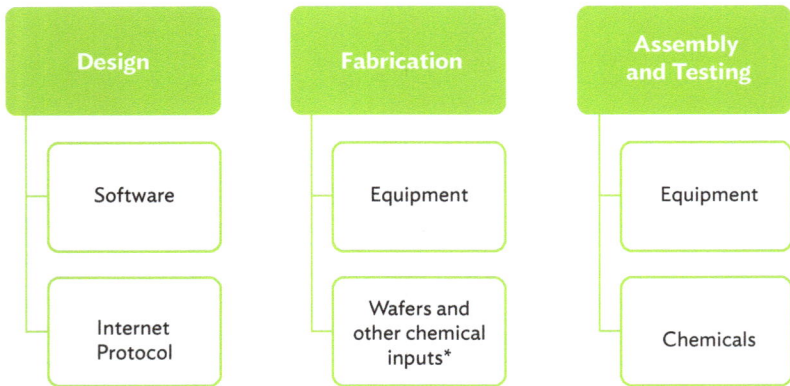

Figure 4.14: Semiconductor Value Chain

* Inputs include silicon, glass, plastics, packaging materials, metal, and other chemicals.
Source: Kleinhans and Baisakova (2020).

Chip design relies on design software tools called electronic design automation. Three US companies—Cadence Design System, Synopsys, and Mentor—with their deep knowledge of the fabrication process, work closely with fabrication companies as well as equipment manufacturers for these foundries. Chip designers also rely on intellectual property access from companies that develop semiconductor internet protocol (IP) blocks, e.g., processor cores or small IP blocks for standard functionality like networking interfaces or graphic cores. Chip design also relies on the close relationship with foundries that match their design to a particular process node in a fabrication plant.

Fabless companies like Nvidia, Qualcomm, and Advanced Micro Devices, which specialize in chip design, work with foundries like a semiconductor manufacturing company based in Taipei,China; and Samsung, among others. A change of a foundry's process node can mean a new chip design and vice versa.

The chip design is sent to a fabrication plant for manufacturing. The main differentiating factor among foundries is their capacity to do increasingly complex design with a greater number of transistors that can be squeezed into smaller and smaller chips. Samsung and TSMC are fabs that can produce 7 nanometer (nm) and smaller ICs, the powerful, cutting-edge chips with tens of millions of transistors; while other foundries like those in the PRC can only do the larger, less powerful semiconductor chips such as 40nm–250nm ICs.[1] In turn, cutting-edge manufacturing capacity requires dozens of very expensive equipment, which make the fabrication industry highly capital intensive; each fabrication facility costs billions of dollars to build.[2] To be sustainable, fabrication relies on volume and economies of scale.

The A&T phase of the process is where the cutting, testing, and packaging of the silicon wafers that exit fabrication facilities are carried out. This back-end work is labor intensive with very low profit margins. As such, they are mostly outsourced to low-wage developing countries. Companies involved in this are called outsourced semiconductor assembly and test (OSAT) companies—which are either MNC branches or outsourced third parties. These companies also rely on equipment and chemicals but cost less to set up than foundries. Since 2009, the PRC has taken significant market share in this part of the semiconductor value chain at the expense of other developing countries like those in ASEAN. Some foundries also carry out some back-end activities like advanced wafer packaging instead of having it done by OSAT companies.

---

[1] Nanometer size refers to the line width between transistors on a chip. The smaller the width, the more cutting-edge the chips are, but also the more challenging and expensive to develop (Liew 2020).

[2] Different semiconductor manufacturing equipment fabricate ICs on a silicon wafer. They are used for deposition (putting material on the wafer), lithography, and etching. For example, the Netherlands manufacturer ASML has a monopoly in photolithography equipment, especially extreme ultraviolet lithography, indispensable for producing chips smaller than 7nm. ASML technology "burns" a blueprint of transistors onto a silicon wafer, a crucial technology for cutting-edge chips manufacturing. Equipment vendors like ASML, in turn, rely on thousands of highly specialized suppliers across the world, as well as on a few buyers in Taipei,China; the Republic of Korea; and increasingly the PRC.

Box 4.5: Understanding the Semiconductor Industry and Technologies

There are seven broad categories of semiconductors: memory, logic, micro, analog, optoelectronics, discrete, and sensors. The more common—known as chips or integrated circuits (ICs)—are memory, logic, micro, and analog semiconductors. For these digital ICs, the pressure is on constant technological development to fit more transistors on smaller and smaller silicon wafers. ICs are produced in three distinct steps: design, fabrication, and assembly and testing.

Different types of players constitute the semiconductor industry. Few do design, fabrication, and assembly in-house. Those that do are called integrated device manufacturers (IDMs). Intel and Samsung are examples of IDMs. Other companies, called fabless, only design chips; examples are Qualcomm and Nvidia United States [US] and HiSilicon People's Republic of China [PRC]. Foundries do the chip fabrication or manufacturing; example is TSMC, a semiconductor manufacturing company based in Taipei,China. After fabrication, the chip is tested, assembled, and packaged. This is done usually by outsourced semiconductor assembly and test companies.

Each step has different characteristics. Chip design is skill intensive and requires high research and development expenditures. Fabrication is capital intensive due to equipment costs. Assembly and testing is labor intensive.

Likewise, each semiconductor chip has specific characteristics:

- DRAM chips are for temporarily storing data being processed (short-term memory chips). Smart phones, supercomputers, autonomous vehicles, and airplanes all need access to DRAM chips. The DRAM market is oligopolistic, where the top eight manufacturers have 97% of the market. Samsung is the technology leader; followed by SK Hynix of the Republic of Korea, and Micron (US). All DRAM makers are IDMs.
- NAND flash memory chips are long-term memory chips for computing devices. Like DRAM, NAND requires production volume and economies of scale to survive; hence, NAND makers are also IDMs. It is less concentrated than the DRAM market. Top manufacturers are from the Republic of Korea, the US, and Japan.

continued on next page

Box 4.5 (continued)

- Analog ICs generate or transform signals from electricity to radio waves or light and are usually designed for specific tasks, such as music listening from a computer or mobile phone. Most devices that need electricity depend on analog ICs. The analog IC market is less concentrated than the memory chip or processor market because of the lack of pressure to invest in cutting-edge fabs that are able to pack as many transistors into a smaller-sized wafer. Some analog IC manufacturers are IDMs; others are fab-lite, outsourcing fabrication of certain chips. Top producers are the US, EU, and Japan.

- Micro semiconductor or processors, often called central processing units (CPUs) or application processing units (APUs), are the brain of any computing device. Its design is based on the instruction set architecture which defines the processors' inner workings. Software is compatible with only a certain processor architecture; hence, there has been a strong tendency toward vendor lock-in. For example, Microsoft Windows was made for x86-based computer processors. In smartphones, tablets and the Internet of Things, the dominant processors are based on ARM blueprints, licensed by the developer ARM Limited, for other chip designers to develop and sell their own processors for mobile, laptops, and workstations. Other special chips are the so-called artificial intelligence (AI) chips, a type of application-specific integrated circuit used for machine learning tasks like facial recognition. Here there is no dominant architecture yet, as AI chips differ substantially, each is specially designed for specific machine learning platforms.

The industry is characterized by strong interdependencies. No country has access to all important types of semiconductors: ICT systems depend on DRAM from the Republic of Korea, NAND from Japan, analog chips from the US, and intellectual property such as ARM blueprints from the United Kingdom. The semiconductor value chain is globally distributed, highly efficient and innovative, but specializations have led to oligopolies and even monopolies, where few suppliers (sometimes just one) dominate the production of certain types of semiconductors. This made the industry efficient but not so resilient, and thus subject to supply chain disruptions caused by natural disasters, pandemics, or trade restrictions.

Source: Kleinhans and Baisakova (2020).

ASEAN in the Electronics and Electrical Value Chain

The E&E industry is important for ASEAN economies. It is responsible for 8.4% of the region's gross domestic product. But in exporting countries like Malaysia, the Philippines, Thailand, and Viet Nam, its estimated share ranges from 10% (Malaysia) to 23% (Viet Nam). Its workforce is in the hundreds of thousands across exporting ASEAN countries, totaling 2.4 million across the region. In 2021, E&E accounted for 26% of ASEAN exports, with the Philippines holding the largest share at 51% (ASEAN-Japan Centre 2021).[3] Chapter 3 estimates that the industry's GVC-related employment is close to 80% of the total, which means it caters mostly to international markets with investments that are mostly GVC-related.

Malaysia, the Philippines, Thailand, and more recently, Viet Nam are ASEAN's main E&E exporters. Although joining relatively late, Viet Nam's E&E exports are now greater than those from other ASEAN economies (Box 4.6). Cambodia and the Lao PDR are just entering the GVC, while Indonesia's GVC is more geared to its huge domestic market.

While E&E exports are large, the industry also imports large amounts of foreign inputs and technology, resulting in foreign value added of 53% of the industry's exports (ASEAN-Japan Centre). The PRC (19% of exports) and Japan (15%) are the main contributors of foreign value added. However, ASEAN's value added has increased over time, from 6% in 1990 to 12% in 2017 due to Japan, US, and EU manufacturers relocating to ASEAN, along with contributions from domestic companies (Figure 4.15). Still, development has been primarily driven by MNCs which located some of their manufacturing in the ASEAN region beginning in the 1970s.

ASEAN's contribution to the E&E value chain is mostly in the A&T segment—it has not developed significant capability in design or fabrication. The region contributes more than 10% to global semiconductor component exports (Table 4.4).[4] Malaysia is the biggest exporter but its contribution is largely in assembly, testing, and packaging. The exception is Singapore, which successfully attracted major global firms to set up businesses there, thus adding to its value chain contribution, especially in chip design.

---

[3] Based on HS 85 sector group for ASEAN exports. Other industry products are scattered across different HS groups and are not included in the estimate.

[4] Based on 2017 data when the export figures were less distorted by supply chain bottlenecks due to the pandemic.

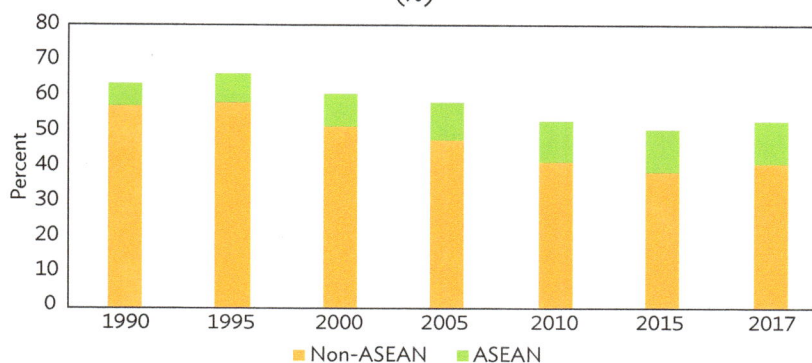

Figure 4.15: Foreign Value Added in ASEAN Electronics and Electronics Exports
(%)

ASEAN = Association of Southeast Asian Nations.
Source: Author. Based on Table 3, ASEAN–Japan Centre (2021).

Table 4.4: ASEAN Semiconductor Component Exports By Category, 2018

Subsector	HS Codes	World Exports ($ billion)	Share in world exports (%)			
			Malaysia	Philippines	Thailand	Viet Nam
Passive (resistors, capacitors)	8532, 8533	43.66	3.05	1.72	1.22	0.15
Printed Circuit Boards	8534	50.95	2.32	0.84	2.75	1.48
Active: tubes/ valves	8540					
Discrete/ Semiconductors	8541	111.00	7.91	2.68	1.67	2.00
Integrated Circuits	8542	691.77	6.64	1.99	1.21	1.14
Total		**897.39**	**6.38**	**1.99**	**1.35**	**1.22**

ASEAN = Association of Southeast Asian Nations.
Note: HS codes are based on HS2002 classification.
Source: Author. Based on World Bank data. https://wits.worldbank.org/ (accessed 31 March 2022).

Among destination markets, the PRC gained importance for ASEAN electronics component exports starting in 2007 (Figure 4.16). After joining the World Trade Organization in 2002, the PRC attracted large amounts of foreign direct investment and eventually embedded itself in the E&E GVC, becoming the subassembly or final assembly destination for components exported from ASEAN. Since then, the PRC has entered low-end semiconductor fabrication and high-end chip design. Nevertheless, the rest of the world, especially Japan, the US, and EU remain ASEAN's major export destinations. ASEAN's global exports continued to climb until 2020 before supply chain bottlenecks and the trade conflict between the PRC and the US brought exports down sharply in 2021.

Figure 4.16: ASEAN Electronic Components Exports to the People's Republic of China and the Rest of the World, 2002–2021
($ billions)

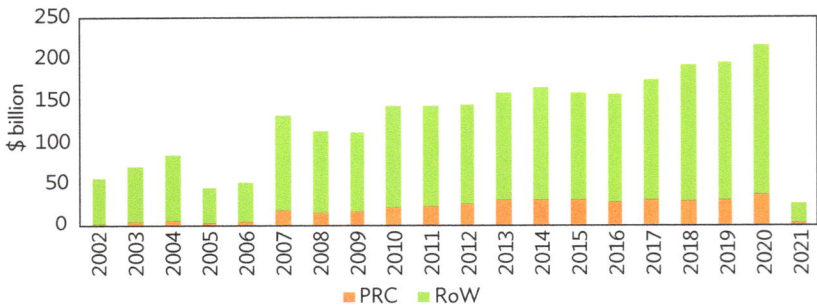

ASEAN = Association of Southeast Asian Nations, PRC = People's Republic of China, RoW = rest of the world.
Notes: See Table 4.4 for HS classification.
Source: Author. Based on World Bank data. https://wits.worldbank.org/ (accessed 10 February 2022).

Box 4.6: Viet Nam's Rapid Growth in the Electronics and Electrical Global Value Chain

Viet Nam's economic growth has been comparable to the People's Republic of China (PRC) over the past decade. In recent years it has attracted the second highest net foreign direct investment inflows in the Association of Southeast Asian Nations (ASEAN) (Box Figure). Its economic growth is consistently robust, averaging 6.3% since 1984. It has continuously improved its infrastructures, especially airports, ports, and highways to meet projected increases in foreign arrivals and trade. Its population is young and growing. Its labor force is cost competitive. Viet Nam's ranking in the World Bank's former Ease of Doing Business Survey rose from 104th in 2007 to 70th in 2020, reflecting government reforms and its determination to improve the economic environment. It liberalized many sectors, allowing 100% foreign ownership, improved government efficiency, and reduced taxes.

continued on next page

Box 4.6 (continued)

Perhaps most important, it is one of four ASEAN members in the Comprehensive and Progressive Agreement for Trans-Pacific Partnership. It also has bilateral trade agreements with the United States, European Union, Japan, and the Republic of Korea. It has joined the Regional Comprehensive Economic Partnership with ASEAN, the PRC, the Republic of Korea, Japan, Australia, and New Zealand. Trade agreements generally signal an economy is "open for business," bringing greater confidence to foreign investors.

Viet Nam also benefits from the PRC+1 risk management strategy of multinational companies that seeks to provide alternative manufacturing locations in the region. Having a base in Viet Nam is strategic: besides its stable and open economic environment—it shares a border with the PRC. It is also close to many international shipping routes.

Box Figure: Foreign Direct Investment
(net, $ milliion)

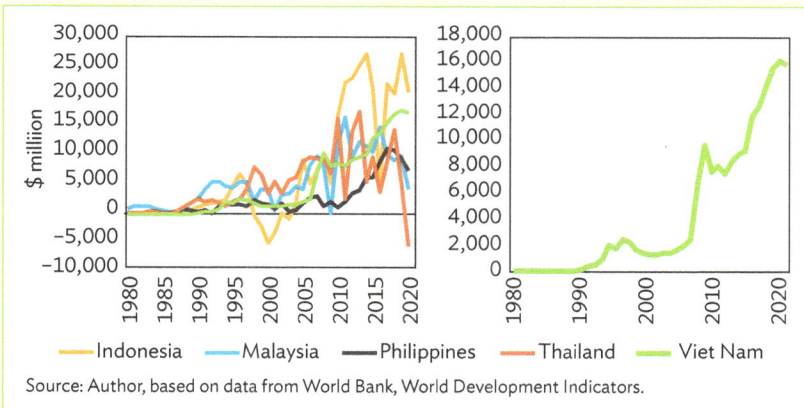

Source: Author, based on data from World Bank, World Development Indicators.

In electronics, Viet Nam succeeded in attracting big technology firms. Samsung was an early entrant in 2014, investing more than $600 million in a manufacturing plant. Since then, it increased its investments to $17.3 billion and attracted its own suppliers to open plants. Apple and Xiaomi also moved some production to the country. These investments helped Viet Nam rise in electronics, computers, and component exports, making it the 10th largest electronics exporter in 2020.

Electronics imports also rose in tandem. Because Viet Nam focuses on the assembly of finished products for export—with components and design done elsewhere—value added remains low. More foreign direct investment in component inputs will help Viet Nam increase its electronics value added.

Source: Leung (2022).

What Can ASEAN Expect in a Transformed Electronics and Electrical Value Chain?

There are several questions looming over ASEAN's participation in the E&E value chain: where is the industry heading and can ASEAN retain its current significant role? Specifically, can ASEAN continue to produce parts and components for emerging and innovative markets? Or will it be stuck producing components for sunset industries? What are the opportunities to upgrade its GVC participation? Semiconductors may be part of the answer.

What drives demand for semiconductors?

Semiconductor manufacturing will continue to grow. Demand is expected to accelerate as the share of electronic products used in daily life proliferates. Semiconductors are like the "power behind the throne" of all technology products—be they low-, medium-, or high-tech. Higher-tech products such as AI or autonomous cars are ratcheting up demand for advanced semiconductors.

The major end-markets for semiconductors are in computers and telecommunications, automotive, consumer and industrial products (Figure 4.17). Laptops, desktops, servers, and the cloud are semiconductor-intensive and critical drivers for semiconductor demand. Likewise, telecommunications need high-speed connectivity that requires increasingly novel semiconductor solutions. Consumer electronics from refrigerators and washing machines to smartphones and gaming consoles all require ever-more powerful small chips. 5G and 6G require secure chips for high-speed voice and data traffic. And the automotive sector is adding to the spiraling semiconductor demand, whether for safety or entertainment, engine power and control, and eventually more autonomous driving. Across industries, more automated manufacturing requires cutting-edge chips to power robots and other industrial IoT.

Innovations like the IoT and AI—with all their myriad potential applications—are expected to drive semiconductor demand over the coming decades. Examples of IoT and AI applications include smart factories, connected homes, and IoT devices, which together are forecast to rise from 7.7 billion in 2019 to 25.4 billion by 2030 (Statista, accessed 1 April 2022). Data from these devices will be stored, analyzed, and processed, adding to demand for servers and cloud computing. Consumer electronics such as 5G phones require 20%–50% more chip content compared with 4G phones, again increasing demand for chips. EVs require twice the value of semiconductors used in internal combustion engine vehicles. In addition, advanced driver assistance systems (ADAS)—which apply brakes if it senses an imminent crash, maintain a consistent distance from the car ahead, or keep vehicles in lane—are chip intensive. More EVs and ADAS, and eventually more fully autonomous vehicles require interconnected radar, sensors, and cameras for road safety, thus requiring even higher semiconductor content.

Figure 4.17: End-market Share in Global Semiconductor Demand, 2019

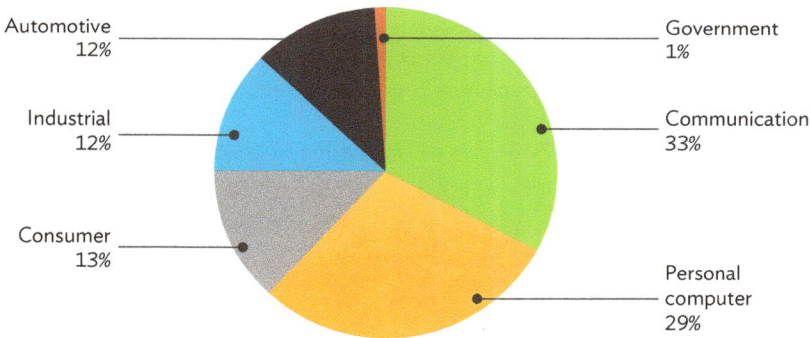

Automotive 12%
Industrial 12%
Consumer 13%
Government 1%
Communication 33%
Personal computer 29%

Source: Statista. https://www.statista.com/ (accessed 31 March 2022).

All these innovations suggest demand for semiconductors will be almost infinite. Wireless communication, IoT, AI, machine learning, data centers and storage, robotics, drones, cloud computing, or augmented reality will continue to boost the chip industry. Different and some new end-markets—medical, industrial, aerospace, and others—further expand semiconductor demand.

ASEAN's Role as Semiconductors Move into More Innovative Sectors

This high and growing demand for semiconductors offers ASEAN—as part of the semiconductor GVC—a vast array of opportunities. Foreign MNCs are, in addition, pivoting to PRC+1 strategies, meaning ASEAN should work toward attracting more foreign direct investments in the semiconductor value chain, especially those with the capability to upgrade ASEAN's role in the GVC.

Frederick et al. (2017) identified various types of upgrades that will help increase a country's value addition in a GVC. These are classified as functional, process, product, or end-market upgrades. The country can also increase its backward and forward linkages with the industry. Functional upgrading refers to taking on other nodes in the GVC process to increase its value contribution. For example, Singapore, from being an OSAT location in the 1980s, progressively grew into a hub for design and R&D. Process upgrading refers more to productivity enhancements while product upgrading signals a shift toward higher value-added, custom-made products instead of, or in addition to, producing low-value, high-volume homogeneous products. End-market upgrading occurs as a country diversifies buyers or end-markets, selling to other geographic markets or other industry levels, such as supplying medical device manufacturers in addition to computer manufacturers. Backward and forward linkages develop as more domestic suppliers join the value chain (Table 4.5).

Table 4.5: Types of Upgrades in ASEAN

Upgrading	Examples in ASEAN
Functional upgrading: advance to more value-adding activities	Singapore: progressively increased value added and now deeply involved with design and R&D
Process upgrading: reduce costs, increase productivity, and improve flexibility by investing in new or better machinery or logistics technology	Malaysia and the Philippines: focusing on process upgrading and improving productivity
Product upgrading: shifting to customized products, higher quality inputs and others that increase product value or competitiveness	Viet Nam: focusing on final products (mobile phones) and specific parts
Backward/forward linkages: vertical integration, more domestic suppliers/sources	Philippines: manufacturing electronic and electrical companies establishing business process outsourcing Malaysia: government-promoted, establishing wafer fabrication
End-market upgrading: market diversification—either new buyers (new industry verticals) or geographic markets	Malaysia: moved from high-volume, low-mix (typically consumer electronics) to high-mix, low volume operations (typically for specific verticals) More ASEAN components now go to the People's Republic of China

ASEAN = Association of Southeast Asian Nations, R&D = research and development
Sources: Author. Based on Frederick et al. (2017); Duke CGCC (2016).

ASEAN's experience thus far in upgrading has been mixed. On one hand, Singapore effectively pivoted to more knowledge-intensive and higher value-added segments of design and R&D from assembly and testing.

From being a location for OSAT services, it grew to become a global hub for the E&E industry. It has 21 wafer fabrication plants, including two of the top three wafer foundries in the world. Nonetheless, it still does assembly and testing and is host to three of the top global OSAT companies. Its value chain participation is in diversified products ranging from storage and memory chips to microelectromechanical systems. Singapore has research institutes working with top chip designers like Nvidia or Infineon in areas like Industry 4.0, AI, and autonomous vehicles. The value chain ecosystem is also rich and includes materials, equipment, and electronics manufacturing services.

On the other hand, Malaysia and the Philippines would not be considered textbook cases of "successful" upgrading. Malaysia tried to increase its value contribution through local wafer fabrication as well as chip design, but so far is not competitive with top global companies in Taipei,China or the Republic of Korea. However, Malaysian backward linkages have increased production capacity and contributions from domestic firms, relative to the Philippine experience. Within OSAT, Malaysia accounts for 13% of global chip packaging and testing. And 7% of the world's semiconductor trade passes through Malaysia (Liew 2020), either for assembly or final packaging.

The risk, going forward, is that ASEAN gets stuck in the semiconductor segment that has little room for growth, either because it manufactures components that serve less innovative end-markets or their existing technologies are old. The majority of Philippine exports, for example, are in computer-related office equipment and hard disk drives considered "sunset products" with less room for innovation (World Bank 2015). Hard disk drives, also a key export of Thailand, are being replaced with hybrid or solid-state drives for use in data centers. This is part of the trend toward cloud computing rather than storage on a local or personal electronic device. By contrast, Viet Nam is involved in the fast-growing smartphone and tablet markets which offer more opportunities for expansion and growth. ASEAN's challenge is to attract more MNC investments that cater to new and innovative products, particularly those needed for Industry 4.0, AI, and the IoT. The question is whether ASEAN can offer enough skilled manpower that these types of investments require.

Another challenge, especially for economies with no fabrication capability, is the growing forward linkage expansion of foundries (pure play fabs) that include assembly, testing, and packaging that had previously been outsourced to third parties and third markets. These fabs have the capacity to provide 2.5D/3D packaging, a packaging methodology for including multiple ICs inside the same package, especially for cutting-edge chips. Fabs' push into the back-end business will compete with external OSAT businesses from ASEAN, further threatening their value-added contribution to the GVC. But it can also push ASEAN companies to upgrade their technologies and become more competitive.

The Human Capital and Innovation Challenge

Technology is both a disruptor and facilitator for businesses, jobs, and employment. The case studies of automotive and semiconductor manufacturing discussed in this chapter point to a transformation in traditional employment that requires new skillsets (Box 4.7). Some jobs are expected to disappear while new ones emerge. Countries that want to keep employment up need to invest in retraining and upskilling if they want to attract technology-driven GVCs. They must have the production and technology capabilities that require more skilled labor. There are policies that developing countries can consider to attract foreign investments—especially for future industries.

Core factors for investment remain but skilled labor is ever more important

The core factors that determine MNC investments—such as cost, size and growth of the market, adequate infrastructure, and connectivity—remain important considerations even with the ongoing digital revolution. Government support through tax and fiscal incentives also play important roles, but they cannot compensate for a poor business environment, including trade openness (OECD 2016; Chuan-Fong Shih et al. 2007). International connectivity like airport and port infrastructure, reliable power and communication technology that facilitate GVC operations, and knowledge flows are also critical. Cost factors like wage levels—including for skilled employees—as well as the cost and quality of living such as land prices, rents, and population density are also important for attracting foreign investment.

Increasingly, available skilled labor has become an important determinant for locating technology-driven businesses and for putting more value in the value chain. Without a skilled workforce, GVC upgrading is stymied. In Malaysia, for example, the backward linkage push toward wafer fabrication was an opportunity to leapfrog up the technology ladder. But the lack of qualified personnel to do high-level R&D saddled its integration into the more knowledge-intensive stages of the semiconductor value chain (Liew 2020). This shows that a "critical mass of capabilities" is

Box 4.7: Changing Skill Requirements in the Job Market

With advances in technology, reskilling and upskilling labor in manufacturing must take place, just as users and service providers must learn and adapt to new technologies. With the advent of electronic vehicles (EV), for example, drivers of buses or passenger cars will need to understand the diagnostic data that sensor-filled vehicles provide onboard. EV driver tasks have changed from checking water and fuel levels to understanding how to maximize battery use. Likewise, instead of being experts with coolants and filters, service technicians need to be more adept at handling automotive software applications, especially diagnostic software that identify parts that need replacement. Of course, in the case of autonomous cars, drivers are no longer needed.

Examples of automotive skills required

	Skills needed in internal combustion engine vehicles	Skills needed in electric vehicles
Drivers	Drive; check water and fuel to run engine	Drive; understand onboard diagnostic data provided by smart sensors; Understand how to maximize battery use
Service technicians	General service: changing filters, check/replace coolant	Update software, run diagnostics to identify parts that need replacement or recalibration. Understand automotive electronics and automotive software applications

Source: Author. Based on Karra (2020).

In manufacturing, machine operators need to understand the basics of machine programming and remote maintenance to run diagnostics using big data or do 3D printing. Those with more sophisticated knowledge of artificial intelligence and other software applications are also needed. In sales, digital trade specialists need an effective online sales pitch. But there will always be a need for soft skills such as communication, decision making, and negotiating capabilities.

Among the skills and knowledge under high demand in technology-driven sectors are engineering, computer science, programming, and complex data analytics (math/statistics). In the digital economy, there is also a particularly acute shortage for workers with problem-solving skills that can integrate applications and systems (Frederick, Bamber, and Cho 2018). Sometimes, these skills need to be practiced creatively, with business acumen, as well as soft skills to rise to the C-suite cited earlier.

Source: Karra (2020); Frederick, Bamber and Cho (2018)

often needed to grow in specific value chain segments. In the Philippines, manufacturing engineers are quick to work abroad because of higher wages, which affects the country's ability to attract MNCs to make more advanced products locally (Sturgeon et al. 2016). Similarly, in the EV value chain, having enough people with the needed technical and software capabilities can spell the difference between high- or low-value participation in the EV GVC.

Innovation policies and human capital development must be supported

What can governments and the private sector do to alleviate the shortage of qualified labor needed to upgrade technology-driven value chains? First, both the private sector and government need to work together. Private sector involvement allows governments to better understand the transforming technological landscape, what the future economy will look like, as well as the corresponding skills required in the workplace. Government and business must together understand the skills needed now and in the future to better guide a person's career or training decisions. Because skills can quickly become obsolete, education systems must continually refresh curricula to adapt to future job requirements. Currently, for example, there is ample need for training in coding, AI skills, as well as soft skills, creative problem solving, critical thinking, and collaboration. These can be bridged in the short term, either through short courses or hands-on training; or in the long-term through the educational system adjustments. University partnerships with the private sector are also important. Businesses can work with academic institutions and specify the skills they need so university curricula and training can be regularly updated. As part of the partnership, companies can provide paid internships to expose students to the nature of industry work and thus help focus their skills acquisition.

Governments can provide more funding for doctoral students involved in research as well as attract those teaching at universities abroad to return and share their knowledge in their home country. They can provide R&D incentives through entrepreneurships, providing generous tax rebates and/or grants.

Companies can also have targeted upskilling and reskilling programs as long-term investments (Kovacs-Ondreikovic et al. 2019). In technology industries where digital capabilities are increasingly being developed, in-house training is essential. Support, including financial, for acquiring skills by employees from third party education providers, whether online or in-person, should also be encouraged. Government incentives for internal employee upskilling can help companies do more. Strack, et al. (2019) of the Boston Consulting Group suggest having an individual learning account—akin to a portable provident fund—from which individuals can draw to pay for training or upskilling and receive certifications from third-party providers, with individuals, companies, and the government all contributing. This is worth exploring.

Government-private sector collaboration is critical in the policy discovery process

Besides what government and private sector partnerships can do for training human capital, it is also important to unify government policies that promote innovation. Private sector involvement is crucial because industry and innovation policies often go beyond public sector competencies while the private sector usually has a more in-depth understanding of what is needed. For example, governments need to appreciate how the IoT is changing the way data are collected and used. They need to be able to promulgate appropriate data policies, including cross-border data flows, that allow industries to grow and at the same time respect data privacy and security. Blockchain and digital ledger technology require open and voluntary interoperability of standards—another policy need that must be better understood. Better use of financial technology requires financial inclusion to grow, but it also requires proactive government effort and support to curb financial scams and cybercrime that can disrupt payment systems.

Innovation policies also take time to deliver results, often exceeding the length of electoral cycles (Radosevic 2017). Yet, political support is just as important as expanding the technological base. Private sector involvement can help sustain political support for innovation policies and projects. They can pressure the government to work on better innovation policy management which, unlike other government policies, requires interdepartmental and intersectoral collaboration. It requires human capital training and talent retention along with budget support, government investment, and appropriate laws and regulations. For example, in testing new technologies such as AI in cars or in fintech, governments have the wherewithal to create regulatory sandboxes, providing a limited space for innovators to test technology in the market without endangering financial stability (in the case of fintech) or lives and traffic (in the case of autonomous vehicles).

If governments are not tightly bound by fiscal constraints, public research investments should be made. Government-funded R&D tends to focus more on big-picture inventions that may take longer but can benefit entire industries, unlike specific business-funded research that has less economy-wide payoffs.

Protecting intellectual property rights and easing registration for patent protection are also incentives for innovation. Governments should invest in building academic and public sector capacity in patent examinations. They can also support regional initiatives such as the ASEAN Patent Examination Co-operation that facilitate registration across multiple jurisdictions.

Technology is changing GVCs. Low-skilled labor will no longer offer strong competitive advantage for developing economies that want to increase their value participation in GVCs. The automotive and E&E sector case studies in this chapter show examples of skills that may become obsolete in transformed GVCs, and highlight trends that could upend ASEAN's earlier comparative advantages in specific parts of the value chain. Improving the core determinants of investment growth such as infrastructure and connectivity remain universal for continued growth in GVC participation. But a critical set of technological skills is increasingly required. Government and private sector partnerships can upskill employees, bolster human capital development, and promote and sustain innovation policies.

References

AlixPartners. 2021. *Shortages Related to Semiconductors to Cost the Auto Industry Billions*. https://www.alixpartners.com/media-center/press-releases/press-release-shortages-related-to-semiconductors-to-cost-the-auto-industry-210-billion-in-revenues-this-year-says-new-alixpartners-forecast/.

ASEAN-Japan Centre. 2021. *Paper 13: Global Value Chains in ASEAN: Electronics*. Tokyo: ASEAN-Japan Centre.

Autor, D., D. Mindell, and E. Reynolds. 2020. *The Work of the Future: Building Better Jobs in an Age of Intelligent Machines*. https://workofthefuture.mit.edu/wp-content/uploads/2021/01/2020-Final-Report4.pdf.

Bamber, P., J. Daly, S. Frederick, and G. Gereffi. 2018. The Philippines: A Sequential Approach to Upgrading in Manufacturing Value Chains. In *Development with Global Value Chains*. eds. Dev Nathan, Meenu Tewari, and Sandip Sarkar, eds. 102–131.

Burkacky, O., S. Lingemann, and K. Pototzky. 2021. Coping with the Auto-Semiconductor Shortage: Strategies for Success. *McKinsey & Company*. https://www.mckinsey.com/industries/automotive-and-assembly/ our-insights/coping-with-the-auto-semiconductor-shortage- strategies-for-success. March 21.

Campbell, P., P. Waldmeir, and K. Inagaki. 2018. The Unlikely Partnerships that are Shaping the Car Industry. *Financial Times*. 18 January. https://www.ft.com/content/fd96456a-fc2b-11e7-9b32-d7d59aace167.

Carnell, R., and I. Pang. 2021. *The Cost of Greening Asia's Transport and Generation Capacity*. ING. https://think.ing.com/uploads/reports/H_Asias_race_to_net_zero_carbon_060921_h.pdf.

Chuan-Fong, S., E. K. Kraemer, and J. Dedrick. 2007. Research Note—Determinants of Country-Level Investment in Information Technology. *Management Science*. No. 53(3): 521–528.

Conigliaro, D. 2019. Automotive, *This is How Employment in the Car Industry is Changing*. https://www.morningfuture.com/en/2019/04/15/automotive-innovation-change-work/.

Deloitte. 2019. Caution ahead: Transformation and disruption for automotive suppliers. *Deloitte Insights*. https://www2.deloitte.com/content/dam/ insights/us/articles/6303_Transformation-and-disruption-for- automotive-suppliers/DI_Caution-ahead.pdf.

————. 2021. *Full Speed Ahead: Supercharging Electric Mobility in Southeast Asia*. https://www2.deloitte.com/content/dam/ Deloitte/sg/Documents/strategy/sea-strategy-operations-full- speed-ahead-report.pdf.

Deloitte Consulting. 2022. *2022 Global Automotive Consumer Study*. January. https://www2.deloitte.com/global/en/pages/consumer-business/articles/global-automotive-consumer-study.html.

Duke University Center on Globalization, Governance and Competitiveness (Duke CGGC). 2016. *The Philippines in the electronics & electrical global value chain*. May. https://scholars.duke.edu/display/pub1138334.

Dyer, S. 2021. If You Build Them, They will Drive. *American Chamber of Commerce Shanghai Magazine*. https://docs.alixpartners.com/view/485312451/.

Eisenstein, P. 2019. Electric Vehicles Pose 'Real Risk' for Autoworkers, With Fewer Parts—and Jobs—Required. *NBC News*. https://www.nbcnews. com/business/autos/electric-vehicles-pose-real-risk-autoworkers- halving-number-people-required-n1060426.

Frederick, S., P. Bamber, L. Brun, J. Cho, G. Gereffi., and J. Lee. 2017. *Korea |in Global Value Chains: Pathways for Industrial Transformation*. Korea: Korea Institute for Industrial Economics and Trade and Duke University Global Value Chains Center. September.

Frederick, S., P. Bamber, L. Brun, and J. Cho. 2018. *The Digital Economy, Global Value Chains, and Asia*. Korea: Korea Institute for Industrial Economics and Trade and Duke University Global Value Chains Center. December.

Heppelmann, J. 2014. How the Internet of Things could Transform the Value Chain. *McKinsey & Company*. https://www.mckinsey.com/industries/technology-media-and-telecommunications/our-insights/how-the-internet-of-things-could-transform-the-value-chain.

Karra, S. 2020. *Technology–Changing the Landscape of Skills Requirement in the Automotive Industry*. https://www.nationalskillsnetwork.in/technology-changing-the-landscape-of-skill-requirement-in-the-automotive-industry/.

Kleinhans, JP., and N. Baisakova. 2020. *The Semiconductor Value Chain: A Technology Primer for Policymakers*. Stiftung Neue Verantwortung. October.

Kovacs-Ondreikovic, O., R. Strack, P. Antebi, A.L. Gobernado, and E. Lyle, 2019. *Decoding Global Trends in Upskilling and Reskilling*. US: Boston Consulting Group. https://www.bcg.com/publications/2019/decoding-global-trends-upskilling-reskilling. November.

Leung, S. 2022. Vietnam Wires into Global Electronics. *East Asia Forum*. https://www.eastasiaforum.org/2022/10/25/vietnam-wires-into-global-electronics/. October 25.

Liew J.T. 2020. Where are the Malaysian Players in the Semiconductor Value Chain? *The Edge Malaysia*. https://www.theedgemarkets. com/article/cover-story-where-are-malaysian-players- semiconductor-value-chain.

McKinsey Global Institute (MGI). 2015. *The Internet of Things: Mapping the value beyond the hype.*

O'Flynn, S. 2020. An ICE-y Road to an Electric Future. *Automotive World Magazine*. https://www.automotiveworld.com/articles/an-ice-y- road-to-an-electric-future/.

Organisation for Economic Co-operation and Development. 2016. Where to Locate Innovative Activities? Does Co-Location Matter? *Policy Note. Directorate for Science, Technology and Innovation*. December.

Priddle, A. 2021. What Happened with the Semiconductor Chip Shortage— and How and When the Auto Industry will Emerge. Motor Trend. https://www.motortrend.com/news/automotive-car-industry- semiconductor-chip-shortage-reasons-solution/.

Radosevic, S. 2017. Assessing EU smart specialization policy in a comparative perspective. In *Advances in the Theory and Practice of Smart Specialization, eds.* Radosevic, et al. Academic Press.

Rodrik, D. 2018. New Technologies, Global Value Chains, and the Developing Economies. *Pathways for Prosperity Commission Background Paper Series No. 1*. Oxford. United Kingdom: Pathways for Prosperity Commission.

Schroer, A. 2022. Artificial Intelligence in Cars: Examples of AI in the Auto Industry. *Builtin*. https://builtin.com/artificial-intelligence/ artificial- intelligence-automotive-industry.

Sierzchula, W., S. Bakker, K. Maat, and B. van Wee. 2014. The Influence of Financial Incentives and Other Socio-Economic Factors on Electric Vehicle Adoption. *Energy Policy*. Vol 68. May. pp. 183–194.

Strack, R., P. Antebi, N. Kataeva, O. Kovacs-Ondrejkovic, A. L. Gobernado, and D. Welch. 2019. Decoding Digital Talent. *Boston Consulting Group*. https://www.bcg.com/publications/2019/ decoding-digital- talent. May.

Sturgeon, T., S. Frederick, J. Daly, P. Bamber, and G. Gereffi. 2016. *The Philippines in the Automotive Global Value Chain*. May. https://www.researchgate.net/publication/305000071_The_ Philippines_in_the_Automotive_Global_Value_Chain.

Vittori, C., G. Evans, and M. Fini. 2021. Electrical Steel—Another Temporary Supply Chain Shortage or a Threat to OEMs' Electrification Plans? *IHS Market Research and Analysis*. https://ihsmarkit.com/ research-analysis/electrical-steel-another- temporary-supply-chain- shortage.html?hsid=be0ebe65-3385-48e3- a574-3521ccea5cf9.

Wayland, M. 2019. Automakers Investing Billions in Partnerships as Industry Races toward Autonomous and Electric Vehicles. *CNBC*. 7 December. https://www.cnbc.com/2019/12/07/gm-lg-venture-adds-to-multibillion-dollar-partnerships-on-evs-avs.html

World Bank. 2015. Philippine Economic Update: Making Growth Work for the Poor. *World Bank Report*. No. 93-530 PH. https://www.worldbank.org/content/dam/Worldbank/document/EAP/Philippines/PEU%20Jan%202015%20PDF.pdf.

World Economic Forum. 2020. *The Future of Jobs Report*. https://www3.weforum.org/docs/WEF_Future_of_Jobs_2020.pdf.

5

Decarbonization and Global Value Chains in ASEAN

Sindhu Bharathi, Sumathi Chakravarthy, and Badri Narayanan Gopalakrishnan

Introduction

Many of the world's ecosystems are on the verge of extinction. Climate-related threats to health, livelihoods, food security, water availability, human security, and economic growth are increasing due to global warming. The impact of climate change and its solutions are heavily linked to sustainable development, which aims to balance social well-being, economic prosperity, and environmental conservation. The damage caused by human-driven climate change is determined by both its magnitude and potential irreversibility. A decline would harm the economic well-being of countries that thrive on biodiversity and ecosystems. Thus, it is imperative we reverse this trend.

Globally, net-zero transition and decarbonization have become an integral part of every country's economic growth and development strategy. This is both due to the tangible impact climate change has on more severe weather events and other disasters across the world, as well as a resolute consensus among nearly all countries to limit further degradation.

Lamb et al. (2022) shows that while greenhouse gas (GHG) emissions continued to rise between 1970 and 2018, 24 countries managed to reduce their carbon dioxide (CO_2) and GHG emissions. The list includes several developed countries like the United States (US), the United Kingdom (UK), Switzerland, and the European Union (EU) members. Globally, 119 countries are committed to the climate change plans of the United Nations Development Programme (UNDP). Among members of the Association of Southeast Asian Nations (ASEAN), Singapore reduced its GHG emission by 19.6% between 2010 and 2020.

There is also an evolving concern over how climate actions may affect economies, given several instances of forced resource reallocation to reduce emissions. Prominent examples include a move from fossil fuels to renewable energy that may more severely disrupt an economy dependent on fossil fuel exports.

Nevertheless, there are at least two reasons to welcome this transition even from a purely economic perspective. First, there is really no choice. Any failure to reduce emissions will likely further aggravate climate change and consequent disasters—natural, economic, and social—that can cause massive deaths and injuries. A World Meteorological Organization (WMO) Atlas of Mortality and Economic Losses from Weather, Climate and Water Extremes (1970–2019) shows that climate change and extreme weather accounted for 50% of all disasters and 45% of associated deaths.

In addition, 74% of reported economic losses are due to climate change and any disasters that followed (WMO 2021).

Second, renewable energy could lead to an entirely new economic system able to make up for the jobs and income lost as fossil fuel production is replaced. Several initiatives have been taken, such as the US's Inflation Reduction Act and India's Production Linked Incentives scheme to boost green production by increasing subsidies and providing tax incentives to encourage investments that enhance research and development. While these schemes definitely promote green development, they may also distort investment decisions and trade globally, which is why several measures are opposed by other countries.

The EU has come up with a Carbon Border Adjustment Mechanism that specifically focuses on taxing imports based on carbon intensity. This is to incentivize both green trade globally and green sectors within EU economies. Some of these measures have already been challenged within the World Trade Organization (WTO), given the trade distortions that can result from these policies.

The positive and negative disruptions to global trade from climate actions come on top of recent trends against free trade. Starting from the UK's 2020 departure from the EU (Brexit) to recent import tariff hikes by the US and the People's Republic of China (PRC)—along with many other countries—the world retreated into a protectionist mood deviating from a decades-long movement toward freer trade. Even before this happened, the rules-based transparent multilateral trading system of the WTO suffered from an existential crisis, given the greater proliferation of regional trade agreements and some plurilateral ones.

With these developments, an already complex web of global value chains (GVCs) became even more complicated due to these constantly changing incentives, cost structures, and disruptions globally, shaped by both evolving climate change strategies and shifts in trade policy.

Given this background, the relationship between GVCs and the green economy itself has become increasingly complex and interesting. On one hand, the fragmented cost-efficient production process that defines these GVCs may play an important role in shaping the future of the green economy globally. On the other hand, meticulously crafted and implemented climate strategies can help mitigate disaster risks that can in turn create more robust GVCs. This is possible as the ripple effects from disasters affecting one GVC node may be outweighed by the resilience built up by the stronger, more flexible GVC diversification these policies helped create.

Since international climate discussions began in earnest, global emissions have risen dramatically. Moralizing about climate change resulted in bold Paris Climate Agreement targets, such as limiting warming to 1.5 degrees Celsius (2.7 degrees Fahrenheit) above pre-industrial levels. But beyond the platitudes and targets, the real problem is to act urgently to significantly reduce GHG emissions. This requires rewiring incentives for governments and firms to change their behavior and decarbonize the global economy. Decarbonizing supply chains is one important way businesses can put zero-emission promises into action.

Over the past 10–20 years, the possibility of decarbonizing transportation, buildings, and energy has greatly increased. Potential zero-emission technologies such as wind and solar power, electric transportation systems, zero-energy buildings, and advanced biofuels have developed rapidly as markets expanded, with the co-benefits of mitigation generally understood (Intergovernmental Panel on Climate Change 2014). Having recognized the long-term ill effects and damage from hazardous emissions, most countries have channeled their efforts, resources, and investments toward decarbonization and zero emissions. Carbon pricing, as experts propose, is the most cost-effective way to drastically reduce GHG emissions (Stiglitz et al. 2017).

Many factors influence the amount of GHG emissions generated through international trade. These include an economy's size, sectoral composition of foreign trade, level of participation in GVCs, mode of transportation used for imports and exports, and the energy efficiency of production processes. All are influenced by environmental and energy policies. GHG emissions emanate from the production, transportation, distribution, and consumption of traded goods and services. Pollutants are created during the production and transit of these goods and services. Embedded GHG emissions are all indirect—from the production and transportation of manufactured inputs to the final products or services consumed—in addition to the direct power used during manufacturing. When the exporting country's GHG emissions are less than what the importing economy would have released by producing the same goods and services, the amount of trade-related emissions can still be less than the importing economy's had the product been produced domestically. An economy with a lower share of imported GHG emissions in its exports is less involved in GVCs yet has large GHG emissions embedded in domestic production. The carbon emissions buried within a product include direct GHG emissions from final production, assembly, packaging, and shipment to consumers. On the other hand, economies that rely on exported commodities and services as inputs for domestic production will likely be net importers of GHG emissions. As it turns out, in recent years the international carbon emission transfer from industrialized to developing countries has fallen due to improved energy efficiency. Emissions from a product as basic as chocolate cookies, for example, come from a variety of sources. The energy used in preparing, baking, and packing the cookies, as well as their delivery to clients, creates GHG emissions. Similarly, the inputs used to make these ingredients—for example, changing land use to cultivate cocoa beans, fertilizers for wheat, energy for grinding and toasting cocoa, among others—all emit greenhouse gases.

Analyzing just how dependent we are on these engrained yet destructive services require models that stress the importance of deep decarbonization, a net-zero carbon footprint, environmental sustainability, and social inclusion. They must assess the broad economic impact from a global, regional, domestic, and local perspective.

The Paris Agreement was a landmark in that, for the first time, a binding agreement was signed to bring all nations together to combat climate change and adapt to its inevitable effects. It was adopted at the 21st Conference of the Parties to the United Nations Framework Convention on Climate Change by 196 signatories in Paris, 12 December 2015. It entered into force 4 November 2016. The policies and investments resulting from the agreement will reshape national economies, economic development, and GVCs. To meet its global warming targets, countries aim to stop GHG emission growth as soon as possible to create a climate-neutral world by mid-century.

Governments are obliged to report their progress in cutting GHG emissions, adopt adaptation measures, and provide help under the enhanced transparency framework beginning in 2024. Under the Global Stocktake framework, most countries are only now beginning to work toward meeting their new CO_2 emission reduction goals.

Under the unconditional Paris pledges for GHG reductions, ASEAN faces an emissions gap of around 400 metric tons of CO_2 equivalent ($MtCO_2e$). This means the region must reduce emissions by 11% of what current forecasts estimate by 2030. Under the more ambitious conditional pledges, the emissions gap is about 900 $MtCO_2e$, or a need to reduce emissions by 24% before 2030 (Paltsev et al. 2018).

This chapter attempts to measure the impact of emission targets and reduction plans on economic and global value chain parameters.

A computable general equilibrium (CGE) model is constructed under the Global Trade Analysis Project (GTAP) framework. The standard GTAP model is a multiregional, multisector model that accounts for linkages between economic agents—including households, governments, and the rest of the world. The GTAP-electricity (E)-Power model is linked to the GTAP-value-added (VA) model to study how reducing carbon emissions may affect GVCs.[1] The potential for renewable energy to substitute for emission-intensive sources is also examined given the Paris Agreement goals and commitments.

The latest available GTAP database covers 141 countries and 65 sectors up to 2014. To make the model more usable, it is calibrated and scaled to 2020 using gross domestic product (GDP) data from the International Monetary Fund (IMF), other global sources, and national statistics.

The impact of decarbonization on GVCs are estimated under two scenarios: (i) a business-as-usual (BAU) scenario where each country reduces carbon emissions from 2020 to 2030 by the same amount they did from 2010 to 2020 (or the same 2020 amount, if emissions rose)[2]; and (ii) a nationally determined contribution (NDC) scenario which estimates the economic and value chain impact of reducing emissions as specified by NDC targets (using a 2010 constructed baseline).

The method aims to take advantage of the features and abilities inherent across the GTAP-E, GTAP-Power, and GTAP-VA model frameworks. It came out of an extensive review of existing models to analyze how the energy–environment–economy is connected. Policy insights are determined based on the implications of a decline in emissions on various macroeconomic parameters like GDP, sector output, trade, employment, and value-added components of trade.

The BAU scenario shows that should ASEAN economies maintain the same level of emissions between 2020 and 2030, GDP will increase slightly (by $194 million). The NDC model shows that achieving NDC targets will cost ASEAN members much more ($50.1 billion). Rennert et al. (2022) estimate that the social cost of carbon is $185 per $MtCO_2e$. ASEAN emissions

---

[1]   The GTAP-E-Power model is an electricity-detailed economy-wide model which combines GTAP-E—the energy-environment version of the GTAP model—and the GTAP-Power model built to analyze the economic impact of reduced carbon emissions. The GTAP-VA model—also an extension of the standard GTAP model—decomposes traded products into their value-added content. By linking the GTAP-E-Power model to the GTAP-VA model, the impact of reduced emissions on GVCs can be analyzed as the GTAP-VA model separates the value-added components of gross trade.

[2]   Data on ASEAN CO_2 emissions show that only Singapore reduced emissions (by 19.6%) between 2010 and 2020. The rest increased emissions, with countries like Cambodia doubling its GHG emissions and the Lao People's Democratic Republic (Lao PDR) increasing emissions tenfold.

were 1,651.9 MtCO$_2$e in 2020, meaning the aggregate social cost from carbon emissions was about $306 billion. When countries achieve their NDC targets, the social cost savings will outweigh the estimated GDP loss of $255 billion. Investments in renewables reduce investments available elsewhere, particularly those energy intensive. The results of the GTAP-VA model shows that meeting NDC targets could cost ASEAN economies $165.2 billion in domestic value-added and $1.65 billion in foreign value-added.

Though the capital cost of transitioning to renewable energy sources might seem high, the long-term benefits and savings in terms of social costs are far higher. Also, as these technologies mature, their efficiency improves, and capital costs decline.

The following sections present a literature review, methodology, results, and analysis of the chapter study.

Literature Review

There are extensive and persuasive studies, data, and research on climate change—its causes, related hazards, and the need for mitigating risks. GHG emissions from fossil fuels are one of the main causes of climate change. Thus, it is useful to examine the literature to better understand and analyze the impact of greenhouse gas emissions, climate change mitigation strategies, the growth of renewables, and related economic issues.

A report by the International Energy Agency (IEA) (2020) says that, to reduce emissions, trading in biofuels and hydrogen may become a better choice for long-distance trade logistics. Now is the time for countries to adopt more efficient and innovative production methods by diffusing lower-carbon goods and services.

Most ASEAN economies are developing countries with over 95% of firms categorized as micro, small, and medium-sized enterprises (MSMEs), adding to the emission problem. Generally, these MSMEs cannot meet the high investment costs needed to join low-carbon projects. Also, strong competition leaves those who want to invest scrambling to countries with flexible climate change policies. As a result, sustainability standards are frequently compromised by countries as they attempt to attract more investments. Another barrier hampering many developing countries from greening their economies is the lack of available information on costs, inputs, technology, the benefits of decarbonization, and sustainability (Marchi and Zanoni 2017).

A goal of the study by Rasiah et al. (2018) was to assess the repercussions of climate change on economic growth based on two scenarios: (i) no action, and (ii) the combined NDCs presented by ASEAN members to the United Nations Framework Convention on Climate Change (UNFCCC) using the Regional Integrated Model of Climate and the Economy. The study evaluated the efficiency of ASEAN members' NDCs in reducing climate change while maintaining economic development. The first scenario considers the temperature impact based on BAU for ASEAN until 2060—no additional interventions in the climate regime. The second incorporates interventions required by ASEAN members to achieve their NDCs. The BAU scenario found that atmospheric carbon concentrations in parts per million (ppm) will decline from 390 ppm in 2010 to 287 ppm between 2035 and 2045 before increasing to 351 ppm in 2060. Carbon concentration follows the BAU pattern from 2010 to 2045, with 390 ppm in 2010, and 287 ppm in 2035 and 2045. In the best-case scenario, however, carbon concentrations rise to a lower 329 ppm in 2060. The impact of the NDCs on carbon concentration is minimal because it is only 6.3% less than the BAU scenarios by 2060.

The Global Value Chain Development Report lists the four important channels associated with GVCs that add to rising global emissions emissions (Solingen, Meng, and Xu 2021). First, GVC supply and production have longer distances to travel between source, production, and distribution networks. Longer transportation means greater emissions. The study estimates that these extra emissions are responsible for 3.5% of global emissions (Cristea et al. 2013). The second important aspect of GVC emissions is the rise in energy use due to backward linkages. The third is the movement of production facilities to countries with more flexible climate change regulations. These facilities also add to carbon leakages and undermine the purpose of having climate mitigation targets. The fourth channel is the waste generated from extra production to maximize benefit from the GVC cost advantage. Around 57.4 million metric tons of electronic waste was generated worldwide in 2021, up by 21% from 2020 (Geneva Environment Network 2021).

According to an IEA assessment, carbon capture, utilization, and storage can help cut emissions and fulfill ASEAN's climate targets. The Scope 3 Standard of the Greenhouse Gas Protocol analyzes the value chain emissions of a company—from the raw material purchases to finished product sales. Those that focus on Scope 3 emissions and use cleaner energy will soon have the upper hand in GVCs (Greenhouse Gas Protocol 2021).

Climate change creates the most damage to the environment, and energy consumption is one of the main factors contributing to the changing climate. Researchers and studies point out the causal relationship between economic growth, CO_2 emissions, and environmental impact. ASEAN has been an epicenter for economic development and population growth, increasing its energy dependency and consumption. An analysis of the evolution of economic growth, energy consumption, and carbon emissions—and their interlinkages—was done using the Cointegration and Causality model. Energy consumption, GDP, population, and CO_2 emissions are the main variables used. The study by Chontanavat (2019) uses annual data (1971 to 2015) from the IEA database for Brunei Darussalam, Indonesia, Malaysia, Myanmar, the Philippines, Singapore, Thailand, and Viet Nam (Cambodia and the Lao People's Democratic Republic [Lao PDR] are excluded due to lack of data). The results are obtained from three tests—unit root, cointegration, and causality tests. The cointegration results show there is a long-term relationship between energy consumption and economic activities and CO_2 emissions. The causality analysis results show a unidirectional causality running from economic growth to energy consumption. As a result, policies that reduce energy consumption can help reduce CO_2 emissions without affecting economic growth.

Improving the environmental quality damaged by human activity is urgent. Fluctuating CO_2 gas emissions represents this shift in environmental quality. The purpose of another study (Hariani, Febriyastuti, and Tamonsang 2022) was to examine the impact of economic growth, increasing urban populations, and high-tech imports and exports on CO_2 emissions in five ASEAN economies (Indonesia, Malaysia, Myanmar, Thailand, and Viet Nam) from 2011 to 2018. It uses panel data for econometric regressions using the Chow test and Hausman test. The classical assumption test was done to check the credibility of the data and model including the normality test, multicollinearity test, heteroscedasticity test, and autocorrelation test. The results showed that the city population has positive and significant effects on CO_2 emissions—while independent variables like a growing economy, high-tech imports, and exports do not significantly affect CO_2 emissions.

Another report, by Zhang et al. (2021), shows that the construction and building sectors are critical to meeting emission objectives as they contribute significantly to GHG emissions. Shifting toward zero energy buildings (ZEBs) remains the most effective way to lower damaging emissions. A comparison of ZEB advances over the previous decade was conducted for the top five Asia-Pacific Economic Cooperation (APEC) members—Canada, Japan, the PRC, the Republic of Korea (ROK), and the US. Their carbon-neutral objectives for 2050 will substantially affect future building and construction. It suggests that government investment, market financing, and raising construction standards to net-zero energy consumption can help.

One way to lower emissions is to switch to renewable energy, reducing dependency on fossil fuels. In the past, renewables have generally been more expensive. But new clean energy technologies are cutting costs and helping countries move away from fossil fuels.

ASEAN is committed to covering its forecast 50% increase in energy demand over the current decade by increasingly using renewables—it is targeting 23% in renewable primary energy by 2025, up from 9.4% in 2014. However, current policies, including those under discussion, will only be able to reach slightly less than 17% renewables, a critical six percentage points below what is needed. For this reason, the International Renewable Energy Agency (IRENA) and the ASEAN Centre for Energy (ACE) agreed to work together on a study using IRENA's REmap analytical tools to generate a Renewable Energy Outlook—to supplement the January 2016 4th ASEAN Energy Outlook (AEO4). The study explores the feasibility of using renewable energy technologies across all ASEAN energy systems to meet the 23% renewable share (IRENA and ACE 2016). It also assesses costs and expenditures, environmental benefits, and some major barriers to scaling up renewables. The research was first presented in September 2016 at the 34th ASEAN Ministers of Energy Meeting in Nay Pyi Taw, Myanmar. ASEAN members agreed with the report's conclusions—that the target is attainable and growing dependence on renewables will lower overall costs, provide for cleaner cities, and ensure a more secure and strong energy supply. They also agreed to create solid national frameworks to meet the renewable energy target on time.

Another ASEAN study found there was widespread belief that renewable energy technologies are not competitive with conventional technology, working against its widespread deployment. The study wanted to raise awareness, emphasizing that with advances in technology and increased availability, the costs of renewable energy have made it far more competitive (ASEAN Centre for Energy 2016). The research analyzed the levelized cost of electricity (LCOE) from renewable energy for selected ASEAN members and recommended policies to further boost competitiveness. It focused on solar photovoltaics (PV), biomass, and hydropower. These technologies were chosen because they matched (i) resource potential, (ii) government goals, (iii) legal and regulatory frameworks, and (iv) energy capacity added over the previous 3 years. The study examined 64 projects from six ASEAN countries. It estimated the LCOE of these projects from project and technical costs such as installation, operating and maintenance charges, and capacity factors. When compared to biomass and hydropower projects, solar PV plants had the highest regional installation costs. The regional average for operating and maintenance expenditures for biomass power was greatest while PV plants had the lowest. A hydroelectric project typically costs twice as much as a solar PV plant. The regional average capacity factor for solar PV projects was lowest, while biomass power plants were greatest. Solar PV plants had the highest LCOE regional mean value ($0.22 per kilowatt-hour [kWh]) while hydropower had the lowest ($0.044 per kWh).

ASEAN faces the fundamental challenge of satisfying rising demand safely, cost effectiveness, and over the long term. Liu et al. (2019) focus on ASEAN to gain a better understanding of how and to what extent three pillars—strengthening regional energy commerce, ensuring investment in renewable energy, and increasing energy efficiency—can help strengthen energy security in developing countries. It examined bilateral trade in the two most traded fossil energy sources—crude oil and natural gas—taking account of six energy trade factors. It found that the two most important elements in bilateral trade were distance and economic scale. It looked at the factors influencing energy commerce in terms of energy efficiency, renewable energy deployment, and economic integration. The study wanted to find important empirical patterns associated with global energy trade and their implications for ASEAN. It used an augmented gravity model (Tinbergen 1962) to incorporate sustainability, affordability, and secure supply into the concept of energy security. It analyzed annual data from 440 countries (218 energy-exporting and 222 energy-importing) collected over 22 years (1995–2016). The findings were used to offer policy recommendations to help ASEAN formulate future energy security plans.

The Paris Agreement led many economies to seek decarbonization— ways to reduce energy intensity and reduce CO_2 emissions. APEC, which accounts for 60% of world energy demand, wants to reduce energy intensity by 45% over 30 years from 2005 to 2035 and increase use of renewable energy between 2010 and 2030 (Zhang et al. 2021).

Consumers have become more conscious of their environment and have begun to favor companies that use stringent measures to combat climate change and protect the planet. This shift led more firms and governments worldwide to push policies like carbon-reduction targets and green legislation to meet decarbonization targets and climate goals. The EU plans to become climate neutral by 2050 under its European Green Deal. Another initiative is carbon pricing, already adopted by nearly 40 countries.

Handayani et al. (2022) assess ways to reach net-zero emissions by 2050, focusing on ASEAN using the Low Emissions Analysis Platform (LEAP). It considers two scenarios: first, the Renewable Energy Scenario, which follows ASEAN member's renewable energy targets, their respective NDCs, and power development plans; and second, the Net Zero Emissions Scenario where ASEAN goes beyond current NDCs to reach net zero by 2050. The LEAP simulations show GHG emissions rising to a peak in 2029, before declining gradually to zero by 2050. The emission abatement cost is $16 per $MtCO_2e$ in the renewable energy scenario and $12 per $MtCO_2e$ in the net-zero scenario.

Some research offers insights on how best to mitigate the effects of climate change.

Overland et al. (2021) access ASEAN's climate-energy nexus using a multisectoral qualitative analysis and policy integration analysis for climate mitigation. The study compares strengths and weaknesses of various sectors of an economy. It finds ASEAN's mitigation work inadequate given the threat members face. The most important reason is that their NDCs are too low, with renewable energy holding just a modest share of the energy mix. A move toward electric vehicle (EV) use will reduce micro-level pollution and reduce environmental costs due to GHG internal combustion engine emissions. While the challenges are by no means insurmountable, there is only a narrow window of opportunity before the economic, reputational, ecological, and political consequences of climate change become unmanageable.

The policy brief by Arino et al. (2022) discusses the ASEAN State of Climate Change Report (ASCCR), which lists several mitigation objectives: (i) achieve net-zero GHG emissions this century, and (ii) reach peak GHG emissions by 2030 to ensure net zero is met on time. However, the 6th ASEAN Energy Outlook shows target discrepancies. In 2018, fossil fuel combustion accounted for three-fifths of ASEAN GHG emissions, with land use accounting for the remaining two-fifths. This necessitates a change in energy and land use to meet the goals of the Paris Agreement and Climate Action Plan. Some of the important initiatives to do this by 2050 include:

- raising targets after meeting the near-term ASEAN Plan of Action for Energy Cooperation 2016–2025 renewable energy target;
- developing a strategy for achieving net-zero energy and land-use systems;
- enhancing the many co-benefits of a clean energy transition;
- tracking and resolving the inverse link between energy and emission intensity reductions; and

- increasing synergies between mitigation and adaptation actions for adjusting land-use.

Finally, Ota and Akagi (2021) examines Japan's proposed mitigation measures since the UNFCCC entered into force in 1994—intending to reduce GHG emissions by 26% from 2013 levels by 2030 and achieve a decarbonized society by 2050. The Ministry of Environment introduced its Zero Carbon City program, in which the mayor or local government set the goal of reaching net zero by 2050. As a result, 31 local governments in Japan's Kyushu prefecture are committed to a Zero Carbon City. To meet the target, they pursue programs to meet zero waste, the sustainable development goals (SDGs), catastrophe avoidance, and mitigation. However, some of the costs and obstacles they face are related to both measuring existing emissions and the unpredictability of future emissions. It is impossible to predict future city emission levels when technical innovation, energy conversion, and social change continually evolve. How far emissions will fall depends on national and global trends.

The extensive literature review thus far shows that GHG emissions are a major factor behind global climate change. ASEAN members are highly vulnerable due to their growing populations and continued economic growth. While the Paris Agreement encourages nations to shift to greener and cleaner energy sources, this cannot happen without continued regional and national government initiatives. Therefore, it is important to understand the economic costs and benefits of shifting to greener energy sources and the impact on GVCs.

Nihayah et al. (2022) studied carbon emissions in Indonesia to link CO_2 emissions, urbanization, and economic activity, and assess whether the pollution haven hypothesis is true (that foreign investors look for the cheapest location in terms of resources, labor, and flexible regulations). The study uses time-series data from 1971 to 2019 in a vector error correction model to determine the long- and short-run interplay using cointegration and the Granger causality approach. The results suggest a long-term relationship with CO_2 emissions, with unidirectional causality occurring from urbanization, economic growth, exports, and foreign direct investment to CO_2 emissions in the short term. Overall, the model concludes that the Paris Agreement will succeed if countries can transform their economies to net-zero carbon emissions.

Understanding the impact of energy-related environmental issues is critical. GTAP remains one of the most advanced quantitative top-down models that can cover these global economic issues.

The GTAP-E model is an advanced version of the standard GTAP model, incorporating the inter-fuel and fuel-factor substitution in the standard version. A review shows how the GTAP-E model is effective in energy-environment policy analysis and decision making. Do Dinh and Kim (2012) construct a general equilibrium model for evaluating energy policy using GTAP-E for Viet Nam. It simulates the impact of imposing a carbon tax for Viet Nam aggregating 17 sectors. Barbe (2017) estimates the effects of restricting coal consumption on coal exports and GHG emissions using a GTAP-E model. The study focuses on measuring how the overall impact of restricting coal consumption in the US affect foreign welfare and emission levels, as a restriction on US consumption would drive exports.

Siriwardana (2015) used the GTAP-E model to measure the economic and environmental impact of two free trade agreements Australia signed in 2014 with Japan and the Republic of Korea. The study simulates two scenarios: a free trade scenario that eliminates tariffs between the countries and a green trade scenario which also includes an emission trading scheme.

Based on all these studies, the model constructed in this chapter can capture the impact of a change in carbon emissions considering the Paris Agreement and other climate change policies on both economic parameters and GVC aspects by linking the GTAP-E-Power model and GTAP-VA model. By doing so, the costs of shifting to renewable sources by region and sector can be better understood, as well as the impact on GVCs due to the massive shift in energy sources.

Methodology

The standard GTAP framework CGE model can capture the impact on GVCs from policies that promote deep decarbonization, a zero-carbon footprint, and environmental sustainability. This widely used modeling approach was designed and developed by the Center for Global Trade Analysis in Purdue University (Hertel 1997). CGE models are preferred as they can capture interactions and linkages between economic agents, including households, governments, and the rest of the world.

The GTAP 10 database used here contains global data for 141 regions and countries, covering 65 sectors taken from country input–output tables along with international sources and national statistics up to 2014. Both models used—GTAP-E-Power and GTAP-VA—are extensions of the standard GTAP framework.

Modeling the nexus between energy, the environment, and trade is an integral part of applied economic modeling. GTAP-E models capture the economic impact of climate policies and the change in carbon emissions. The GTAP-E database integrates global energy data compiled by the IEA into the trade and input–output tables of the standard GTAP database.

Energy as an intermediate input in the standard model is a value-added input in the GTAP-E model. Also, GTAP-E allows for both alternative fuel substitutions and substitutions for factors like capital and labor that affect aggregate energy. On consumption, energy commodities in the GTAP-E model are separate from non-energy commodities and use different substitution elasticities. The GTAP-E model incorporates CO_2 emissions estimated by fuel type and user category for every region or country in the standard GTAP model. Thus, the model can be used to assess the impact of global, regional, and national climate policies, carbon mitigation policies, the imposition of carbon taxes, and other environmental policies.

Climate change policies and regulations try to partially or completely replace emission-intensive sources for generating electricity with better technologies or mechanisms. This requires elaborate, in-depth modeling and analysis of the electricity sector. The standard GTAP model sets up an aggregate representation of the sector, including fuel, capital, and other production inputs. The GTAP-Power model extends the standard GTAP model by disaggregating electricity into nine sectors—transmission, distribution, and seven base load technologies such as NuclearBL, CoalBL, GasBL, HydroBL, OilBL, WindBL, and OtherBL. It includes four peak load technologies covering GasP, OilP, HydroP, and SolarP. The problem with electricity is that supply must instantly rise to meet demand, which varies by season, work hours, day and night, for example. Coal power plants cannot instantly adjust to demand while gas or solar power can cover during peaks. Also, it is unrealistic to assume that solar or nuclear power can meet all power demand given their operational constraints. Thus, some generation is split into base- and peak-load technologies.

The GTAP-Power database covers 76 sectors (as opposed to 65 in the GTAP database). The GTAP-Power model allows substitution between various transmission, distribution, and generation technologies. The model accounts for sectoral differences as each differs in fuel efficiency and investment requirements.

The GTAP-E-Power model incorporates the best of both the GTAP-E and GTAP-Power models. It extends the GTAP-E model to disaggregate electricity into the nine sectors mentioned above. Thus, the model uses the GTAP-Power database in a CGE setting to account for emissions as well as substitutions between electricity-generating technologies. It uses direct electric power substitution as well as indirect substitutions of capital energy and energy fuel. It makes GTAP-E power sector outcomes and electricity capabilities clearer. Thus, the model has all the GTAP-E capabilities and can be used effectively in policies that affect climate change, carbon emissions, and other energy-related mechanisms.

The GTAP-Power database is aggregated into 41 economies, with the 76 sectors aggregated into 49. It retains overall database granularity.

Peters (2016a) shows how the GTAP-E-Power model offers greater capabilities and dimensions for modeling the electricity sector. It also accounts for substitution between fossil fuels and renewable energy sources through capital–energy substitution, unlike the GTAP-E model which accounts for substitution between coal and gas power sources.

Aggregation is also done using the GTAP-E database to merge emissions data and parameters into the model and map the electricity sector in the GTAP-E model to the 11 expanded sectors in the power database. As the latest available GTAP-Power database runs through 2014, GDP data from the IMF and programs from Center for Policy Studies are used to extend the database to 2020.

The output from renewables is updated using IRENA data for all regions. The difference between 2020 output levels and 2014 levels are calculated with the model updated to reflect the latest renewable power capacities. According to IRENA estimates, the cost of solar power has dropped by 85% and wind power by 52.8%—the model is updated accordingly.

Once the model is set, the reduction in emissions is calculated and used to shock the global value of the CO_2 quota under two scenarios:

Scenario 1—BAU scenario

To estimate the economic impact of the change in emissions from 2020 to 2030, the economic impact of the decrease in emissions from 2010 to 2020 is modeled using territorial emissions data from the Global Carbon Project (2021). This is more realistic for estimating achievable targets for each country's Paris Agreement commitment. For countries that increased emissions during 2010–2020, no change in emissions is expected between 2020 and 2030.

Scenario 2—NDC scenario

NDCs require each country to outline its climate action plans and target commitments to reduce GHG emissions. These are collected from various national statistics and commission websites and then fed into the model as emissions shocks.

After estimating the economic impact of emission reductions using the GTAP-E-Power model, the GTAP-VA model is used to check the impact of the decline on GVCs. The GTAP-VA model extends the standard GTAP framework by decomposing and deconstructing traded products in terms of their value-added content. The standard GTAP model database has input–output data for each country and region covering bilateral trade flows, firms' intermediate input costs, and finished goods bought by households or the government. Data are collected at the border and not at the consumption point whereas, in the GTAP-VA model, they are collected at the agent level. The model covers the origin of value-added for total exports—value in the exporting country—which is reflected back to the importing economy. Value-added is split between domestic and foreign value added. There is direct value added (from the exporter or producer) and indirect value added embedded in domestic products or inputs, along with foreign value-added content. That way, a policy shock on gross exports or imports is distributed across all value-added components involved across the entire supply chain. The GTAP-VA model is preferred for measuring and analyzing the impact of emission targets on GVCs. The change in energy exports from the GTAP-E-Power model now becomes a shock in the GTAP-VA model.

GTAP-E Power is a guide on how to use the GTAP-Power database in a CGE model to substitute different technologies that influence economic, energy, and climate policies. GTAP-E-Power can use this database capability; but it comes at the cost of increased computing complexity and time. Combining the GTAP-E Power model with the GTAP-VA model further helps identify the emissions generated and value added at each stage of production, but it can also identify the unique trade routes through which value is added and emissions are generated.

The social costs of emissions are calculated and compare with the GDP gains (losses) estimated by the model for scenario 1 and scenario 2 to arrive at the net impact of meeting NDC targets.[3]

---

[3] The social costs are computed with respect to the baseline emissions from 2030. In the baseline, on the other hand, we do not explicitly change emissions and therefore, we assume the baseline for emissions in 2030 as being the same as our initial baseline emissions in 2020.

Results and Analysis

The updated model uses the latest available macroeconomic data covering GDP, exports, and imports, along with increased production capacities of renewable power plants and decreases in the cost of solar and wind power.

ASEAN's aggregate solar capacity jumped by a factor of 13 between 2014 and 2020 (Table 5.1). The biggest increase was in Viet Nam with 16,660 megawatts (MW) of solar power capacity. By 2020, Thailand had an aggregate solar power capacity of 2,988 MW, Malaysia 1,483 MW, and the Philippines 1,058 MW. Cambodia also saw its capacity rise rapidly in 2020 to 315 MW, up from just 9 MW in 2014. The aggregate solar power capacity in Asia was 410,000 MW, nearly six times more than in 2014.

Table 5.1: ASEAN's Renewable Power Capacity

Renewable Energy	2014 (MW)	2020 (MW)	% Change
Solar power	1,628	23,146	1,321.74
Hydro power	39,400	52,820	34.06
Wind power	616	2,622	325.65

MW = megawatt.
Source: International Renewable Energy Agency.

ASEAN's hydropower capacity was 52,820 MW in 2020, 34% more than in 2014. Viet Nam again had the most capacity (20,817 MW in 2020), followed by the Lao PDR (7,583 MW), Malaysia (6,197 MW), Indonesia (6,141 MW), the Philippines (3,780 MW), and Thailand (3667 MW). The Lao PDR increased its hydropower capacity by 136% between 2014 and 2020. The aggregate hydropower generation capacity among Asian economies was 569,778 MW, up 18.8% between 2014 and 2020.

ASEAN had wind power generation capacity of 2,622 MW in 2020, with Thailand leading (1,507 MW), followed by Viet Nam (518 MW), and the Philippines (443 MW). The aggregate wind power generation capacity across Asia was 332,302 MW in 2020, an increase of 167.3% from 2014.

The following subsections offer a country-level view of renewable energy generation capacities, along with the impact a policy shock would have on macroeconomic indicators and supply chain parameters. All results correspond to the policy shock in the respective scenarios relative to the baseline(2030).

Brunei Darussalam

All of Brunei Darussalam's energy supply comes from nonrenewable sources. Given its rich oil and gas reserves, there is little interest to diversify or substitute with renewables. The country does not produce wind power or hydropower, and it produces less than 1 MW of solar (Table 5.2). It had 10.2 million $MtCO_2e$ in 2020 (23.2 $MtCO_2e$ per capita), up 26.1% since 2010.

Table 5.2: Emissions and Renewable Power Capacity— Brunei Darussalam

Indicator	Value
Emissions in 2010	8.06 MT
Emissions in 2020	10.16 MT
NDC target as per Paris Agreement	−20%
Scenario 1 Shock	0%
Scenario 2 Shock	−20%
Solar power capacity	1 MW
Wind power capacity	0 MW
Hydropower capacity	0 MW

MT = metric ton, MW = megawatt, NDC = nationally determined contribution.
Source: Author's calculations based on GTAP simulations.

Table 5.3: Change in Macroeconomic Variables—Brunei Darussalam

Economic Indicator	Scenario 1 % Change	Scenario 1 Absolute Value ($ million)	Scenario 2 % Change	Scenario 2 Absolute Value ($ million)
GDP	−0.02	−2	−5.86	−776
Exports	−0.01	−1	5.98	571
Imports	−0.18	−9	6.21	318
Domestic Value Added	2.81	246	0.53	47
Foreign Value Added	1.69	13	6.90	53
Social cost of carbon emissions 2020 (in $ billions) Emissions in $MtCO_2e$ * $1,853	1.88			
Net Savings (in $ billion) = Social Cost - GDP gains/+GDP losses	1.88		1.10	

CO_2 = carbon dioxide, GDP = gross domestic product, $MtCO_2e$ = metric tons of CO_2 equivalent.
Source: Author's calculations based on GTAP simulations.

Figure 5.1a: Percent Change in Investment in Brunei Darussalam—Scenario 1

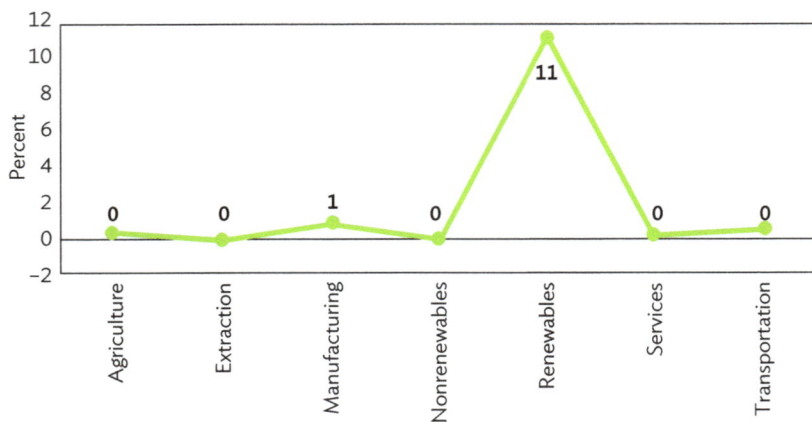

Source: Author's calculations based on GTAP simulations.

Figure 5.1b: Percent Change in Investment in Brunei Darussalam—Scenario 2

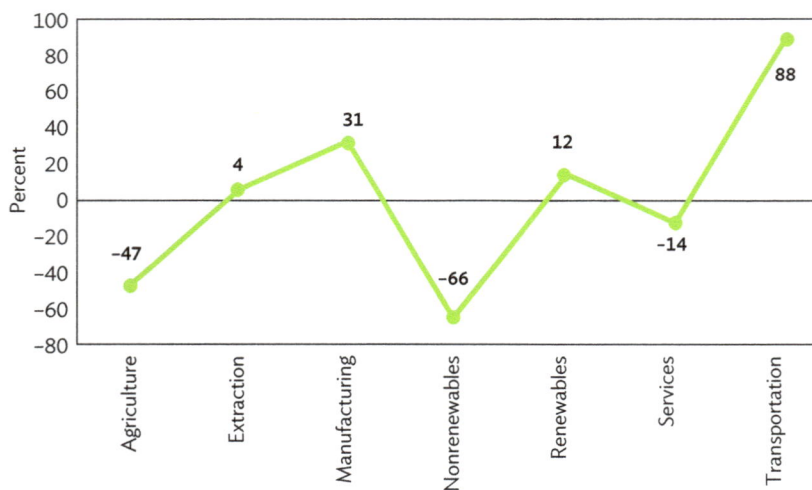

Source: Author's calculations based on GTAP simulations.

In the BAU scenario, emissions in 2030 are the same as in 2020, as they increased over the previous decade.

The model estimates a decline of 0.02% in its GDP, or about $2 million. This stems from a decline in its constituent parameters—exports and investments. There is a 0.08% decline in employment.

To meet its NDC targets, Brunei Darussalam is committed to reduce 20% of its 2020 emissions by 2030. As a shock, the model estimates a 5.9% decline in GDP, or $1.5 billion, largely due to a decline in investment and consumption of nonrenewable energy sources and related sectors. The output of renewable power sources increases by 20% while that of nonrenewable power sources declines by 66% (Figure 5.2). Investments flow to renewable power generation as well as extraction of oil and gas. A simultaneous decline is seen in investments in nonrenewable energy, agriculture, and services—also driving output down. Aggregate employment falls 18%. Although employment from renewable investments increases, there is a simultaneous decline in employment in other sectors.

Figure 5.2: Percent Change in Output—Brunei Darussalam

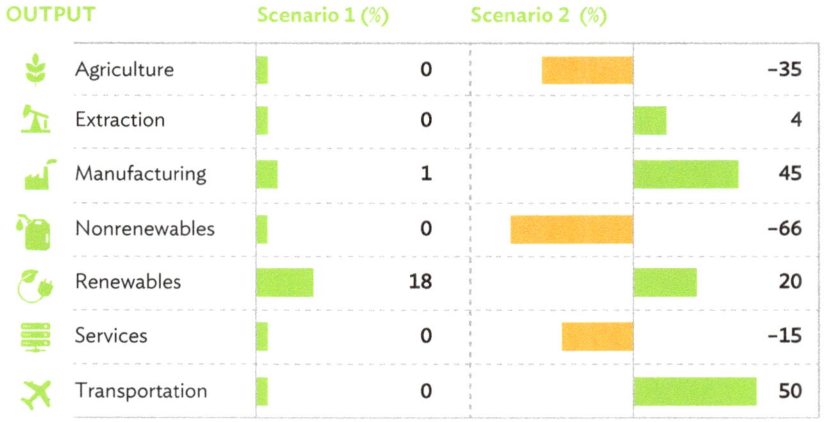

OUTPUT	Scenario 1 (%)	Scenario 2 (%)
Agriculture	0	−35
Extraction	0	4
Manufacturing	1	45
Nonrenewables	0	−66
Renewables	18	20
Services	0	−15
Transportation	0	50

Source: Author's calculations based on GTAP simulations.

Brunei Darussalam is highly dependent on the fossil fuel trade. Therefore, when renewable sources become less costly, the country's fossil fuel sectors suffer, along with other sectors.

The social cost of carbon is estimated to be $185 per $MtCO_2e$. Brunei Darussalam's emissions in 2020 were 10.2 $MtCO_2e$, with a social cost of

$1.9 billion. While the country will lose $776 million to meet its emission goals, it saves $1,879 million in social costs, leaving net savings of $1.1 billion (Table 5.2).

Domestic value added in Brunei Darussalam exports equals 91.9% ($813.12 million) with just 8% foreign value added (Table 5.4). Most domestic value added comes from oil and gas. Of the total domestic value added, 53.4% derives from oil and 41.9% from gas. Brunei Darussalam's domestic value added content is highest in its exports to Japan (31.9%), India (18.3%), the ROK (14.1%), Thailand (10.3%), and Indonesia (5.4%). In scenario 2, there is a 24.8% decline in domestic value added to oil and an increase of 29.3% in value added to gas. Within ASEAN, Brunei Darussalam's domestic value added is high in exports of oil to Indonesia and Thailand. Outside ASEAN, it is higher in exports to Australia, India, and the ROK. Japan; Malaysia; Taipei,China; the EU; and the ROK are the major importers of gas. Brunei Darussalam's domestic value added is significant in its gas exports to these economies Thus, other economies in the supply chain could benefit. Given that gas produces less carbon emissions, it could help the country meet its NDC targets. The foreign value added to oil exports decreases by 9.4%; gas increases by 3.6%. Because more than 96% of oil content and 89.5% of gas comes from domestic value added, the impact might not be as pronounced as with domestic value added.

Table 5.4: Percent Change in Domestic and Foreign Value Added— Brunei Darussalam

Sector	Domestic Value Added		Foreign Value Added	
	Scenario 1	Scenario 2	Scenario 1	Scenario 2
Grains and Crops	29.97	−1.48	34.76	−27.75
Meat Products	0.28	0.04	0.28	−2.63
Forestry and Mining	0.32	0.06	0.29	0.46
Coal	0.4	0	0.33	−0.11
Oil	2.78	24.87	1.11	−9.42
Gas	2.58	29.3	0.63	3.57
Processed Food	13.84	48.4	11.85	36.96
Textiles and Apparel	7.19	29.64	7.82	−18.93
Light Manufacturing	5.22	25.11	4.41	6.68
Oil Products	1.87	14.58	2.54	14.62
Heavy Manufacturing	5.63	41.61	5.65	72.34
Electricity	0.17	0.01	0.17	0.52
Utility and Construction	35.19	−38.99	34.77	−35.15
Transport and Communication	6.9	46.31	5.23	17.7
Services	3.9	22.06	2.47	17.13

Source: Author's calculations based on GTAP simulations.

Beyond its NDC targets, Brunei Darussalam has a target of at least 30% renewable energy in its power generation mix by 2035.[4] It has already started monitoring energy consumption in commercial buildings and has set high tariffs to discourage high household energy consumption. It is also promoting the sale of EVs. As a major exporter of oil and gas, there is the chance of emissions leakages by way of exports to countries with lower NDC targets, reducing its dependence on oil and gas exports. India, Japan, and the ROK consume oil and gas from Brunei Darussalam, so when they reduce consumption of nonrenewable energy to achieve their NDC targets, Brunei Darussalam could see losses if it does not diversify. Well thought-out plans and investment strategies to diversify and reduce dependence on oil and gas can help Brunei Darussalam mitigate the economic losses resulting from its own and others' transition.

Cambodia

Cambodia significantly increased its solar power generation, from a capacity of 9 MW in 2014 to 315 MW in 2020 (Table 5.5). Hydropower generation also increased from 929 MW to 1,330 MW. Despite the increase in the generation of renewable power, Cambodia almost quadrupled its emissions between 2010 and 2020—to 5.10 million metric tons in 2020. Its per capita emissions was 0.92 $MtCO_2e$.

Table 5.5: Emissions and Renewable Power Capacity—Cambodia

Indicator	Value
Emissions in 2010	5.10 MT
Emissions in 2020	15.33 MT
NDC target as per Paris Agreement	−41.7%
Scenario 1 Shock	0%
Scenario 2 Shock	−41.7%
Solar power capacity	315 MW
Wind power capacity	0 MW
Hydropower capacity	1,330 MW

MT = metric ton, MW = megawatt, NDC = nationally determined contribution.
Source: Author's calculations based on GTAP simulations.

As emission levels increased between 2010 and 2020, there will be no changes in emission levels in 2030 under the BAU scenario. Cambodia's GDP will increase by 0.14% or about $34 million in absolute terms, mostly from an increase in exports and investments (Table 5.6). Exports increase by 0.23% and imports by 0.21%. There is a 0.1% increase in employment.

[4]   Narayan (2021).

Table 5.6: Change in Macroeconomic Variables—Cambodia

Economic Indicator	Scenario 1 % Change	Scenario 1 Absolute Value ($ millions)	Scenario 2 % Change	Scenario 2 Absolute Value ($ millions)
GDP	0.14	34	−3.85	−914
Exports	0.23	53	−12.91	−2,972
Imports	0.21	51	−9.43	−2,246
Domestic Value Added	1.02	123	−30.38	−3,670
Foreign Value Added	0.86	94	−18.23	−1,992
Social cost of carbon emissions ($ billion) = 2020 Emissions $MtCO_2e$ * $185		2.84		
Net Savings (in $ billion) = Social Cost - GDP gains/+GDP losses		2.87		1.92

CO_2 = carbon dioxide, GDP = gross domestic product, $MtCO_2e$ = metric tons of CO_2 equivalent.
Source: Author's calculations based on GTAP simulations.

Investments in renewables increase with a decline in investments for nonrenewable energy, extraction, and energy-intensive manufacturing like textiles and apparel (Figure 5.3a and Figure 5.3b). The positive impact remains given the ample renewable sources available, so it is far easier for the country to maintain its emission level. This will help Cambodia diversify.

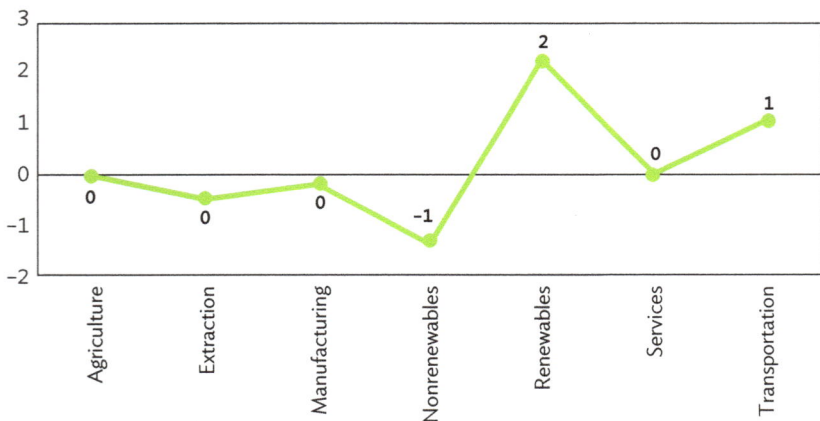

Figure 5.3a: Percent Change in Investment in Cambodia—Scenario 1

Source: Author's calculations based on GTAP simulations.

Figure 5.3b: Percent Change in Investment in Cambodia—Scenario 2

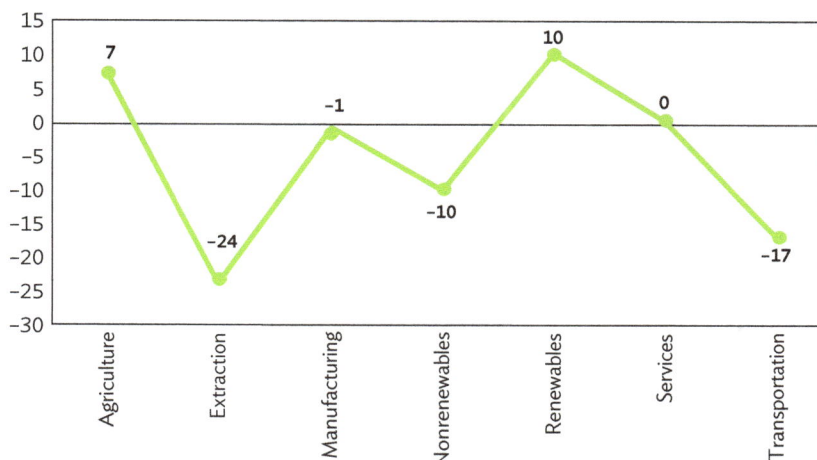

Source: Author's calculations based on GTAP simulations.

Cambodia aims to reduce its 2020 BAU emissions by 41.7% in 2030. In scenario 2, the model estimates a decline of 3.9% in GDP. This comes from a 12.9% decline in exports and 9.4% decline in aggregate imports. Though Cambodia's emission targets in percentage value remains large, the value of reducing emission is quite low (3.2 $MtCO_2e$).

There is a 10% increase in investments for renewable power sources with a corresponding decline in investments in nonrenewable energy, extraction, and services. By sector, there is a 37% decline in output from transportation, a 13% decline in nonrenewable power sources, a 30% decline in extraction (that includes coal, oil, and gas), and a 6% decline in manufacturing (Figure 5.4). There is a 4.7% decline in employment, stemming from the decline in energy-intensive sectors. As the prices of renewables decline along with the increase in renewable energy investments, substitution by renewable energy sources is likely.

A baseline analysis of Cambodia's GVCs shows that 52.5% comes from domestic value added mainly from exports to the EU (37.5%), the US (22.4%), the PRC (6.6%), and Japan (4.6%). Textiles take up 48.1% of its domestic value added, with 16% in transport and communication. Textile exports contain 49.1% in domestic value added with the rest (50.8%) foreign value added. In scenario 2, domestic value added declines by 30.4% while foreign value added declines by 18.2%. In general, textiles and heavy manufacturing suffer. Textiles' domestic value added declines by 32.2%, services by 36.2%, and heavy manufacturing by 37.7% (Table 5.7). There is significant foreign value added in textiles and apparel, light manufacturing, transportation, and communications. Foreign value added in textile exports falls by 16.9%, light manufacturing by 12.8%, and transportation by 45.0%. Both foreign and domestic value added in textiles decline, possibly affecting major importers such as the US, EU, Canada, and Japan.

Figure 5.4: Percent Change in Output—Cambodia

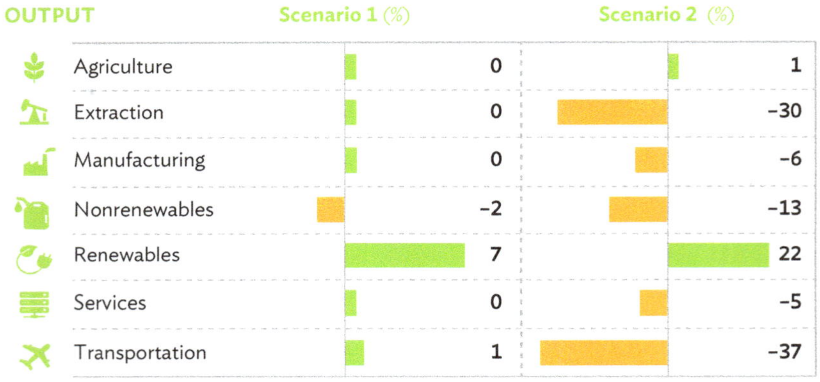

OUTPUT	Scenario 1 (%)	Scenario 2 (%)
Agriculture	0	1
Extraction	0	−30
Manufacturing	0	−6
Nonrenewables	−2	−13
Renewables	7	22
Services	0	−5
Transportation	1	−37

Source: Author's calculations based on GTAP simulations.

Table 5.7: Percent Change in Domestic and Foreign Value Added— Cambodia

Sector	Domestic Value Add		Foreign Value Add	
	Scenario 1	Scenario 2	Scenario 1	Scenario 2
Grains and Crops	0.35	−18.89	0.54	5.94
Meat Products	0.34	−11.85	0.69	−39.71
Forestry & Mining	−0.44	−29.58	−0.23	−0.46
Coal	0.41	0.04	0.13	0.01
Oil	0.55	0.02	0.89	0.01
Gas	0.23	0.03	0.29	0.01
Processed Food	0.43	−15.49	0.70	−18.37
Textiles and Apparel	0.21	−32.18	0.15	−16.92
Light Manufacturing	0.58	−21.09	0.76	−12.83
Oil Products	0.36	0.77	0.41	0.01
Heavy Manufacturing	1.61	−37.70	1.89	−1.30
Electricity	0.66	0.02	0.65	0.01
Utility and Construction	1.94	−44.65	1.95	−17.38
Transport and Communication	4.19	−30.67	3.89	−45.50
Services	0.98	−36.20	0.82	−22.63

Source: Author's calculations based on GTAP simulations.

Cambodia's emissions equaled 15.33 $MtCO_2e$ in 2020. With the estimated $185 per $MtCO_2e$ social cost of emissions, the aggregate cost of emissions amounts to $2.8 billion. Thus, the overall $914 million GDP loss is well covered by $1,920 million   in savings from the social cost of emissions. Comparing the economic losses and disruptions against the long-term benefits of larger solar power generation, the cost looks affordable. Located in the middle of the Greater Mekong Subregion, the vast river and water networks are a blessing to Cambodia. Potential wind and solar power resources remain underutilized. Agriculture also produces residues that can be used for power generation. Cambodia has no refineries and limited facilities for oil exploration, so much of its electricity is imported, keeping it relatively expensive. Though there has been a decline in electricity imports in recent years, energy demand has increased investments in solar and other renewable resources like wind and biomass—along with declining costs of renewables—substitution can help reduce much of its spending on imported electricity. An increase in investments in renewables could also reduce investments in other sectors, leading to a drop in output and exports in some energy-dependent manufacturing industries. Yet, over the long run, Cambodia would benefit from cheaper electricity, which, when fed into manufacturing, product exports will become more competitive. Also, many people in Cambodia still lack access to electricity. Increasing output from renewable power sources, amid declining costs, could help reduce inequality, foster greater inclusion, and improve livelihoods. While an increase in investments in renewables may disrupt the supply chain and economic activities in the short term, the country would benefit from reduced imports and cheaper electricity in the long run.

Indonesia

Indonesia is ASEAN's largest country by many measures, including level of emissions. In 2020, the country produced 589.5 $MtCO_2e$, up 30.4% from 2014. With a population of 273.5 million, per capita emissions equaled 2.16 $MtCO_2e$. Indonesia has 185 MW capacity of solar power, well up from the 42 MW it had in 2014. Its hydropower capacity was 6,141 MW in 2020, a 17% increase from 2014. Wind power capacity also increased to 154 MW in 2020. Only 12% of the power generated in the country comes from renewable sources. By 2025, it wants to meet its ambitious 23% target (Table 5.8).

Table 5.8: Emissions and Renewable Power Capacity—Indonesia

Indicator	Value
Emissions in 2010	451.93 MT
Emissions in 2020	589.50 MT
NDC target as per Paris Agreement	−29%
Scenario 1 Shock	0%
Scenario 2 Shock	−29%
Solar power capacity	185 MW
Wind power capacity	0 MW
Hydropower capacity	6,141 MW

MT = metric ton, MW = megawatt, NDC = nationally determined contribution.
Source: Author's calculations based on GTAP simulations.

With an increase in emissions between 2010 and 2020, the BAU scenario assumes the same level of emissions between 2020 and 2030. In that case, the model estimates that the GDP would increase by 0.18%, which in absolute terms amounts to $183 million. Exports increase by 0.71% and imports by 0.07%. There is a 9% increase in investments in renewable power and an 11% increase in output. There is also a 0.04% increase in employment (Table 5.9).

Table 5.9: Change in Macroeconomic Variables—Indonesia

Economic Indicator	Scenario 1		Scenario 2	
	% Change	Absolute Value ($ million)	% Change	Absolute Value ($ million)
GDP	0.18	183	−1.84	−18,782
Exports	0.71	203	−0.50	−1,416
Imports	0.07	13	−8.96	−16,655
Domestic Value Added	0.42	1,070	−33.92	−85,539
Foreign Value Added	1.79	555	39.31	12,231
Social cost of carbon emissions ($ billion) = 2020 Emissions in $MtCO_2e * \$185$	109.06			
Net Savings (in $ billion) = Social Cost - GDP gains/+GDP losses	109.24			90.28

CO_2 = carbon dioxide, GDP = gross domestic product, $MtCO_2e$ = metric tons of CO_2 equivalent.
Source: Author's calculations based on GTAP simulations.

Under the NDC scenario, Indonesia reduces GHG emissions by 29% against the BAU scenario in 2030. GDP would decline by 1.84%, also due to a decrease in nonrenewable energy and extraction industry output (Figure 5.5a and Figure 5.5b). Renewable power increases by 140%, primarily from an increase in hydropower. Nonrenewable power output from coal and oil declines by 27% (Figure 5.6). Yet the increase in renewable power does not compensate for the drop in nonrenewable power and other energy-intensive extraction such as coal, oil, and gas. Coal is important to Indonesia, and a decline in output drives down GDP. The country must increase investment in renewables by 211% to meet its NDC targets. This would mean investments in nonrenewables would drop by 21% and extraction by 43%. Under this scenario, employment declines by 2.9%.

Figure 5.5a: Percent Change in Investment in Indonesia—Scenario 1

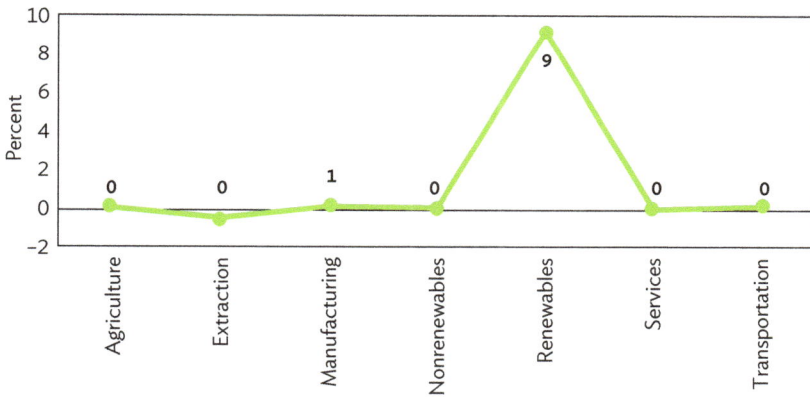

Source: Author's calculations based on GTAP simulations.

Figure 5.5b: Percent Change in Investment in Indonesia—Scenario 2

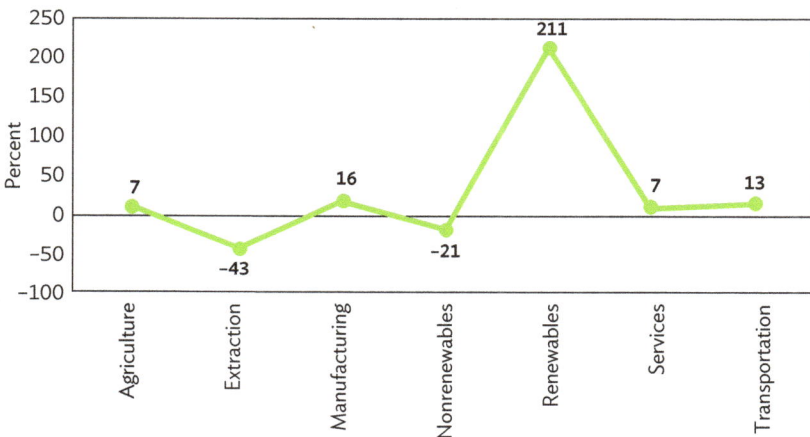

Source: Author's calculations based on GTAP simulations.

Figure 5.6: Percent Change in Output—Indonesia

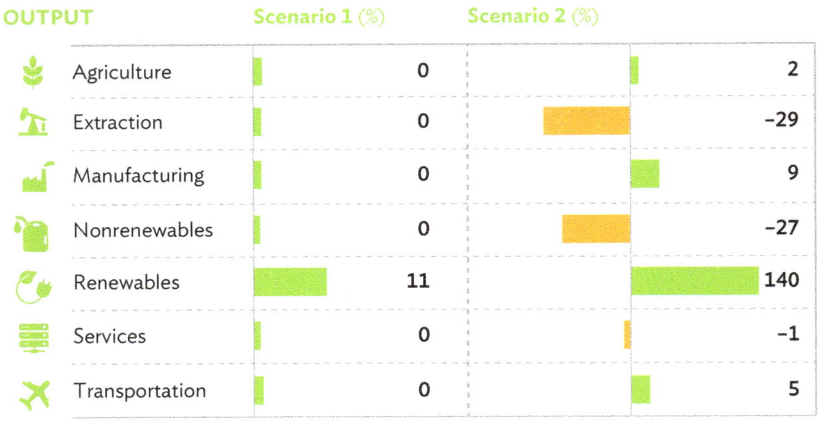

OUTPUT	Scenario 1 (%)	Scenario 2 (%)
Agriculture	0	2
Extraction	0	−29
Manufacturing	0	9
Nonrenewables	0	−27
Renewables	11	140
Services	0	−1
Transportation	0	5

Source: Author's calculations based on GTAP simulations.

Around 89.0% of Indonesia's exports derive from domestic value added with the remainder (11.0%) from foreign value added. Major exports include coal (17.4%), processed food (15.0%), gas (8.8%), oil (6.4%), and textiles and apparel (5.9%). Domestic value added accounts for almost 99% of coal, oil, and gas exports. It is 89.2% in processed food, and 69.2% in textiles. The largest export markets include Japan (13.5%), the PRC (11.2%), the EU (10.8%), India (9.8%), and the US (9.5%). The scenario 2 (NDC) results expect domestic value added will decline by 33.9% while foreign value added will increase by 39.3%. Domestic value added declines across almost all sectors (Table 5.10). Heavy manufacturing declines by 35.6%, followed by light manufacturing (54.4%), gas (37.3%), coal (31.3%), and oil (16.9%). Foreign value added to heavy manufacturing increases (57.09%), followed by light manufacturing (80.8%), coal (49.3%), oil (25.8%), and gas (15.6%). Large imports in heavy and light manufacturing come from Japan, Singapore, Thailand, the EU, the PRC, and the ROK—and they will increase.

When pegged at \$185 per $MtCO_2e$, the aggregate social cost of carbon emissions comes to \$109.1 billion as Indonesia emitted 589.5 $MtCO_2e$ in 2020. Compared to the \$18.8 billion cost of transitioning to renewables and meeting its NDCs, it is quite affordable—a net \$90.3 billion benefit over the long term.

Table 5.10: Percent Change in Domestic and Foreign Value Added—Indonesia

Sector	Domestic Value Add		Foreign Value Add	
	Scenario 1	Scenario 2	Scenario 1	Scenario 2
Grains and Crops	0.80	−22.31	1.26	21.53
Meat Products	1.82	−23.55	2.47	48.37
Forestry and Mining	1.38	−39.52	1.30	0.17
Coal	−2.85	−31.37	−0.36	49.32
Oil	0.12	−16.88	0.19	25.76
Gas	−0.34	−37.34	0.23	15.62
Processed Food	1.34	−35.42	1.90	17.26
Textiles and Apparel	1.23	−14.55	1.64	−3.61
Light Manufacturing	1.67	−54.41	2.22	80.80
Oil Products	0.92	−27.14	−1.85	−22.82
Heavy Manufacturing	1.50	−35.56	1.95	57.09
Electricity	0.88	0.05	87.59	0.01
Utility and Construction	1.15	−41.45	1.66	22.79
Transport and Communication	2.47	−25.46	2.41	15.39
Services	1.65	−30.91	1.94	31.35

Source: Author's calculations based on GTAP simulations.

Indonesia's energy consumption has been growing, partly due to the government's 100% electrification target by 2022. Indonesia remains the third largest coal producer globally. To reduce oil and petroleum product imports, Indonesia is using more coal to meet energy demand. Coal made up just 10% of the energy mix in the early 2000s. It is now more than 30%. And it contributes some 28% to global coal trade—more than 15% of Indonesia's exports. Fossil fuel dependence stems from ample nonrenewable supplies—and relatively high subsidies. During 2005–2014, energy subsidies accounted for about 10%–20% of central government expenditures and around 3% of GDP. It has declined since, but the government recently announced an increase. This could throw Indonesia off the path to meet its NDC target. Indonesia should instead consider investing in renewable energy and diversify energy sources away from coal, for example. Japan; Malaysia; Taipei,China; the PRC; and the ROK are major coal importers. As these economies reduce fossil fuel imports and consume more renewables as they move toward their NDC targets, Indonesia may suffer. Coal's emerging supply chain disruption is a case in point. Diversifying its energy sources by investing in renewables is a good way forward.

Lao People's Democratic Republic

The Lao PDR is landlocked. It has a high concentration of renewable energy resources, such as hydropower and biomass. In 2015, biomass consumption was the country's most abundant energy resource, with most used in rural areas. Power is also generated by hydro dams, which have increased production by 136% since 2014. Solar power also adds to the renewable energy mix: 34 MW in 2020 from 2 MW in 2014 (Table 5.11). Oil products are the second most common source of energy. With no oil refineries, Lao PDR imports from Thailand and Viet Nam. Between 2014 and 2020, the country's emissions increased by 30.9 $MtCO_2e$, reaching 33.9 $MtCO_2e$. With a population of 7.3 million, the country's per capita emissions are 4.7 $MtCO_2e$.

Table 5.11: Emissions and Renewable Power Capacity— Lao People's Democratic Republic

Indicator	Value
Emissions in 2010	3 MT
Emissions in 2020	33.85 MT
NDC target as per Paris Agreement	−60%
Scenario 1 Shock	0%
Scenario 2 Shock	−60%
Solar power capacity	34 MW
Wind power capacity	0 MW
Hydropower capacity	7,583 MW

MT = metric ton, MW = megawatt, NDC = nationally determined contribution.
Source: Author's calculations based on GTAP simulations.

Again, as emissions increased between 2010 and 2020, the BAU scenario assumes no change in emissions between 2020 and 2030. The baseline results show a 0.17% increase in GDP, or about $30 million (Table 5.12). Exports increase by 0.67% and imports by 0.39%. Investments in renewables increase by 11% with output up by 12%. Nonrenewable energy output also increases, attributed to a relatively higher increase in emissions. With the same level of emissions in 2030, domestic value added increases by 12.8% and foreign value added by 4.9%. Employment rises by just 0.067%.

**Table 5.12: Change in Macroeconomic Variables—
Lao People's Democratic Republic**

Economic Indicator	Scenario 1		Scenario 2	
	% Change	Absolute Value ($ million)	% Change	Absolute Value ($ million)
GDP	0.17	30	1.49	264
Exports	0.67	36	0.60	53
Imports	0.39	33	0.98	51
Domestic Value Added	12.75	495	14.14	550
Foreign Value Added	4.94	72	-37.04	-543
Social cost of carbon emissions ($ billion) = 2020 Emissions in $MtCO_2e$* \$185		6.26		
Net Savings (in \$ billion) = Social Cost - GDP gains/+GDP losses		6.29		6.53

CO_2 = carbon dioxide, GDP = gross domestic product, $MtCO_2e$ = metric tons of CO_2 equivalent.
Source: Author's calculations based on GTAP simulations.

Lao PDR is the only ASEAN country where GDP rises under NDC scenario 2. Its NDC target is 60%, the highest among ASEAN members. Its emissions fall to 10.2 $MtCO_2e$, as unlike other ASEAN countries, it emits little to begin with. Renewable power increases by 127%, mostly due to hydropower. From 2014 to 2020, hydropower capacity increased by 136%, according to IRENA. Between 2020 and 2030, the model estimates the Lao PDR will increase its hydropower capacity by 126%. Exports are estimated to increase by 0.98%. Transportation output increases by 12%, with agriculture and extraction up 2% each (Figure 5.8). Manufacturing output drops by 3% (Figure 5.7a and Figure 5.7b). Though there is a decline in manufacturing, it does not impact GDP as it is covered by growth in other sectors. With investments in renewables already relatively high, there is plenty of room to invest in other sectors. The drop in prices for renewable power and the increase in investments in renewables help meet the Lao PDR NDC target at virtually no cost. The country emitted 33.9 $MtCO_2e$ in 2020. Compared with the increase in GDP estimated at $264 million, it is easy to conclude that meeting its NDC target will save Lao PDR $6.5 billion. Employment also increases by 3.2% (162,000 jobs).

Figure 5.7a: Percent Change in Investment of Lao People's Democratic Republic—Scenario 1

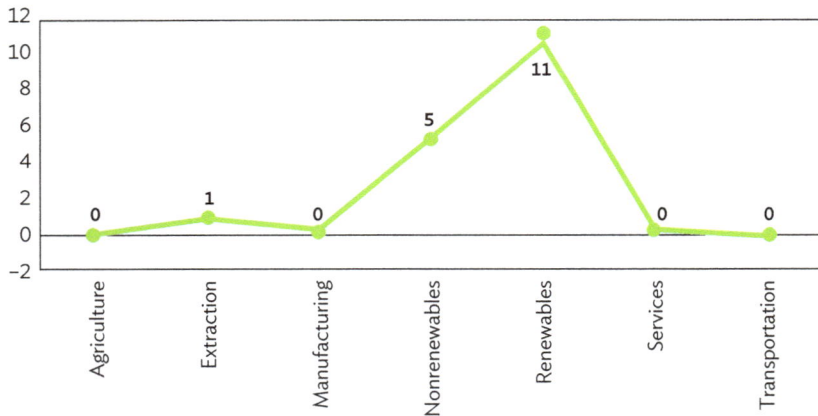

Source: Author's calculations based on GTAP simulations.

Figure 5.7b: Percent Change in Investment in Lao People's Democratic Republic—Scenario 2

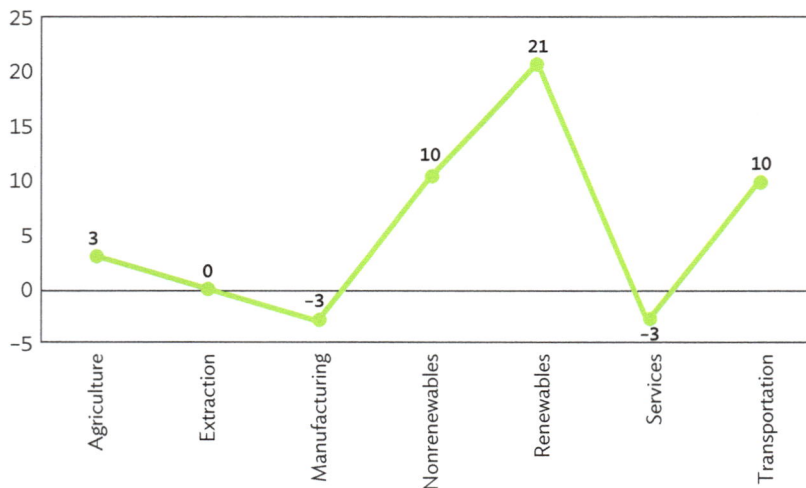

Source: Author's calculations based on GTAP simulations.

**Figure 5.8: Percent Change in Output—
Lao People's Democratic Republic**

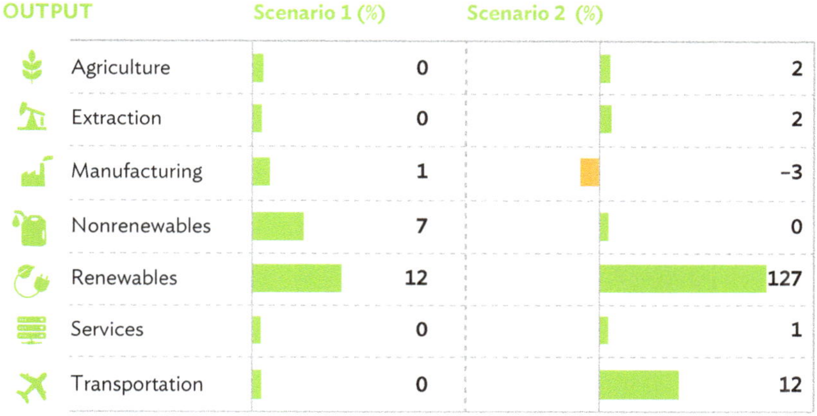

OUTPUT	Scenario 1 (%)	Scenario 2 (%)
Agriculture	0	2
Extraction	0	2
Manufacturing	1	-3
Nonrenewables	7	0
Renewables	12	127
Services	0	1
Transportation	0	12

Source: Author's calculations based on GTAP simulations.

Forestry, wood and lumber, gas, oil, and nonferrous metals together make up 64.7% of the Lao PDR exports, with 34.4% going to Thailand, the EU, the PRC, the US, and Viet Nam. The domestic value-added component is 72.6%, with foreign value added comprising the remaining 27.4%. When NDC emission targets are used, the model shows domestic value added increases by 14.1%, with foreign value added declining by 37.1%. By sector, domestic value added increases most in forestry and mining, gas, heavy manufacturing, and transport and communication (Table 5.13). The foreign value added declines mainly in textiles and apparel, heavy manufacturing, oil products, and light manufacturing. A major share in foreign value added overall comes from the PRC, Thailand, and Viet Nam.

While the Lao PDR lacks access to conventional sources of energy like natural gas or petroleum, it is blessed with abundant sources of renewable energy including hydropower and solar power. As it moves up the development ladder, the Lao PDR can tap its renewable sources to make electricity more widespread and inclusive, thus improving livelihoods. It should diversify beyond hydropower as it is vulnerable to erratic rainfall and other climate risks. Emissions also stem from forestry and land use.

Table 5.13: Percent Change in Domestic and Foreign Value Added—Lao People's Democratic Republic

Sector	Domestic Value Add		Foreign Value Add	
	Scenario 1	Scenario 2	Scenario 1	Scenario 2
Grains and Crops	11.50	13.33	4.52	66.10
Meat Products	13.04	10.71	9.37	1.10
Forestry and Mining	12.72	15.39	1.56	37.47
Coal	0.14	-16.02	46.62	-16.27
Oil	-6.13	-10.82	-1.45	-12.46
Gas	14.15	14.25	2.87	-13.26
Processed Food	10.66	11.65	8.61	12.50
Textiles and Apparel	10.04	11.70	11.94	-53.58
Light Manufacturing	12.32	13.88	2.16	-50.52
Oil Products	7.03	24.73	0.40	-24.32
Heavy Manufacturing	17.74	13.89	8.44	-86.38
Electricity	14.91	6.04	7.72	34.67
Utility and Construction	20.20	6.80	11.89	14.11
Transport and Communication	11.96	14.20	1.63	37.88
Services	11.95	12.11	2.99	-39.59

Source: Author's calculations based on GTAP simulations.

Malaysia

In 2019, Malaysia was the second largest oil and natural gas producer in Southeast Asia and the world's fifth largest exporter of liquefied natural gas. Natural gas, coal, oil, and diesel have been the primary sources of nonrenewable energy for Malaysia's power networks. To diversify its energy dependence, Malaysia instituted several renewable energy projects. Hydropower accounts for a major source of renewable energy and about 15% of its energy output—capacity grew by 30% between 2014 and 2020. Wind power is negligible as Malaysia is in a region with lower wind speeds and faces several obstacles in developing wind energy. With a population of 32 million, the country generated 272.61 $MtCO_2e$ in 2020, or 8.42 $MtCO_2e$ per capita. Emissions increased by 26.2% from 2010 to 2020.

Along with every ASEAN country except Singapore, Malaysia increased its emissions between 2014 and 2020, meaning the baseline BAU scenario uses the 2020 emissions level through 2030. The model estimates that GDP will increase by 0.04% or around $141 million. Investments in renewable power increases by 11%, driving a 15% increase in output. Employment increases by 0.1%. Supply chain parameters show that domestic value added increases by 0.77% and foreign value added by 0.73%.

Malaysia's NDC target is to reduce emissions by 45%. Estimation results show that GDP declines by 1.9% (Table 5.15). The output of renewables doubles (up 101%) as both hydropower and solar power double as well. Malaysia has already made significant investments in solar and hydro energy capacity between 2014 and 2020 (Table 5.14). The model expects investment in renewables to increase by 95%. Output from nonrenewable sources would drop by 31% due to a decline in Myanmar gas and coal power. Oil and gas extractions decline by 12.8% and 18.0%, which helps explain the drop in Malaysia's GDP. Overall, extraction declines by 18%, and services by 2% (Figure 5.10). Construction, communication, processed food, and chemicals also decline, again adding to the decline in GDP. Employment declines by 5.2%.

Table 5.14: Emissions and Renewable Power Capacity—Malaysia

Indicator	Value
Emissions in 2010	214.94 MT
Emissions in 2020	272.61 MT
NDC target as per Paris Agreement	-45 %
Scenario 1 Shock	0%
Scenario 2 Shock	-45%
Solar power capacity	1,483 MW
Wind power capacity	0 MW
Hydropower capacity	6,197 MW

MT = metric ton, MW = megawatt, NDC = nationally determined contribution.
Source: Author's calculations based on GTAP simulations.

Table 5.15: Change in Macroeconomic Variables—Malaysia

	Scenario 1		Scenario 2	
Economic Indicator	% Change	Absolute Value ($ million)	% Change	Absolute Value ($ million)
GDP	0.04	141	-1.95	-6,698
Exports	0.11	307	-0.67	-1,820
Imports	0.09	203	-1.30	-3,004
Domestic Value Added	0.77	1,325	8.94	15,322
Foreign Value Added	0.73	709	-26.36	-25,766
Social cost of carbon emissions ($ billion) = 2020 Emissions in $MtCO_2e$ * \$185	50.43			
Net Savings (in $ billion) = Social Cost - GDP gains/+GDP losses	50.57			43.73

CO_2 = carbon dioxide, GDP = gross domestic product, $MtCO_2e$ = metric tons of CO_2 equivalent.
Source: Author's calculations based on GTAP simulations.

Figure 5.9a: Percent Change in Investment of Malaysia— Scenario 1

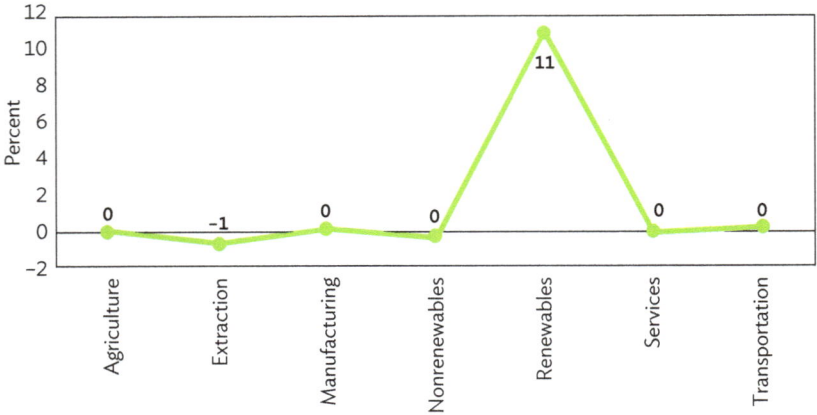

Source: Author's calculations based on GTAP simulations.

Figure 5.9b: Percent Change in Investment in Malaysia— Scenario 2

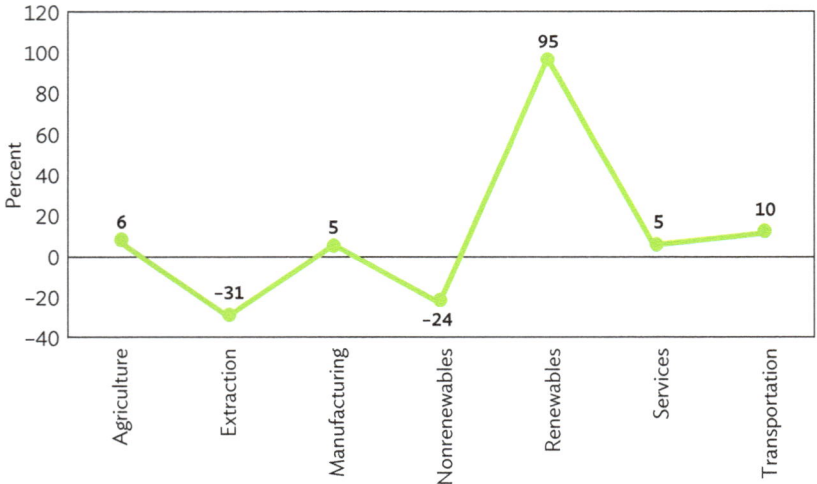

Source: Author's calculations based on GTAP simulations.

Figure 5.10: Percent Change in Output—Malaysia

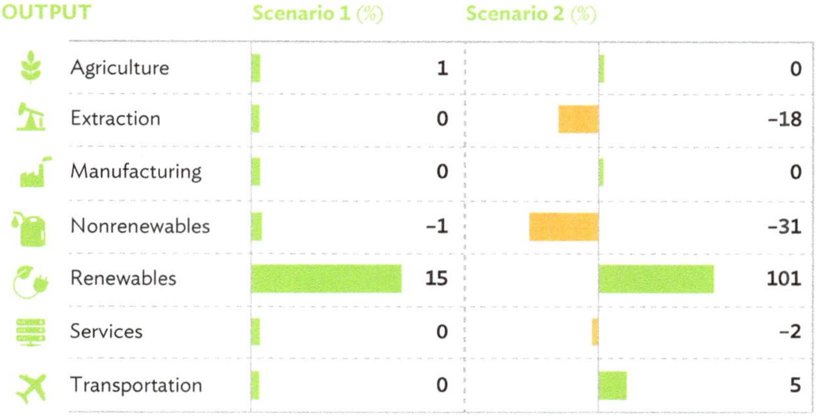

OUTPUT	Scenario 1 (%)	Scenario 2 (%)
Agriculture	1	0
Extraction	0	−18
Manufacturing	0	0
Nonrenewables	−1	−31
Renewables	15	101
Services	0	−2
Transportation	0	5

Source: Author's calculations based on GTAP simulations.

Exports mainly go to the PRC (19%), but the US, the EU, and Japan are also important destinations. Exports are mostly heavy manufacturing— particularly computer, electronic, and optical products—chemicals, rubber, and electrical equipment. Processed food and extracted gas are also notable exports. Nearly two-thirds (63.7%) of export content comes from domestic value added with the rest (36.3%) as foreign value added content. Results show that the domestic value-added component increases by 8.9% while the foreign value added declines by 26.4%. The increase is mostly in heavy manufacturing and processed food, with declines in energy-intensive sectors like oil products, coal, oil, gas, and electricity (Table 5.16). The foreign value-added portion declines largely in textiles and apparel, services, oil, forestry, and mining. Much extra-ASEAN value added comes from the PRC, with Indonesia and Viet Nam contributing most from within. Again, this derives from the decline in exports and output in energy-intensive sectors.

Table 5.16: Percent Change in Domestic and Foreign Value Added—Malaysia

Sector	Domestic Value Added		Foreign Value Added	
	Scenario 1	Scenario 2	Scenario 1	Scenario 2
Grains and Crops	11.50	13.33	4.52	66.10
Meat Products	13.04	10.71	9.37	1.10
Forestry and Mining	12.72	15.39	1.56	37.47
Coal	0.14	-16.02	46.62	-16.27
Oil	-6.13	-10.82	-1.45	-12.46
Gas	14.15	14.25	2.87	-13.26
Processed Food	10.66	11.65	8.61	12.50
Textiles and Apparel	10.04	11.70	11.94	-53.58
Light Manufacturing	12.32	13.88	2.16	-50.52
Oil Products	7.03	24.73	0.40	-24.32
Heavy Manufacturing	17.74	13.89	8.44	-86.38
Electricity	14.91	6.04	7.72	34.67
Utility and Construction	20.20	6.80	11.89	14.11
Transport and Communication	11.96	14.20	1.63	37.88
Services	11.95	12.11	2.99	-39.59

Source: Author's calculations based on GTAP simulations.

Malaysia's emissions in 2020 reached 272.61 $MtCO_2e$. With the social cost of carbon emissions pegged at $185 per $MtCO_2e$, the social cost was estimated at $50.4 billion. Compared to the cost of meeting NDC targets (estimated to be $6.7 billion), it shows the benefits of the transition outweigh its costs, with $43.7 billion in net savings. Malaysia wants its capacity from renewable sources to account for 31% of all power generated. The government is working to diversify out of nonrenewable energy using decentralized solar power systems, hydroelectric projects, and initiatives like its Green Electricity Tariff Program to help drive Malaysia's transition to green energy.

Philippines

With around half of its primary energy supply imported, the Philippines is highly vulnerable to oil price fluctuations. In terms of CO_2 emissions, the Philippines ranked fifth among ASEAN countries in 2020, with 136 $MtCO_2e$—up 64.0% from 2014 (Table 5.17). With a population of 109.6 million, per capita emissions was 1.24 $MtCO_2e$ in 2020. There was 1,058 MW of solar power capacity, up from 28 MW in 2014. Hydropower capacity was 3,780 MW in 2020, up 5% from 2014. Wind power also increased to 443 MW in 2020. With renewables only 30% of the country's energy mix, the government's National Renewable Energy Plan aims to triple renewable capacity to 15,304 MW by 2030.

Table 5.17: Emissions and Renewable Power Capacity—Philippines

Indicator	Value
Emissions in 2010	82.95 MT
Emissions in 2020	136.02 MT
NDC target as per Paris Agreement	−2.71%
Scenario 1 Shock	0%
Scenario 2 Shock	−2.71%
Solar power capacity	1,058 MW
Wind power capacity	443 MW
Hydropower capacity	3,780 MW

MT = metric ton, MW = megawatt, NDC = nationally determined contribution.
Source: Author's calculations based on GTAP simulations.

In the BAU scenario, which uses 2020 emissions, if there was an increase since 2014, there would be no change in emissions for the Philippines between 2020 and 2030. Results show GDP increasing by $49 million, with exports declining slightly to $55 million (Table 5.18). When looking at the impact on supply chains, it shows a 0.72% decline in domestic value added and about 0.53% decline in foreign value added. Employment increases by 0.04%.

Table 5.18: Change in Macroeconomic Variables—Philippines

Economic Indicator	Scenario 1		Scenario 2	
	% Change	Absolute Value ($ million)	% Change	Absolute Value ($ million)
GDP	0.01	49	0.20	700
Exports	−0.07	−55	0.19	148
Imports	0.00	2	−1.01	−1481
Domestic Value Added	−0.72	−354	24.08	12,213
Foreign Value Added	−0.53	−144	14.74	4,052
Social cost of carbon emissions ($ billion) = 2020 Emissions in MtCO$_2$e* $185	25.16			
Net Savings (in $ billion) = Social Cost - GDP gains/+GDP losses	25.21			25.86

CO$_2$ = carbon dioxide, GDP = gross domestic product, MtCO$_2$e = metric tons of CO$_2$ equivalent.
Source: Author's calculations based on GTAP simulations.

Figure 5.11a: Percent Change in Investment in the Philippines—Scenario 1

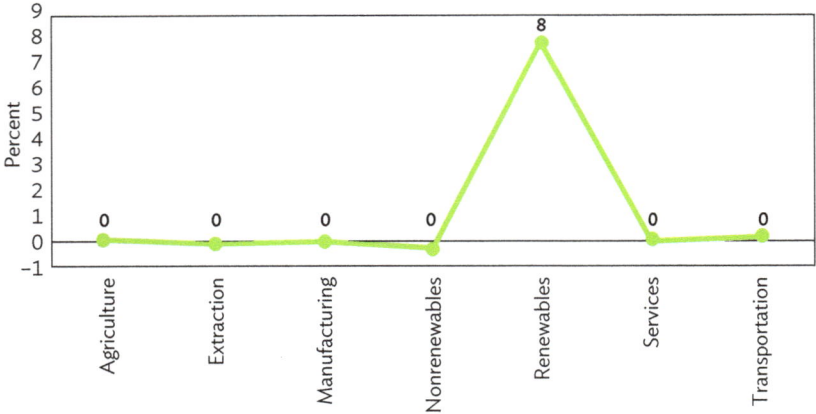

Source: Author's calculations based on GTAP simulations.

Figure 5.11b: Percent Change in Investment in the Philippines—Scenario 2

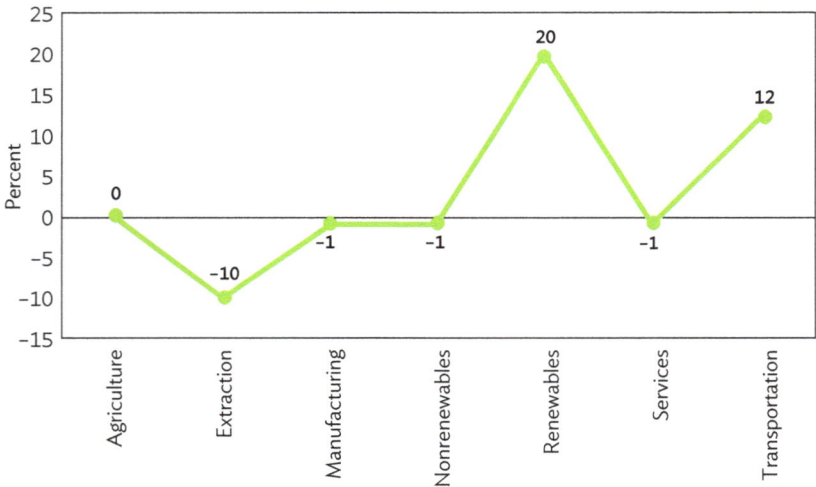

Source: Author's calculations based on GTAP simulations.

Figure 5.12: Percent Change in Output—Philippines

OUTPUT	Scenario 1 (%)	Scenario 2 (%)
Agriculture	0	0
Extraction	0	–10
Manufacturing	0	0
Nonrenewables	0	–2
Renewables	9	21
Services	0	0
Transportation	0	16

Source: Author's calculations based on GTAP simulations.

The Philippine NDC's unconditional target is to reduce emissions by 2.7%, while its conditional target is 72.3%. To be more realistic, the unconditional NDC target is used as a shock to the model. Results show a 0.2% increase in GDP ($700 million). Exports increase by $148 million. There is a 20% increase in investments for renewables with output also increasing by around 21%. Employment increases by 0.75%. Though there is a decline in extraction, the net GDP impact is positive, possibly due to the rise in renewable output to a level good enough to meet the country's energy demand. It could also be due to the relatively low emission target the Philippines set compared to other ASEAN economies. Also, the Philippines has already invested more in renewable energy sources, already tapping solar and hydropower to help supply power needs. With the decline in prices for renewables, it is likely the country will try to shift away from nonrenewable sources.

Baseline data show export composition split, with 64.9% from domestic input and 35.1% from foreign value added (Table 5.19). Computer, electronic, and optical products make up 30% of exports. Heavy manufacturing like electrical equipment and machinery is also strong, with 51.9% domestic value added and 48.1% foreign value added. Though the results of the E-Power model show an increase in exports, they also show a decline in exports of heavy manufacturing. The results of the GTAP-VA model show a 3.0% decline in domestic value added and an 11.6% increase in foreign value added for heavy manufacturing. Foreign value added comes from a rise in imports from Japan, and the ROK. Domestic value added increases by 24.1% and foreign value added by 14.7%.

Table 5.19: Percent Change in Domestic and Foreign Value Added—Philippines

Sector	Domestic Value Add		Foreign Value Add	
	Scenario 1	Scenario 2	Scenario 1	Scenario 2
Grains and Crops	−0.94	29.11	−0.70	12.69
Meat Products	−0.98	35.66	−0.84	19.81
Forestry and Mining	−0.47	28.57	−0.20	15.54
Coal	−2.17	−55.47	−5.45	10.34
Oil	0.32	−69.93	−1.44	−61.55
Gas	0.42	0.11	0.42	0.97
Processed Food	−0.98	37.16	−0.92	26.45
Textiles and Apparel	−1.09	21.58	−0.88	13.65
Light Manufacturing	−0.88	49.10	−0.71	41.01
Oil Products	3.82	−14.99	−0.66	−62.81
Heavy Manufacturing	−0.67	−3.03	−0.52	11.62
Electricity	0.95	62.65	87.87	1.38
Utility and Construction	−1.13	39.09	−0.86	36.08
Transport and Communication	−0.30	82.47	0.38	46.68
Services	−1.23	32.27	−1.07	19.08

Source: Author's calculations based on GTAP simulations.

Electricity demand is expected to more than triple by 2040. With coal-powered plants expected to supply a lower power share, substituting nonrenewable sources with renewable energy could lower energy costs as well as enhance sustainability. With 136.02 $MtCO_2e$ in 2020, the social cost amounts to \$25.2 billion. The model estimates the Philippines could add another \$700 million to GDP if it meets its NDC target. Savings are much higher at current prices, adding more than \$25.9 billion.

Singapore

Singapore has relatively few nonrenewable resources and relies almost entirely on natural gas to provide power. It does not have access to hydro resources and wind speeds, and the mean tidal range limits wind power options. Solar power is the main source of Singapore's renewable energy program. In 2020, it produced 45.50 $MtCO_2e$, down 19.6% from the 56.6 $MtCO_2e$ in 2010 (Table 5.20). In 2020, Singapore logged 8 $MtCO_2e$ per capita, a decrease of 3.2 $MtCO_2e$ from the 11.1 $MtCO_2e$ per person in 2010. Singapore's solar power capacity increased from 25 MW in 2014 to 336 MW in 2020.

Table 5.20: Emissions and Renewable Power Capacity—Singapore

Indicator	Value
Emissions in 2010	56.62 MT
Emissions in 2020	45.50 MT
NDC target as per Paris Agreement	-36%
Scenario 1 Shock	-19%
Scenario 2 Shock	-36%
Solar power capacity	336 MW
Wind power capacity	0 MW
Hydropower capacity	0 MW

MT = metric ton, MW = megawatt, NDC = nationally determined contribution.
Source: Author's calculations based on GTAP simulations.

With a 19% emission reduction between 2010 and 2020, the BAU scenario assumes that the same amount would fall between 2020 and 2030. The model estimates a 0.22% decline in GDP ($771 million) (Table 5.21). Only Singapore among ASEAN countries reduced emissions between 2010 and 2020. The model estimates a 10% increase in investments in renewables, resulting in a 137% increase in renewable power output (Figure 5.13a and Figure 5.13b). Employment under this scenario declines by 0.72%.

Table 5.21: Change in Macroeconomic Variables—Singapore

Economic Indicator	Scenario 1		Scenario 2	
	% Change	Absolute Value ($ million)	% Change	Absolute Value ($ million)
GDP	-0.22	-771	-3.62	-12,703
Exports	-2.74	-10,424	-23.81	-90,565
Imports	-2.73	-9,202	-26.02	-87,710
Domestic Value Added	-1.05	-1,952	-33.40	-61,856
Foreign Value Added	-0.67	-1,294	-38.18	-74,246
Social cost of carbon emissions ($ billion) = 2020 Emissions in $MtCO_2e$ * $185	8.42			
Net Savings (in $ billion) = Social Cost - GDP gains/+GDP losses	7.65		-4.29	

CO_2 = carbon dioxide, GDP = gross domestic product, $MtCO_2e$ = metric tons of CO_2 equivalent.
Source: Author's calculations based on GTAP simulations.

Figure 5.13a: Percent Change in Investment in Singapore— Scenario 1

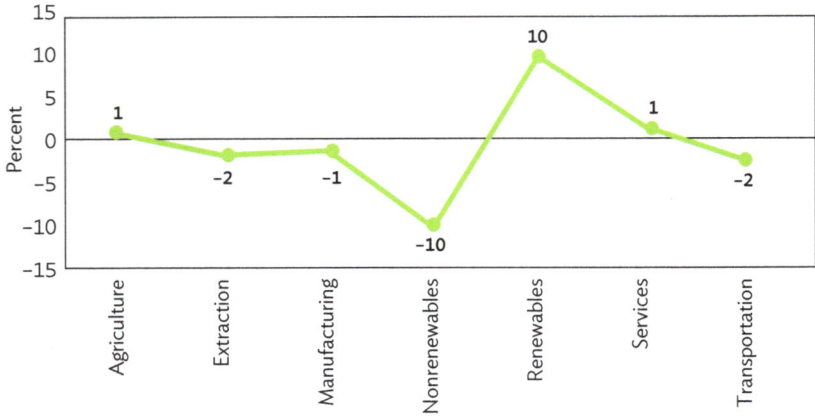

Source: Author's calculations based on GTAP simulations.

Figure 5.13b: Percent Change in Investment in Singapore— Scenario 2

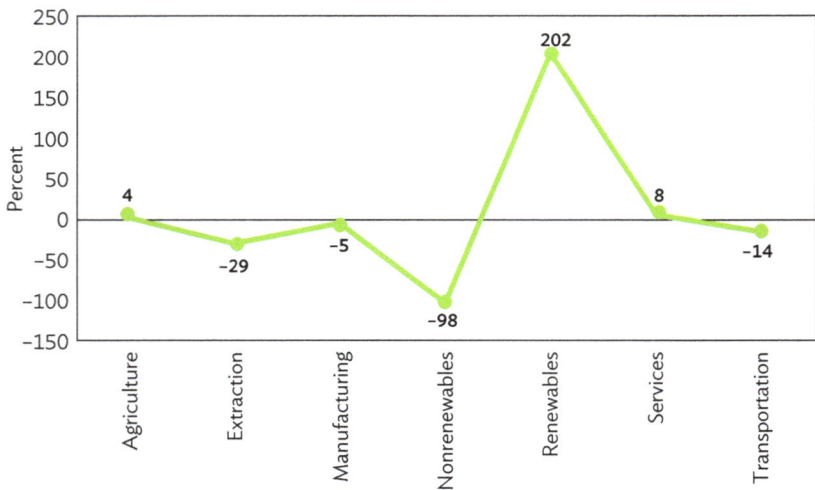

Source: Author's calculations based on GTAP simulations.

GDP declines by 3.6% under the NDC scenario based on Singapore meeting its 36% emissions reduction target. The output of renewable power generation (solar) must increase by 150%, with nonrenewable sources declining by 90%. There is a drop in the output of energy-intensive sectors like extraction (–54%), transportation (–32%), and manufacturing (–27%). Services and agriculture also decline. As the country diverts labor, capital, and other resources toward increasing solar power capacity, the model shows other sectors declining. To achieve its NDC target, investment in renewable power must increase by 202% with investment in nonrenewable power decreasing by 98% (Figure 5.14). Investments in extraction, manufacturing, and transportation also decline. The drop in investment and output of energy-intensive sectors is the main cause of the decline in GDP. Employment declines by 9.5%.

Figure 5.14: Percent Change in Output—Singapore

OUTPUT	Scenario 1 (%)	Scenario 2 (%)
Agriculture	0	–5
Extraction	–6	–54
Manufacturing	–3	–27
Nonrenewables	–12	–90
Renewables	137	150
Services	0	–5
Transportation	–6	–32

Source: Author's calculations based on GTAP simulations.

Services, electronic, computer, and optical products, oil products, and chemicals, are the main export categories, with Malaysia, the EU, the PRC, and the US as the top export destinations. Within Singapore's exports, 48.8% comes from domestic value added while 51.2% comes from foreign value added (Table 5.22). The foreign value-added share is predominantly higher in heavy manufacturing and oil products. Scenario 2 shows that in meeting its NDC target, Singapore registers a decline in both domestic and foreign value-added components. The aggregate domestic value-added component in exports falls by 33.4% with foreign value added declining by 38.2%. In heavy manufacturing, domestic value added drops by 23.0% and foreign value added declines by 28.5%. For oil products, domestic value added falls by 12.6% and foreign value added drops by 55.4%. This could disrupt the supply chains for both heavy manufacturing (going to Malaysia, the EU, the PRC, and the US) and oil products (heading to Indonesia, Malaysia, Thailand, and the PRC).

Table 5.22: Percent Change in Domestic and Foreign Value Added—Singapore

Sector	Domestic Value Added		Foreign Value Added	
	Scenario 1	Scenario 2	Scenario 1	Scenario 2
Grains and Crops	−0.77	−15.12	−0.20	−5.61
Meat Products	−1.59	−43.48	−1.03	−48.90
Forestry and Mining	−3.79	−85.35	−0.74	−67.14
Coal	0.14	−0.01	0.14	0.63
Oil	0.28	0.41	0.27	0.45
Gas	0.66	0.38	0.66	0.52
Processed Food	−1.21	−24.25	−0.62	−19.08
Textiles and Apparel	−3.21	−83.19	−2.66	−89.71
Light Manufacturing	−1.33	−31.92	−0.90	−28.18
Oil Products	12.59	−12.57	−0.22	−55.39
Heavy Manufacturing	−1.05	−23.03	−0.60	−28.49
Electricity	27.25	−49.46	27.52	−8.68
Utility and Construction	−1.43	−34.68	−0.91	−32.21
Transport and Communication	−1.95	−59.16	−1.60	−59.58
Services	−0.92	−30.04	−0.56	−29.84

Source: Author's calculations based on GTAP simulations.

Singapore has limited access to renewable energy so there are limits on what it can do to reduce carbon emissions. Yet, the country has successfully reduced emissions by relying on natural gas (one of the cleanest fossil fuels) for 95% of its electricity. The country is accelerating use of solar power while working on ways to increase the carbon efficiency of natural gas. Singapore emitted 45.5 $MtCO_2e$ in 2020 and with the social cost of carbon at $185 per $MtCO_2e$, the overall cost comes to $8.42 billion, way higher than the estimated GDP losses in both scenario 1 ($771 million) and scenario 2 ($12.70 billion). The net savings amount to $7.7 billion in scenario 1 and $4.3 billion in scenario 2. Though the initial cost of mitigation and renewable power might seem a bit higher, the savings and the long-term benefits are quite high.

Thailand

The government promotes renewable resources to replace fossil fuels—mainly natural gas—to reduce damage to the environment. Thailand emitted 257.8 $MtCO_2e$ in 2020, with per capita emissions reaching 3.7 $MtCO_2e$, slightly below the 3.8 $MtCO_2e$ per capita in 2010 (Table 5.23). As of 2020, Thailand's hydropower capacity was 3,667 MW, solar capacity 2,988 MW, and wind power capacity 1,507 MW. Thailand targets 30% of its energy consumption by 2036 to come from renewable resources.

Table 5.23: Emissions and Renewable Power Capacity—Thailand

Indicator	Value
Emissions in 2010	255.40 MT
Emissions in 2020	255.57 MT
NDC target as per Paris Agreement	−20%
Scenario 1 Shock	0%
Scenario 2 Shock	−20%
Solar power capacity	2,988 MW
Wind power capacity	1,507 MW
Hydropower capacity	3,667 MW

MT = metric ton, MW = megawatt, NDC = nationally determined contribution.
Source: Author's calculations based on GTAP simulations.

Emissions in 2020 were nearly the same as in 2010, so, for the BAU scenario, the same level of emissions is expected between 2020 and 2030. The model estimates a 0.03% increase in GDP and 0.11% increase in exports (Table 5.24). There is an 8% increase in investments made in renewable energy sources and a 16% increase in output (Figure 5.15a and Figure 5.15b). Employment increases by 0.06%.

Table 5.24: Change in Macroeconomic Variables—Thailand

Economic Indicator	Scenario 1 % Change	Scenario 1 Absolute Value ($ million)	Scenario 2 % Change	Scenario 2 Absolute Value ($ million)
GDP	0.03	157	−0.22	−1,062
Exports	0.11	33	−0.29	−872
Imports	0.45	123	−7.25	2,206
Domestic Value Added	0.19	353	5.50	9,989
Foreign Value Added	−0.04	−39	32.86	37,060
Social cost of carbon emissions ($ billion) = 2020 Emissions in $MtCO_2e * \$185$	47.69			
Net Savings (in $ billion) = Social Cost − GDP gains/+GDP losses	47.84			48.75

CO_2 = carbon dioxide, GDP = gross domestic product, $MtCO_2e$ = metric tons of CO_2 equivalent.
Source: Author's calculations based on GTAP simulations.

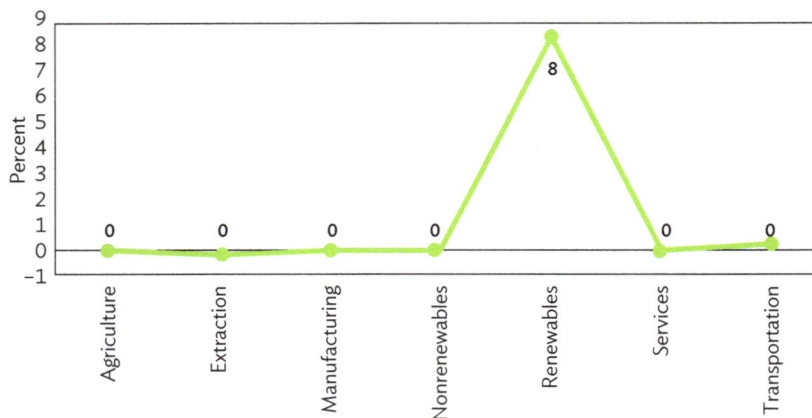

Figure 5.15a: Percent Change in Investment in Thailand—Scenario 1

Source: Author's calculations based on GTAP simulations.

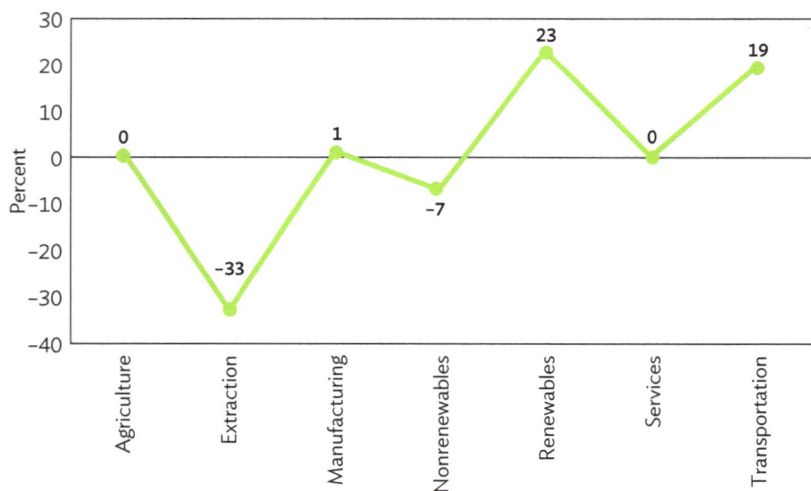

Figure 5.15b: Percent Change in Investment in Thailand—Scenario 2

Source: Author's calculations based on GTAP simulations.

Thailand's NDC aims to reduce its emissions in 2030 by 20%. The model results show a 0.22% decline in GDP, or $1.1 billion. The output of renewables increases by 31% with nonrenewable power sources declining by 5% (Figure 5.16). This comes from a 23% increase in investment in renewable power sources and a corresponding 33% decrease in investments in nonrenewable power sources. Extraction output declines by 33% due to an 18% decline in coal and a 76% decline in gas. There is an increase in transportation output (22%) and manufacturing (1%). The decline estimated for sectors like grains, processed food, rubber and plastics, and electronic equipment are behind the overall decline in GDP. The decline in energy-intensive sectors is largely covered by an increase in manufacturing. Employment declines by 0.31%.

Figure 5.16: Percent Change in Output—Thailand

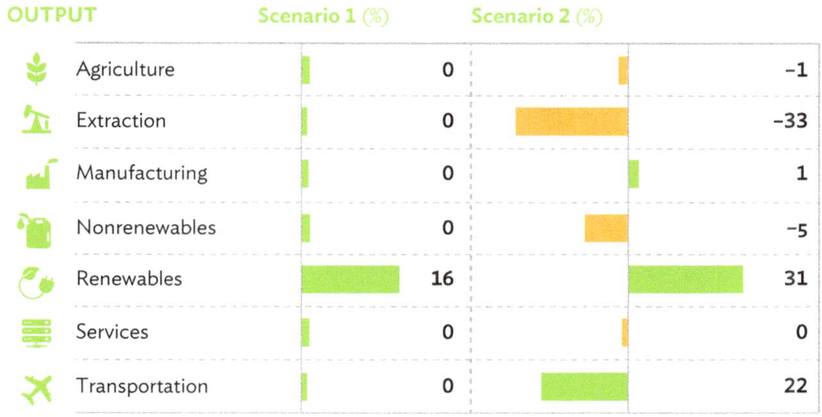

OUTPUT	Scenario 1 (%)	Scenario 2 (%)
Agriculture	0	−1
Extraction	0	−33
Manufacturing	0	1
Nonrenewables	0	−5
Renewables	16	31
Services	0	0
Transportation	0	22

Source: Author's calculations based on GTAP simulations.

More than 44% of exports are in heavy manufacturing and 18.8% in light manufacturing. Within manufacturing, electronics, computer, and optic products ("ele" in GTAP), heavy vehicles, machinery, and equipment, and processed food are exported. Top destinations are Japan, the EU, the PRC, and the US. Exports contain 61.7% domestic value added and 38.3% foreign value added (Table 5.25). Scenario 2 results show domestic value added increases by 5.5% and foreign value added by 36.2%. By sector, there is a decline in domestic value added in energy-intensive sectors, producing a ripple effect across other sectors such as processed food, manufacturing, and textiles. This could disrupt supply chains and increase dependence on Japan, the EU, and the PRC outside ASEAN, and Malaysia and Viet Nam within ASEAN.

Table 5.25: Percent Change in Domestic and Foreign Value Added—Thailand

Sector	Domestic Value Add		Foreign Value Add	
	Scenario 1	Scenario 2	Scenario 1	Scenario 2
Grains and Crops	−0.14	56.60	−0.01	31.35
Meat Products	−0.15	84.74	−0.06	48.35
Forestry and Mining	0.05	−4.98	0.30	25.36
Coal	0.67	0.82	56.60	−0.16
Oil	−0.60	−26.79	−1.94	−0.28
Gas	−5.15	−5.45	−6.41	−0.20
Processed Food	−0.07	−4.51	0.01	40.44
Textiles and Apparel	−0.21	−3.57	−0.19	55.76
Light Manufacturing	−0.03	−2.53	−0.23	31.23
Oil Products	3.57	−4.80	0.25	−7.01
Heavy Manufacturing	0.21	−2.77	−0.07	34.97
Electricity	−3.65	−1.78	−6.34	55.50
Utility and Construction	0.08	−3.28	0.02	40.66
Transport and Communication	0.84	−8.80	0.97	48.87
Services	−0.37	53.02	−0.29	32.78

Source: Author's calculations based on GTAP simulations.

Gas-based thermal power accounts for more than 61% of Thailand's power generation. Though the country produces natural gas and oil, hydrocarbon imports are needed to meet the rising demand for fuel. Thailand's natural gas reserves are getting depleted while the country grapples with rising import costs. Hundreds of wells must be drilled to meet natural gas demand. If no wells are found, the country may find it difficult to meet energy demand. Thus, investing more in renewables will help the country reach its NDC targets, reduce dependence on fossil fuels, and lower import costs. Thailand has an array of renewable resources so it does not have to depend on a single source like hydro or solar, unlike some of its neighbors. Thailand emitted 257.8 MtCO$_2$e in 2020. The social cost amounts to $47.7 billion. Comparing this against the losses estimated by the model ($1.1 billion), the transition looks highly affordable as savings from social cost outweigh the short-term economic losses estimated in the model. The net savings after accounting for GDP losses estimated in scenario 2 is $48.8 billion. It may seem costly initially, but the long-term benefits outweigh short-term effects.

Viet Nam

As of 2021, Viet Nam has been extremely successful in attracting investments in renewable energy. It has diverse renewable power resources with hydropower capacity in 2020 of 20,817 MW, solar power capacity of 16,660 MW (from just 5 MW in 2014), and wind power capacity of 518 MW (Table 5.26). Even though it has been working rapidly to develop renewable capacity, CO_2 emissions increased due to high use of coal in power generation. As of 2020, its per capita emission was 2.7 $MtCO_2e$, up from 1.6 $MtCO_2e$ in 2010. In 2020, emissions totaled 254.3 $MtCO_2e$.

Table 5.26: Emissions and Renewable Power Capacity—Viet Nam

Indicator	Value
Emissions in 2010	138.59 MT
Emissions in 2020	254.30 MT
NDC target as per Paris Agreement	–9%
Scenario 1 Shock	0%
Scenario 2 Shock	–9%
Solar power capacity	16,660 MW
Wind power capacity	518 MW
Hydropower capacity	20,817 MW

MW = megawatt, MT = metric ton, NDC = nationally determined contribution..
Source: Author's calculations based on GTAP simulations.

Though renewable power capacity increased rapidly between 2014 and 2020, emissions also grew substantially. In 2010, its CO_2 emissions were 138.6 $MtCO_2e$, reaching 254.3 $MtCO_2e$ in 2020, or an increase of 83.5%. Under the BAU scenario, there will be no change in emissions between 2020 and 2030. The model estimates a 0.14% increase in GDP, 0.25% increase in exports, and 0.18% increase in employment (Table 5.27). The results show a 4% increase in investments in renewables with output increasing by 8%.

Table 5.27: Change in Macroeconomic Variables—Viet Nam

	Scenario 1		Scenario 2	
Economic Indicator	% Change	Absolute Value ($ million)	% Change	Absolute Value ($ million)
GDP	0.14	332	−2.14	−5,229
Exports	0.25	662	3.62	9,438
Imports	0.18	488	−0.36	−972
Domestic Value Added	1.44	1,707	−36.18	−42,946
Foreign Value Added	1.00	1411	34.34	48,621
Social cost of carbon emissions ($ billion) = 2020 Emissions in $MtCO_2e$ * $185	47.05			
Net Savings (in $ billion) = Social Cost - GDP gains/+GDP losses		47.38		41.82

CO_2 = carbon dioxide, GDP = gross domestic product, $MtCO_2e$ = metric tons of CO_2 equivalent.
Source: Author's calculations based on GTAP simulations.

Under Viet Nam's 9% unconditional NDC target (conditional pledges are less realistic), the model estimates that GDP will decline by 2.1%. There is also a 2.7% decline in employment. By sector, renewable power output increases by 24% (Figure 5.18), with other sectors like transportation, manufacturing, and agriculture also increasing. Renewable sources like solar and hydropower notably increase while extractions like oil and coal decline. Although manufacturing, agriculture, and transportation output rise, the decline in GDP comes from the drop in oil, construction, and services—a significant portion of the economy. Investments in renewables rise by 19% and in transportation by 21% (Figure 5.17a and Figure5.17b). This reduces the capital available for investment in other sectors like extraction.

Textiles and apparel, electronic, computer, and optical manufacturing (aggregated under heavy manufacturing) contribute much to Viet Nam's exports. Its exports primarily go to Japan, the EU, the PRC, and the US. There is 45.6% of domestic value added, with the remaining 54.4% foreign value added (Table 5.28). Under scenario 2, the model estimates a 36.2% decline in the domestic value added with an increase of 34.3% in foreign value added. In textiles, domestic value-added component declines by 27.5% but foreign value-added increases by 15.6%, possibly due to an increase in textile imports from Taipei,China; the PRC; and the ROK.

Figure 5.17a: Percent Change in Investment in Viet Nam— Scenario 1

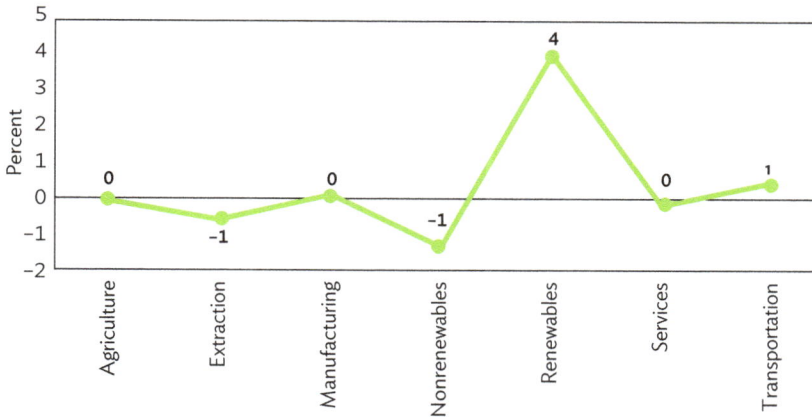

Source: Author's calculations based on GTAP simulations.

Figure 5.17b: Percent Change in Investment in Viet Nam— Scenario 2

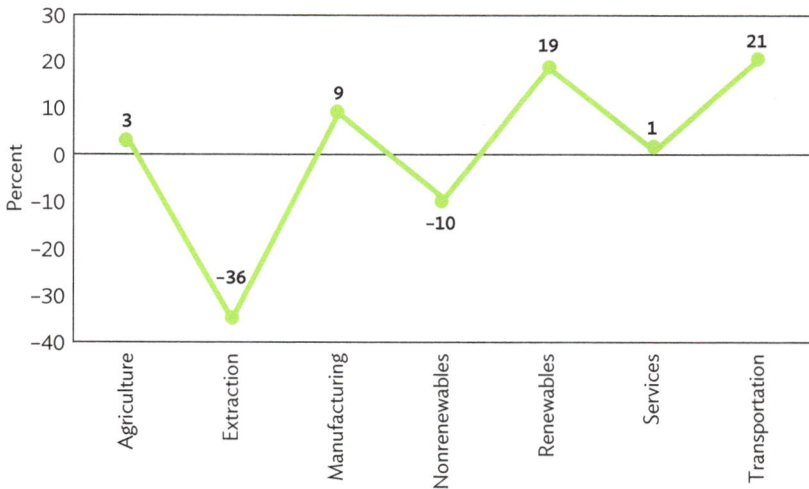

Source: Author's calculations based on GTAP simulations.

Figure 5.18: Percent Change in Output—Viet Nam

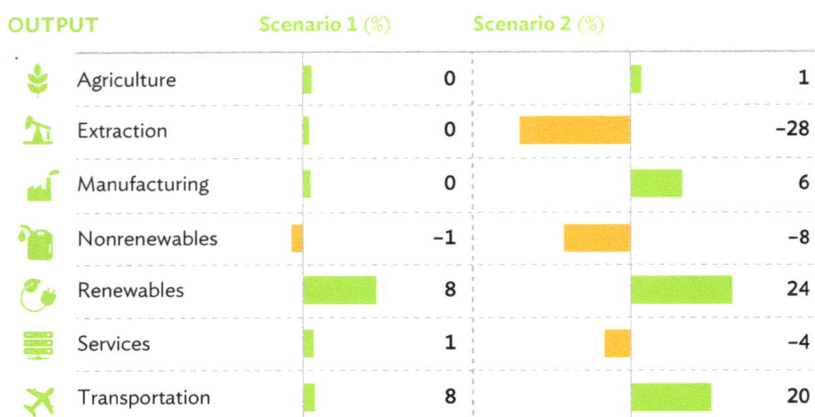

OUTPUT	Scenario 1 (%)	Scenario 2 (%)
Agriculture	0	1
Extraction	0	−28
Manufacturing	0	6
Nonrenewables	−1	−8
Renewables	8	24
Services	1	−4
Transportation	8	20

Source: Author's calculations based on GTAP simulations.

Table 5.28: Percent Change in Domestic and Foreign Value Added—Viet Nam

Sector	Domestic Value Added		Foreign Value Added	
	Scenario 1	Scenario 2	Scenario 1	Scenario 2
Grains and Crops	1.00	−0.36	0.78	25.51
Meat Products	0.98	−17.86	1.04	34.62
Forestry and Mining	1.42	−14.56	0.87	63.37
Coal	−2.79	−37.21	−3.38	−14.21
Oil	−0.52	−8.84	−0.53	17.81
Gas	0.14	−46.29	134.17	−45.78
Processed Food	1.53	−53.51	1.30	82.54
Textiles and Apparel	1.31	−27.45	0.96	15.65
Light Manufacturing	1.57	−61.15	0.85	46.11
Oil Products	1.84	−9.82	1.90	15.99
Heavy Manufacturing	2.18	−56.57	1.09	32.81
Electricity	5.11	−51.04	3.42	57.35
Utility and Construction	2.63	−23.14	1.65	23.55
Transport and Communication	3.61	0.02	2.79	38.31
Services	1.61	−2.73	0.65	30.33

Source: Author's calculations based on GTAP simulations.

Economic growth and development over the past decade almost doubled CO_2 emissions. Coal remains the major energy source, and among all Greater Mekong Subregion countries, Viet Nam has the largest coal power capacity. The continuous rise in energy demand forces Viet Nam to import fossil fuels. Hydropower remains a major source of renewable energy, followed by solar and wind power. Viet Nam needs to add more renewable energy to its energy mix to meet its NDC target. Viet Nam emitted 254.3 $MtCO_2e$ in 2020 with the social cost of emissions reaching $47.1 billion. Against the estimated GDP loss of $5.2 billion, the transition looks affordable. The net savings from social costs after accounting for GDP losses amount to $41.8 billion. Also, the future lower costs for renewable technologies mean capital costs should fall. This allows Viet Nam to save a lot more over the long run as it continues to shift to renewables.

Conclusion

Except for Singapore, each ASEAN member increased its carbon emissions from 2010 to 2020. As a region, emissions rose by 34.2%. This is alarming. If left alone, it will reduce long-term socioeconomic prosperity. The cost of meeting the NDC target levels of each ASEAN member is estimated to be $50.1 billion, or 1.7% of ASEAN GDP. Value chain disruptions could cost $166.9 billion.

Yet, despite all this, the costs are quite affordable given the socioeconomic and biodiversity losses if nothing is done. With the social cost of carbon estimated at $185 per $MtCO_2e$, maintaining the 1,651.9 $MtCO_2e$ ASEAN produced in 2020 would cost $306 billion. Thus, savings from social costs outweighs GDP and supply chain losses—or an estimated savings of $256 billion.

Emission reduction targets can be met with strong investment and capacity building. Well thought-out strategies and policies that reduce emissions— for example, by replacing fossil fuel energy sources with solar, wind, and hydroelectric power—has already been a priority for countries with good renewable energy infrastructure. Carbon leakages from those with lower NDC targets must be plugged if the region is to create a truly green economy.

Coal remains the dominant energy source for ASEAN economies. Electricity generation technologies and power sources should be a priority in carbon mitigation policies and emission reduction plans. Increasing investments in high efficiency, low emission, and renewable power generating technologies is essential to meet the increasing energy demand from expanding populations and rapidly developing economies—all while reducing emissions to the agreed Paris Agreement NDCs. Shifting subsidies from fossil fuel consumption to incentives for renewable power development would make the allocation of scarce resources far more efficient.

Within ASEAN generally, electronic, computer, and optical manufacturing, along with oil products, textiles, wearing apparel, and processed food are the major exported goods (aside from services). ASEAN's foreign value added is 30.3% of the value of exports heading outside the region. Foreign sources provide 55.8% of inputs to petroleum, coal, and oil products; 41.5% to textiles and apparel; and 39.9% to heavy manufacturing. Of the aggregate value of foreign inputs to ASEAN products, more than one-fifth ends up in exports to the PRC (21.6%), with the rest going to the EU (18.2%), the US (14.8%), Japan (9.9%), the ROK (4.5%), India (3.6%), and other economies (see GTAP 10 database).

ASEAN value added from within is $122.0 billion. Singapore uses the most value added from other ASEAN economies in its exports ($51.6 billion), followed by Thailand ($26.5 billion), Malaysia ($17.8 billion), and Viet Nam ($15.0 billion).

This underscores just how complex ASEAN supply chains are—entangled with both developed and developing economies. Disruptions produce ripple effects across the value chain and require adjustments at each segment.

Reducing emissions to meet NDC targets could cost $165.2 billion in domestic value-added components, with a $1.7 billion decline in foreign value-added inputs. Much of the drop in domestic value added is energy-intensive like coal, gas, manufacturing, and oil products. ASEAN's export share in coal, for example, equals 31.7% of global exports; 17.3% of gas exports; 8.2% in textiles and apparel; 6.5% of global exports for oil; and 4.9% in light manufacturing. This affects exports to Japan, the Republic of Korea, the EU, the PRC, and the US as they hold the highest domestic value-added content from ASEAN. If these countries substitute imports from other countries with lower NDC targets, it could lead to greater global carbon leakage.

Foreign value-added components have increased in textiles, light manufacturing, coal, oil, processed food, and heavy manufacturing, among others. Both domestic and foreign value-added components have increased in exports of non-energy-intensive products like grains, other crops, and meat. In energy-intensive sectors, ASEAN economies may grow more dependent on foreign value-added components.

Some countries like Brunei Darussalam and Indonesia are highly dependent on fossil fuel trade. They could lose as other countries reduce fossil fuel imports to meet NDC targets. Thus, investing in renewables will allow them to both meet their NDC targets and reduce dependence on fossil fuels. As the capital costs of renewable technologies continue to fall as they mature, estimated GDP losses would decrease further.

Policy Implications

There are five major implications for ASEAN policy makers:

1. Substituting nonrenewable with renewable energy sources and cleaner fossil fuels offers a huge opportunity to the GVCs related to these sectors. While in aggregate, a 32% rise in renewable investments drives a 36% increase in ASEAN's renewable output, it is most prominent in Singapore (150%), Indonesia (140%), the Lao PDR (127%), and Malaysia (101%). There is also an increase in employment in these sectors. The supply chain analysis shows how ASEAN economies are highly entangled with other developed and developing economies. It reveals a paradigm shift toward an increase in output and exports of non-energy-intensive commodities with a simultaneous decline in energy-intensive sectors. Meeting NDC targets is an opportunity for ASEAN economies to decarbonize their supply chains as a precursor to creating greener technologies and products.
2. At their rates of emissions, ASEAN members will need to cover an estimated social cost of about $306 billion. When weighed against the estimated costs of achieving NDCs, the savings reaches $256 billion. As these savings eventually boost private consumption, it also boosts overall productivity, which would in fact compensate for some of the losses in the sectors and variables cited. Thus, it makes sense for ASEAN members to set efficient policies that will channel these savings to create a virtuous cycle leading to greater investments in renewables. If ASEAN members can do this from their savings, they can lead the way toward greater emissions reduction.
3. This virtuous cycle offers a future roadmap to an achievable net zero, as plans may already appear overly ambitious.
4. ASEAN members should help lead GVC decarbonization. This analysis assumes no reduction in trade barriers. But if trade barriers are eliminated, particularly across the renewables GVC, reduced costs will clearly help reach net zero. Policy makers should focus on reducing trade barriers in the renewables supply chain to make the transition easier.

5.   This chapter does not comprehensively capture the opportunity cost of climate change on GVCs. If this were done, there may be spiralling economic losses globally in addition to the direct costs faced in those regions facing climate disasters. For example, if Viet Nam is severely affected by climate change, all manufacturing products—from textiles to automobiles—will jump in price, heavily affecting importing countries. Thus, the findings on net social benefits further reinforces the virtuous cycle as decarbonization leads to social benefits that further strengthen GVCs.

In sum, policy makers should strengthen their decarbonization strategies by leveraging GVCs. By doing so, they are reinforced and will boost the use of renewables globally.

Appendix

Sectoral and Regional Aggregation

Regions	GTAP E-Power Aggregation Sectors	GTAP VA Aggregation Sectors
Australia	Grain crops	Grain crops
New Zealand	Meat and animal products	Meat and animal products
Pacific	Forestry	Forestry, fishing, and other mining
People's Republic of China	Fishing	Coal
Hong Kong, China	Coal	Oil
Japan	Oil	Gas
Republic of Korea	Gas	Processed food
Mongolia	Extraction	Textiles and apparels
Taipei,China	Processed food	Light manufacturing
Rest of East Asia	Textile and apparels	Oil products
Brunei Darussalam	Leather	Heavy manufacturing
Cambodia	Wood products	Electricity
Indonesia	Paper products, publishing	Utility and construction
Lao People's Democratic Republic	Petroleum, coal products	Transport and communication
Malaysia	Chemical products	Other services
Philippines	Basic pharmaceutical products	
Singapore	Rubber and plastic products	
Thailand	Mineral products	
Viet Nam	Ferrous metals	
Rest of Southeast Asia	Metal	
Bangladesh	Metal products	
India	Computer, electronic, and optical products	
Nepal	Electrical equipment	
Pakistan	Machinery and equipment	
Sri Lanka	Motor vehicles and parts	
Rest of South Asia	Transport equipment	
Canada	Other manufactures	
United States	transmission and distribution	
European Union 28	Nuclear baseload	
Switzerland	Coal baseload	
Norway	Gas baseload	
Russian Federation	Wind baseload	
Kazakhstan	Hydro baseload	
Kyrgyz Republic	Oil baseload	
Tajikistan	Other power	

continued on next page

Table (continued)

Regions	GTAP E-Power Aggregation Sectors	GTAP VA Aggregation Sectors
Rest of Central Asia	Gas peak load	
Armenia	Hydro peak load	
Azerbaijan	Oil peak load	
Georgia	Solar peak load	
Türkiye	Water	
	Construction	
	Trade	
	Accommodation, food, and service activities	
	Other transport	
	Water transport	
	Air transport	
	Warehousing	
	Communication	
	Other services	

GTAP = Global Trade Analysis Project, VA = value added
Source: GTAP.

References

Aguiar, A., M. Chepeliev, E. Corong, R. McDougall and D. van der Mensbrugghe. 2019. The GTAP Data Base: Version 10. *Journal of Global Economic Analysis*. 4 (1). pp. 1–27. https://doi.org/10.21642/JGEA.040101AF.

Antimiani, A., I. Fusacchia, and L. Salvatici. 2018. GTAP-VA: An Integrated Tool for Global Value Chain Analysis. *Journal of Global Economic Analysis*. 3 (2). pp. 69–105. https://doi.org/10.21642/JGEA.030202AF.

Arino, Y., P. Sivapuram Ventaka Rama Krishna, Y.Y. Lee, M. Ikeda, and E. Zusman. 2021. ASEAN State of Climate Change Report. https://asean.org/wp-content/uploads/2021/10/ASCCR-e-publication-Correction_8-June.pdf.

ASEAN Centre for Energy. 2016. *Levelised Cost of Electricity of Selected Renewable Technologies in the ASEAN Member States*. https://agep.aseanenergy.org/wp-content/uploads/2018/04/Levelised-Cost-of-Electricity-of-Selected-Renewable-Technologies-in-ASEAN-Member-States.pdf.

Barbe, A. 2017. The Effects of Restricting Coal Consumption on Coal Exports and Greenhouse Gas Emissions. *U.S. International Trade Commission Working Paper. 2017-05-A*. https://www.usitc.gov/publications/332/working_papers/081117_coal.html.

Birur, D., T. W. Hertel, and W.E. Tyner. 2007. *The Biofuels Boom: Implications for World Food Markets*. https://www.academia.edu/6205255/The_Biofuels_Boom_Implications_for_World_Food_Markets.

Burniaux J., and T. Truong. 2002. *GTAP-E: An Energy-Environmental Version of the GTAP Model*. Global Trade Analysis Project (GTAP). https://www.gtap.agecon.purdue.edu/resources/res_display.asp?RecordID=923.

Chontanawat, J. 2019. Relationship between Energy Consumption, CO_2 Emission and Economic Growth In ASEAN: Cointegration and Causality Model. https://doi.org/10.1016/j.egyr.2019.09.046.

Cristea, A., D. Hummels, L. Puzzello, and M. Avetisyan. 2013. Trade and the Greenhouse Gas Emissions from International Freight Transport. Journal of Environmental Economics and Management, 65(1), pp.153-173.

Do Dinh, L., and S. Kim. 2012. A General Equilibrium Model for Energy Policy Evaluation Using GTAP-E for Vietnam. https://eneken.ieej.or.jp/3rd_IAEE_Asia/pdf/abstract/059_ab.pdf.

Geneva Environment Network. 2021. The Growing Environmental Risks of E-Waste. https://www.genevaenvironmentnetwork.org/resources/updates/the-growing-environmental-risks-of-e-waste/.

Handayani, K., P. Anugrah, F. Goembira, I. Overland, B. Suryadi, and A. 2022. Moving Beyond the NDCs: ASEAN Pathways to a Net-Zero Emissions Power Sector in 2050. Applied Energy, 311, p.118580.

Hariani, E., W. R. Febriyastuti, and M. Tamonsang. 2022. An Analysis of Factors that Affect CO_2 Emissions in 5 ASEAN Countries in 2011–2018. https://doi.org/10.12928/optimum.v12i1.5824.

Hertel, T.W. 1997. Global Trade Analysis: Modeling and Applications. Cambridge University Press.

Intergovernmental Panel on Climate Change. 2014. Climate Change 2014: Mitigation of Climate Change. https://www.ipcc.ch/site/assets/uploads/2018/03/WGIIIAR5_SPM_TS_Volume-3.pdf.

International Energy Agency (IEA). 2020. Energy Technology Perspectives 2020. IEA. https://iea.blob.core.windows.net/assets/04dc5d08-4e45-447d-a0c1-d76b5ac43987/Energy_Technology_Perspectives_2020_-_Special_Report_on_Clean_Energy_Innovation.pdf.

International Renewable Energy Agency (IRENA) and ASEAN Centre for Energy (ACE). 2016. *Renewable Energy Outlook for ASEAN: a REmap Analysis.* IRENA, Abu Dhabi and ACE, Jakarta.

Lamb, W., M. Grubb, F. Diluiso, and J. Minx. 2022. Countries with Sustained Greenhouse Gas Emissions Reductions: An Analysis of Trends and Progress by Sector. *Climate Policy.* 22 (1). pp. 1–17. https://doi.org/10.1080/14693062.2021.1990831.

Liu, Y., Z. Sheng, and D. Azhgaliyeva. 2019. Toward Energy Security in ASEAN: Impacts of Regional Integration, Renewables, and Energy Efficiency. *ADBI Working Paper.* No. 1041. Tokyo: Asian Development Bank Institute. https://www.adb.org/publications/toward-energy-security-asean.

Marchi, B., and S. Zanoni. 2017. Supply Chain Management for Improved Energy Efficiency: Review and Opportunities. Energies, 10. no. 10: 1618. https://doi.org/10.3390/en10101618.

McDougall, R., and A. Golub. 2007. *GTAP E: A Revised Energy-Environmental Version of the GTAP Model.* GTAP. https://www.gtap.agecon.purdue.edu/resources/download/4212.pdf.

Narayan, M. 2021. Renewables to Make Up 30% of Brunei's Power Generation by 2035-Minister. Reuters. https://www.reuters.com/world/asia-pacific/renewables-make-up-30-bruneis-power-generation-by-2035-minister-2021-10-25/.

Nihayah, D.M., I. Mafruhah, L. Hakim, and S. Suryanto. 2022. CO_2 Emissions in Indonesia: The Role of Urbanization and Economic Activities towards Net Zero Carbon Economies, 10, No. 4: 72. https://doi.org/10.3390/economies10040072.

Ota, J., and J. Akagi. 2021. *Commitment to Net Zero Carbon Emissions by 2050 by Local Governments in the Kyushu Region of Japan.* https://www.iges.or.jp/en/publication_documents/pub/issue/en/11193/KUC+Issue+Brief_Kyushu+zero+carbon_rev.20210226_en.pdf.

Overland, I., H.F. Sagbakken, H.Y. Chan, M. Merdekawati, B. Suryadi, N.A. Utama, and R. Vakulchuk. 2021. The ASEAN Climate and Energy Paradox. Energy and Climate Change, 2, p.100019.

Paltsev, S., M. Mehling, N. Winchester, J. Morris and K. Ledvina. 2018. Pathways to Paris: ASEAN. *MIT Joint Program Special Report.* http://globalchange.mit.edu/publication/17160.

Peters, J. 2016a. GTAP-E-Power: An Electricity-detailed Economy-wide Model. *Journal of Global Economic Analysis.* 1 (2). 156–187. https://doi.org/10.21642/JGEA.010204AF.

_____. 2016b. *The GTAP-Power Data Base: Disaggregating the Electricity Sector in the GTAP Data Base. Journal of Global Economic Analysis.* https://www.gtap.agecon.purdue.edu/resources/res_display. asp?RecordID=4619.

Rasiah, R., A. Al-Amin, A. Chowdhurry, F. Ahmed, and C. Zhang. 2018. Climate Change Mitigation Projections for ASEAN. *Journal of the Asia Pacific Economy.* 23 (2). pp. 1–18.

Rennert, K., F. Errickson, B. Prest, L. Rennels, R. Newell, W. Pizer, C. Kingdon et al. 2022. Comprehensive Evidence Implies a Higher Social Cost of CO_2. *Nature* 610. pp. 687–692. https://doi.org/10.1038/s41586-022-05224-9.

Siriwardana, M. 2015. Australia's New Free Trade Agreements with Japan and South Korea: Potential Economic and Environmental Impacts. *Journal of Economic Integration.* 30 (4). https://www.e-jei.org/upload/JEI_30_4_616_643_2013600083.pdf.

Solingen, E., B. Meng, and A. Xu. 2021. *Global Value Chain Development Report 2021: Beyond Production.* World Trade Organization (WTO). https://www.wto.org/english/res_e/booksp_e/08_gvc_ch5_dev_report_2021_e.pdf.

Southeast Asia Energy Outlook 2019. 2019. https://iea.blob.core.windows.net/assets/47552310-d697-498c-b112-d987f36abf34/Southeast_Asia_Energy_Outlook_2019.pdf.

Stiglitz, J.E., N. Stern, M. Duan, O. Edenhofer, G. Giraud, G.M. Heal, E.L. La Rovere, A. Morris, E. Moyer, M. Pangestu, and P.R. Shukla, 2017. Report of the High-Level Commission on Carbon Prices. https://doi.org/10.7916/d8-w2nc-4103.

World Meteorological Organization (WMO). 2021. *WMO Atlas of Mortality and Economic Losses from Weather, Climate and Water Extremes (1970–2019).* https://library.wmo.int/index.php?lvl=notice_display&id=21930#.ZADIo-xBxao.

Zhang, S., K. Wang, W. Xu, X. Wei, U. Iyer-Raniga, A. Athienitis, H. Ge, D. Cho et al. 2021. Policy Recommendations for the Zero Energy Building Promotion towards Carbon Neutral in Asia-Pacific Region. *Energy Policy.* 159. https://doi.org/10.1016/j.enpol.2021.112661.

6

Scenarios for a Global "New Normal" and ASEAN Global Value Chains

Peter Petri and Michael Plummer

Diverging Prospects

Economic development in the Association of Southeast Asian Nations (ASEAN) has been long predicated on an outward-oriented production strategy. Over the past half century, this approach benefited from a steep drop in global trade barriers, deepening regional integration, and new extra-regional free–trade agreements. In this conducive economic environment, ASEAN firms built lucrative new industries by joining global and regional value chains (GVCs and RVCs). Yet, a series of recent developments empirically analyzed in this paper—spanning economic shocks and geopolitical tensions—now pose serious threats to the strategy.

High-stakes environment

The stakes are demonstrated by Viet Nam's stunning development. Viet Nam launched its *doi moi* program of economic liberalization in 1986, after decades of isolation from world markets. Since then, it has become the most open large developing economy in the world.[1] Viet Nam's trade-to-gross domestic product (trade-to-GDP) ratio rose from 19% in 1989 to 209% in 2020, and its inward foreign direct investments (FDI) grew from $15 billion in 2000 to $193 billion in 2021. Its forward and backward participation in GVCs has risen from 38.5% in 2007 to 52.3% in 2017 (AMRO 2021). For example, Viet Nam is now launching major manufacturing facilities for Apple iPhones and tablets.[2] The overall economic effects are rightly seen as a miracle: GDP expanded from $6 billion in 1989 to $363 billion in 2021;[3] per capita income levels grew from $95 to $3,700; and the poverty headcount fell from 37% of the population in 2002 to 2% in 2018.[4]

Today, progress faces enormous headwinds. Multilateral trade and investment liberalization are at an impasse, with the World Trade Organization (WTO) Appellate Body still not functioning and only modest gains from the 12th WTO Ministerial Conference.[5] The coronavirus disease (COVID-19) pandemic sharply disrupted international trade, fanning demand for reshoring and other policies to fragment international markets.

---

[1] Data cited in this paragraph are from World Bank. TCdata360. https://tcdata360.worldbank.org/indicators/NE.TRD.GNFS.ZS?country=BRA&indicator=1127&countries=VNM&viz=line_chart&years=1960,2020 (accessed 23 August 2022) and UNCTAD. 2022. *World Investment Report 2022 - International Tax Reforms and Sustainable Investment (Annex Table 2)*. New York: UN Publications. https://unctad.org/system/files/official-document/wir2022_en.pdf.

[2] See, for example, Hinojales (2021).

[3] World Bank. GDP (current $) - Viet Nam. https://data.worldbank.org/indicator/NY.GDP.MKTP.CD?locations=VN (accessed 23 August 2022).

[4] World Bank. Viet Nam - Country Data. https://data.worldbank.org/country/vietnam?view=chart (accessed 23 August 2022).

[5] Accomplishments included limits on fishery subsidies, food security, e-commerce, and a partial intellectual property rights waiver for coronavirus disease (COVID-19) vaccines.

The Russian invasion of Ukraine, followed by severe retaliatory sanctions, raised barriers to trade and geopolitical tensions. Related supply chain disruptions led to surges in the prices of energy, food, and other critical raw materials, driven by shortages and uncertainties about the future. These shocks are now fueling global inflation and deflationary policies to confront it. Governments are also imposing export bans and creating incentives to bring production home, and companies are reevaluating risks in foreign operations.

But the environment does include green shoots: much of Asia, increasingly led by ASEAN, continues to prioritize economic cooperation. The Regional Comprehensive Economic Partnership (RCEP), a historic, "ASEAN-centric" 15-member agreement, went into effect in January 2022, and the Comprehensive and Progressive Agreement for Trans-Pacific Partnership (CPTPP) survived the exit of the United States (US) and went into force in December 2018. The CPTPP has already received applications from Europe (the United Kingdom [UK]); Latin America (Ecuador, Costa Rica); and Asia (the People's Republic of China [PRC]; the Republic of Korea [ROK]; and Taipei,China). Indonesia, Thailand, and the Philippines have also expressed interest in joining. Notwithstanding the headwinds, ASEAN and like-minded partners are mounting a spirited defense of economic cooperation.

This study uses a newly constructed medium-term simulation model—an updated and improved alternative to the computable general equilibrium (CGE) model we used in earlier studies—to examine recent shocks and the sharply divergent policy options noted above, which will shape global trends in the coming decade and beyond.[6] An innovative technical aspect of the model is a Multiregional Input–Output (MRIO) subsystem that traces the effects of CGE simulations on the value chain structures that support contemporary trade.

Preview of results

To motivate the details that follow we begin by summarizing three sets of results. A first set describes a *new normal baseline* to account for shocks reflecting the Russian invasion of Ukraine and the recent surge in natural resource prices. The second examines proposed *geopolitical interventions* in trade that reflect political interests and concerns about supply chains. This set explores the implications of reshoring, near-shoring, and friend-shoring trade—widely discussed but still poorly understood alternatives for raising barriers among countries. The third analyzes

---

[6] For example, Park, Petri, and Plummer (2021) and a series of studies listed on asiapacifictrade.org.

enhanced economic cooperation options, including the implementation of the RCEP; two enlargements of the CPTPP adding seven economies; and massive agreements that bring the PRC, the US, the European Union (EU), and Taipei,China into the CPTPP and India into RCEP. This last, admittedly unrealistic, alternative defines a benchmark for renewed global cooperation.

The trends and policy alternatives examined in this chapter are highly uncertain. Results are best read for insights on qualitative changes—i.e., the relative implications of different policies for countries, industries, and variables—rather than quantitative detail. To build confidence in the results, the chapter tries to highlight data, relationships, and intuition behind key conclusions. Careful interpretation is especially important for stylized policy scenarios, such as friend-shoring, which so far lack implementation details like those available for tariff rates used to model RCEP.

Figures 6.1 through 6.3 summarize GDP simulations for selected country groups (ASEAN, CPTPP, RCEP, NATO+)[7] and in one case the Russian Federation. Later sections discuss further details and the mechanisms behind them. Relevant scenarios are described briefly in this section, but readers may wish to consult the next section and specifically Tables 6.1, 6.2A, and 6.2B for additional information. Results for scenarios are presented in real US dollar terms for 2035 *relative to baseline outcomes* for that year—for example, a 5% decline in real incomes in a scenario does not mean an absolute decline below 2021 levels, only that the trajectory will be 5% below the baseline trajectory in 2035.

The new normal scenario in Figure 6.1 shows the cumulative, long-term effects of the Russian invasion of Ukraine, higher resource prices, and their macroeconomic consequences. Global GDP, not shown in this figure, would fall by 2.2%. Even though real resource prices are likely to retreat somewhat from their levels in 2021 and 2022, the resource price surge will have widespread and persistent negative effects, especially for the resource-importing economies of ASEAN and RCEP. By contrast, NATO+ countries face milder effects; they include Australia, Canada, and the US, which are roughly self-sufficient in primary products. Despite higher energy prices, even Russian Federation real incomes decline, due to reduced exports of resource-intensive products, lower real wages, and employment losses. The invasion scenario depresses intermediate-term incomes for most regions, but except for the Russian Federation, this shock has modest effects.

---

[7] In this paper, the "NATO+" group is composed of NATO members and their allies. Section II, Table 6.1 lists the specific model regions included in this group and explains the group's role in the new normal scenario. In addition, Appendix B lists the composition of all groups referenced in this paper.

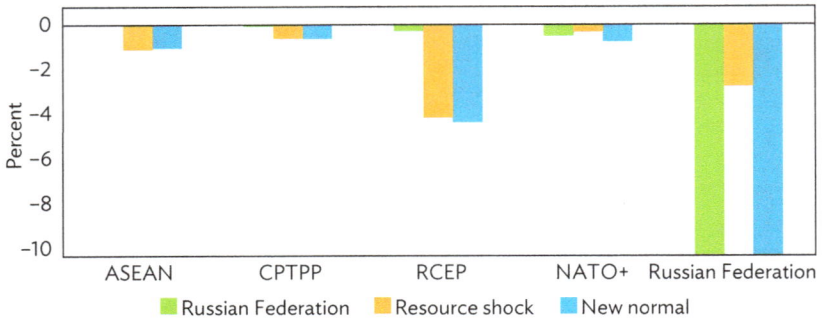

Figure 6.1: Recent Shocks and the New Normal: Income Changes

ASEAN = Association of Southeast Asian Nations, CPTPP = Comprehensive and Progressive Agreement for Trans-Pacific Partnership, NATO+ = North Atlantic Treaty Organization and their member allies, RCEP = Regional Comprehensive Economic Partnership.
Notes: Definitions of baseline scenario components and the regions directly affected by them are in Table 6.1. Definitions of the ASEAN, CPTPP, RCEP, and NATO+ groups are in Appendix B. Results for the Russian Federation are not fully shown for the Russian Federation and new normal shocks; their values are –22.4% and –23.4%, respectively.
Source: Authors' simulations.

Geopolitical interventions are reported in Figure 6.2.[8] These scenarios are calibrated to mimic policies used in the US–PRC trade tension. Reflecting current policy trends, the three interventions are formulated as raising barriers to undesired trade (rather than eliminating existing barriers to desired trade) and would therefore generate significantly negative global results. Among them, near-shoring generates global income losses of 1.2% (–$1.6 trillion), reshoring 0.9% (–$1.2 trillion), and friend-shoring 0.6% (–$0.8 trillion). These income changes are largely driven by large net declines in global trade, ranging up to 11.1% (–$4.0 trillion) under the near-shoring scenario. Trade-dependent economies in ASEAN and RCEP, including especially the PRC, fare worst. The interventions have the least damaging effects when they seek to reinforce already strong trade relationships.

Finally, Figure 6.3 analyzes opportunities for enhanced trade cooperation.[9] Here, all income and trade effects are positive, consistent with past experience from Asia and Pacific economic cooperation. RCEP increases members' incomes by 0.6% ($245 billion), although its trade-diversion effects reduce net global gains by about one-third. ASEAN economies fare especially well, with income gains of 1.3%, despite FTAs already in place with other members. CPTPP enlargements likewise generate meaningful

---

[8] Table 6.2A offers detail on geopolitical intervention scenarios and defines the economies affected.

[9] Table 6.2B offers detail on trade cooperation scenarios and defines the economies participating in them.

benefits: the first raises global incomes by $101 billion, while the second adds $57 billion, for a total increase of $158 billion relative to the baseline. Four of the seven prospective CPTPP countries are members of ASEAN. The massive "global reach" scenario raises incomes by 1.1% ($1.4 trillion) worldwide, including by 4.0% ($0.2 trillion) in ASEAN. The results confirm a well-known pattern: the bigger the agreement, the better the outcome.

Figure 6.2: Geopolitical Interventions in Trade: Income Changes

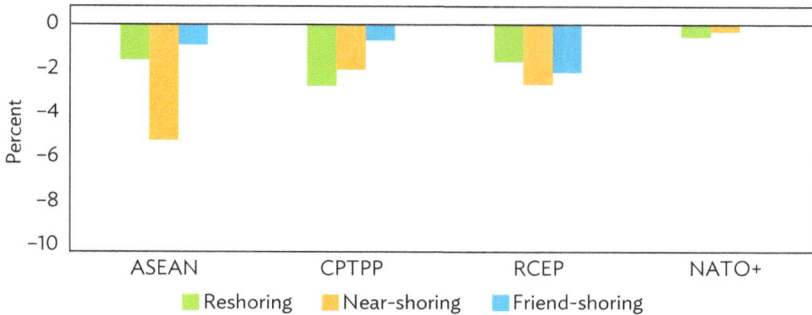

ASEAN = Association of Southeast Asian Nations, CPTPP = Comprehensive and Progressive Agreement for Trans-Pacific Partnership, NATO+ = North Atlantic Treaty Organization and their member allies, RCEP = Regional Comprehensive Economic Partnership.
Notes: Definitions of scenarios and regions directly affected by them are in Table 6.2A. Definitions of the ASEAN, CPTPP, RCEP, and NATO+ groups are in Appendix B.
Source: Authors' simulations.

Figure 6.3: New Cooperation Alternatives: Income Changes

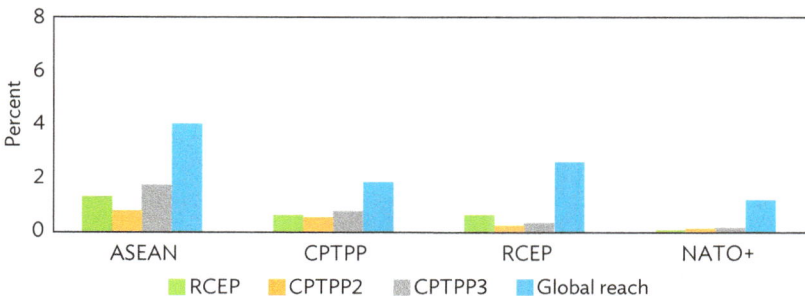

ASEAN = Association of Southeast Asian Nations, CPTPP = Comprehensive and Progressive Agreement for Trans-Pacific Partnership, NATO+ = North Atlantic Treaty Organization and their member allies, RCEP = Regional Comprehensive Economic Partnership.
Notes: Definitions of scenarios and the model regions directly affected by them are in Table 6.2B. Definitions of the ASEAN, CPTPP, RCEP, and NATO+ groups are in Appendix B.
Source: Authors' simulations.

Unique features of our model also show how different policies would affect GVCs. On the negative side, geopolitical interventions would severely disrupt GVCs by increasing the cost of fragmented production, reducing global GVC participation at rates ranging from 4.5% to 9.0%. The economies most affected would be small, open, manufacturing economies like those in ASEAN. On the positive side, lowering trade costs by extending economic cooperation agreements would increase GVC participation. In other words, GVCs play a key role in determining the effects of trade policies, especially in regions like ASEAN.

In sum, the study finds that recent global shocks and potential geopolitical trade interventions, developments mostly beyond ASEAN's control, could sharply disrupt growth in ASEAN, Asia and the Pacific generally, and similar economies elsewhere. (The chapter does not examine the non-economic effects of these policies, their principal motivation). At the same time, the chapter finds that other future policy choices—principally trade cooperation in Asia and expanding it into other regions—are sizeable and could also affect long-term global prospects. Outcomes are not preordained and the stakes are high.

The rest of the chapter is structured as follows: the next section examines methodology, describing the CGE and MRIO models and the construction baselines and scenarios. The succeeding section reviews outcomes in detail. The penultimate section reports results for GVCs and RVCs. The last section concludes.

Research Strategy

CGE models remain the tool of choice for analyzing policies that affect multiple industries and countries. An extensive data infrastructure has become available for such analysis, in applications ranging from trade and resource economics to the environment. Meanwhile, new literature has developed for analyzing value chain linkages among countries. This chapter links these strains of research to examine how trade policy affects value chains. This section explains the logic of the model and its scenarios.

The Computable General Equilibrium model

A CGE model empirically implements relationships that define budget constraints for firms, households, and governments; tracks how agents earn and spend income; and ensures supply–demand balances for goods and factors of production. These equations define a static equilibrium— outcomes consistent with budget constraints, decision rules, and market clearing. CGE models also include parameters like taxes, subsidies, and tariffs, which can be changed in simulations to find new equilibrium solutions.

Assembling the data required for a global CGE model is increasingly beyond the resource constraints of small teams of modelers, so we also left behind the model developed with our own team over the past decade.[10] In its place, we adopted the WTO's Global Trade Model (GTM) (Aguiar et al. 2019) as the basis for a new, comprehensive model for Indo-Pacific trade analysis.

The WTO's GTM model is a state-of-the-art CGE model developed from the Global Trade Analysis Project (GTAP) model (Corong et al. 2017). The WTO team complemented GTAP with new long-term projection approaches, introduced equations to calculate rigorous welfare effects, and developed mechanisms for applying alternative trade-theoretic foundations. In turn, components were added from previous work to quantify changes in tariff and nontariff barriers (NTBs) and introduced a multiregional sub-model for value chain analysis.

The resulting model emphasizes key interactions in the Indo-Pacific with 25 production sectors and 30 regions. It is "dynamic recursive," allowing capital accumulation over time and runs over the 2021–2035 period. It currently uses an Armington production structure (Figure 6.4).[11] Capital endowments are exogenous, based on prior investments, while labor, other factor supplies, and net national savings (or trade balances) are endogenous. However, equations for these latter variables limit adjustments around exogenously projected values. For example, labor supply equations are anchored on consensus forecasts of the labor force but allow solutions to deviate inelastically from these norms based on real wages. As with other CGE models, our model only calculates relative prices and fixes the 2014 US Consumer Price Index as a stable numeraire benchmark.

---

[10] The core model was developed by Zhai (2008) and expanded and adapted by Petri, Plummer, and Zhai (2012) to study trade initiatives in the Asia and Pacific region. It has been used most recently to model the economic effects of the US-PRC trade tension and RCEP (Park, Petri, and Plummer 2021).

[11] This may change in the future; our earlier model used the Melitz trade model.

Figure 6.4: Production Structure of the Global Trade Model

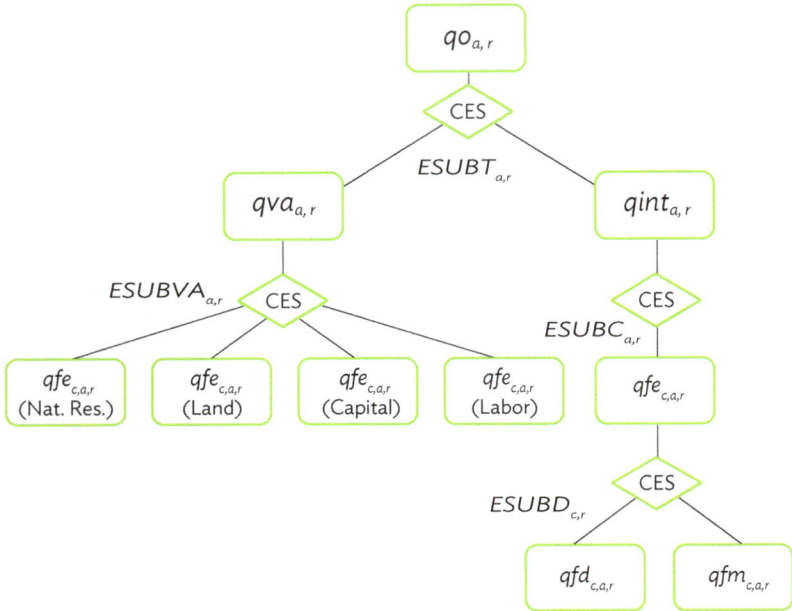

Notes: Starting at the top, output levels by activity (*a*) and region (*r*) are determined as constant elasticity of substitution (CES) aggregates of value added and intermediate input bundles; the value-added bundle is a CES aggregate of sector-specific resources, land, capital, and two types of labor; the intermediate input bundles are CES aggregates of individual intermediate goods bundles; and intermediate goods bundles are CES aggregates of domestic and import bundles. In the trade structure, import bundles are determined as CES aggregates of imports from different regions.
Source: Aguiar et al. (2019).

A novel feature of the model is an associated MRIO system for analyzing value chains. Our approach uses CGE results to construct MRIO tables and then analyzes how scenario changes affect value chains (Figure 6.5). As a first step, the CGE model generates outcomes for one or more scenarios. The second step extracts the MRIO tables implicit in the solution. The third step conducts the MRIO analysis—for example, to calculate backward and forward GVC participation rates. The system potentially supports many other exercises, including regional analysis of value chains, assessments of upstream and downstream positioning of sectors and countries, and computations of the length and cost of value chain activities.[12]

---

[12] Although the model is not yet set up this way, the GVC equations could be directly incorporated into the CGE equation system, enabling, for example, exogenous targets for GVC participation to determine tariffs endogenously.

Figure 6.5: Structure of Global Value Chain and Regional Value Chain Analysis

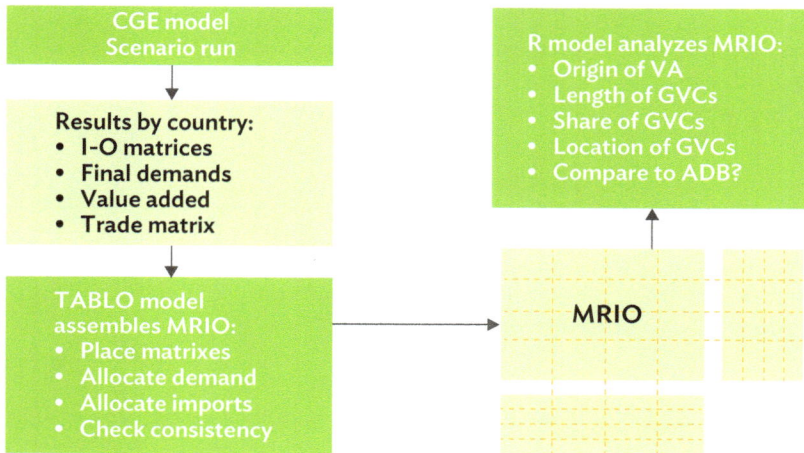

CGE model
Scenario run

Results by country:
• I-O matrices
• Final demands
• Value added
• Trade matrix

TABLO model
assembles MRIO:
• Place matrixes
• Allocate demand
• Allocate imports
• Check consistency

R model analyzes MRIO:
• Origin of VA
• Length of GVCs
• Share of GVCs
• Location of GVCs
• Compare to ADB?

MRIO

ADB = Asian Development Bank, CGE = Computable General Equilibrium, GVC = global value chain, I–O = input–output, MRIO = Multiregional Input–Output, RVC = regional value chain, VA = value added. Source: Authors.

The goal of the methodology is to base GVC analysis on the results of the CGE modeling process, rather than on separate MRIO tables that cannot be adjusted through CGE simulations. However, by relying on GTAP data to construct the MRIO table, the model does not fully exploit all available trade data. GTAP data, as currently implemented, include detailed, consistent information for bilateral trade flows, but do not distinguish among *end users* of these flows, that is, whether an import is sold for intermediate production, consumption, or investment. This information is available in some databases and potentially improves value chain measures.

If import sourcing differs significantly among final users, then GTAP's method of using average sourcing parameters for all end users may yield distortions. Fortunately, differences in the GVC measures calculated from the current model and other data sets are not large. Researchers have rebuilt the GTAP model to use end-user information (Carrico 2017), but that approach still lacks the advantages associated with a widely used, frequently refreshed, GTAP data system.

Specifying (and respecifying) the baseline

Dynamic models require the modeler to specify how the parameters of a single-year model will change over time. Potentially time-varying parameters include factor supplies, technological coefficients, prices in controlled markets, and policy interventions. In static models, these parameters are usually recovered from base-year data; in dynamic models, projecting them requires considerable effort.

Time-varying data are typically collected from external research. In the current model, these requirements have been filled by International Monetary Fund (IMF) projections (intermediate-term projections of economic growth, population and employment, resource prices, and net national savings); the Shared Socioeconomic Pathways collaborative (longer-term projections of growth and population); the International Trade Centre (tariff barriers under current agreements), the Design of Trade Agreements Database (NTBs under current agreements); as well as studies conducted by the authors of the GTM (sector and regional structure of productivity changes) and this chapter (tariff and NTBs under current and new trade agreements).

Even if these data sources are reliable individually, their consistency cannot be taken for granted. Hence, most dynamic models—including our past model and the GTM—further adjust dynamic parameters to yield overall growth rates based on plausible projections. This involves running the model first in "calibration mode," that is, with growth rates set to exogenous projections while adjustment factors for time-varying parameters are found endogenously. For example, the calibration process may calculate multipliers for rates of technological progress to ensure that overall growth matches projections. After calibration, the model's closure is reversed to make calibrated multipliers exogenous and growth outcomes again endogenous.

This chapter took an unexpected turn in early 2022: the calibrations used to construct its original baseline in mid-2021—just months before this application began—were disrupted by consequential global shocks in late 2021 and early 2022, making the baseline an inappropriate starting point for analysis. We therefore decided to use the 2021 baseline to calculate another baseline scenario that incorporates recent "news." This new baseline scenario, which we call the "new normal," incorporates shocks between mid-2021 and mid-2022; it models the isolation of the Russian Federation economy following the Russian invasion of Ukraine; updates the long-run path of oil and natural resource prices (Appendix C [a] and [b]); and potentially introduces adjustments for macroeconomic policy changes.

The new normal serves two aims: (i) to estimate the effects of recent shocks, and (ii) to update the model's baseline for further analysis.

The assumptions behind the 2021 baseline and the new normal shock are summarized in Table 6.1. Care has been taken to incorporate the best available information for different elements of each scenario, but some assumptions are especially uncertain. For example, the effects of sanctions on the Russian Federation are difficult to quantify, the willingness of countries to enforce sanctions over long periods is uncertain, and little is known about the Russian Federation's ability to circumvent them. We simply judged the ad valorem equivalent of the sanctions to be twice as high as the tariffs applied by the US and PRC in their recent trade tension.

The macroeconomic effects of recent shocks are especially uncertain; the continuing global battle against inflation (as of end-2022) could have unpredictable growth effects. The expected macroeconomic effects of recent shocks is measured by calculating how much the IMF had to downgrade its GDP projections since early 2021. This approximately matched the GDP declines also calculated just from the new normal simulations based on the Russian invasion of Ukraine and resource price shocks. Therefore, no negative effects were added for the macroeconomic policy responses themselves. This modeling decision may eventually prove too optimistic.[13]

---

[13] While assumptions about global macroeconomic policy decisions could significantly change projected growth rates, they often have little effect on results for unrelated policy changes. For example, *variations* calculated in a country's GDP due to new trade areas will be affected only modestly by its *level* of GDP.

Table 6.1: Specification of Alternative Baselines

Scenario	Principal Shocks (sources in parentheses)
Common baseline assumptions	• Productivity growth rates calibrated to external projections of per capita GDP and population growth (IMF through 2025 and SSP thereafter) • Fixed relative sector productivity growth rates by region (WTO) • Scheduled trade barrier reductions for trade agreements in place in 2021 (ITC and DESTA) • Scheduled trade barrier reductions under CPTPP agreements ratified by 2021 (authors) • Estimated trade cost savings from the implementation of the WTO Trade Facilitation Agreement from 2017 to 2031 (GTM)
2021 baseline assumptions	• Exogenous real prices for oil and other natural resource sectors for 2022–2025 projected using 2010–2021 price data (IMF, authors)
New normal baseline	• Exogenous real prices for oil and other natural resource sectors for 2022–2025 projected using 2010–2022 price data (IMF, authors) • Sanctions on trade between the Russian Federation and NATO+ model regions (Australia, Canada, Europe, Japan, New Zealand, the Republic of Korea, the UK, and the US) are implemented in two steps in 2022 and 2023 and then maintained through 2035 (authors) 　□ 40% AVE penalties on imports from the Russian Federation 　□ 40% AVE penalties on exports to the Russian Federation 　□ 10% AVE added transaction costs on trade with the Russian Federation by all trade partners • 2022–2025 macroeconomic outlook revisions (IMF, used for information only)

AVE = ad valorem equivalent, CPTPP = Comprehensive and Progressive Agreement for Trans-Pacific Partnership, DESTA = design of trade agreement, GDP = gross domestic product, GTM = global trade model, IMF = International Monetary Fund, International Trade Centre, NATO+ = North Atlantic Treaty Organization and their member allies, SSP = Statement of Surveillance Priories, UK = United Kingdom, US = United States, and WTO = World Trade Organization.
Notes: Resource price projections are described in Appendix C Figures a and b
Source: Authors.

Specifying geopolitical interventions in trade

Over the past half-century, world trade has doubled as a percentage of GDP, from 25% in 1972 to 52% in 2020,[14] but this trend peaked around the 2008–2009 global financial crisis and has given way to disagreements about the role trade plays in economic development. In the US and other advanced economies, leaders have since emphasized worsening wage disparities, higher risks in supply chains, and transfers of industry and technology to geopolitical adversaries. In most of Asia's emerging economies, however, the commitment to economic integration remains intact as the region emerges as the leader of cooperation initiatives.

---

[14] World Bank. Trade (% of GDP). https://data.worldbank.org/indicator/NE.TRD.GNFS.ZS (accessed 21 August 2022).

These contrasting trends are examined in two groups of policy simulations in this chapter. The first group considers *geopolitical interventions,* reflecting the shifting priorities of globally influential economies from trade liberalization to policies that increasingly account for geopolitical interests. A second group, discussed in the next section, addresses *enhanced trade cooperation* scenarios, primarily focused on the Indo-Pacific.

Each of the three geopolitical intervention scenarios has historical precedents as well as current proponents (Table 6.2A). Theoretical and empirical work shows that trade—as any innovation or economic change—can harm activities or groups even if society benefits overall. Thus, groups that expect to be harmed have long opposed liberal trade policies. However, with growing evidence on the reasonably wide distribution of trade benefits, protectionism declined substantially over the post-World War II period. More recently, opposition to trade has again strengthened, especially in advanced countries. Critics blame trade for job losses, wage inequality, supply chain risks, and the growth of adversaries, among others. Some of these problems are real, but advocates quickly (and often wrongly) jump to trade restrictions as solutions. Even historical champions of open trade are today adopting new restrictions.

We examine three stylized approaches to managing trade. The first is *reshoring*, an old idea for protecting domestic industry under a new name. The approach seeks to incentivize agents to make and buy products at home. These policies traditionally attract support from workers and employers in industries that are losing competitiveness. But critics now also focus on national security and supply chain risks. Until recently, advocates of protectionism have been outweighed by national interest, but the US administration under former president Trump shifted this balance in the US—and perhaps globally—by equating reshoring with national welfare. The US has continued to support reshoring even during the current administration; for example, in August 2022 President Biden signed into law both the CHIPS Act, the largest subsidy program in US history, and the Inflation Reduction Act, which also has inward-looking features. Both are already leading to tensions with partners in Asia and Europe. The PRC and the EU are also ramping up related industrial policies.

Table 6.2A: Specification of Geopolitical Interventions

Scenario	Model Regions Affected	Major Shocks
Reshoring	Large economies: PRC, Europe, Japan, India, Russian Federation, the US	• All large economies impose 15% AVE penalties on sensitive imports (7.5% on other imports) from all other regions, introduced gradually over 2022–2026
Near-shoring	Eight world regions: North America (Canada, Mexico, US); Latin America (Chile, Colombia, Peru, Latin America nes); Northeast Asia (PRC; Hong Kong, China; Japan; the Republic of Korea; Taipei,China); Southeast Asia (Australia, Brunei Darussalam, Indonesia, Malaysia, New Zealand, the Philippines, Singapore, Viet Nam); South Asia (India, Asia nes); Africa (Africa, ½ Middle East); Europe (Europe, UK, ½ Middle East); Others (Russian Federation, Rest of World)	• Each of the eight world regions imposes 15% AVE penalties on all sensitive extraregional imports (7.5% on other imports), introduced gradually over 2022–2026 • No new barriers are imposed on intraregional trade
Friend-shoring	Three global geopolitical groups: PRC-led (PRC; Hong Kong,China; 1/2 ASEAN nes; Africa; Russian Federation); US-led (Canada, Mexico, the US, Australia, Japan, New Zealand, the Republic of Korea, Europe, UK); Neutral (all 17 other regions)	• The PRC-led and US-led groups impose 15% AVE penalties on sensitive imports from the other group (7.5% on other imports) • The PRC-led and US-led groups impose half of the above penalties on imports from Neutral regions, introduced gradually over 2022–2026 • Neutral regions impose no barriers

ASEAN = Association of Southeast Asian Nations, AVE = ad valorem equivalent, nes = not elsewhere specified, PRC = People's Republic of China, UK = United Kingdom, US = United States.
Notes: Economy groups used in scenarios and in presentation tables are also presented in more comprehensive form in Appendix B.
Source: Authors.

The *near-shoring* approach assumes that trade risks rise with distance and incentivizes trade within a regional neighborhood. Near-shoring has gained currency in the wake of the COVID-19 pandemic; proponents believe that the supply shocks would have been less severe with shorter supply chains connecting nearby firms. It is difficult to find empirical evidence for this argument, but it has popular appeal as some consumer-oriented companies, like Zara, Samsung, LG, Boeing, and Hasbro, claim to have benefited.[15] The policy may be also attractive to large countries because they believe they have leverage over nearby partners.

---

[15] Haar. (2021.).

The *friend-shoring* approach, proposed by US Treasury Secretary Janet Yellen in 2021[16] and recently defended by Canadian Deputy Prime Minister Chrystia Freeland,[17] is the most explicitly geopolitical of the alternatives. The approach intends to restrict trade that might be subject to political manipulation and to deny economic and strategic benefits to political competitors, chiefly by replacing part of trade with geopolitical adversaries with trade among friendly countries.

Despite the new name, historical examples of friend-shoring are numerous and notably include trade agreements adopted by ASEAN and the EU. What makes early examples different from current proposals is that they *lowered* barriers between partners rather than *raised* them against outsiders. Today's examples are less generous. Even the Indo-Pacific Economic Framework for Prosperity,[18] launched in May 2022 to enhance trade relations among the US and 12 regional partners, stipulated that it would not include market access concessions. Rather, it proposed negotiations on regulating supply chains, electronic commerce, environmental protection, and other commercial sectors, like those that might have been included in previous US FTA negotiations. If such agreements are concluded, they could be interpreted as regulatory concessions that partners make in exchange for merely maintaining existing access to US markets.

We represent the three geopolitical scenarios with increases in barriers against undesirable partners rather than reductions in barriers against desirable partners (say, through trade agreements). This reflects the current policy emphasis on associating negative externalities with many types of trade, while in other time periods, the goal of trading with regional or political partners led to agreements to liberalize trade. We implement the three scenarios with tariffs that restrict trade in line with scenario objectives (Table 6.2). Tariffs should be understood as the ad valorem equivalents of various barriers that policy makers may actually apply with similar protectionist effects.

---

[16] Atlantic Council. 2022. *Transcript: US Treasury Secretary Janet Yellen on the next steps for Russia sanctions and 'friend-shoring' supply chains.* 13 April. https://www.atlanticcouncil.org/news/transcripts/transcript-us-treasury-secretary-janet-yellen-on-the-next-steps-for-russia-sanctions-and-friend-shoring-supply-chains/.

[17] US Department of the Treasury. 2022. Transcript of Fireside Chat of U.S. Treasury Secretary Janet L. Yellen and Deputy Prime Minister and Minister of Finance Chrystia Freeland Hosted by Canada 2020. 20 June. Press release. https://home.treasury.gov/news/press-releases/jy0830.

[18] Office of the US Trade Representative. Indo-Pacific Economic Framework for Prosperity (IPEF). https://ustr.gov/trade (2021)-agreements/agreements-under-negotiation/indo-pacific-economic-framework-prosperity-ipef

- *Reshoring.* Simulated barriers against all imports into large economies, applying protection levels of 7.5% to general imports (15% to sensitive imports), or about half as severe as the protection applied in the US–PRC trade tension.
- *Near-shoring.* Simulated policies to encourage regional trading blocs. The model's 30 regions are divided into seven larger blocs (North America, South America, Europe, East Asia, Southeast Asia, South Asia, and Others). Each is assumed to apply protection levels of 7.5% to general imports (15% to sensitive imports) on all extra-regional trade.
- *Friend-shoring.* Two blocs, one led by the US and the other by the PRC, are constructed from their close allies (Table 6.2A). Although usual trade barriers continue no added tariffs are imposed on trade within blocs, but a 7.5% penalty is applied to imports (15% on sensitive imports) to trade between blocs. Regions not included in either bloc—considered neutral economies—face half the tariffs on trade with bloc members.

Scenarios have yet to be developed that target risk reductions through diversification rather than managing partners (which unfortunately is often politically preferred).[19] This requires carefully identifying risks, which correspond partly but certainly not entirely with the political groupings in our current scenarios.

Specifying enhanced trade cooperation

Despite anti-trade headwinds, Asian economies, especially those in East Asia, continue to support economic integration. We therefore consider four explicit cooperation scenarios (Table 6.2B). The first is RCEP implementation by its 15 signatories starting in 2022. The second is an enlargement of the CPTPP in 2024, adding four countries to the eight that ratified the agreement before 2022. The third is an additional CPTPP enlargement in 2027, admitting three more countries. The fourth is an admitted "reach" scenario, a globalization home run in 2030 that would add four major economies to the CPTPP—including the PRC, with India joining RCEP.

---

[19]   See, for example, D. Malacrino, A. Mohommad, and A. Presbitero. 2022. Global Trade Needs More Supply Diversity, Not Less. *IMF Blog.* 12 April. https://www.imf.org/en/Blogs/Articles/2022/04/12/blog041222-sm2022-weo-ch4

Table 6.2B: Specification of Trade Cooperation Scenarios

Scenario (launch)	Model Regions Affected	Major Shocks (sources in parentheses)
RCEP (2022)	Australia, Brunei Darussalam, the PRC, Indonesia, Japan, Malaysia, New Zealand, the Philippines, the Republic of Korea, Singapore, Thailand, ASEAN nes	• RCEP 15-member trade agreement comes into force in 2022 with negotiated tariff schedules (World Bank) and estimated NTBs (authors)
CPTPP2 (2024)	Baseline CPTPP members are Australia, Brunei Darussalam, Canada, Japan, Mexico, New Zealand, Peru, Singapore, Viet Nam. This scenario adds Chile, Malaysia, the Republic of Korea, the UK	• CPTPP membership takes effect for two remaining signatories under negotiated tariffs schedules (Peterson Institute) and estimated NTBs (authors) • CPTPP admits the UK and the Republic of Korea under tariff schedules and NTBs similar to those of current members (authors)
CPTPP3 (2027)	This scenario adds Indonesia, the Philippines, Thailand to CPTPP2	• CPTPP admits the three remaining "ASEAN-5" economies under tariffs schedules and NTBs similar to those of current members (authors)
Global Reach (2030)	This scenario adds the PRC; Europe; Taipei,China; and the US to CPTPP3, and adds India to RCEP	• CPTPP admits the PRC, the EU, and the US with tariffs schedules and NTBs similar to those of current members (authors) • RCEP admits India with tariff schedules and NTBs similar to those of current members

ASEAN = Association of Southeast Asian Nations, CPTPP = Comprehensive and Progressive Agreement for Trans-Pacific Partnership, EU = European Union, nes = not elsewhere specified, NTB = nontariff barrier, PRC = People's Republic of China, RCEP = Regional Comprehensive Economic Partnership, UK = United Kingdom, US = United States.
Notes: Economy groups used in scenarios and in presentation tables are also presented in more comprehensive form in Appendix B.
Source: Authors.

These scenarios are implemented using the detailed negotiated tariff levels for the RCEP and the CPTPP. For potential future agreements where negotiated estimates are unavailable, we construct estimates based on similar economies participating in similar agreements.

- *RCEP.* The implementation of the RCEP is simulated with all 15 signatories. Indonesia and the Philippines have ratified the RCEP in January and February 2023, respectively.[20] The simulation uses estimated NTB parameters (Park, Petri, and Plummer 2021), but introduces new tariff details.
- *CPTPP2 (first enlargement).* The policy effects of the CPTPP with eight members are included in the model's baseline. We now simulate the accession of four new members in 2024, including

[20] All ASEAN economies have ratified RCEP as of March 2023.

two new applicants (the UK and the Republic of Korea) and two signatories (Chile and Malaysia) that had not yet ratified the agreement when the simulations were conducted.[21] New countries are assumed to join under liberalization templates equivalent to those of the original signatories.

- *CPTPP3* (second enlargement). We simulate the admission of three more members into the CPTPP in 2027: Indonesia, the Philippines, and Thailand. All have followed the agreement since its inception and are likely to apply in the intermediate term.
- *Global reach*. Lastly, we simulate a massive expansion of the CPTPP to include the PRC; the US; Taipei,China; and the EU, with a parallel expansion of RCEP to include India. Ambitious agreements have long been part of an Indo-Pacific vision for an APEC-wide FTA of the Asia Pacific (FTAAP), as well as other initiatives. Despite recent political setbacks, this vision continues to attract support, including from the APEC Business Advisory Group. And even if the agreement is unrealistic for now, its results can serve as a benchmark for extensive integration.

Simulation Results

The world economy was struggling even before mid-2021 with the effect of the pandemic. Forecasts then were nevertheless optimistic, expecting a sharp rebound from the downturn in 2021 and 2022, and a return to normal growth in 2–3 years. These assumptions were reflected in the 2021 baseline constructed for this chapter. The baseline clearly underestimated the delayed effects of the pandemic, including persistent supply chain disruptions and the inflationary impact of pandemic-related stimulus not to mention the shocks resulting from the Russian invasion of Ukraine. The new normal baseline attempts to repair these deficits to create a plausible point of departure for future policy choices.

Baseline projections

Even the more optimistic 2021 baseline suggested a marked deceleration in growth over the medium term. But the shocks in the new normal baseline further depress global prospects. Changes are especially marked in the early part (2021–2025) of the projection period as past shocks are absorbed (Table 6.3). The deceleration associated with the 2022 shocks is evident in changes of the new normal from the 2021 baseline (the last three columns of Table 6.3). Global growth declines by 0.37% between the projections for

---

[21]   Malaysia completed the ratification process in late 2022 and for Chile on 20 February 2023.

2021–2025, or by 1.48% in total, with most changes expected in 2022 and 2023. The largest burden falls on raw material importers such as the PRC, Japan, and India. The setbacks in growth are smaller in later subperiods but continue until 2035.

Despite slowing growth rates, the projections continue some recent development trends. The center of the world economy continues to shift toward Asia—the shares of India and the RCEP together in world GDP increase from 32.3% in 2021 to 35.1% in 2035, while the shares of NATO+ developed countries decline from 57.9% to 51.8% over the same period. World exports under the new normal baseline expand by 46%, roughly as much as GDP, and include India's 145% jump and ASEAN's 66% increase.[22]

A more detailed view of the new normal, comparing 2035 results with the 2021 baseline, separates the effects of the Russian invasion of Ukraine shock and the natural resource price shock (the two are not independent, so the new normal total is not merely their sum) (Table 6.4). The Russian Federation's economy is medium-sized—a little smaller than Canada's—but is an important supplier of strategic energy and agricultural products. The Russian Federation and Ukraine together constitute one-third of global exports of wheat and corn, one-fifth of mineral fertilizers and natural gas, and 11% of oil (OECD 2022 March). In 2035, the Russian Federation's GDP is projected to fall below the baseline by 22.4% ($580 billion), dragging world GDP down by 0.6% ($784 billion). After the Russian Federation, the regions with the largest losses include Europe, Japan, and the Republic of Korea; those experiencing gains include resource suppliers like Brunei Darussalam, Australia, and countries in the Middle East. Most other economies, including the US and the PRC, are not affected much.

---

[22] These trade data are from modeling results not presented in the tables.

Table 6.3: World Growth under Baseline Scenarios
($ billions and annual rates)

	Base Year GDP		New Normal GDP		New Normal Growth Rates			Change from 2021 Baseline		
	2021	%	2035	%	2021–2025	2025–2030	2030–2035	2021–2025	2025–2030	2030–2035
World	87,258	100.0	126,252	100.0	2.85	2.79	2.42	−0.37	−0.09	−0.07
United States	20,874	23.9	27,160	21.5	2.09	1.98	1.66	−0.02	0.00	−0.01
Europe	17,067	19.6	21,999	17.4	2.25	1.65	1.68	−0.19	−0.03	−0.02
PRC	14,240	16.3	23,349	18.5	4.10	4.01	2.78	−1.12	−0.23	−0.18
Japan	4,448	5.1	4,944	3.9	0.85	0.84	0.60	−0.48	−0.08	−0.06
India	3,009	3.4	5,803	4.6	5.40	4.84	4.28	−0.88	−0.17	−0.13
ASEAN (8 regions)	3,095	3.5	5,492	4.4	4.71	4.23	3.71	−0.14	−0.05	−0.04
CPTPP (11 regions)	10,909	12.5	14,496	11.5	2.33	2.03	1.85	−0.09	−0.03	−0.03
RCEP (13 regions)	25,210	28.9	38,556	30.5	3.43	3.36	2.53	−0.76	−0.17	−0.13
NATO+ (8 regions)	50,556	57.9	65,400	51.8	2.16	1.82	1.65	−0.12	−0.02	−0.02

ASEAN = Association of Southeast Asian Nations, CPTPP = Comprehensive and Progressive Agreement for Trans-Pacific Partnership, GDP = gross domestic product, NATO+ = North Atlanic Treaty Organization and their member allies, PRC = People's Republic of China, RCEP = Regional Comprehensive Economic Partnership.
Source: Authors' simulations.

Table 6.4: Elements of the New Normal Baseline, 2035

	Baseline GDP	Income Changes from Baseline ($ billion)			% Changes from Baseline		
		Russian Federation Sanctions	Resource Shock	New Normal	Russian Federation Sanctions	Resource Shock	New Normal
Americas	**39,044**	**39,051**	**39,044**	**39,055**	**0.0**	**0.0**	**0.0**
Canada	2,551	2,559	2,558	2,565	0.3	0.3	0.5
Chile	408	409	410	412	0.3	0.6	1.0
Colombia	685	690	714	722	0.7	4.3	5.3
Mexico	1,902	1,907	1,885	1,891	0.3	−0.9	−0.6
Peru	335	335	335	336	0.3	0.2	0.5
United States	27,197	27,175	27,175	27,160	−0.1	−0.1	−0.1
Latin America nes	5,967	5,975	5,966	5,970	0.1	0.0	0.1
Asia and Oceania	**49,095**	**48,973**	**47,080**	**47,031**	**−0.2**	**−4.1**	**−4.2**
Australia	2,307	2,315	2,359	2,364	0.3	2.2	2.5
Brunei Darussalam	23	24	26	27	2.6	14.7	15.5
PRC	24,861	24,825	23,365	23,349	−0.1	−6.0	−6.1
Hong Kong, China	481	480	470	469	−0.2	−2.4	−2.5
Indonesia	2,078	2,081	2,099	2,100	0.1	1.0	1.1
India	6,085	6,055	5,803	5,803	−0.5	−4.6	−4.6
Japan	5,075	5,040	4,968	4,944	−0.7	−2.1	−2.6
Malaysia	715	715	700	701	0.0	−2.0	−1.9
New Zealand	280	280	280	280	−0.1	0.1	0.0
Philippines	738	738	731	731	0.0	−1.0	−0.9
Singapore	525	524	519	518	−0.2	−1.2	−1.3
Republic of Korea	2,223	2,200	2,142	2,127	−1.0	−3.7	−4.3
Thailand	780	778	741	742	−0.3	−5.1	−4.9
Taipei,China	743	740	717	717	−0.4	−3.4	−3.5
Viet Nam	472	471	459	459	−0.1	−2.6	−2.7
ASEAN nes	214	214	215	215	0.1	0.4	0.3
Asia nes	1,496	1,495	1,487	1,487	−0.1	−0.6	−0.6
Other Regions	**40,904**	**40,234**	**40,740**	**40,166**	**−1.6**	**−0.4**	**−1.8**
Africa nes	3,480	3,499	3,522	3,541	0.6	1.2	1.8
Europe nes	22,209	22,023	22,133	21,999	−0.8	−0.3	−0.9
United Kingdom	3,968	3,954	3,968	3,962	−0.3	0.0	−0.2
Middle East, North Africa	7,395	7,461	7,379	7,432	0.9	−0.2	0.5
Russian Federation	2,594	2,014	2,524	1,987	−22.4	−2.7	−23.4
Rest of World	1,258	1,283	1,213	1,246	2.0	−3.5	−1.0

continued on next page

Table 6.4 (continued)

	Baseline GDP	Income Changes from Baseline ($ billion)			% Changes from Baseline		
		Russian Federation Sanctions	Resource Shock	New Normal	Russian Federation Sanctions	Resource Shock	New Normal
World	**129,043**	**128,259**	**126,864**	**126,252**	**−0.6**	**−1.7**	**−2.2**
Memorandum							
ASEAN (8 members)	5,544	5,544	5,489	5,492	0.0	−1.0	−0.9
CPTPP (11 members)	14,591	14,579	14,500	14,496	−0.1	−0.6	−0.7
RCEP (15 members)	40,291	40,204	38,603	38,556	−0.2	−4.2	−4.3
NATO+ (8 members)	65,810	65,546	65,583	65,400	−0.4	−0.3	−0.6

ASEAN = Association of Southeast Asian Nations, CPTPP = Comprehensive and Progressive Agreement for Trans-Pacific Partnership, GDP = gross domestic product, NATO+ = North Atlantic Treaty Organization and their member allies, nes = not elsewhere specified, PRC = People's Republic of China, RCEP = Regional Comprehensive Economic Partnership.
Notes: Definitions of scenarios and regions directly affected by them are in Table 6.1.
Source: Authors' simulations.

The natural resource price shock, the second major element of the new normal, is about 2.5 times as large as the Russian Federation shock, leading to a global GDP shortfall of $2.1 trillion in 2035. In this shock, the largest negative effects are felt by the PRC (−6.0%), Thailand (−5.1%), the Republic of Korea (−3.7%) and other economies that export manufactures and depend on imported primary materials. Perhaps surprisingly, the Russian Federation's GDP is somewhat negatively affected by the primary material shock. Russian export revenues would expand due to higher resource prices, but these gains would be partly offset by lower international demand. Real income measures would then fall slightly, as consumer prices are pushed higher.

The effects of the new normal are dominated by raw material price changes and their effects on economies' terms of trade. World GDP falls below the 2021 baseline, which itself includes significant raw material price increases (by 2.2% by 2035). The beneficiaries are raw material exporters (Brunei Darussalam, Colombia, and countries in Africa and the Middle East, a region that includes both raw materials producers and importers), while those suffering losses are manufactures exporters that import raw materials. Since these economies are concentrated in Asia, the region suffers more than the rest of the world.

Geopolitical interventions

Our scenarios of geopolitical interventions further amplify the adverse effects of the new normal projections. These reflect policy goals such as increased domestic production, stronger competitive positions compared to geopolitical adversaries, and reduced supply chain risks. Overall, policies used to achieve these goals often lead to the fragmentation of trade and reduce global efficiency, output, real incomes, and especially international trade. Whatever their nationalist effects, their economic results are large and negative.

Even with negative global averages, a few regions benefit, including those applying protection as well as those subject to it. The results depend on whether the product and bilateral configuration of protection in a scenario turns the terms of trade in a region's favor. The simulations shed light on these differences; they explore the implications of different approaches to protection and their impact on different regions (Tables 6.5 and 6.6).

Table 6.5: Geopolitical Alternatives, Income 2035

	New Normal GDP	Income Changes from Baseline ($ billion)			% Changes from Baseline		
		Reshoring	Near-shoring	Friend-shoring	Reshoring	Near-shoring	Friend-shoring
Americas	**39,055**	**−73**	**−60**	**82**	**−0.2**	**−0.2**	**0.2**
Canada	2,565	−79	−6	−1	−3.1	−0.2	0.0
Chile	412	−7	−18	−4	−1.7	−4.3	−1.0
Colombia	722	5	5	−31	0.6	−0.4	0.2
Mexico	1,891	−69	38	12	−3.6	2.0	0.6
Peru	336	−2	−6	−1	−0.5	−1.9	−0.4
United States	27,160	64	−11	67	0.2	0.0	0.2
Latin America nes	5,970	15	−54	8	0.2	−0.9	0.1
Asia and Oceania	**47,031**	**−696**	**−1,177**	**−772**	**−1.5**	**−2.5**	**−1.6**
Australia	2,364	−26	−63	−36	−1.1	−2.7	−1.5
Brunei Darussalam	27	−1	−1	−1	−3.3	−4.2	−3.4
PRC	23,349	−369	−511	−627	−1.6	−2.2	−2.7
Hong Kong, China	469	−16	−19	−18	−3.4	−4.0	−3.9
Indonesia	2,100	14	−20	7	0.6	−1.0	0.3
India	5,803	−40	−113	46	−0.7	−1.9	0.8
Japan	4,944	−125	−13	−33	−2.5	−1.5	−0.7
Malaysia	701	−20	−57	−9	−2.9	−8.1	−1.2

continued on next page

Table 6.5 (continued)

	New Normal GDP	Income Changes from Baseline ($ billion)			% Changes from Baseline		
		Reshoring	Near-shoring	Friend-shoring	Reshoring	Near-shoring	Friend-shoring
New Zealand	280	0	−7	−1	−0.1	−2.5	−0.5
Philippines	731	−7	−31	−2	−1.0	−4.3	−0.3
Singapore	518	−20	−43	−14	−3.9	−8.3	−2.7
Republic of Korea	2,127	−27	−66	−46	−1.3	−3.1	−2.2
Thailand	742	−13	−60	−11	−1.7	−8.1	−1.5
Taipei,China	717	−13	−17	−3	−1.8	−2.4	−0.5
Viet Nam	459	−25	−44	−12	−5.4	−9.7	−2.6
ASEAN nes	215	−3	−11	−2	−1.3	−5.2	−1.0
Asia nes	1,487	−5	−40	−9	−0.3	−2.7	−0.6
Other Regions	**40,166**	**−320**	**−311**	**−103**	**−0.8**	**−0.8**	**−0.3**
Africa nes	3,541	−33	−127	−32	−0.9	−3.6	−0.9
Europe nes	21,999	−61	10	10	−0.3	0.0	0.0
United Kingdom	3,962	−61	11	13	−1.5	0.3	0.3
Middle East, North Africa	7,432	−84	−46	−54	−1.1	−0.6	−·0.7
Russian Federation	1,987	−51	−13	−24	−2.6	−3.1	−1.2
Rest of World	1,246	−30	−86	−16	−2.4	−6.9	−1.3
World	**126,252**	**−1,089**	**−1,548**	**−793**	**−0.9**	**−1.2**	**−0.6**
Memorandum							
ASEAN (8 members)	5,492	−75	−268	−43	−1.4	−4.9	−0.8
CPTPP (11 members)	14,496	−373	−280	−101	−2.6	−1.9	−0.7
RCEP (15 members)	38,556	−622	−988	−787	−1.6	−2.6	−2.0
NATO+ (8 members)	65,400	−315	−205	−27	−0.5	−0.3	0.0

ASEAN = Association of Southeast Asian Nations, CPTPP = Comprehensive and Progressive Agreement for Trans-Pacific Partnership, GDP = gross domestic product, NATO+ = North Atlantic Treaty Organization and their member allies, nes = not elsewhere specified, PRC = People's Republic of China, RCEP = Regional Comprehensive Economic Partnership.
Notes: Definitions of scenarios and regions directly affected by them are in Table 6.2A.
Source: Authors' simulations.

Table 6.6: Geopolitical Alternatives, Exports 2035

	New Normal Exports	Export Changes from Baseline ($ billion)			% Changes from Baseline		
		Reshoring	Near-shoring	Friend-shoring	Reshoring	Near-shoring	Friend-shoring
Americas	**5,140**	**–876**	**–786**	**–262**	**–17.0**	**–15.3**	**–5.1**
Canada	734	–85	–36	–16	–11.5	–4.9	–2.2
Chile	122	–11	–17	–7	–9.2	–13.6	–5.4
Colombia	83	–10	–14	–6	–11.4	–17.1	–6.9
Mexico	586	–65	–17	–7	–11.1	–2.8	–1.3
Peru	74	–8	–12	–5	–10.3	–16.7	–6.2
United States	2,670	–602	–529	–165	–22.6	–19.8	–6.2
Latin America nes	872	–95	–161	–57	–11.0	–18.5	–6.5
Asia and Oceania	**11,709**	**–1,720**	**–1,953**	**–1,229**	**–14.7**	**–16.7**	**–10.5**
Australia	544	–56	–78	–47	–10.3	–14.3	–8.7
Brunei Darussalam	16	–1	–1	–1	–9.6	–7.9	–7.6
PRC	3,896	–767	–715	–665	–19.7	–18.3	–17.1
Hong Kong, China	274	–25	–28	–·24	–9.0	–10.2	–8.7
Indonesia	397	–41	–62	–23	–10.2	–15.7	–5.9
India	1,006	–185	–201	–56	–18.4	–20.0	–5.5
Japan	1,336	–237	–173	–116	–17.7	–13.0	–8.7
Malaysia	482	–47	–94	–23	–9.8	–19.5	–4.9
New Zealand	80	–7	–10	–5	–8.4	–12.6	–6.0
Philippines	153	–18	–37	–9	–11.5	–24.4	–5.8
Singapore	517	–42	–88	–25	–8.1	–17.1	–4.9
Republic of Korea	1,105	–116	–144	–126	–10.5	–13.0	–11.4
Thailand	481	–41	–89	–25	–8.5	–18.4	–5.3
Taipei,China	585	–61	–64	–31	–10.5	–10.9	–5.3
Viet Nam	373	–35	–96	–16	–9.4	–25.8	–4.4
ASEAN nes	109	–9	–15	–8	–8.5	–14.1	–7.4
Asia nes	355	–31	–57	–28	–8.7	–16.2	–7.9
Other Regions	**14,763**	**–1,224**	**–1,255**	**–605**	**–8.3**	**–8.5**	**–4.1**
Africa nes	894	–85	–187	–73	–9.6	–20.9	–8.1
Europe nes	9,524	–656	–546	–281	–6.9	–5.7	–3.0
United Kingdom	951	–115	–84	–41	–12.1	–8.8	–4.3
Middle East, North Africa	2,365	–238	–230	–145	–10.1	–9.7	–6.1
Russian Federation	546	–80	–994	–38	–14.6	–18.1	–6.9
Rest of World	483	–50	–108	–28	–10.4	–22.4	–5.8

continued on next page

Table 6.6 (continued)

	New Normal Exports	Export Changes from Baseline ($ billion)			% Changes from Baseline		
		Reshoring	Near-shoring	Friend-shoring	Reshoring	Near-shoring	Friend-shoring
World	**31,612**	**–3,820**	**–3,994**	**–2.097**	**–12.1**	**–12.6**	**–6.6**
Memorandum							
ASEAN (8 members)	2,528	–235	–483	–132	–9.3	–19.1	–5.2
CPTPP (11 members)	4,863	–594	–623	–269	–12.2	–12.8	–5.5
RCEP (15 members)	9,490	–1,418	–1,603	–1,091	–14.9	–16.9	–11.5
NATO+ (8 members)	16 945	–1,874	–1,600	–796	–11.1	–9.4	–4.7

ASEAN = Association of Southeast Asian Nations, CPTPP = Comprehensive and Progressive Agreement for Trans-Pacific Partnership, NATO+ = North Atlantic Treaty Organization and their member allies, nes = not elsewhere specified, PRC = People's Republic of China, RCEP = Regional Comprehensive Economic Partnership.
Notes: Definitions of scenarios and regions directly affected by them are in Table 6.2A.
Source: Authors' simulations.

Reshoring. In this scenario, large countries turn more protectionist—the PRC, the US, Europe, India, Japan, and the Russian Federation apply protection to all trade, regardless of partner. Only the US gains 0.2% ($64 billion) in national income; every other region loses. Most large regions depend on others for exchange; the US is the only one that happens to be both large enough and well endowed enough across all economic sectors to slightly gain. Global incomes decline by nearly 1% ($1.2 trillion), with ASEAN and most other relatively small economies losing far more. Global exports decline by a much higher 12.1% ($3.8 trillion) and decreases are also significant for all economies. The reshoring countries themselves contribute almost two-thirds of the losses, the US falling by $602 billion, the PRC by $767 billion, Japan by $125 billion, and Europe by $656 billion. Despite the large share of world trade destroyed by such policies, income effects are smaller due to the continuing importance of domestic services in global consumption.

Near-shoring. The near-shoring scenario allows more opportunities for specialization than reshoring by permitting barrier-free trade within each of the seven regional blocs. However, its results are even worse. Large economies discriminate among large groups of foreign suppliers. In addition, smaller economies, as well as larger ones, apply regionally targeted trade policies. Due to these multiple distortions, real incomes fall even for the US and every other region except those with strong regional ties (Indonesia, Mexico, Europe, and the UK). Global real incomes fall by 1.2%; the largest losers are ASEAN members, including Viet Nam,

Singapore, Thailand, and Malaysia. Global exports contract by 12.6% ($4.0 trillion), suggesting even more retrenchment than under general protectionism. ASEAN exports decline by 19.1%, as members often trade with distant partners in Northeast Asia, Europe, and North America. Exports of other emerging regions are also hit hard, including those in Africa, Latin America, and the rest of the world.

Friend-shoring. This scenario envisions that frictions between the PRC and the US eventually split the world economy into two camps, with relatively few economies remaining neutral (so far, ASEAN has maintained neutrality). The implementation assumes no new intra-bloc barriers, but each bloc is assumed to penalize trade with members of the other bloc, and to a lesser extent with neutral economies. For the world, the implications of friend-shoring are less severe than those of the two other scenarios, as trade among "friends" already appears to be important. Nevertheless, global incomes decline by 0.6% ($793 billion) in 2035.

The effects of friend-shoring are especially negative for real incomes in the PRC-led bloc as this grouping has fewer and economically smaller members than the US-led bloc. In addition, economies that trade intensively with the PRC also face adverse effects, including ASEAN. Only a few neutral economies benefit; India, for example, is not as closely linked to the PRC as ASEAN and gains from trade diverted from the PRC by the US-led bloc. World exports decline by 6.6% ($2.1 trillion), the least among the three intervention scenarios, but still high.

In sum, the geopolitical interventions modeled have widespread negative effects. Global incomes and trade contract and no economy reaps systematic gains. Some face major losses, including the PRC and ASEAN's outward-oriented and relatively independent economies. It is important to remember that these are simple, stylized scenarios rather than those that might emerge from more extensive negotiations and analysis. Without such refinements, there is great potential for extensive, unintended damage to industries at home and abroad. If noneconomic goals need to be pursued, policies should be carefully designed to minimize collateral damage. That will require, at a minimum, sophisticated export and investment regulatory regimes.

Enhanced trade cooperation

In contrast to the previous section, the four cooperation scenarios generate solid wins for partners and the world economy (Tables 6.7). In general, the wider and deeper the agreement, the greater the benefits, with gains from the large (and improbable) global reach scenario particularly strong.

Table 6.7: Cooperation Alternatives, Income 2035

	New Normal GDP	Income Changes from Baseline ($ billion)				% Changes from Baseline			
		RCEP	CPTPP2	CPTPP3	Global Reach	RCEP	CPTPP2	CPTPP3	Global Reach
Americas	**39,055**	**−25**	**4**	**2**	**193**	**−0.1**	**0.0**	**0.0**	**0.5**
Canada	2,565	−1	5	8	12	0.0	02	0.3	0.5
Chile	412	0	3	3	5	−0.1	0.7	0.8	1.1
Colombia	722	−1	0	0	−9	−0.1	0.0	−0.1	−1.2
Mexico	1,891	−2	6	7	12	−0.1	0.3	0.4	0.6
Peru	336	0	1	1	1	−0.1	0.2	0.3	0.4
United States	27,160	−14	−8	−13	241	−0.1	0.0	0.0	0.9
Latin America nes	5,970	−6	−2	−4	−69	−0.1	0.0	−0.1	−1.1
Asia and Oceania	**47,031**	**224**	**64**	**115**	**977**	**0.5**	**0.1**	**0.2**	**2.1**
Australia	2,364	0	7	8	9	0.0	0.3	0.4	0.4
Brunei Darussalam	27	0	0	0	0	0.8	0.8	0.9	1.3
PRC	23,349	90	−29	−46	615	0.4	−0.1	−0.2	2.6
Hong Kong, China	469	0	0	0	−6	−0.1	0.0	0.0	−1.4
Indonesia	2,100	6	−2	11	17	0.3	−0.1	0.5	0.8
India	5,803	−8	−4	−7	−14	−0.1	−0.1	−0.1	−0.2
Japan	4,944	53	17	26	89	1.1	0.3	0.5	1.8
Malaysia	701	21	24	29	59	3.0	3.5	4.1	8.4
New Zealand	280	1	4	3	7	0.4	1.4	1.2	2.4
Philippines	731	12	−1	13	27	0.7	−0.1	1.8	3.7
Singapore	518	6	7	10	25	1.2	1.4	1.9	4.9
Republic of Korea	2,127	22	33	37	66	1.1	1.6	1.7	3.1
Thailand	742	6	−2	20	35	0.8	−03	2.7	4.7
Taipei, China	717	−3	−1	−1	26	−0.5	−0.1	−0.2	3.7
Viet Nam	459	16	11	14	49	3.4	2.4	3.0	10.7
ASEAN nes	215	5	0	−1	−1	2.2	−0.1	−0.3	−0.4
Asia nes	1,487	−2	−1	−2	−24	−0.2	−0.1	−0.1	−1.6
Other Regions	**40,166**	**−35**	**20**	**22**	**231**	**−0.1**	**0.0**	**0.1**	**0.6**
Africa nes	3,541	−2	0	−1	−24	−0.1	0.0	0.0	−0.7
Europe nes	21,999	−20	−10	−16	244	−0.1	0.0	−0.1	1.1
United Kingdom	3,962	−3	33	42	108	−0.1	0.8	1.1	2.7
Middle East, North Africa	7,432	−6	−2	−2	−70	−0.1	0.0	0.0	−0.9
Russian Federation	1,987	−2	0	0	−15	−0.1	0.0	0.0	−0.8

continued on next page

Table 6.7 (continued)

	New Normal GDP	Income Changes from Baseline ($ billion)				% Changes from Baseline			
		RCEP	CPTPP2	CPTPP3	Global Reach	RCEP	CPTPP2	CPTPP3	Global Reach
Rest of World	1,246	−1	0	0	−12	−0.1	0.0	0.0	−1.0
World	**126,252**	**164**	**87**	**140**	**1,401**	**0.1**	**0.1**	**0.1**	**1.1**
New members		238	93	156	1,427	0.6	1.3	1.4	1.6

ASEAN = Association of Southeast Asian Nations, CPTPP = Comprehensive and Progressive Agreement for Trans-Pacific Partnership, GDP = gross domestic product, nes = not elsewhere specified, PRC = People's Republic of China, RCEP = Regional Comprehensive Economic Partnership.
Notes: Definitions of scenarios and regions directly affected by them are in Table 6.2B.
Source: Authors' simulations.

RCEP. Members' real incomes will rise by 0.6% ($238 billion) due to RCEP, although world GDP will increase by just 0.1% ($164 billion) relative to the baseline. This comparison shows that RCEP has negative consequences for non-members due to trade diversion and preference erosion. The largest losses appear in Europe ($20 billion) and the US ($14 billion), but these are minor compared to GDP. The greatest gains occur in the PRC ($90 billion), Japan ($53 billion), and the Republic of Korea ($22 billion). All smaller ASEAN economies also benefit, led by Malaysia ($22 billion), Viet Nam ($16 billion), and the Philippines ($12 billion). Exports mirror income members' exports increase by 1.9% ($185 billion), slightly short of global gains.[23] The PRC receives the biggest boost in exports ($67 billion) and nearly all ASEAN economies increase exports by 1% to 6%.

CPTPP2. The nine-member CPTPP that went into effect in 2019 was included in the baseline projection and is not reported as a separate scenario. Rather, CPTPP2 is the first enlargement of the CPTPP, which adds Chile, Malaysia, the UK, and the Republic of Korea beginning in 2024. The new members' income gains by 2035 reach $93 billion, somewhat more than the $87 billion in global gains. The differences include both losses for outsiders, including the PRC; the US; Europe; and Taipei,China as well as gains for existing CPTPP members such as Japan. Export effects are small; overall, the agreement creates more trade for both new members and other economies, although some slight trade diversion is evident for the PRC, the US, and Southeast Asian economies.

---

[23] Trade effects were expected to be larger than income effects—in conventional analysis, the "triangles" that measure net benefits are smaller than the rectangles that measure trade changes. However, terms of trade effects also matter, and NTB reductions, which dominate gains from modern agreements, also have direct productivity effects.

CPTPP3. We define the second enlargement of the CPTPP as adding three more members, Indonesia, the Philippines, and Thailand in 2027. The results of the CPTPP3 scenario include CPTPP2, the first enlargement, so the net effects of adding the three economies can be calculated as the benefits of CPTPP3 less those of the CPTPP2. CPTPP3 generates $156 billion in gains for all members, incrementally adding $63 billion to CPTPP2. The marginal gains of ASEAN economies are significant, as all three new CPTPP members are ASEAN members. The incremental gains are significant for Indonesia (from –$2 billion to $11 billion), the Philippines (from –$1 billion to $15 billion), and Thailand (from –$2 billion to $20 billion).

Global reach. The CPTPP2 and CPTPP3 enlargements are feasible and arguably likely. But is there hope—as there was only a decade ago—for a breakthrough agreement that offers an even more solid step toward global liberalization? This question prompted a scenario that brings both the PRC and the US into the CPTPP, along with Taipei,China (which has applied) and Europe (which has bilateral FTAs with some CPTPP members), and at the same time adds India to RCEP (which it left after virtually signing a deal in November 2019). The simulation of this huge amalgam is essentially a "globalization benchmark" (Tables 6.7 and 6.8). By 2035, the agreement would add an annual $1.4 trillion to global incomes and $1.6 trillion to international trade. Members' real incomes would expand by 1.6%, with the PRC, the US, and Europe appearing as the largest beneficiaries, sharing more than $1 trillion in benefits. Other economies with large gains include the UK, Japan, Malaysia, the Republic of Korea, and Viet Nam. Export gains would also be large, with the US, the PRC, the Philippines, and Viet Nam all seeing a double-digit rise in exports. Nevertheless, there would be trade diversion effects, including in Latin America and the Middle East. Even India would lose, despite joining RCEP, by remaining outside the greatly expanded CPTPP.

Table 6.8: Cooperation Alternatives, Exports 2035

	New Normal GDP	Export Changes from Baseline ($ billion)				% Changes from Baseline			
		RCEP	CPTPP2	CPTPP3	Global Reach	RCEP	CPTPP2	CPTPP3	Global Reach
Americas	**5,140**	**5**	**7**	**10**	**366**	**0.1**	**0.1**	**0.2**	**7.1**
Canada	734	1	3	4	15	0.1	0.4	0.6	2.1
Chile	122	0	2	2	4	0.1	1.2	1.4	3.5
Colombia	83	0	0	0	1	0.2	0.1	0.1	1.4
Mexico	586	0	3	4	9	0.1	0.4	0.6	1.5
Peru	74	0	1	1	3	0.0	0.8	1.0	3.8

continued on next page

Table 6.8 (continued)

	New Normal GDP	Export Changes from Baseline ($ billion)				% Changes from Baseline			
		RCEP	CPTPP2	CPTPP3	Global Reach	RCEP	CPTPP2	CPTPP3	Global Reach
United States	2,670	3	−1	−1	335	0.1	0.0	−0.1	12.5
Latin America nes	872	1	0	1	−1	0.1	0.1	0.1	−0.1
Asia and Oceania	**11,709**	**181**	**82**	**136**	**914**	**1.5**	**0.7**	**1.2**	**7.8**
Australia	544	2	6	7	15	0.3	1.1	1.3	2.8
Brunei Darussalam	16	0	0	0	0	0.5	0.6	0.7	1.6
PRC	3,896	67	−2	−2	485	1.7	−0.1	−0.1	12.5
Hong Kong, China	274	0	0	0	−1	0.0	0.1	0.1	−0.4
Indonesia	397	6	0	11	34	1.4	−0.1	2.7	8.6
India	1,006	0	0	0	39	0.0	0.0	0.0	3.9
Japan	1,336	40	14	22	99	3.0	1.0	1.6	7.4
Malaysia	482	12	17	19	43	2.5	3.5	4.0	9.0
New Zealand	80	1	3	2	6	1.0	3.4	2.9	7.2
Philippines	153	5	0	6	16	3.2	−0.1	4.0	10.2
Singapore	517	3	5	6	12	0.6	1.0	1.2	2.3
Republic of Korea	1,105	23	31	35	58	2.1	2.8	3.2	52
Thailand	481	6	−2	18	30	1.3	−0.4	3.6	6.3
Taipei,China	585	−4	−1	−1	41	−0.6	−0.1	−0.2	7.1
Viet Nam	373	17	12	13	52	4.5	3.1	3.5	13.9
ASEAN nes	103	3	0	0	−2	2.4	−0.1	−0.3	−1.6
Asia nes	355	−1	0	0	−14	−0.1	−0.1	−0.1	−4.1
Other Regions	**14,763**	**6**	**20**	**26**	**338**	**−0.0**	**0.1**	**0.2**	**23**
Africa nes	894	1	1	1	−4	0.1	0.1	0.1	−0.4
Europe nes	9,524	2	1	0	272	0.0	0.0	0.0	2.9
United Kingdom	951	1	16	21	74	0.1	1.7	2.2	7.8
Middle East, North Africa	2,365	3	2	3	−3	0.1	0.1	0.1	−0.1
Russian Federation	546	1	0	1	1	0.1	0.1	0.1	0.2
Rest of World	483	0	0	0	−2	0.0	0.0	0.1	−0.4
World	**31,612**	**192**	**108**	**171**	**1.618**	**0.6**	**0.3**	**0.5**	**5.1**
New members		185	66	112	1,432	1.9	2.5	3.0	6.7

ASEAN = Association of Southeast Asian Nations, CPTPP = Comprehensive and Progressive Agreement for Trans-Pacific Partnership, GDP = gross domestic product, nes = not elsewhere specified, PRC = People's Republic of China, RCEP = Regional Comprehensive Economic Partnership.
Notes: Definitions of scenarios and regions directly affected by them are in Table 6.2B.
Source: Authors' simulations.

The solutions of the regional cooperation scenarios are much more optimistic than the geopolitical interventions. They offer a counterweight to trade fragmentation and a bulwark against further harmful shocks. Ambitious liberalization, as under the global reach scenario, could nearly offset the losses of the trade fragmentation scenarios.

Employment and wages

When political choices among economic policies prioritize economic issues, they tend to focus on labor market outcomes rather than welfare calculations, such as changes in real national income. Employment and wage increases, rather than efficiency, are the principal arguments for trade policies ranging from reshoring to new trade agreements.

The model estimates employment levels and wage rates by region for skilled and unskilled labor. Labor demands are derived from the production side of the model, which adjusts demand depending on real wages. Labor supplies mainly follow exogenously specified trends but can move above or below projected trends whenever labor market equilibrium requires real wages to rise above or fall below trends. As these supply relationships are inelastic, employment results generally remain close to projected levels. In the intermediate term, the equilibrating mechanisms of the model (and indeed the economy) tend to keep employment close to normal. The projected trajectories are derived from detailed estimates of demographic variables, labor force participation, and real wage trends.

Employment and wage results for both skilled and unskilled labor are shown for selected simulations—the 2021 baseline, the new normal baseline, friend-shoring interventions, and the global reach trade cooperation scenario (Appendixes D and E). All results are expressed as 2035 values as a percent of 2021 values, and typically exceed 100%. The results are reasonably similar across simulations. This is expected, since demographic and productivity trends that are common across scenarios are the most important drivers of employment and real wage changes over time. Since labor markets cut across all economic sectors, the differential effects of trade policy changes are muted in most regions. Employment effects vary less than wage effects since labor supply functions have low wage elasticities.

All scenarios show *increases in global employment from 2021 to 2035, especially for skilled workers* (most 2035 employment levels exceed 100% of 2021 levels). In the new normal scenario, for example, global employment of unskilled workers in 2035 ("World" region) is 13.4% higher, and for skilled workers 65.3% higher than 2021 employment. In other words, the share of skilled workers is projected to grow worldwide and for every region in the model. To be sure, there are large variations across economies in employment growth rates—from –34.8% (Singapore) to 47.7% (Africa nes) for unskilled workers and from 12.2% (Japan) to 115.4% (Africa nes) for skilled workers. However, variations are much less across different scenarios in a region. Consider Viet Nam, an open economy with relatively rapid employment growth. Unskilled employment growth in Viet Nam ranges from 2.4% to 7.0% across scenarios, and skilled employment growth ranges from 44.4% to 47.6%. As noted above, employment growth rates are primarily driven by long-term demographic and productivity assumptions and much less by trade policy assumptions.

All scenarios also show *significant increases in global real wages from 2021 to 2035, especially for unskilled workers.* Unskilled real wages rise by 38.3% and skilled real wages by 11.2% for the world and by similar amounts in most regions. Thus, real wage gaps between unskilled workers and skilled workers will tend to narrow. Also, there is much less cross-economy variation in real wage growth results than in the employment results. These are interesting and hopeful findings; given the projected global shift in employee qualifications from unskilled to skilled categories, supply changes may make unskilled workers relatively *more scarce* than skilled workers, warranting larger wage gains over time, in percentage terms.

Comparisons of *labor market effects across scenarios reinforce earlier findings* in this chapter. The employment and wage results rank the baseline, global reach, and friend-shoring scenarios in the same order as real income results. For example, the global unskilled employment growth rates with the new normal (13.4%), global reach (13.6%), and friend-shoring (13.0%) scenarios suggest more-than-normal global job growth with ambitious cooperation, and less-than-normal job growth with trade fragmentation. Similarly, global unskilled wage growth under the new normal (38.3%), global reach (39.0%), and friend-shoring (37.3%) scenarios suggest more-than-normal global wage growth with cooperation and less-than-normal wage growth with trade fragmentation. Comparable results are also found for skilled workers. Importantly, the model offers no evidence that unskilled and skilled workers would have different priorities in making these trade policy choices.

To be sure, these results need further validation. Would they hold under different assumptions about employment and wage determination? Are they sensitive to the model used to determine bilateral trade flows? Do they depend on the details used to model labor? For now, they confirm an intriguing finding from a different model (Petri and Plummer 2016), that in practice, good trade policy not only improves productive efficiency but also raises wages and employment across different job categories.

Implications for Global Value Chains

The emergence of GVCs particularly benefited ASEAN. They facilitate the flow of information on technologies and markets among companies and enable even small countries to find specialized market beachheads. The CGE/GVC framework here lets us examine how economic shocks such as trade policy changes affect GVC participation at the country and industry level.

Trade policy shocks need not affect simple trade and GVC trade similarly. Effects will vary depending on the specifics of barriers; for example, barriers imposed on directly consumed products will have less effect on GVC participation than indiscriminate barriers on intermediate inputs, even if both have similar overall trade effects. Broadly applied barriers, like geopolitical interventions, appear to be especially harmful to GVC trade.

This analysis of value chains builds on a large literature on Multiregional Input–Output (MRIO) modeling; recent reviews and mathematical restatements by Antras and Chor (2021) and Borin and Mancini (2019) offer valuable overviews. In turn, this work rests on contributions by Hummels et al. (1998), Koopman, Wang, and Wei (2014), and others. Extensive recent empirical applications include the WTO's *Global Value Chain Development Reports* and the World Bank's 2020 *World Development Report*. Organizations maintain MRIO databases, including the WTO/OECD and ADB.[24]

Analysis of global value chain participation

Although CGE and GVC models share an ancestry in input–output analysis, few applications link the two methodologies, and those that do often focus simply on adjusting CGE databases using MRIO data sources (for example Carrico 2017). Yet, CGE applications often involve policy changes that significantly affect GVCs because their production arrangements require frequent border crossings. Thus, CGE simulations of trade policy experiments may substantially distort the MRIO tables that implicitly underly all CGE models. By extracting MRIO tables from CGE results and calculating scenario-related changes, we can directly identify how GVC characteristics such as participation rates are affected.

---

[24]   See for example studies by de Vries et al. (2019) and by Zhong and Su (2021).

We rely on four commonly applied measures of GVC participation to examine GVC effects (Appendix F). The appendix uses the notation of Borin and Mancini (2019) and the World Bank (2020). Conceptually, the measures are:

- Backward GVC participation, imported inputs directly or indirectly contained in exports, expressed as a percentage of exports. These products cross at least two borders, once as imported inputs and then as exports (see Appendix F, equation [6])
- Forward GVC participation, domestic value added contained in exports further exported by the destination country, expressed as a percentage of exports. These products also cross at least two borders, once as exports and later as exports of the destination country (see Appendix F, equation [8])
- Total GVC participation, the sum of backward and forward participation (see Appendix F, equation [9])
- Value-added exports, domestic value added embedded directly or indirectly in products absorbed in final demand abroad. This value added crosses at least one border and is usually expressed as a percentage of domestic value added (see Appendix F, equation [12]).

The global average GVC participation rate under the new normal baseline is 39.1% (Figure 6.6).[25] One important takeaway is that the model does not project significant changes in GVC participation between 2021 and 2035, or across the alternative baselines. This is because baseline projections do not anticipate unusual changes in trade costs, GVC-related technologies, or trade barriers, that is, in factors that would change the international structure of production. However, these changes do appear in the simulated policy alternative scenarios.

The ordering of economies on the GVC participation ladder is also interesting. At the top are small, open economies, with specialized manufacturing industries well integrated into global production. Most ASEAN economies are in this top group, with GVC participation rates that show more than half of exports tied to international value chains. At the bottom are large, geographically isolated, and/or natural-resource-specialized economies. Large and distant economies tend toward self-sufficiency, while natural resource exporters typically have modest backward linkages and may export directly to final users (say, consumers of gasoline and food).

---

[25] Although these results are based on an MRIO data set derived from Global Trade Analysis Project (GTAP) data, they are like those calculated with specialized MRIO databases. Nevertheless, further comparisons are needed to determine whether and where significant differences appear.

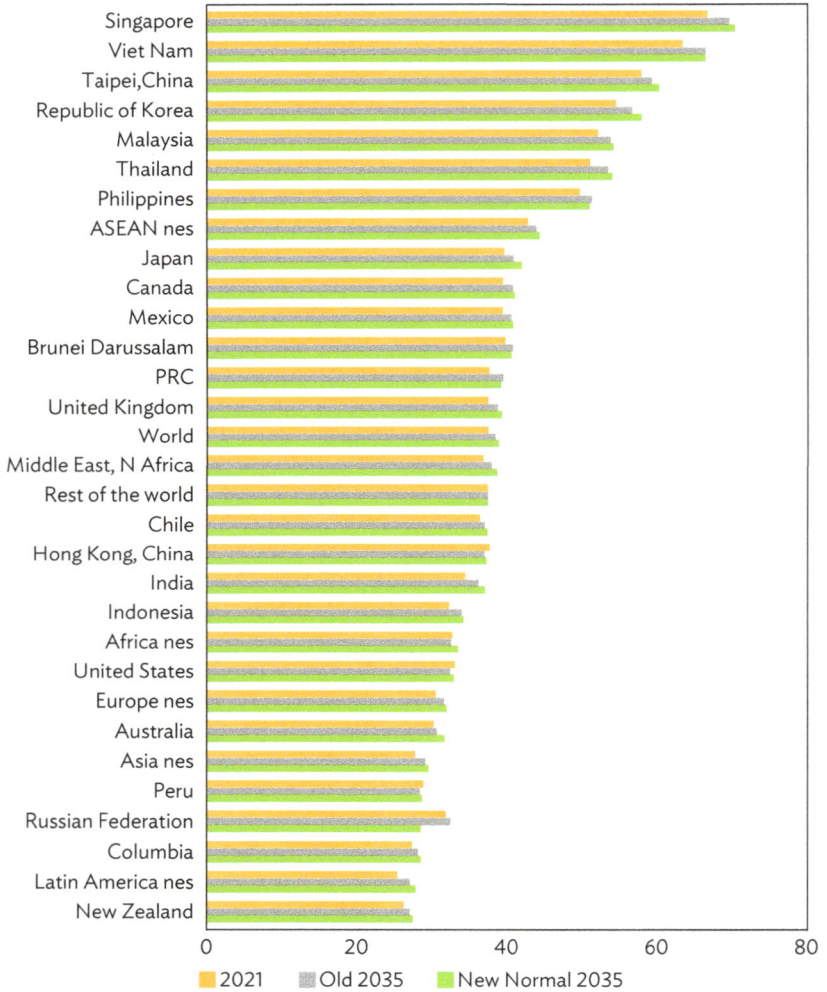

Figure 6.6: Participation in Global Value Chains, Baseline 2021 and 2035 (percent exports)

ASEAN = Association of Southeast Asian Nations, nes = not elsewhere specified, PRC = People's Republic of China.
Notes: Total global value chain participation rates are calculated using equation (9) in Appendix F.
Source: Authors' simulations.

Effects of policy experiments on global value chains

Geopolitical interventions that reduce global incomes as they decrease trade and make it less profitable now shows that these interventions also undermine GVCs, in some scenarios more than they affect trade in general (Tables 6.9 and 6.10). All simulations of geopolitical interventions show declining GVC participation rates worldwide and in individual regions. The world average GVC participation rate would decrease by 4.5% to 9.0% by 2035, depending on the geopolitical intervention scenario. In these results, firms substitute costlier domestic processing for outsourcing, with both the firm and its partner losing the efficiency benefits of GVC production and information flows.

Table 6.9: Geopolitical Interventions: Changes in Global Value Chain Participation, 2035

	New Normal	Geopolitical Interventions			% Changes		
		Reshoring	Near-shoring	Friend-shoring	Reshoring	Near-shoring	Friend-shoring
Americas	**34.3**	**32.7**	**32.4**	**33.1**	**−4.8**	**−5.4**	**−3.7**
Canada	41.2	38.8	39.0	40.0	−5.8	−5.2	−2.7
Chile	37.5	34.9	34.1	33.7	−6.9	−9.1	−10.0
Colombia	28.7	26.8	25.1	25.5	−6.6	−12.3	−10.9
Mexico	40.9	39.4	38.8	39.8	−3.6	−5.0	−2.6
Peru	28.8	26.5	25.0	24.9	−8.1	−13.4	−13.5
United States	32.9	31.8	31.1	31.7	−3.3	−5.5	−3.6
Latin America nes	27.8	25.5	24.5	24.4	−8.4	−12.0	−12.2
Asia and Oceania	**44.9**	**43.8**	**42.0**	**40.3**	**−2.4**	**−6.4**	**−10.2**
Australia	31.8	28.0	29.7	30.0	−12.0	−6.5	−5.7
Brunei Darussalam	40.8	43.1	39.2	38.2	5.7	−3.7	−6.3
PRC	39.3	38.9	36.5	34.4	−0.9	−7.2	−12.4
Hong Kong, China	37.4	35.8	35.4	35.1	−4.3	−5.3	−6.1
Indonesia	34.2	32.9	32.4	30.1	−3.7	−5.4	−12.0
India	37.1	35.2	32.8	32.8	−5.1	−11.6	−11.8
Japan	42.1	40.5	39.8	38.6	−3.8	−5.5	−8.2
Malaysia	54.4	53.3	51.1	49.3	−1.9	−6.1	−9.3
New Zealand	27.5	26.8	25.5	25.9	−2.6	−7.4	−6.0
Philippines	51.3	39.6	47.6	46.5	−3.3	−7.2	−9.3
Singapore	70.5	70.1	67.2	65.9	−0.6	−4.8	−6.5
Republic of Korea	58.0	56.4	55.3	53.5	−2.9	−4.8	−7.8
Thailand	54.2	53.3	51.4	49.3	−1.6	−5.1	−9.1
Taipei,China	60.4	58.2	57.9	55.2	−3.7	−4.1	−8.7

continued on next page

Table 6.9 (continued)

	New Normal	Geopolitical Interventions			% Changes		
		Reshoring	Near-shoring	Friend-shoring	Reshoring	Near-shoring	Friend-shoring
Viet Nam	66.7	66.1	62.5	61.4	−0.9	−6.4	−8.0
ASEAN nes	44.6	41.9	43.0	40.9	−6.0	−3.5	−8.1
Asia nes	29.5	27.8	26.5	26.6	−6.0	−10.2	−9,8
Other Regions	**34.5**	**32.0**	**31.0**	**31.4**	**−7.3**	**−10.2**	**−9.1**
Africa nes	33.5	30.3	29.7	29.6	−9.4	−11.3	−11.6
Europe nes	32.1	29.4	28.2	29.2	−8.4	−12.0	−8.8
United Kingdom	39.3	37.0	36.9	37.6	−5.7	−6.1	−4.3
Middle East, North Africa	38.8	36.3	35.5	35.2	−6.4	−8.5	−9.1
Russian Federation	28.7	26.1	25.6	24.9	−9.1	−10.6	−13.0
Rest of World	37.6	34.8	33.0	33.2	−7.5	−12.2	−11.8
World	**39.1**	**37.3**	**36.2**	**35.6**	**−4.5**	**−7.3**	**−9.0**
ASEAN	55.2	53.7	51.9	50.1	−2.6	−5.9	−9.2

ASEAN = Association of Southeast Asian Nations, nes = not elsewhere specified, PRC = People's Republic of China.
Notes: Definitions of scenarios and regions directly affected by them are in Table 6.2A.
Source: Authors' simulations.

Interestingly, the relative ranking of different geopolitical scenarios changes from those observed earlier (Tables 6.5 and 6.7). The yardstick of comparison was national income and by this measure, friend-shoring minimized global losses compared to reshoring or near-shoring. In Table 6.9, the GVC participation yardstick suggests a different ranking: friend-shoring is more damaging than the alternatives. A possible explanation lies in the type of trade eliminated. Friend-shoring has large negative effects on trade between the PRC and NATO+ countries, a key source of current GVC trade. However, it may expand final-goods trade among geopolitical partners. Thus, friend-shoring seems to replace trans-Pacific GVC trade with simpler trade with other regions.

In Table 6.10, GVC participation effects of trade cooperation alternatives reinforce earlier results. The results for trade cooperation are smaller than those for geopolitical interventions, as they have smaller effects and apply to fewer trade flows than the geopolitical scenarios. GVC participation is positively affected in all cooperation scenarios, but the table does show small negative GVC effects for a few economies excluded from new trade agreements, like the US and the PRC in the CPTPP scenarios. Relatively large increases in GVC participation are projected for economies with major GVC headquarters (such as Japan and the Republic of Korea) in the case of CPTPP enlargement scenarios.

Table 6.10: Enhanced Trade Cooperation: Changes in Global Value Chain Participation, 2035

| | New Normal | Trade Cooperation Initiatives | | | | % Changes | | | |
		RCEP	CPTPP 2024	CPTPP 2027	CPTPP 2030	RCEP	CPTPP 2024	CPTPP 2027	CPTPP 2030
Americas	**34.3**	**34.3**	**34.3**	**34.3**	**35.0**	**0.0**	**0.0**	**0.0**	**2.0**
Canada	41.2	41.2	41.2	41.2	41.9	0.1	0.0	0.0	1.9
Chile	37.5	37.6	37.4	37.4	38.2	0.3	−0.3	−0.2	2.0
Colombia	28.7	28.7	28.7	28.7	29.6	0.1	0.0	0.0	3.1
Mexico	40.9	40.9	40.9	40.9	41.5	0.0	0.1	0.2	1.7
Peru	28.8	28.9	28.8	28.9	29.7	0.3	0.1	0.2	3.2
United States	32.9	32.9	32.9	32.9	33.6	0.0	−0.1	−0.1	2.1
Latin America nes	27.8	27.9	27.9	27.9	28.8	0.2	0.1	0.2	3.4
Asia and Oceania	**44.9**	**45.2**	**45.1**	**45.1**	**45.7**	**0.6**	**0.4**	**0.5**	**1.7**
Australia	31.8	32.0	31.8	31.9	32.7	0.6	0.1	0.3	2.9
Brunei Darussalam	40.8	41.0	41.0	41.0	41.7	0.6	0.5	0.7	2.4
PRC	39.3	39.8	39.2	39.2	40.1	1.2	−0.1	−0.1	2.0
Hong Kong, China	37.4	37.4	37.4	37.4	38.1	0.1	0.0	0.0	2.0
Indonesia	34.2	34.3	34.2	34.7	34.5	0.4	−0.1	1.5	1.0
India	37.1	37.1	37.1	37.1	38.1	−0.1	−0.1	−0.1	2.6
Japan	42.1	42.3	42.5	42.6	43.0	0.6	1.1	1.2	2.1
Malaysia	54.4	54.5	54.7	54.7	55.0	0.2	0.5	0.6	1.1
New Zealand	27.5	27.7	27.5	27.7	28.1	0.7	0.0	0.7	2.1
Philippines	51.3	51.3	51.3	51.3	51.5	0.0	0.0	0.0	0.3
Singapore	70.5	70.4	70.6	70.5	70.5	−0.2	0.0	0.0	−0.1
Republic of Korea	58.0	58.4	58.7	58.7	59.3	0.7	1.1	1.2	2.2
Thailand	54.2	54.3	54.1	54.1	54.1	0.2	−0.1	−0.2	−0.1
Taipei,China	60.4	60.3	60.4	60.4	61.4	−0.2	−0.1	−0.1	1.6
Viet Nam	66.7	67.2	67.1	67.0	67.9	0.7	0.5	0.4	1.8
ASEAN nes	44.6	44.7	44.6	44.5	44.6	0.3	0.0	−0.1	0.2
Asia nes	29.5	29.5	29.5	29.5	30.4	0.0	0.0	0.1	3.0
Other Regions	**34.5**	**34.5**	**34.6**	**34.6**	**35.5**	**0.1**	**0.1**	**0.2**	**2.9**
Africa nes	33.5	33.6	33.5	33.5	34.6	0.2	0.1	0.1	3.2
Europe nes	32.1	32.1	32.1	32.1	33.2	0.0	0.0	0.0	3.6
United Kingdom	39.3	39.3	39.4	39.4	40.0	0.0	0.3	0.3	1.9
Middle East, North Africa	38.8	38.9	38.8	38.9	39.8	0.3	0.2	0.3	2.7

continued on next page

Table 6.10 (continued)

		Trade Cooperation Initiatives				% Changes			
	New Normal	RCEP	CPTPP 2024	CPTPP 2027	CPTPP 2030	RCEP	CPTPP 2024	CPTPP 2027	CPTPP 2030
Russian Federation	28.7	28.7	28.7	28.7	29.3	0.2	0.0	0.1	2.3
Rest of World	37.6	37.7	37.6	37.6	38.4	0.1	0.0	0.0	2.1
World	**39.1**	**39.3**	**39.2**	**39.3**	**40.0**	**0.5**	**0.3**	**0.4**	**2.3**
ASEAN	55.2	55.3	55.4	55.3	55.5	0.3	0.3	0.3	0.6

ASEAN = Association of Southeast Asian Nations, CPTPP = Comprehensive and Progressive Agreement for Trans-Pacific Partnership, PRC = People's Republic of China, RCEP = Regional Comprehensive Economic Partnership.
Notes: Definitions of scenarios and regions directly affected by them are in Table 6.2B.
Source: Authors' simulations.

Value-added exports measure regions' dependence on the world by calculating the total direct and indirect domestic value added incorporated in foreign final demand, netting out the many stages of production and trade that separate an economy's value added from the final users of these inputs (Table 6.11). The ratio of world value-added exports to world GDP in 2035 (in the new normal scenario) is 15.6% compared to 25.0% for world exports divided by world GDP. In other words, 38% of the value added embedded in gross exports is ultimately returned to economies' own final demand through production linkages.

Table 6.11: Geopolitical Interventions: Share of Value-Added Exports, 2035

		Geopolitical Interventions			% Changes		
	New Normal	Reshoring	Near-shoring	Friend-shoring	Reshoring	Near-shoring	Friend-shoring
Americas	**10.1**	**9.1**	**8.7**	**9.2**	**-9.5**	**-13.9**	**-9.2**
Canada	20.5	22.7	19.5	19.9	10.4	-5.0	-2.9
Chile	23.0	26.0	22.0	21.9	13.2	-4.2	-4.7
Colombia	10.4	14.2	8.7	8.5	36.8	-16.4	-18.0
Mexico	21.8	24.9	20.8	21.1	14.2	-4.7	-3.1
Peru	20.1	22.0	17.6	17.1	9.7	-12.0	-14.9
United States	7.8	6.1	6.6	7.2	-22.3	-16.0	-8.1
Latin America nes	10.9	13.5	8.6	8.8	24.2	-20.7	-19.3
Asia and Oceania	**17.6**	**14.6**	**16.2**	**16.0**	**-17.4**	**-8.0**	**-9.1**
Australia	19.0	21.2	17.6	17.9	11.6	-7.4	-5.6
Brunei Darussalam	46.5	48.6	45.8	45.9	4.4	-1.6	-1.4

continued on next page

Table 6.11 (continued)

		Geopolitical Interventions			% Changes		
	New Normal	Reshoring	Near-shoring	Friend-shoring	Reshoring	Near-shoring	Friend-shoring
PRC	13.0	7.8	11.7	11.5	−39.9	−10.0	−11.6
Hong Kong, China	39.0	41.3	38.1	38.2	6.1	−2.2	−2.1
Indonesia	15.5	19.0	13.8	13.4	22.4	−11.3	−13.9
India	14.7	13.3	13.2	13.1	−9.6	−10.1	−10.8
Japan	18.7	21.8	17.6	17.7	16.9	−5.6	−5.2
Malaysia	45.0	46.5	43.5	42.8	3.4	−3.3	−4.9
New Zealand	23.8	26.7	22.4	22.8	12.2	−6.0	−4.3
Philippines	14.9	17.2	13.3	12.8	15.6	−10.5	−14.2
Singapore	32.8	34.8	33.7	33.3	6.2	2.7	1.6
Republic of Korea	27.9	31.0	27.3	27.4	11.1	−2.3	−1.8
Thailand	39.7	41.8	38.5	38.3	5.4	−3.0	−3.5
Taipei,China	43.7	46.8	43.3	43.7	7.1	−0.9	0.1
Viet Nam	39.3	41.9	38.5	38.2	6.5	−2.1	−2.8
ASEAN nes	38.2	40.3	37.7	37.4	5.6	−1.3	−2.0
Asia nes	21.0	23.1	18.8	18.8	9.6	−10.6	−10.6
Other Regions	**18.8**	**18.3**	**16.7**	**16.9**	**−3.0**	**−11.4**	**−10.0**
Africa nes	20.1	22.1	17.4	17.7	10.0	−13.1	−12.0
Europe nes	16.7	14.4	14.6	15.1	−13.3	−12.5	−9.3
United Kingdom	17.1	19.7	16.0	16.2	15.1	−6.7	−5.2
Middle East, North Africa	23.0	25.9	20.6	20.1	12.4	−10.7	−12.8
Russian Federation	22.5	21.1	20.9	21.7	−6.1	−6.9	−3.5
Rest of World	27.6	30.0	25.2	25.2	8.7	−8.9	−8.9
World	**15.6**	**14.0**	**13.9**	**14.1**	**−10.5**	**−10.8**	**−9.8**
ASEAN	26.7	29.4	24.9	24.4	10.5	−6.4	−8.5

ASEAN = Association of Southeast Asian Nations, nes = not elsewhere specified, PRC = People's Republic of China.
Notes: Definitions of scenarios and regions directly affected by them are in Table 6.2A.
Source: Authors' simulations.

This also helps explain the mechanisms behind the geopolitical scenarios. For example, the reshoring column shows the potential pushback that large countries face as they bring trade home. It indicates that the PRC's withdrawal from trade, in this scenario decreasing its dependence on the world by 39.9%, would push other economies (especially competitors like Indonesia, Japan, the Philippines, and the Republic of Korea) toward deeper trade. American reshoring would do the same for countries in North and South America and European reshoring would similarly affect nearby economies. This new competition would erode the terms-of-trade benefits that reshoring economies might have expected. Rather than strengthening their economies, reshoring would create stronger foreign competitors. As earlier noted, only the US would be a (slight) net winner from reshoring policies.

In other words, the CGE-linked MRIO system generates valuable insights into the effects of policy changes on value chain strategies. Important applications remain to be investigated, including the regional decomposition of value chain activities and changes in them. That could create a new toolset for analyzing the drivers and implications of GVC linkages.

Conclusions

As of this writing, the world economy is grappling with conflicting trends and great uncertainty. Global shocks are appearing with increasing frequency: the acute phase of the COVID-19 pandemic quickly gave way to the Russian invasion of Ukraine, followed by global surges in natural resource prices, and now by global inflation and increased chances for a sharp economic downturn. Diverging views on future trade policy add to the uncertainty. On one hand, the political backlash against globalization has intensified and found new rationales with geopolitical tensions. Prominent leaders call for bringing production home and restricting trade to politically desirable partners. On the other hand, economic cooperation continues to attract vigorous support in parts of the world, especially East Asia and ASEAN. The outcome of these trends is especially important for ASEAN and similar economies that depend on active global engagement.

To help make sense of these developments, this chapter offers a quantitative analysis of recent trade-related shocks and emerging policy responses. It calculates intermediate-term projections of global economic growth using a new, medium-term CGE model that also traces effects on international production chains. Based on scenarios ranging from proposals for reshoring, near-shoring, and friend-shoring, to proposals for new trade agreements in Asia and the Pacific, three broad findings emerge:

(i)   Recent shocks, including geopolitical threats and surging natural resource prices, are likely to persist. They favor resource-rich economies and will create significant, though manageable, challenges for ASEAN's international supply chains, and more generally for its manufacturing-based development model.

(ii) Current proposals for deeper geopolitical interventions in trade—ostensibly to ease concerns about employment, national security, and supply chain stability—are not well defined, and in some configurations could substantially weaken the world trading system. Much will depend on the details of these interventions, but the risks from them are high. As often in the past, ASEAN must anticipate new global frameworks, analyze their implications, and respond pragmatically.

(iii) Although global interest in economic cooperation has waned, its sturdy base in East Asia offers opportunities for working around global anti-trade trends. Plausible regional initiatives, from the aggressive implementation of the RCEP to the creative enlargements of the CPTPP, are feasible and desirable.

Throughout its history, ASEAN has had to manage difficult environments, some not unlike those today. The difference is that the region now has assets—economic momentum, institutions, policy experience, and international opportunities—that are far stronger than it had for overcoming past challenges.

Appendixes

Appendix A: Model Sectors and Regions (20 August 2022)

Sectors			Regions		
1	CRO	Crops	1	AFR	Africa
2	LVS	Livestock	2	AUS	Australia
3	OIL	Oil	3	BRU	Brunei Darussalam
4	ONR	Natural resources, nes	4	CAN	Canada
5	PRF	Food, beverages	5	CHL	Chile
6	P_C	Petroleum and coal	6	CLM	Cambodia, Lao People's Democratic Republic, Myanmar
7	CHM	Chemicals	7	COL	Colombia
8	PRP	Pharmaceuticals	8	EUR	Europe
9	TWP	Textiles, apparel	9	HKG	Hong Kong, China
10	OTG	Wood and paper	10	INO	Indonesia
11	MET	Metals	11	IND	India
12	EEQ	Electrical machinery	12	JPN	Japan
13	ELE	Electronics	13	KOR	Republic of Korea
14	OME	Machinery	14	MEX	Mexico
15	MVH	Motor vehicles	15	MIN	Middle East, North Africa
16	OTN	Transport equipment, nes	16	MAL	Malaysia
17	UTC	Constructon, utilities	17	NZL	New Zealand
18	TRD	Trade	18	OAS	Asia, nes
19	ARS	Accommodation, food	19	OLA	Latin America, nes
20	TRA	Transport	20	PER	Peru
21	COM	Communications	21	PHI	Philippines
22	RSE	Real estate	22	PRC	People's Republic of China
23	OBS	Business services	23	ROW	Rest of World
24	FIN	Finance	24	RUS	Russian Federation
25	OTS	Social services	25	SIN	Singapore
			26	THA	Thailand
			27	TAP	Taipei,China
			28	UK	United Kingdom
			29	US	United States
			30	VIE	Viet Nam

nes = not elsewhere specified.
Source: Authors.

Appendix B: Groups Used in Simulation and Presentations (14 September 2022)

	ASEAN	CPTPP	RCEP	NATO+	US-Led	The PRC-Led	Neutral	Large Regions	Region
Americas									
Canada		yes		yes	yes				N America
Chile		maybe					yes		S America
Colombia							yes		S America
Mexico		yes			yes				N America
Peru		yes					yes		S America
United States		maybe		yes	yes			yes	N America
Latin America nes							yes		S America
Asia and Oceania									
Australia		yes	yes	yes	yes				SE Asia
Brunei Darussalam	yes	yes	yes				yes		SE Asia
PRC		maybe	yes			yes		yes	NE Asia
Hong Kong, China						yes			NE Asia
Indonesia	yes	maybe	yes				yes		SE Asia
India			maybe				yes	yes	S Asia
Japan		yes	yes	yes	yes			yes	NE Asia
Malaysia	yes	maybe	yes				yes		SE Asia
New Zealand		yes	yes	yes	yes				SE Asia
Philippines	yes	maybe	yes				yes		SE Asia
Singapore	yes	yes	yes				yes		SE Asia
Republic of Korea		yes	yes	yes	yes				NE Asia
Thailand	yes	maybe	yes				yes		SE Asia
Taipei,China		maybe					yes		NE Asia
Viet Nam	yes	yes	yes				yes		SE Asia
ASEAN nes	yes		yes		yes				SE Asia
Asia nes					1/2	1/2			S Asia
Other Regions									
Africa nes					1/2	1/2			Africa
Europe nes		maybe		yes	yes		yes	yes	Europe
United Kingdom		maybe		yes	yes		yes		Europe
Middle East, North Africa							yes		Africa/Europe
Russian Federation						yes		yes	Others
Rest of World							yes		Others

ASEAN = Assocation of Southeast Asian Nations, CPTPP = Comprehensive and Progressive Agreement for Trans-Pacific Partnership, NATO+ = North Atlantic Treaty Organization and their member allies, nes = not elsewhere specified, PRC = People's Republic of China, RCEP = Regional Comprehensive Economic Partnership. Source: Authors.

Appendix C: Oil Price and Natural Resource Price Forecasts, 2014=100

(a) Oil Price Forecasts

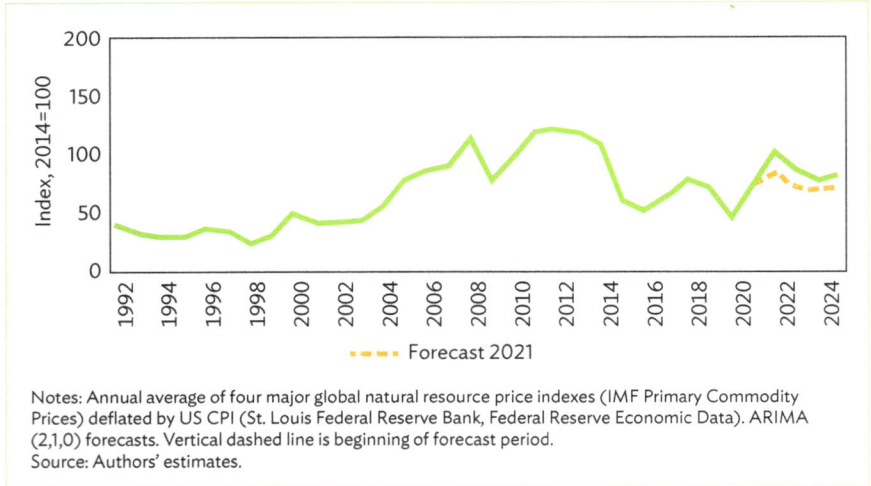

Notes: Annual average of four major global natural resource price indexes (IMF Primary Commodity Prices) deflated by US CPI (St. Louis Federal Reserve Bank, Federal Reserve Economic Data). ARIMA (2,1,0) forecasts. Vertical dashed line is beginning of forecast period.
Source: Authors' estimates.

(b) Natural Resource Price Forecasts

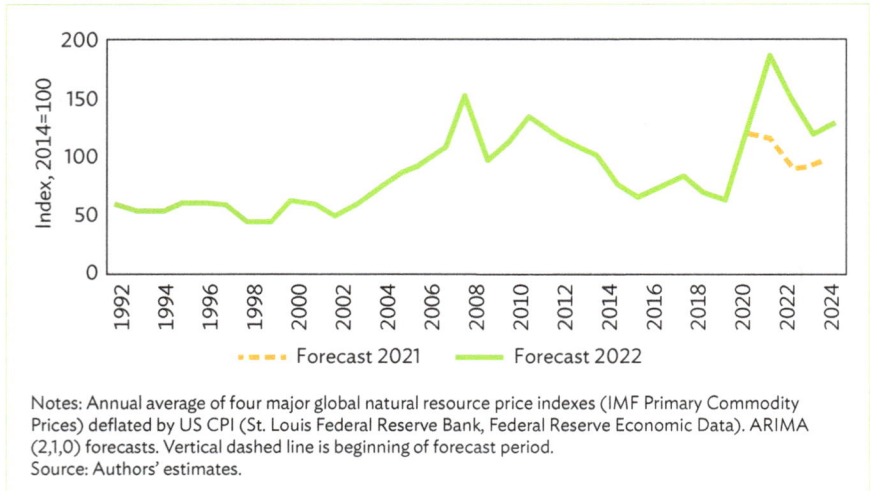

Notes: Annual average of four major global natural resource price indexes (IMF Primary Commodity Prices) deflated by US CPI (St. Louis Federal Reserve Bank, Federal Reserve Economic Data). ARIMA (2,1,0) forecasts. Vertical dashed line is beginning of forecast period.
Source: Authors' estimates.

Appendix D: Employment under Selected Alternatives, 2035 as Percent of 2021

	Unskilled employment, % of 2021				Skilled employment, % of 2021			
	2021 Baseline	New Normal	Global Reach	Friend-shoring	2021 Baseline	New Normal	Global Reach	Friend-shoring
Americas	**105.2**	**105.1**	**104.9**	**105.1**	**139.4**	**139.2**	**139.2**	**139.3**
Canada	96.0	95.9	96.0	95.7	117.8	117.7	117.8	117.7
Chile	94.9	94.8	95.2	94.6	135.9	135.9	136.1	135.7
Colombia	103.9	106.0	105.3	106.2	148.8	150.7	150.1	150.8
Mexico	113.5	112.7	113.0	112.6	160.1	159.6	160.0	159.6
Peru	105.0	104.7	104.9	104.6	140.9	140.6	140.6	140.5
United States	100.7	100.6	100.9	100.6	122.9	122.8	123.0	122.8
Latin America nes	107.7	107.3	106.7	107.4	146.6	146.4	145.9	146.4
Asia and Oceania	**112.6**	**110.8**	**111.4**	**110.3**	**168.8**	**167.3**	**167.9**	**166.8**
Australia	100.9	101.1	101.2	100.7	129.4	129.5	129.6	129.3
Brunei Darussalam	99.2	102.4	102.8	101.5	142.3	144.7	144.9	144.0
PRC	93.8	90.9	92.2	89.4	149.6	146.8	148.1	145.4
Hong Kong, China	80.1	79.5	79.3	78.3	129.3	128.9	128.7	128.0
Indonesia	115.7	115.5	115.9	115.7	175.5	175.5	175.7	175.6
India	133.7	131.8	131.8	132.0	195.5	194.2	194.3	194.4
Japan	79.7	79.1	79.5	78.7	112.6	112.2	112.5	112.0
Malaysia	106.8	105.3	109.8	104.8	183.1	181.5	186.0	181.0
New Zealand	99.2	99.1	99.8	98.8	122.4	122.3	122.7	122.1
Philippines	120.9	120.4	121.7	120.3	170.4	170.1	171.1	170.0
Singapore	65.4	65.2	66.1	64.7	127.6	127.4	128.2	127.0
Republic of Korea	73.5	72.7	73.5	72.0	135.8	135.0	135.8	134.4
Thailand	92.8	90.6	93.1	90.0	142.7	140.5	142.7	140.0
Taipei,China	67.6	67.0	67.8	66.9	124.8	124.3	124.9	124.2
Viet Nam	104.1	103.1	107.0	102.4	145.6	144.9	147.6	144.4
ASEAN nes	116.5	116.1	115.6	115.2	174.5	174.3	173.9	173.6
Asia nes	122.0	121.5	121.0	121.1	171.9	171.6	171.4	171.3
Other Regions	**121.8**	**121.1**	**120.9**	**120.8**	**173.4**	**173.4**	**172.7**	**172.6**
Africa nes	147.2	147.4	147.0	146.9	215.4	215.6	215.4	215.3
Europe nes	85.6	85.2	85.5	85.0	116.6	116.3	116.5	116.2
United Kingdom	93.3	93.1	93.9	93.0	124.7	124.6	125.1	124.5
Middle East, North Africa	117.6	117.0	116.4	116.8	173.2	172.8	172.3	172.5

continued on next page

Appendix D (continued)

	Unskilled employment, % of 2021				Skilled employment, % of 2021			
	2021 Baseline	New Normal	Global Reach	Friend-shoring	2021 Baseline	New Normal	Global Reach	Friend-shoring
Russian Federation	91.8	83.3	82.9	83.0	106.5	99.0	98.7	98.7
Rest of World	101.1	100.3	100.0	100.0	122.9	122.5	122.4	122.3
World	**114.6**	**113.4**	**113.6**	**113.0**	**166.3**	**165.3**	**165.6**	**165.0**
Memorandum								
ASEAN (8 members)	111.7	111.0	112.4	110.8	166.7	166.2	167.2	166.0
CPTPP (11 members)	97.0	96.3	97.5	95.9	139.5	138.9	139.9	138.7
RCEP (15 members)	97.9	95.9	97.1	94.9	152.0	150.1	151.2	149.1
NATO+ (8 members)	90.2	89.9	90.2	89.7	119.8	119.6	119.8	119.5

ASEAN = Association of Southeast Asian Nations, CPTPP = Comprehensive and Progressive Agreement for Trans-Pacific Partnership, NATO+ = North Atlantic Treaty Organization and their member allies, nes = not elsewhere specified, PRC = People's Republic of China, RCEP = Regional Comprehensive Economic Partnership.
Notes: Definitions of scenarios and the regions directly affected by them are in Tables 6.1, 6.2A, and 6.2B. Aggregates are population-weighted averages of regional results.
Source: Authors' simulations.

Appendix E: Real Wages under Selected Alternatives, 2035

	Unskilled Wages, % of 2021				Skilled Wages, % of 2021			
	2021 Baseline	New Normal	Global Reach	Friend-shoring	2021 Baseline	New Normal	Global Reach	Friend-shoring
Americas	**132.2**	**131.9**	**131.8**	**131.8**	**108.2**	**107.9**	**108.0**	**107.9**
Canada	141.7	141.2	141.8	140.6	121.5	121.0	121.6	120.4
Chile	154.0	153.7	155.2	152.5	119.2	118.7	119.9	117.7
Colombia	151.8	155.8	154.5	156.0	115.3	119.0	117.9	119.2
Mexico	128.1	127.0	127.4	126.8	101.4	100.6	101.2	100.6
Peru	151.4	150.8	151.1	150.6	125.2	124.5	124.7	124.5
United States	124.1	123.6	124.7	123.5	107.3	106.8	107.9	106.7
Latin America nes	134.3	133.8	132.8	133.9	107.2	106.8	106.0	106.9
Asia and Oceania	**148.2**	**143.7**	**145.3**	**142.5**	**116.4**	**112.3**	**114.0**	**111.2**
Australia	138.4	139.5	139.9	137.6	115.4	116.4	116.8	114.7
Brunei Darussalam	191.4	209.8	211.8	204.7	138.9	155.3	157.0	150.8
PRC	164.9	158.5	161.3	155.3	120.3	114.8	117.2	112.0

continued on next page

Appendix E (continued)

	Unskilled Wages, % of 2021				Skilled Wages, % of 2021			
	2021 Baseline	New Normal	Global Reach	Friend-shoring	2021 Baseline	New Normal	Global Reach	Friend-shoring
Hong Kong, China	175.4	171.9	170.2	164.5	125.0	122.4	121.2	116.5
Indonesia	158.6	158.2	159.4	158.8	122.7	122.7	123.5	123.0
India	134.0	128.6	128.7	129.4	111.3	106.4	107.0	107.0
Japan	136.5	133.6	135.6	132.0	105.5	103.0	104.8	101.8
Malaysia	153.7	150.9	159.0	150.1	104.6	102.4	108.9	101.7
New Zealand	124.9	124.4	126.9	123.4	108.3	107.7	110.1	106.8
Philippines	149.5	148.0	152.6	147.6	125.0	123.5	128.3	123.1
Singapore	150.3	148.6	154.6	145.6	93.3	92.2	96.3	90.2
Republic of Korea	173.5	167.8	173.5	163.1	110.2	105.9	110.0	102.8
Thailand	174.3	169.0	174.8	167.6	130.5	125.5	130.3	124.2
Taipei,China	167.1	163.0	168.8	162.3	111.0	107.9	111.9	107.4
Viet Nam	156.6	152.3	169.4	149.2	132.3	128.0	144.8	125.1
ASEAN nes	118.2	116.9	115.6	114.3	94.4	93.5	92.2	91.0
Asia nes	135.4	134.0	132.4	132.6	117.4	116.1	114.8	114.7
Other Regions	**133.5**	**131.8**	**131.5**	**131.0**	**112.5**	**110.6**	**110.4**	**109.8**
Africa nes	120.5	120.8	120.1	119.7	105.4	105.8	105.3	104.9
Europe nes	143.2	141.2	142.8	140.5	115.4	113.7	115.1	113.0
United Kingdom	141.1	140.3	143.5	140.0	113.9	113.2	116.1	112.8
Middle East, North Africa	140.7	139.7	138.8	139.5	108.9	108.3	107.5	107.8
Russian Federation	155.0	137.2	136.5	136.6	143.8	119.8	119.0	118.8
Rest of World	149.4	146.1	144.9	144.9	137.3	134.5	133.4	132.9
World	**141.3**	**138.3**	**139.0**	**137.3**	**114.0**	**111.2**	**112.0**	**110.3**
Memorandum								
ASEAN (8 members)	153.3	151.4	156.1	150.6	120.7	119.1	123.4	118.3
CPTPP (11 members)	144.2	141.9	146.5	140.3	112.5	110.5	114.8	109.2
RCEP (15 members)	159.7	155.0	158.3	152.5	119.3	115.2	118.2	113.1
NATO+ (8 members)	137.7	136.1	137.8	135.3	111.7	110.3	111.8	109.6

ASEAN = Association of Southeast Asian Nations, CPTPP = Comprehensive and Progressive Agreement for Trans-Pacific Partnership, NATO+ = North Atlantic Treaty Organization and their member allies,nes = not elsewhere specified, PRC = People's Republic of China, RCEP = Regional Comprehensive Economic Partnership.
Notes: Definitions of scenarios and the regions directly affected by them are in Tables 6.1, 6.2A, and 6.2B. Aggregates are population-weighted averages of regional results.
Source: Authors' simulations.

Appendix F: Global Value Chain Management

Value chain accounting tracks the movement of value added across production stages and borders. We mostly follow Borin and Mancini's (2019) notation for a multiregional input–output (MRIO) system consisting of N sectors and G countries.

Value added is related to gross output by the equation:

$$(1) \quad VA_s = u_N V_s X_s$$

where VA_s is the value added from country s embedded in its own gross output
X_s is an $Nx1$ vector of gross output of country s
V_s is an NxN matrix of value added/output coefficients in country s
u_N is a $1xN$ row vector of "1"s

Vs has values only on its diagonal; by definition, industries only use their own value added. The output vector is equal to output sold to domestically to other industries, final users, and internationally to foreigners:

$$(2) \quad X_s = A_{ss}X_s + Y_{ss} + \Sigma_{r \neq s}E_{sr}$$

where A_{sr} is the NxN matrix of inputs required from country s per unit of output in country r
Y_{sr} is the $Nx1$ vector of country s outputs needed for final demand in country r
E_{sr} is the $Nx1$ vector of exports from country s to country r

Solving **(2)** for X_s and substituting the result into **(1)** gives:

$$(3) \quad VA_s = u_N V_s (I - A_{ss})^{-1} Y_{ss} + u_N V_s (I - A_{ss})^{-1} \Sigma_{r \neq s} E_{sr}$$

where the first term in **(3)** is value added absorbed domestically in country s and the second term is value added absorbed in exports. This second term is denoted DVA_s.

Part of DVA_s is absorbed in immediate destination countries and is denoted $DAVAX_s$. It is given by:

$$(4) \quad DAVAX_s = u_N V_s (I - A_{ss})^{-1} [Y_{sr} + A_{sr}(I - A_{rr})^{-1} Y_{rr}]$$

Note that the first term in the brackets of **(4)** is the final demand for the products of country s in country r and the second term is exports from country s to country r for the purpose of domestically producing r's final demand for its own products.

The backward GVC content of the exports of country r is defined as:

$$(5) \quad GVCB_s = \Sigma_{r \neq s} E_{sr} - DVA_s$$

where $GVCB_s$ is the backward GVC content of exports

(5) defines the portion of the value of exports that had already crossed a border, that is, the part of exports that is *not* domestic value added. GVC content is usually expressed not as a value, as in **(5)**, but rather as a ratio of exports:

$$(6) \quad GVCB_{sr} = 1 - \frac{\Sigma_G DVA_{sr}}{\Sigma_G E_{sr}}$$

The forward GVC content of exports from s to r is equal to the forward value added content of exports, defined as DVA_s less **(4)** which is the part of this value added that is absorbed in the immediate destination country and hence does not cross further borders. It is:

$$(7) \quad GVCF_s = DVA_s - DAVAX_s$$

where $GVCF_s$ is the forward GVC content of exports

Like backward content, forward GVC content is also usually defined as a percentage of exports:

$$(8) \quad GVCF_{sr} = \frac{\Sigma_G (DVA_{sr} - DAVAX_{sr})}{\Sigma_G E_{sr}}$$

Total GVC content is found by adding (6) and (8):

$$(9) \quad GVCT_{sr} = 1 - \frac{\Sigma_G DAVAX_{sr}}{\Sigma_G E_{sr}}$$

While the computations so far involved only national input-output systems and inverses, the computation of value added that is absorbed directly or indirectly by final demand abroad, no matter what borders or production stages it crosses, is found using the full interdependence relationships of the MRIO model. This requires defining the *GNxGN* matrix A:

$$(10) \quad A = \begin{bmatrix} A_{1,1} & \cdots & A_{1,G} \\ \vdots & & \vdots \\ A_{G,1} & \cdots & A_{G,G} \end{bmatrix}$$

and finding the inverse:

$$(11) \quad B = (I - A)^{-1}$$

The elements of B enable the calculation of the direct and indirect value added in s required to produce final demand abroad:

$$(12) \quad VAX_s = u_N V_s \Sigma_q \Sigma_{r \neq s} B_{sq} Y_{qr}$$

where VAX_s is the value added of country s directly or indirectly absorbed abroad.

References

Aguiar, A. et al. 2019. The WTO Global Trade Model: Technical documentation. *World Trade Organization Staff Papers.*

ASEAN+3 Macroeconomic Office (AMRO). 2021. *AMRO Annual Consultation Report: Viet Nam (2020)*. https://www.amro-asia.org/wp-content/uploads/2021/05/AMRO-Annual-Consultation-Report-on-Vietnam-2020.pdf.

Antras, P., and D. Chor. 2019. On the Measurement of Upstreamness and Downstreamness in Global Value Chains. In L. Y. Ing and M. Yu, eds. *World Trade Evolution: Growth, Productivity and Employment.* Routledge. Chapter 5, pp. 126–194.

_____. 2021. Global Value Chains. *NBER Working Paper.* No. 28549. http://www.nber.org/papers/w28549.

Borin, A., and M. Mancini. 2019. Measuring What Matters in Global Value Chains and Value-Added Trade. *World Bank Policy Research Working Paper.* No.8804.

Carrico, C. 2017. Enhandced Analytical Framework for Evaluating the Effects of Trade Costs along Global Value Chains. *Journal of Global Economic Analysis.* 2 (2). 43–111.

Cigna, S., V. Gunnella, and L. Quaglietti. 2022. Global vValue Chains: Measurement, Trends, and Drivers. *European Central Bank Occasional Paper Series.*

Corong, E. 2020. The GTAPv7 Multi Region Input –Output (MRIO) Model. *GTAP Research Memorandum No. 36.* Center for Global Trade Analysis. Purdue University.

Corong, E. L., T.W. Hertel, R. McDougall, M.E. Tsigas, and D. van der Mensbrugghe. 2017. The Standard GTAP Model, Version 7. Journal of Global Economic Analysis. 2 (1):1-119. https://doi.org/10.21642/JGEA.020101AF.

De Vries, G. et al. 2019. Do Asian Countries Upgrade in Global Value Chains? A Novel Approach and Empirical Evidence. *Asian Economic Journal.* 33(1). 13–37.

Haar, J. 2021. Nearshoring: Panacea, Quick Fix or Something in Between? *The Hill.* 22 November. https://thehill.com/opinion/international/582542-nearshoring-panacea-quick-fix-or-something-in-between.

Hinojales, M.M. 2021. Viet Nam's Route to Moving up Global Value Chains. *AMRO Blog.* 16 June. https://www.amro-asia.org/vietnams-route-to-moving-up-global-value-chains/.

Hummels, D., D. Rapoport., and K.M. Yi. 1998. Vertical Specialization and the Changing Nature of world Trade. Economic Policy Review. 4. (Jun), 79-99.

Hummels, D., J. Ishii, and K. M. Yi. 2001. The Nature and Growth of Vertical Specialization in World Trade. *Journal of International Economics 54* (1), 75–96.

Johnson, R. C. 2018. Measuring Global Value Chains. *Annual Review of Economics.* 10 (1). 207–236.

Koopman, R., Z. Wang, and S. J. Wei. 2014. Tracing Value-Added and Double Counting in Gross Exports. *American Economic Review.* 104(2). 459–494.

Miller, R. E., and I. Temurshoev. 2017. Output Upstreamness and Input Downstreamness of Industries/Countries in World Production. *International Regional Science Review.* 40(5). 443–475.

Organisation for Economic Co-operation and Development (OECD). 2022. OECD Economic Outlook, Interim Report March 2022: Economic and Social Impacts and Policy Implications of the War in Ukraine. OECD Publishing. Paris. https://doi.org/10.1787/4181d61b-en.

Park, C.Y., P.A. Petri, and M.G. Plummer. 2021. The Economics of Conflict and Cooperation in the Asia-Pacific: RCEP, CPTPP and the US-PRC Trade. *East Asian Economic Review.* 25(3). 233–272. September.

Petri, P.A., and M.G. Plummer. 2016. Economics of the Trans-Pacific Partnership: Distributional impact. *VoxEU.* 30 Apr 2016. https://cepr.org/voxeu/columns/economics-trans-pacific-partnership-distributional-impact.

_____. 2020. East Asia Decouples from the US: Trade War, COVID-19, and East Asia's New Trade Blocs. *Peterson Institute for International Economics Working Paper.* 20-9 (June). https://www.piie.com/sites/default/files/documents/wp20-9.pdf.

Petri, P.A., M.G. Plummer, and F. Zhai. 2012. The Trans-Pacific Partnership and Asia-Pacific Integration: A Quantitative Assessment. *Policy Analyses in International Economics.* No. 98. Washington: Peterson Institute for International Economics.

World Bank. 2020. World Development Report 2020: Trading for Development in the Age of Global Value Chains, Washington: World Bank.

Zhai, F. 2008. Armington Meets Melitz: Introducing Firm Heterogeneity in a Global CGE Model of Trade. *Journal of Economic Integration.* 23(3). pp. 575–604.

Zhong, S., and B. Su. 2021. Investigating ASEAN's Participation in Global Value Chains: Production Fragmentation and Regional Integration. *Asian Development Review.* 38(02). pp. 159–188.

www.ingramcontent.com/pod-product-compliance
Lightning Source LLC
Chambersburg PA
CBHW082348230326
41599CB00058BA/7153